CULTURAL DIFFERENCE ON TRIAL

To Juliette, with love

Cultural Difference on Trial

The Nature and Limits of Judicial Understanding

ANTHONY J. CONNOLLY
Australian National University, Australia

Routledge
Taylor & Francis Group
LONDON AND NEW YORK

First published 2010 by Ashgate Publishing

Published 2016 by Routledge
2 Park Square, Milton Park, Abingdon, Oxon OX14 4RN
711 Third Avenue, New York, NY 10017, USA

Routledge is an imprint of the Taylor & Francis Group, an informa business

British Library Cataloguing in Publication Data
Connolly, Anthony J.
Cultural difference on trial : the nature and limits of judicial understanding. -- (Applied legal philosophy)
1. Judicial process. 2. Judges--Attitudes. 3. Culture and law.
I. Title II. Series
347'.012-dc22

Library of Congress Cataloging-in-Publication Data
Connolly, Anthony J.
Cultural difference on trial : the nature and limits of judicial understanding / by Anthony J. Connolly.
p. cm. -- (Applied legal philosophy)
Includes bibliographical references and index.
ISBN 978-0-7546-7952-3 (hardcover)
1. Justice, Administration of. 2. Minorities--Legal status, laws, etc. 3. Judicial process. 4. Culture and law. I. Title.
K2100.C667 2009
347'.012--dc22

200903080

IBSN 9780754679523 (hbk)

Contents

Series Editor's Preface

The objective of the Applied Legal Philosophy series is to publish work which adopts a theoretical approach to the study of particular areas or aspects of law or deals with general theories of law in a way which focused on issues of practical moral and political concern in specific legal contexts.

In recent years there has been an encouraging tendency for legal philosophers to utilize detailed knowledge of the substance and practicalities of law and a noteworthy development in the theoretical sophistication of much legal research. The series seeks to encourage these trends and to make available studies in law which are both genuinely philosophical in approach and at the same time based on appropriate legal knowledge and directed towards issues in the criticism and reform of actual laws and legal systems.

The series will include studies of all the main areas of law, presented in a manner which relates to the concerns of specialist legal academics and practitioners. Each book makes an original contribution to an area of legal study while being comprehensible to those engaged in a wide variety of disciplines. Their legal content is principally Anglo-American, but a wide-ranging comparative approach is encouraged and authors are drawn from a variety of jurisdictions.

Tom Campbell
Series Editor
Centre for Applied Philosophy and Public Ethics
Charles Sturt University, Canberra

Acknowledgements

The distant origins of this book lie, on the one hand, in the lecture halls, seminar rooms and academic offices of the philosophy faculties of the University of Western Australia and the University of Melbourne which I frequented far too often as an undergraduate student, and, on the other hand, in the courtrooms and community halls and shores and hillsides I attended later as a native title lawyer representing a number of the indigenous peoples of the south of Western Australia. Its origins are at once philosophical and legal, theoretical and practical. It is essentially a work of applied legal philosophy and I am grateful to Tom Campbell and Alison Kirk at Ashgate for including it in this series.

In light of its dual origins, my initial thanks go to those who provided support and friendship back then. Firstly, those philosophers at my undergraduate alma maters who provoked and cultivated my interest in philosophy – notably, Val Kerruish, Uwe Petersen, Chris Cordner, Michael Tooley, Julius Kovesi, Graham Priest and Bob Ewin. Then, my colleagues at the Aboriginal Legal Service of Western Australia in those early exciting years of native title practice in Australia – Greg Benn, David Hyams, Harriet Ketley, Marcus Holmes, Anne De Soyza, Anne Sheehan, Tony Shelley, Catherine Crawford, Margaret Jordan, Greg McIntyre and Rob Riley – and the wise and passionate indigenous people I represented who taught me more about cultural difference, intercultural understanding and indigenous rights than any text could.

The majority of the research for this book was engaged in as part of my doctoral studies in philosophy which I completed at the Philosophy and Social and Political Theory programmes of the Research School of the Social Sciences at the Australian National University. I want to thank my two supervisors over the course of that work, Philip Pettit and Robert Goodin, who, in their own distinctive ways, drew more out of me in the thinking and writing of this book than I would have thought possible. I also want to acknowledge the stimulating and immensely challenging intellectual environment provided by the members of the RSSS philosophy community over the course of my studies there. Of special note here are Daniel Stoljar, Michael Smith, Frank Jackson, Jack Smart, David Chalmers and Kim Sterelny, each of whom served as a role model for me in the dark arts of analytic philosophizing.

I also express my gratitude to the other philosophers, legal and political theorists, lawyers and anthropologists at the many centres and faculties of the ANU who, over the years, offered their insights and provoked my thinking about the issues comprising this book – especially Natalie Stoljar, Adrienne Stone, John Braithwaite, Tim Rouse, Desmond Manderson, Bora Kanra, Larissa Behrendt, David Martin, Paul Burke, Katie Glaskin, James Wiener, Chandran Kukathas and Jon Altman.

The final phases of writing this book took place at the Law School of the Australian National University where I presently work. I am indebted to our Dean, Michael Coper, and to our Head of School, Stephen Bottomley (as well as his predecessor Phillipa Weeks), for providing me with the moral and material support for that process. Others in the Law School who have been supportive over the course of this project include Robin Creyke, John McMillan, Dennis Pearce, Leslie Zines, Peter Bailey, Ann Kent, Daniel Stewart, Mike Kobetsky and Anne MacDuff.

I would like to thank Christos Mantziaris, Leighton McDonald, Declan Roche, Gary Edmond and Rick Bigwood for their friendship and support along the way. Barry Laing has also been a good friend and intellectual comrade for many years now.

My special thanks go to Peter Cane for his longstanding support and guidance over much of the course of my academic life and to Tom Campbell for his faith in this project and my work, generally. Thanks also to Jude Chillman at Ashgate for his editorial assistance.

Finally, I am grateful to my parents, Val and Liam and my sister Tanya (as well as Chris, Grace and Lucy) for their love and support over the course of this project. Most importantly, I thank my daughter Elisabeth for the joy she brought to my life over the latter stages of writing and my wife Juliette for all she has given me over the course of our life together. It is to her that this book is enthusiastically and lovingly dedicated.

Chapter 1
Introduction

The Problematic

It has been asserted by various critical and postmodern theorists over a number of years that the agents of the dominant legal systems of liberal democratic nation states such as the United States, Canada, the United Kingdom and Australia are, to some degree, unable to understand the thought and practice of the members of culturally different minority groups inhabiting those states.[1] With reference to indigenous minorities, for example, the Australian indigenous writer and lawyer, Kado Muir, has claimed that, 'legal institutions do not understand Indigenous society, [they] do not understand their relationship with their land, their belief systems, their history'.[2] In relation to Canada's indigenous peoples, the Canadian lawyer and academic, Mary Ellen Turpel, has similarly stated that 'cultural differences are not such that they can be managed within the dominant legal conceptual-framework'.[3] Likewise, the legal theorist Penelope Pether has asserted that, 'it is a commonplace of accounts of indigenous culture … that connection with the land is at its heart, in a way radically incommensurable with the non-indigenous … legal consciousness'.[4]

One way of making sense of assertions such as these is to construe them as involving the claim that the legal agents of such jurisdictions – including, most notably, judges – are unable to adequately conceptualize the thought and practice (and associated material artefacts) of the members of different cultures. Such agents do not and cannot possess an adequate concept of culturally different phenomena. As a result, they cannot maintain true beliefs about these things – they cannot know them and respond appropriately to them – in any significant sense. This is what their lack of understanding consists of. Given the nature of the problematic under discussion in this book, we may assume (as the theorists just mentioned assume) that the members of culturally different minorities may be identified as such, independently of knowing the contents of their conceptual

---

1 See, for example, Foucault (1980), Young (1990), Connolly (1991), Douzinas and Warrington (1991), Derrida (1992), Cornell (1992), Nunn (1997). It is assumed in these claims, as it will be in the discussion to follow, that the agents of dominant legal systems are not members of the culturally different minority groups they encounter in the course of their official duties.

2 Muir (1999) pp. 3–4.

3 Turpel (1990) p. 24.

4 Pether (1998) p. 118.

scheme – for example, by reference to shared genetic properties, historical origins or experience, geographic location, or to language type or other behavioural features. This approach is not inconsistent with that adopted by many anthropologists and social scientists.[5]

Because possessing a concept of an element of thought or practice involves possessing some set of the concepts actually informing that thought and practice,[6] what this claim amounts to is that in their relations with culturally different groups, legal agents do not possess and are unable to adequately acquire some – perhaps, even any – of the concepts which inform the thought and practice of the members of those groups. They do not possess and cannot acquire what I will term, 'culturally different concepts'. Culturally different concepts are those concepts which, from the point of view of a given agent or group, are possessed by the members of a culturally different group.[7] A situation of conceptual difference exists, analysable in terms of an interpretively significant – and again, perhaps even a global – difference in the contents of the respective conceptual schemes of the legal agents and culturally different minorities in question. Further, some degree of *necessity* obtains in relation to this difference. It cannot be adequately resolved or overcome by the acquisition by legal agents of the concepts they lack – no matter what circumstances they find themselves in, *qua* legal agents. We might conceive of this irresolvable difference between the conceptual schemes of the agents in question in terms of an untranslatability or *incommensurability* between those schemes.[8] On this construal, the abovementioned theorists maintain that a significant degree of conceptual incommensurability obtains in the legal sphere as far as culturally different minorities are concerned, comprising both a difference in conceptual schemes and a cognitive-cum-interpretive incapacity as far as overcoming that difference is concerned.

The truth or falsity of the cultural incommensurabilist view is not merely of academic interest. A great deal of concrete, political, social and economic import hinges on it for the millions of people who constitute the culturally different minorities in question here. For if the incommensurabilists are correct, there is little reason to believe that the legal systems of liberal democratic states are able to provide what they purport to provide culturally different minorities by way of minority rights and the like – namely, the meaningful recognition of their ways of life and their effective protection from interference by members of the dominant culture. It would appear that judges, for example, are not able to appropriately recognize, protect or otherwise formally respond to any culturally different thought

5 See Gamst and Norbeck (1976) and Kuper (1999) on this.

6 I will be demonstrating this in Chapter 4.

7 I will also be using the term conceptually different concepts to refer to those concepts which are not, at a given point in time, possessed by the agents of the legal system.

8 Dorit Bar-on (1994) p. 145 defines what he terms cultural incommensurabilism as the view that 'different cultures view the world through conceptual schemes that cannot be reconciled'.

and practice which might come before them at hearing – except, perhaps, by error or accident. If they are right, it would appear that all legal attempts to address the ongoing disruption of distinctive minority cultures by way of minority rights and the like are futile wastes of effort and resources, doomed to failure. Even more problematically, if the cultural incommensurabilists are correct it would follow that by holding out the *hope* of recognition of culturally different thought and practice through a rights regime, the legal systems in question actually obscure the true situation regarding such recognition, distracting minority groups and their supporters from potentially more effective non-legal means of recognition and protection (assuming, of course, that even these were a viable option). This is because, as will be demonstrated in Chapter 4, any such recognition and protection requires a degree of understanding of the culturally different way of life on the part of those legal agents charged with putting into action that recognition and protection. One cannot properly recognize and protect a set of beliefs or practices which one does not understand – to some sufficient degree, at least.

Few would argue that if a legal system is fundamentally disabled from performing its recognitional and protective role because of an inherent conceptual incapacity on the part of its agents, then that incapacity should be understood and appropriately responded to. And if it turns out that that incapacity is not remediable, then those aspects of the legal system which are grounded on the assumption of a conceptual capacity should be abandoned.[9] Nothing is to be gained by maintaining a public institution whose key professed aims are impossible. Likewise, however, if the cultural incommensurabilists are *wrong* in their diagnosis of the conceptual, epistemic and recognitional potential of the liberal democratic legal system, then, given the influence of their thesis within both the academy and broader community, it is important that their error be investigated, diagnosed and publicized. It is important that their own purportedly demystifying thesis be itself demystified. This is particularly so, given the pessimistic and, potentially, quietistic ethical and political outlook such a thesis is liable to engender in regard to cross-cultural relations within those jurisdictions in which culturally different minorities reside.[10] A legal system which is capable of providing at least *some* degree of recognition and protection to culturally different peoples (and potentially a significant degree) should not be subject to a false and destructive criticism, the effect of which might be that system's disempowerment or dismantlement (at least, as far as that recognition and protection is concerned), together with the loss of those benefits it might have been able to provide minorities – limited though those benefits might be. This is quite apart from any theoretical benefits which might be had from debunking a popular but false account of how the world relevantly is.

9 See, for example, Muir (1999), Pether (1998), Motha (1998), Kerruish and Purdy (1998).

10 On the politically and ethically quietistic dynamic of certain postmodern strands of incommensurabilist thought, see Habermas (1987c), Harvey (1989) p. 117, White (1991) pp. 16–18, Norris (1993) p. 287 and Bauman (1993).

Aim and Structure of the Book

So, are the cultural incommensurabilists right or wrong? Can legal agents come to understand culturally different thought and practice in the course of their duties? If not, why not? And if they can, how does such understanding proceed and what factors at play within the legal system affect their ability to do so? Which conditions governing the engagement of legal agents with culturally different thought and practice are conducive to that understanding and which are obstructive of it? These are the questions this book is concerned with – all provoked by the claims of cultural incommensurabilists such as those mentioned above.

This book's aim, then, is to explore – partly by means of a philosophically and legally informed engagement with the cultural incommensurabilist viewpoint, but more substantively by a sustained positive theorizing of the very nature of thought and practice – the capacity of the modern liberal legal system, through its agents, to understand or conceptualize the thought and practice of culturally different people. More specifically, I want to explore the capacity of what is arguably the key agent within that system, the judge adjudicating a legal hearing in which culturally different thought and practice play a significant role. One common and important kind of such hearing is that involving the adjudication of a formal claim on the part of a culturally different minority for the recognition and protection of some aspect of their culture – for example, a land title claim by indigenous group or a claim for religious rights by an immigrant group. Much of this book is concerned with determining whether, to what extent and (importantly) how a judge in such a case might understand those aspects of the culturally different way of life which are the subject of such a claim and which come before her by way of evidence and argument over the course of a hearing. Despite this focus, though, and by virtue of the structural similarities between such a judicial encounter and the institutionalized encounter of any legal agent – indeed, any public official – with a member of a culturally different minority, this book implicates a more general reflection on and explication of the cross-cultural potential of the state and its agents at large.

As I shall argue in Chapter 2, the thought and practice of a group or a person may be analysed in terms of action and its mental – and, specifically, intentional – content. Thus, a more narrowly formulated aim of this book is to inquire into the capacity of a judge acting within the context of a legal hearing to understand culturally different *actions* – that is, actions performed by the members of other cultures whose intentional content is (necessarily) informed by culturally different concepts. Even more precisely, the focus of much of the discussion to follow will be on those culturally different actions which are informed by concepts which are not, at the commencement of the hearing, possessed by that judge – that is, actions which are both culturally and *conceptually* different as far as the judge is concerned.[11] These pose a particular challenge for a theoretical project such as this and constitute the kind of actions which cultural incommensurabilists are most concerned with. I will argue in Chapter 4 that in order to understand a culturally and conceptually different action a judge must acquire some epistemically sufficient set of the concepts informing that action. Given that the only means by which she can do this over the course of a hearing is by means of her interpreting or otherwise cognitively appropriating relevant and admissible evidence about the action and its conceptual content, this book comprises not merely an inquiry into the judicial understanding of such actions but also an inquiry into the capacity of a judge to acquire culturally different concepts and to interpret evidence about those concepts and the actions they inform. It comprises an integrated inquiry into the epistemic, conceptual and interpretive capacities of judges under conditions of cultural and conceptual difference. As such, it is concerned to outline the epistemic, conceptual and interpretive conditions which prevail within the legal hearing process – its epistemic, conceptual and interpretive architecture, if you like. Its ambitions are that broad.

My inquiry into these things proceeds on the basis of a philosophically naturalistic – and, more precisely, physicalistic – metaphysics and methodology. According to this approach, all of the phenomena invoked in the judicial understanding of culturally different actions – concepts, intentional states, actions, cultural difference and the very process of understanding these – are an integral and ordinary part of the natural world, metaphysically continuous with all of the other things in the world. There is nothing supernatural – that is, metaphysically distinct in the traditional dualist, as well as contemporary postmodern sense – about these things, contrary to what many cultural incommensurabilist theorists seem to believe.[12] They are not (fundamentally, at least) of a different nature from the other things existing in the world – things like tables and chairs, judges and courtrooms. They coexist in the world alongside and in the same way as these other things. Like these other things, they may be usefully theorized as 'higher-order' phenomena, ultimately comprised of and made real (realized) by the basic physical stuff of the universe, and individuated as the specific kind of phenomena they are by their functional relations or causal interaction with other things in the world.

11 Actions which are engaged in by agents from a different culture to that of the judge and which are informed by concepts which the judge does not possess at the commencement of the legal hearing.

12 Historically influential incommensurabilists of a dualist stripe include Sapir (1949), Whorf (1956), Levy-Bruhl (1979), Levinas (1969 and 1985), Foucault (1971 and 1980), Derrida (1976, 1978, 1992 and 1998) and Lyotard (1988). See Norris (1993) and Foley (1997) on the influence on these theorists of the dualist metaphysics of Kant. Of the theorists quoted in the early part of this chapter, both Pether and Motha rely explicitly on the dualistic metaphysics of Derrida.

As natural phenomena, we can gain valuable insights into all of the various things implicated in the judicial understanding of cultural difference by means of our best theories and methodologies to do with the natural world – those of the natural sciences and related social sciences, including neurophysiology, developmental psychology, linguistics and sociology. As a result of its metaphysical and methodological articulation with these sciences, the naturalistic approach adopted in this book is not only able to provide a philosophical understanding of things that is more coherent and consistent with the phenomena than that offered by its dualistic and non-naturalistic rivals, but it is able, over the course of its inquiries, to productively exploit the best findings of our current science about human thought and practice. This is not an insignificant theoretical advantage and I will strive to exploit it as best I can in the discussion to follow. I will have more to say later in this chapter on those aspects of the naturalistic metaphysics and methodology which most importantly inform my later analysis.[13]

That analysis proceeds as follows. In Chapter 2, I provide a naturalistic account of the object of judicial understanding – namely, culturally different action and its associated intentionality. The chapter commences with a simple theory of action informed by certain widely held ideas within contemporary analytic philosophy. On this account, actions – including culturally different actions – comprise an interrelated 'psycho-physical' complex of mental and behavioural events. I go on to analyse the philosophically problematic mental aspect of action in terms of behaviourally causal sets of intentional states – sets of beliefs and desires possessing propositional and conceptual content – governed by law-like regularities we traditionally refer to as rationality. Following this, I pursue a sustained theoretical inquiry into the nature of intentionality with a view to defending both the ontological status of intentional states (together with their conceptual content) within a naturalistic ontology, and the epistemological status of our various expert and folk discourses about such states within a scientifically sound system of knowledge. The substance of my analysis of intentional states here is that they are higher-order, physically realized and behaviourally causal states, individuated by their causal-functional role within a broader 'system' of things comprising the behavioural interaction of an agent with her external environment. This is to say that I elaborate what is known in the philosophy of mind as a functionalist account of intentionality and its conceptual constituents. I close Chapter 2 by supplementing the rather individualistic and atomistic account of actions developed in its early stages with a working model of those collective and more complex culturally different sets of actions most likely to come before a judge as the subject matter of a legal claim – for example, religious and other

13 Some might query why I place so much emphasis on metaphysical matters in a book such as this. My response, simply, is that *metaphysics matters* – both to the quality of our understanding of things and to the nature and effectiveness of our interventions in relation to those things.

cultural practices such as rituals, ceremonies, economic practices and the like. These can only be properly understood in their complex entirety.

The physicalist and functionalist account of action and intentionality offered in Chapter 2 provides a philosophical basis for the analysis of the judicial understanding of culturally different action, the judicial acquisition of culturally different concepts and the judicial interpretation of evidence about such action and concepts which follows in Chapters 4 and 5.[14] Prior, though, to the substantively philosophical discussion of those chapters, Chapter 3 provides a degree of concrete legal context for that discussion by presenting an overview of an area of law within which the judicial understanding of culturally different action is commonly pursued in a number of common law jurisdictions – that of indigenous land title law. By virtue of their relatively standard legal form and content, indigenous land title cases embody the theoretically significant aspects of most kinds of legal matters involving cultural difference. In this chapter the concept of indigenous land title is analysed with a view to clarifying the various properties which a set of culturally different indigenous actions must possess in order to obtain the recognition and protection offered by a positive determination of indigenous land title. The fundamental role played by this concept within the epistemic and interpretive practices of judges is clarified in some detail. Following this, those stages of the indigenous land title determination hearing process in which a judge is called upon to interpret evidence about culturally different concepts and actions (and on that basis, potentially acquire those concepts and understand those actions) are identified. With information in hand about the nature of a paradigm procedural and conceptual context within which a judge is called upon to interpret evidence of culturally different concepts and actions, acquire such concepts, and understand such actions, the legal and practical relevance of the substantially philosophical chapters to do with concept acquisition, cross-cultural understanding and conceptual incommensurability which follow may be better appreciated.

In Chapter 4, I return to a more substantive philosophical discussion by establishing and elaborating on the connection between judicial understanding and concept possession which was mentioned earlier in this chapter. This discussion points to the fact that where a judge does not possess culturally different concepts at the commencement of the determination hearing, she must acquire them over the course of that hearing. That is, under conditions of relevant conceptual difference, judicial understanding necessitates the judicial *acquisition* of culturally different concepts. In order to make sense of the nature and possibilities of any such acquisition, I proceed in the second part of Chapter 4 to outline a general definitionalist account of the nature of concepts. This, in turn, provides the basis for a detailed general account of the possession and acquisition of concepts by agents, including judges, which follows. The discussion throughout this part draws on (and is, I argue, the account most compatible with) the physicalist-functionalist

14 In Chapter 4 I address the first two of these and in Chapter 5, the last.

theory of action and intentionality articulated in Chapter 2. It sets the scene for the account of conceptual difference – its nature and its origins – which follows in the latter part of Chapter 4. I conclude the chapter with some preliminary comments, arising out of the discussion there, about the possible limits of such difference, flagging later detailed discussion in Chapter 6.

In Chapter 4, I argue that where a judge does not possess culturally different concepts at the commencement of the legal hearing, she must acquire them over the course of that hearing. In Chapter 5, I follow this up with an argument that the key *means* by which a judge acquires culturally different concepts over the course of a hearing is by interpreting testimonial evidence about those concepts and the culturally different actions those concepts implicate. Much of that chapter is concerned with presenting a physicalist and functionalist account of the nature of such interpretation. Reflecting the methodologically monist tendencies of physicalist naturalism at large, in Chapter 5 I adopt and defend a methodologically monist view of interpretation according to which it constitutes a mode of the naturalistic explanation of higher-order phenomena – in this case, the explanation of testimonial behaviour with reference to that behaviour's intentional cause – which is in no significant respects different from any other kind of explanation offered in the natural or social sciences. Committing to a theory-theory approach to the interpretation of action which has been highly influential in contemporary analytic philosophy, as well as psychology and linguistics, I explore the role played in judicial interpretation by the judge's (largely) folk-psychological theory of agency, theory of mind and theory of the testimonial agent, noting how these theories are applied by the judge in response to and in interpretation of evidence led at hearing. I explore briefly the role of the notorious 'principle of charity' within the interpretive process and distinguish my views of that role from those of noted interpretation theorists such as Donald Davidson and Daniel Dennett.

Chapter 6 relies heavily on the discussion in Chapters 4 and 5. In it I turn my attention to the important question of the limits of conceptual incommensurability within the legal sphere – that is, the extent to which a judge might be incapacitated from understanding culturally different actions. I do so by critically engaging as a physicalist and functionalist with an (admittedly) extreme but heuristically valuable construal of the cultural incommensurabilist position mentioned earlier. This construal, which I term the radical cultural incommensurability thesis, maintains that as a matter of theoretical necessity no judge possesses or is able to acquire any culturally different concept. Over the course of Chapter 6, I rely on various findings in recent neuroscience and developmental psychology, as well as on certain lines of thought in contemporary analytic philosophy, in mounting a series of arguments rebutting the two limbs of this thesis – that asserting the necessity of a radical conceptual *difference* obtaining between judges and culturally different agents, and that asserting the necessity of a radical conceptual-acquisitive *incapacity* afflicting judges in relation to culturally different concepts. In the course of this discussion, I identify and elaborate on the nature and interrelationship of those factors which affect the judicial understanding of culturally different actions.

It is important to note here that the critique of the radical cultural incommensurability thesis in Chapter 6 is pursued not in order to engage with or rebut the views of any particular incommensurabilist theorist but to provide a strategic and heuristic means by which I might inquire into and provide a positive and naturalistically sound account of the nature and limits of (as well as the factors affecting) judicial understanding under conditions of cultural and conceptual difference. In critically engaging with the thesis I do not mean to imply that it represents the views of any actual theorist, including any of the cultural incommensurabilists mentioned earlier in this chapter. It need not represent any actual theorist's views in order to effectively perform the role I am assigning it in this book. Consequently, no charge can be maintained that in utilizing the thesis in the manner I do I am misrepresenting or distorting the views of any theorist or group of theorists. This is not to say, of course, that the outcome of my inquiries will not be of relevance to the views of any actual incommensurabilists, including more moderate ones. By identifying the naturalistic limits of incommensurability, it certainly will.[15]

The upshot of my critique of the radical cultural incommensurability thesis in Chapter 6 is that a significant (though not a global) degree of conceptual difference between a judge and a culturally different agent or group is contingently possible, but not necessary. The degree of difference which obtains in relation to a given judge and a given set of culturally different concepts at a given point in time depends for the most part on certain contingent facts to do with the judge's prior conceptual development, the nature and relevance of which I describe in Chapter 6. Likewise, it is contingently possible (but again, not necessarily the case) that a judge not be able to acquire a culturally different concept or set of concepts over the course of a legal hearing. Again, whether she can or cannot depends on two contingent factors – the concepts already possessed by the judge at the commencement of the hearing and what I term the epistemic conditions which obtain over the course of the hearing.[16] A failure of judicial understanding – even a widespread failure across the whole of the judiciary in relation to all culturally different actions which might be subject to claim – is entirely possible within the legal sphere. But, equally, a successful exercise in judicial understanding is possible, for any and all judges and for any and all culturally different actions. Everything here depends on the content of the judge's conceptual scheme at the

15 I might add here that the *prima facie* implausibility of the radical cultural incommensurability thesis also provides no grounds for not utilizing it in the manner I intend. The very nature of and reasons for its implausibility are of prime importance to the project I have set myself in this book.

16 These conditions include the sensory and cognitive capacities of the presiding judge, the availability of evidence about the culturally different concept or action in question, the legal norms regulating the use of any such evidence, and the quality of the hearing environment.

commencement of the hearing and on the epistemic conditions which obtain for that judge over the course of the hearing.

What most importantly emerges from Chapter 6 as far as culturally different claimants and their lawyers, presiding judges, responsible law makers and interested citizens are concerned is that the various factors conditioning the capacity of a judge to acquire culturally different concepts and understand culturally different actions are not only contingent, they are amenable to a significant degree of legal regulation. Because of the contingency of these factors, it lies within the power of those responsible for the operation of the legal hearing process to affect them to some degree. The legal system is open to the effective reform of its capacity to understand culturally different actions. As a matter of institutional design it is possible for those presently constituting and controlling the epistemic and interpretive architecture of the legal system act so as to affect both the contents of the conceptual scheme possessed by its judges at the commencement of those hearings they preside over and the epistemic conditions those judges act under over the course of hearings.

In the concluding Chapter 7, I attempt to fulfil the modest practical and critical aspirations of the book, which in earlier chapters remain merely implicit, by identifying a number of key features common to many contemporary legal systems which affect – both favourably and unfavourably – the judicial understanding of culturally different actions. To the extent that a legal system might be oriented towards the improvement of its epistemic and interpretive capacities under conditions of cultural difference, the provision and cultivation of facilitative conditions and the removal or amelioration of obstructing conditions are objectives those controlling and constituting that system might want to pursue. Whilst noting that it is not the primary aim of this book to elaborate a detailed set of reform proposals in relation to legal process but, rather, to provide a philosophically and legally informed *basis* for the development of any such proposals, Chapter 7 identifies a number of lines of thinking in relation to such reform. It completes the book's descriptive project and points the way to future legal analytic and reformist research and practice in this sphere.

Physicalism: A Metaphysics and Methodology

As mentioned above, the stance I adopt throughout the inquiry to follow is a philosophically naturalistic one. At this early stage of things, I want to identify the theoretical foundations on which this book is based and spend some time articulating those aspects of the naturalistic project which directly inform the discussion in later chapters. Important parts of that discussion will not be readily comprehensible to the reader without this prior groundwork. Philosophical naturalism, as I described it earlier, is a broad church, admitting a range of more refined metaphysical and methodological positions. Within that broad church, the brand of naturalism I find most compelling is that known as physicalism.[17] Like naturalism at large, physicalism is a philosophical approach which is concerned with both the nature of reality and our knowledge of that reality. It 'provides a vision, a way of seeing and understanding reality and a way of pursuing knowledge'.[18] As such, physicalism has both an ontological and an epistemological dimension, both of which are important to the inquiry into judicial understanding and cultural difference which is to follow.

The ontological dimension of physicalism is concerned with the questions of what there is in the world (what categories of things actually exist), how those things most fundamentally are and how they are ontologically related to each other. In the course of rendering an account of what it is that renders phenomena real, physicalism is also concerned with articulating a set of standards by which we may judge the ontological status or reality of putative phenomena and discern those that actually exist from those that do not. The epistemological dimension of physicalism is parasitic on the ontological (as our knowledge of the world is parasitic on how the world actually is) and is concerned with determining which claims and theories are actually about real phenomena and are, therefore, theoretically legitimate on that account, as well as what the standards are by which we might assess this. In this mode, physicalism seeks to provide an account of what it is which renders a theory of things or a claim about how things are a legitimate part of our overall body of theorizing and, ultimately, knowledge about the world, enabling us to discern legitimate from illegitimate theories and claims about the world.[19] In pursuing its ontological and epistemological objectives, physicalism distinguishes itself by giving ontic priority to the fundamental physical realm and epistemic priority to our best theory of that realm, physics.[20]

As far as its ontology goes, very simply, physicalism holds that everything in the world which may properly be said to exist, to be real (including, for our purposes, all of the phenomena comprising the judicial understanding of culturally different thought and action) is, *in a sense*, physical. What this 'sense' boils down to is that 'all phenomena occur in nature in virtue of what goes on in the physical domain'.[21] Everything in the world is either a member of that class of phenomena

17 For many contemporary philosophers, naturalism is synonymous with physicalism. See Papineau (1993), Pettit (1992) and (1993a) p. 213. The modern roots of physicalism may be traced to the influential 'naturalizing' programme of Quine (1969) and his successors. See Poland (1994) and Melnyk (2003) for two recent detailed expositions of physicalism.

18 Poland (1994) p. 348. See also Alyssa Ney's (2008) recent article on physicalism as an attitude.

19 As far as its scope and epistemic status is concerned, physicalism aspires to be an *a posteriori* doctrine about the natural world – that is, an empirically justified account of that realm of phenomena in which we humans live and with which we causally interact. Crane and Mellor (1990) p. 185, Post (1991) p. 95, Poland (1994) pp. 227–8 and Melnyk (1997) pp. 635–7 and (2003), Chapter 6.

20 Melnyk (1994) p. 223. Crane (1994) p. 480.

21 Poland (1994) p. 207.

which comprise the most ontologically basic constituents of the world – the set of phenomena described by our best account of the most basic constituents of the world, physics – or is made up of those basic phenomena in some ontologically distinctive way.[22] Everything is either part of the physical base or is ontologically related to that base in the requisite sense as a more complex, so-called *higher-order* phenomenon. There is nothing which exists in the world that is not physical in this sense. The world is ontologically closed.[23] There are no ghosts, supernatural substances or properties, or immaterial minds or meanings or cultural differences, as many religious, philosophical and commonsense accounts of the world of a metaphysically dualist stripe (including certain cultural incommensurabilist accounts) have maintained over the years.

As far as its epistemology goes, physicalism holds that all legitimate claims and theories about the world (including those about the judicial understanding of cultural difference) are discursively related to or grounded in – indeed, in a sense, *reducible to* – the theories and claims of science and, ultimately, physics.[24] What this boils down to, crudely, is that knowledge claims and theories which are about physical and physically realized phenomena are legitimate claims and theories about the world (they may be true or false[25]) and those which are about putative phenomena which do not exist in the physicalist sense are not legitimate claims and theories about the world.[26] Given the physicalist ontology and the parasitic relationship which our knowledge of the world has to the way the world actually

22 Physicalists grant physics 'a unique ontological authority: the authority to tell us what there is'. Crane and Mellor (1990) p. 185. See also Post (1987) p. 159, Pettit (1993b) pp. 213–5 and Lewis (1994) p. 412. The question of the identity of the physical base is one of the most controversial and intractable problems for physicalists at present. I don't propose to discuss it here, other than to say that my preference lies with those who identify it in terms of present day physics (despite the risk of that physics being to some degree incomplete or false). See Crane and Mellor (1990) p. 185, Crane (1994), Poland (1994), ch. 3, Guttenplan (1994b), Melnyk (1997) and (2003) ch. 1 on this.

23 Papineau (1993) pp. 16–17, Braddon-Mitchell and Jackson (1996) p. 15, and Post (1987) pp. 205–6.

24 Physicalism 'is a programme of [epistemic] unification which accords special privilege to physics. It is directed towards development of a system of knowledge within which all aspects of reality have a place and are related to physics in certain specifiable ways'. Poland (1994) p. 10. See also Hellman and Thompson (1975) p. 551, Post (1987) p. 17, Crane and Mellor (1990) p. 185, Melnyk (1994) pp. 17, 223 and (2003) p. 2, Jackson (1998) p. 6. Again, the precise nature of the sense of reducibility at work here is a highly contentious issue for physicalists. Classical bridge-law and identity accounts, which have drawn so much attention from non-physicalists over the years, have been superseded of late and replaced with more sophisticated, more credible and less eliminativist modes of reduction. See for example, the realizationist reductionism of Jaegwon Kim in Kim (1998).

25 Post (1987) p. 17.

26 This is not to say, of course, that such latter claims and theories may not be legitimate in some other, non-descriptive, sense – say, an aesthetic or edificatory sense.

is, this account of what constitutes knowledge within the physicalist schema is to be expected. In seeking to distinguish legitimate from illegitimate claims and theories, physicalism constitutes an epistemologically eliminativist doctrine. However, the realizationist version of physicalism maintained throughout this book is a *modestly* eliminativist one which aims to be as consistent as it can with our best intuitions about what is real and what is not, what claims and theories are legitimately about the world and what are not. The reducibility of all legitimate higher-order claims and theories to physics does not entail that physics or even the natural sciences says all there is to say about the world or that all other theories or disciplines serve as mere placeholders or shorthand for the physical truth.[27] To the extent that the phenomena under discussion in this book are realized by the physical, this book constitutes a legitimate – and I would want to argue, true – account of those phenomena. So too, I might add, is the folk theory of mind utilized by judges in making sense of culturally different actions. Likewise, to the extent that the phenomena posited by dualistic cultural incommensurabilists in their account of understanding and difference are not physically realized, then their account is an illegitimate one.

Physicalists have conceived of the precise nature of the ontological relationship which all existing higher order things bear to the physical base in a number of ways, including those of type-identity, supervenience and realization.[28] For reasons well argued by Kim, Melnyk and Poland, I am most persuaded by that school of physicalist thought which conceives of that relation as one of realization.[29] I hold that all existent phenomena are either elements of the physical base or are realized (made real) by elements of the physical base in a manner still to be fully described here.[30] The phenomena constituting the subject matter of this book fall into the

---

27 Poland (1994) p. 12. 'The universality of [physics] should not be mistaken for a kind of tyranny'. Guttenplan (1994b) p. 77.

28 On type-identity physicalism, see Smart (1959) and Braddon-Mitchell and Jackson (1994). On supervenience see the essays in Savellos and Yalcin (1995). On realization, see Kim (1993) and (1998), Poland (1994) and Melnyk (2003).

29 Ibid. The ontological relationship of realization comprehends or entails a number of weaker modes of ontological relatedness between physical and higher-order phenomena including the relations of dependence (invoking the notion that the existence of higher-order phenomena requires the existence of some or other physical base) and supervenience (invoking the notion that any changes or differences in the higher-order entail changes or differences in the physical base). Encompassing and transcending these weaker relations, realization better satisfies core physicalist intuitions about the ontological primacy of the physical and the proper inventory of existent phenomena by ruling out all unacceptably strong forms of metaphysical dualism. None of this is to deny the challenge that realizationist physicalists face in rebutting their critics and rendering the concept of realization more philosophically sound. See Moreland (1998), Poland (1994), ch. 4, Kim (1998), ch. 1 and Melnyk (2003), ch. 2.

30 Braddon-Mitchell and Jackson (1996) p. 27, Poland (1994) p. 47, Melnyk (2003) pp. 9–11, Kim (1998) p. 19.

latter category. At the heart of the notion of realization (as with most of the other forms of physicalism) lies a common and deeply embedded intuition 'that the various kinds of things in the world are composed of smaller and simpler items [and] that this composition establishes a hierarchy of different levels of thing'.[31] For Jaegwon Kim, physicalism is an expression of the dominant philosophical and scientific paradigm of our age which conceives of the world as 'a hierarchically organised system stratified into levels or orders of entities and their properties, from the bottom level of the most basic bits of matter to higher levels consisting of increasingly complex structures composed of material particles'.[32]

Physicalism reflects and gives theoretical body to this intuition or paradigm, identifying the most basic level in the ontological hierarchy in terms of the phenomena described by physics. Because of its privileging of the physical base in this manner, physicalism may be conceived of as generating an ontological hierarchy of lower- and higher-order phenomena, characterized as such by virtue of their ontological 'altitude' or proximity to that base. For physicalists,

> [t]he bottom level is thought to consist of elementary particles, or whatever our best physics is going to tell us are the basic bits of matter out of which all material things are composed. As we go up the ladder, we successively encounter atoms, molecules, cells, larger living organisms, and so on … entities belonging to a given level, except those at the very bottom, have an exhaustive decomposition, without remainder, into entities belonging to the lower levels. Entities at the bottom level have no physically significant proper parts.[33]

Thus, some of the fundamental physical entities which make up the world may combine to form those higher-level entities we term chemical entities. Likewise, the (relatively) lower-level entities of chemistry may combine to form the even higher-level entities of biology (for example, cells), and some of this set of entities may combine to form the even higher-level entities of physiology and psychology, including those entities we term human beings, their brains and bodies and their intentional states and actions, as well as the understanding of these. This process of the realization of things proceeds up into the social and other super-structural realms of the world, generating all of the phenomena comprising the realms of

31 Pettit (1993b) p. 221.

32 Kim (1998) p. 16. See also Pettit (1993) p. 342 and Kim (2003) p. 565.

33 Kim (1998) p. 15. It is worth noting that some physicalists – including Lewis, Armstrong and Melnyk – deny that physicalism is committed to this layered ontology if, by this, we mean 'the idea that reality constitutes a *neat and tidy* hierarchy of levels in which each level is the bailiwick of a particular branch of science'. Melnyk (2003) p. 30 (my emphasis). I agree that the relationship between layers may be more complex and indeterminate than the simple picture outlined here suggests. However, this picture is, I think, broadly correct and quite an adequate model of things for the purposes of the discussion to follow.

law and other cultural institutions.[34] At every stage, the entities within each of these ontological levels possess certain characteristic properties, engage in certain activities or fulfil certain functions which are, in a way, distinct from the properties, activities or functions of entities at other levels, including the base physical level.[35]

The concept of realization captures the view that all existent higher-order entities are entirely constituted by lower-order and, ultimately, physical entities and that all existent higher-order properties are the properties of such higher-order entities and arise out of and are instantiated solely in virtue of the instantiation of the properties of physical entities.[36] A higher-order phenomenon is realized by a physical phenomenon when it owes its existence and its nature *entirely* to the existence and nature of that physical phenomenon – when no fundamentally non-physical or metaphysically emergent phenomenon plays a role.[37] A higher-order phenomenon exists and is the way it is solely in virtue of the fact that some set of physical phenomena – its physical realizer set – exists and is the way it is. Notwithstanding its fundamentally monist orientation, this brand of physicalism is, however, at the same time, remarkably generous as far as the granting of ontological status is concerned. It is quite compatible with a rich, multifaceted ontology of physical, lower- and higher-order phenomena, including most importantly, the higher-order phenomena comprising the judicial understanding of cultural difference.[38] As I hope to show in Chapter 2, in applying realization physicalism to the realm of intentionality, action and interpretation we are able to

---

34 The ontological relationship here is a transitive one. An existing higher-order phenomenon maintains a relation of realization either directly with the physical base or indirectly with the physical base by virtue of being realized by some set of lower-order physically-based phenomena – that is, some set of lower-order phenomena which is itself directly or indirectly realized by the physical base. Poland (1994) p. 198. Thus, we may conceive of and explain certain legal or social phenomena in terms of the psychological, and psychological phenomena in terms of the neuro-physiological, and these latter phenomena, in turn, in terms of the chemical and physical.

35 Kim (1998) pp. 15–16 states that, 'it is part of this layered picture that at each level there are properties, activities, and functions that make their first appearance, or "emerge", at that level (we may call them the characteristic properties of that level). Thus, among the characteristic properties of the molecular level are electrical conductivity, inflammability, density, viscosity, and the like; activities and functions like metabolism and reproduction are among the characteristic properties of the cellular and higher biological levels; and consciousness and other mental properties make their appearance at the level of higher organisms'.

36 Melnyk (2003) p. 7, Heil (1998) p. 97.

37 Melnyk (2003) p. 7.

38 Post (1987) p. 15. As Poland points out, 'the conception of reality that the physicalist system must accommodate is one which countenances, inter alia, the many kinds of natural and artifactual objects that we encounter in daily life and that we identify in various theoretical and other cultural endeavours'. Poland (1994) pp. 196–7. See also Kim (1998) p. 2 and Post (1987) p. 15.

address Kim's concern that we 'find a way of accommodating the mental within a principled physicalist scheme, while at the same time preserving it as something distinctive – that is, without losing what we value, or find special, in our nature as creatures with minds'.[39]

A striking feature of the realization of higher-order phenomena is that it is importantly conceptual. This is to say that it is importantly – though not exclusively, of course – the result of human conceptualizing activity.[40] What happens is this. Combinations of the basic physical stuff of the world may become the subject of human perception and conceptualization – whether in the course of our everyday engagement with the world or in our scientific practices. These combinational entities and their properties may be perceived and conceptualized by us, individually and collectively, as entities and properties of a given higher-order kind or type. For example, by virtue of our sensory apparatus, as well as our beliefs and our desires, we perceive, think about and act towards those combinations of physical stuff that constitute what we call trees. This is to say that we conceptualize those combinations of physical stuff as trees, coining a term to refer to the class of things that are comprehended by the concept of tree. By doing so, we give ontological status to trees *qua* trees. Within some cognitive and practical context, we accept certain combinations of physical phenomena as comprising part of the furniture of the world. We hold that trees exist.

Different cognitive and practical contexts may generate different inventories of phenomena and different conceptual vocabularies for different communities of agents engaged in this process. In our everyday engagement with the world we perceive, conceive of and give ontological status to a range of higher-level entities such as trees, rocks, rivers and clouds. Likewise, in the course of their cognitive and practical engagement with the world, scientists perceive things which lead them (directly or indirectly) to conceive of and give ontological status to higher-level entities such as molecules, cells and living organisms. Judges too, as well as other agents participating in legal hearings, conceptualize the physical reality they are confronted with in terms of witnesses, testimony, evidence and argument. To the extent that these things are, in fact, constituted by physical phenomena in the requisite sense – that is, realized by the physical – physicalists too may grant those things ontological status and classify them as lower- or higher-order depending on their position within physicalism's ontological hierarchy.

In all of our various higher-order engagements with the world we use 'non-physics' terminology – chemical, biological, intentional, legal and so on – to group and categorize large-scale arrangements of what are fundamentally physical phenomena.[41] Thus, for each ontological level of entities and its characteristic

39 Kim (1998) p. 2.

40 The precise nature of which I will have more to say about in Chapter 4.

41 Papineau (1993) p. 13 captures this aspect of human conceptualizing practice in his comment that, 'the world recognised by physicalism is at bottom a world constituted by physical facts, by particles and fields in motion through space. At this basic level all facts

properties a theory or science may develop (perhaps more than one) which is responsible for identifying and inquiring into the nature of phenomena at that level.[42] 'Each of the many [higher-order theories] has its own characteristic theoretical vocabulary with which, to the extent that it gets things right, it describes a characteristic domain of objects, events, and properties.'[43] The natural science we term physics has arisen and is concerned with the nature of the most fundamental entities which constitute the world, as well as their characteristic properties. The higher-order natural science of chemistry is concerned with the nature of those complexes of the basic physical phenomena which we term chemical phenomena. It is concerned with the properties of atoms and molecules and the like. And so on, through the natural sciences of biology and human physiology into the so-called special sciences of human psychology, sociology, and the like – including, importantly for our purposes, legal philosophy. By virtue of the ontological relation which exists between the phenomena studied by them, these sciences are epistemically related in a manner which is of great interest and of great value to the physicalist inquirer. Specifically, it is by virtue of this relation that the philosophical inquiry constituting this book can later rely so effectively on the findings of relevant natural and social sciences. Just as the physicalist ontology generates a picture of reality as a hierarchical series of lower- and higher-orders, all ultimately grounded in the physical, so the physicalist epistemology generates a picture of our overall system of knowledge as a hierarchical series of lower- and higher-order theories of things, all ultimately grounded in physics.

Although phenomena at the higher orders are ontologically grounded in phenomena at lower orders, including the physical order – although *fundamentally* there is no more to all the higher-order phenomena of the world than the phenomena comprising their physical base – such phenomena are and may legitimately be conceived of as having a certain existence of their own. They are at once ontologically related to lower-order and (ultimately) physical phenomena and – in a way, at least – distinct from them. Of course, they are not so distinct as not to be realized by the physical base in the manner required by physicalism. Higher-order phenomena are real, but in a manner which is subordinate to the reality of the basic physical stuff which ontologically grounds them.[44] The physical has

can be *described* by strictly physical terminology, like "mass", "energy", and "position". However, physicalism, as I have characterized it, allows that we often use non-physical terminology, like "sulphuric acid", "thunderstorm", "elephant", and "thinking of the future", to group and categorise large-scale arrangements of physical facts'.

42 Kim (2003) p. 566.

43 Melnyk (2003) p. 1, Poland (1994) pp. 31–2.

44 One key manifestation of this subordinate ontological status is that higher-order phenomena do not have a *distinct causal role* from that of the physical phenomena they are ontologically related to. In fact, only the physical base is, properly speaking, causally efficacious in the world. This is an important issue in the philosophy of intentionality and action, which regrettably, I only pass over in the next chapter. For the record, I am sympathetic to the views of Kim (1998) on the causal nature of higher-order phenomena.

ontic priority. The ontological autonomy of higher-order phenomena within the physicalist schema is, therefore, a metaphysically attenuated one. If higher order phenomena exist, they exist *by virtue of* their relation to the basic physical stuff and its properties. This is what it is for the physical to have ontic priority in the scheme of things and for the world to be fundamentally physical. Higher-order phenomena exist, but not – in any full sense – *in addition to* the physical phenomena which realize them. This is the sense mentioned above in which higher-order phenomena are physical.

I will have more to say about the ontology of those higher-order phenomena comprising the judicial understanding of cultural difference in the next chapter. For the time being, though, let me offer a rather crude but nonetheless instructive analogy as a way of enabling a better sense of that ontology. Imagine that I place a carved block of coloured glass on a pile of loose papers. It would be correct to say that there is a carved block of coloured glass on the pile of papers. It would also be correct to say that there is a paperweight on the pile. But if asked how many objects there are on the papers, the correct answer would be one, not two. The paperweight does not exist – in any strong sense of the term – *in addition to* the block of glass. It *just is* the block of glass. It is entirely constituted by the block of glass. If, for the sake of discussion, we were to assign ontic priority to the block of glass, then we could conceive of the relation between the two things as one approximating that of realization. It would be correct to say that the paperweight is realized by the block of glass and that it enjoys an ontological status commensurate with being realized in this way. It exists in the attenuated sense referred to above.

At this point, it is useful to consider what paperweights are in a more general sense. That is, we might ask what the type or class of phenomena termed 'paperweight' is. Here we must turn to an authoritative concept or definition of paperweight and identify its content. Let's suppose that according to that concept, a paperweight is an object which (actually or potentially) keeps loose paper in place. The type 'paperweight' is, then, that class of objects described by this concept or definition. Any token object which keeps loose paper in place is a paperweight. A more philosophically abstract way to conceive of a paperweight is as an object which meets certain characteristic conditions, including, for example, playing a certain causal role in relation to other things in the world – in this case, the condition or role of keeping loose paper in place. We may think of these conditions as described by the concept of paperweight – a concept whose content (understood as a set of membership-defining conditions) is determined by the thought and actions of some semantically authoritative set of conceptualizing

We might conceive of the ontological status of higher-order phenomena advocated here as lying between a full-blown realism of the higher-order (which might entail a form of metaphysical dualism) on the one hand, and a higher-order anti-realism on the other (in the mould of Dennett's stance on mental phenomena). Dennett (1987) pp. 37, 103–16. Avoiding the dualistic and anti-realist implications of this position remains a key challenge for realization physicalists, including myself.

agents, some conceptual community for whom the concept plays a role in their worldview and way of life. Any object which meets the characteristic conditions of being a paperweight is a paperweight.[45] The existence of a paperweight *qua* paperweight is, thus, a function of this process of conceptualization.[46]

This is to say that paperweights are importantly conceptual. However, we must keep in mind that this conceptualization does not magically create a new object with the full ontological status of the glass block which comprises or realizes it. As Kim points out, 'by existential quantification over a given domain of properties we do not literally bring into being a new set of properties. That would be sheer magic ... By mere logical operation on our notations, we cannot alter our ontology – we cannot diminish or expand it'.[47] What *most fundamentally* exists in our example (given our assumption of its ontic priority) is the glass block, not the paperweight. Though a process of conceptualization may be a necessary condition of a paperweight existing qua paperweight, it is not *sufficient* for it existing. By virtue of this a full-blown anti-realism in relation to paperweights is avoided. Paperweights do not exist *solely* or even *primarily* by virtue of the conceptualizing practices of some community of agents. They exist most fundamentally because there exist lower-order realizers who meet the conditions definitive of being a paperweight. The physical phenomena constituting the block of glass in our example realize the paperweight because those phenomena are such that they meet the individuating conditions described by the concept of paperweight. They are importantly, but not exclusively or even primarily, conceptual.

Developing this line of thought further, a physical object which we characterize as a paperweight can meet a variety of conditions or play a variety of roles apart from that of holding down paper. It can serve as a doorstop, or a weapon, or a piece of modern art. An important philosophical question arises here in regard to which of the many roles which the physical object can perform (or sets of conditions which it can meet) make it a paperweight and how we might come to know this.[48] The answer is that the conditions or role which makes the object a paperweight (as distinct from a doorstop or a piece of modern art) is determined by the thought and practice of the community of agents who use the concept 'paperweight'. This conceptual community utilizes in their thought and practice the concept of paperweight in response to the way the world around them is and in response to

---

45 To the extent that a range of physical object types can meet these conditions, a paperweight is a multiply realizable higher-order type. Realization physicalism is, therefore, compatible with the multiple realizability of the higher order. This is a point in its favour over other modes of physicalism such as type-identity physicalism. Putnam (1967), Kim (1998) pp. 2–3.

46 In introducing the conceptual dimension of physicalist ontology at this point, I am incidentally providing a metaphysical framework for the important discussion on the nature of concepts and judicial concept acquisition which is to follow in Chapter 4.

47 Kim (1998) p. 103.

48 Braddon-Mitchell and Jackson (1996) p. 45.

how their beliefs and desires about that world are. They have paper, the paper sometimes blows away in a breeze, they desire that it does not blow away, they believe that putting certain kinds of objects on the paper stops it blowing away, they put these objects on the paper. And then, on the basis of these objects' functional capacity to keep paper in place and for the purposes of their future thought and practice they class together these kinds of objects – they conceptualize them – as members of the higher-order type known as paperweights.

Why? Because there is some advantage or value in doing so. The role played by all the physical realizers in keeping papers in place is important enough to the community to ground the adoption of a concept categorizing them all in relation to this role. Kim notes this when he states that higher-order concepts such as paperweight 'may well serve important conceptual and epistemic needs, by grouping properties that share features of interest to us in a given context of inquiry'.[49] The thought and practice of members of this conceptual community is from this point on informed by this concept. It has currency amongst them through their actions. It is this thought and practice which, to a necessary but not sufficient extent, renders any physical object which meets the conditions prescribed by that concept, a paperweight. This is the sense in which paperweights are importantly conceptual.

Our paperweight example can serve as a rough model of the ontological status of all higher-order phenomena – including, most importantly, the phenomena which form the subject matter of our inquiry, culturally different thought and action and judicial understanding. All higher-order phenomena are realized by an ontically prior set of physical phenomena. They exist not in addition to the existence of their physical and lower-order realizers but wholly in virtue of the existence of those realizers.[50] Further, they do so because, like the paperweight in our example, they are phenomena which are fundamentally characterized or individuated with reference to a certain set of conditions specified by the concept of the higher-order phenomenon in question. The set of conditions which individuate all higher-order phenomena – which make them the specific higher-order phenomenon they are – is determined by the thought and practice of some relevant conceptual community of agents. Higher-order phenomena as a whole are, again, importantly conceptual. Invoking certain of Heidegger's ontological views, John Post captures this dimension of things rather well in his comment that 'we bear some responsibility for the way things become part of our world or worlds; for us, things never have their being or their properties by themselves but only through the combined activity of our understanding *and* some undisclosed ground beyond'.[51]

49 Kim (1998) p. 110.

50 An important challenge for theorizing any given higher-order phenomenon is identifying that realizer set.

51 Post (1987) p. 20. Kim (1998) p. 104 goes so far as to suggest that in recognition of this we should speak in terms of higher-order concepts rather than higher-order phenomena, as such. As Sabates (2002) notes, however, Kim's unfortunate view here threatens to collapse into higher-order anti-realism.

Every higher-order type or property has an associated condition or set of conditions, specified by the concept of that type or property. Higher-order types and properties differ from each other by virtue of them being characterized or individuated by different sets of associated conditions. The conceptually-defined individuating conditions of a higher-order phenomenon may involve the possession of certain intrinsic physical properties – having a specific physical composition or internal structure – or, alternatively, the maintenance of certain causal-nomic (regular causal) relations with other phenomena.[52] For some higher-order phenomena the maintenance of such causal-nomic relations may be construed in terms of the occupying or filling of a characteristic causal-nomic role or *function* within a broader set or system of other phenomena. Something occupies a causal role or function within a system of things if it is the subject of regular causal relations with other phenomena within that system; if it 'causally responds in particular ways to causal inputs with particular kinds of output'.[53] Thus, certain higher-order phenomena – and for our purposes, the most important of these are the intentional phenomena comprising the judicial understanding of cultural difference – are functionally characterized. They are importantly functional in nature and are best theorized about from a functionalist perspective. I will have more to say about this in the next chapter.

Having elaborated the ontological and epistemological commitments of physicalism, I hope that the value of the doctrine as a framing metaphysics and methodology for an inquiry such as this has been rendered apparent to some degree. Justifying my choice of metaphysics and methodology nevertheless remains a challenge. At heart – and to put it very crudely – the attraction I and many others have towards physicalism as an ontology lies in the fact that, *all things considered*, it just seems right. Given all we know about the natural world and its evolution, and about human beings and their history, it overwhelmingly appears that we humans and what we do and what we think have historically emerged from and continue to constitute a part of the natural – and, as it turns out, fundamentally physical – world which predates us and continues to surround us. There appears no good reason to suppose that with the historical emergence of human beings into the world, radically novel metaphysical kinds such as minds and meanings also emerged. And with a physicalist ontology thus justified, a parasitic physicalist epistemology and methodology of the kind sketched here follows. Of course, some might find this attempt at justification very slight and rather suspect (a product of my all too

52 Heil (1998) p. 96. Natural kind concepts such as water, for example, fall into the first category of concepts here. Concepts such as paperweight – but also, as we shall see, those of belief, desire and concept itself – fall into the second category.

53 Heil (1998) p. 97. Melnyk (1994) p. 225 argues that *all* higher-order phenomena are functionally individuated, in which case realizationist physicalism of mind entails (for him, at least) functionalism of mind. If he is correct, then this serves as another reason to foreground physicalism and not merely functionalism in any discussion of intentionality, action and understanding.

subjective intuitions or preferences or of an ultimately irrational faith in science). I do not intend to mount a full-scale argument in defence of my comments here. I will, though, at least point to certain other reasons which might be employed in support of physicalism – specifically those that relate to the ends and values of the very activity of theorizing (as these are conventionally understood, at least).

For example, by virtue of its underlying ontological and epistemic monism, a physicalist framework of inquiry is capable of providing theorists with an ontological and theoretical parsimony and unity which is, in turn, able to ground an unequalled degree of theoretical simplicity, consistency, comprehensiveness and synergy across our system of knowledge at large, as well as within its various disciplines. These epistemic values in turn, provide the basis for a substantial increase in our understanding of things – and specifically, the judicial understanding of culturally different action. As Poland points out, 'a unified picture of nature provides more and deeper understanding than does a view of nature that represents it as a disunified aggregate of isolated and disconnected facts'.[54] Such unity also provides for consistency across the system of knowledge; a consistency which ensures maximal truth across theories by more effectively subjecting claims within a discipline and between disciplines to cross-check. An overarching epistemic unity across disciplines of knowledge facilitates an extremely valuable epistemic accountability between and within those disciplines.[55]

Following on from this, by calling on us to understand the nature of the judicial understanding of culturally different action as part of the natural order of things, a physicalist approach enables us, in a way that other approaches do not, to effectively and justifiably draw on the best that the natural and related social sciences have to offer about the various phenomena implicated here. There can be little doubt that the sciences have provided and will continue to provide immense explanatory and predictive power in relation to human thought, action and interaction. The findings of these sciences should not readily be marginalized in any theoretical pursuit. Any credible inquiry into judicial understanding and cultural difference must be prepared to take note of and rely on the findings of our best sciences of the various elements comprising that phenomenon – of neuro-physiology, developmental and cognitive psychology, linguistics, and anthropology. Physicalism provides the most compelling philosophical framework within which to do so.

Some Final Introductory Remarks

The modern liberal legal system has been subjected to a sustained campaign of incommensurabilist critique for a number of years now, a great deal of it arising, as I said earlier, from the postmodernist perspective. Much of this critique has been based (explicitly or implicitly) on what, I would argue, are empirically and

54 Poland (1994) p. 28. See also Kitcher (1981) pp. 529–30.

55 Poland (1994) p. 26.

conceptually unsound metaphysical premises. Many incommensurabilists, for all their *post*modern pretensions, appear to partake of an anachronistic, metaphysically dualist theory of mind and meaning, according to which intentional states and their conceptual components are fundamentally non-natural phenomena whose identity is known by a fundamentally non-natural faculty quite metaphysically distinct from that by which we come to knowledge of the natural world.[56] For example, for many such theorists, the mind (including its intentional and conceptual contents) serves as a filter of sorts through which the noumenal world – the given, the in-itself, and so on – is apprehended and rendered phenomenal and (in circumstances of cultural difference) radically incommensurable.[57] The truth of this dichotic view of mind and world has not only been contradicted by our ever increasing body of scientific knowledge about the physiological and psychological and communicative features of human beings but its very logical coherence has been devastatingly called into question.[58] A not unimportant part of what this book is about lies in rebutting this non-naturalistic mode of understanding the issues here, a mode of understanding which is not only theoretically flawed but ethically and politically counterproductive in its implicit promotion and perpetuation of a quietistic pessimism about the possibilities of legal, political and social reform in relation to cross-cultural matters.[59]

My objective in calling cultural incommensurabilist views into question is not to immunize liberal democratic legal systems from critique but, rather, to provide a sounder basis for the critique of those systems. I share the general concern of incommensurabilist critics of the liberal democratic legal system in relation to the capacity of its agents to adequately understand culturally different action and properly recognize and protect culturally different ways of life. If the interests and expectations of culturally different minorities are to be effectively addressed by a dominant society, appropriate and effective mechanisms must operate. As mentioned, if the legal system is inherently incapacitated from providing such mechanisms, then this incapacity should be properly diagnosed and made public.

---

56 See Dews (1987), Norris (1993) and Foley (1997).

57 See, for example, Stuart Motha's claim that 'the European subject was and is unable to recognize the indigenous relationship to land other than *through their own conceptions of it*' and that 'the actual experience and particularity of the [indigenous] other cannot be accessed *through the concepts* we invent'. Motha (1998) pp. 85, 88 (emphasis added). Likewise, Patton (1997) pp. 94–5 states that 'the full and complete recognition of the other is impossible, since any such recognition will always be carried out *in the language and on the terms of the one party*' (emphasis added). This construal of things resembles the Kantian construal famously critiqued by Davidson (1974c).

58 Most notably by Rescher (1980) and Davidson (1984d).

59 By claiming that cross-cultural understanding on the part of state institutions is impossible, the cultural incommensurabilist position renders us bereft of any good reason to seek to reform state institutions with a view to facilitating such understanding. See Habermas (1987c), Harvey (1989) p. 117, White (1991) pp. 16–18, and Norris (1993) p. 287 on this point.

But any such diagnosis must proceed on the basis of our best account of how the world actually is – a philosophically naturalistic and scientific account. Only on such a basis can we hope to persuade those in control of that system to make changes. Only on such a basis can we hope to make an ongoing and effective difference in the world.

The actual and potential intersection of the philosophical analysis undertaken in this book with the propositions and methodology of the natural and social sciences increases the likely effectiveness of any critique and any reform proposals which might emerge from that analysis. These sciences have given us an unprecedented capacity to understand and constructively intervene in the world across a range of practical contexts. There is no reason to doubt their capacity to enable us to understand and reform judicial epistemic and interpretive practice as effectively and productively as has been the case in these other contexts. Notwithstanding its deep roots in Anglophonic analytical and naturalistic philosophy – a school of philosophy which has been widely caricatured as lacking any capacity for ethical or political critique – the approach taken and the account of things offered by this book provides, I would argue, the best means available for understanding and effectively critiquing the epistemic and interpretive capacity of the legal system.

One of the key advantages of the naturalistic approach to cross-cultural understanding adopted here is that it is (as we shall see) capable of providing ontological space for a substantial degree of conceptual difference whilst, at the same time, providing for the possibility, at least, of some significant part of that difference being recognized and appropriately responded to by the agents and institutions of the liberal state, including its judges. It is capable of making plausible space for the effective reform of the liberal state and its legal system without downplaying the great challenges that may be involved in such reform. The approach taken in this book is capable of sustaining a concern for cultural difference and of providing a reasonable basis for looking forward to and acting in pursuit of the effective and appropriate institutional recognition of that difference. It enables theorists of cultural difference to pursue their theoretical, ethical and political interests without the great theoretical, ethical and political costs demanded by the false and disempowering necessity inherent in the cultural incommensurabilist view.

Chapter 2
Culturally Different Action: An Analysis

A Theory of Action

As I argued in the preceding chapter, we can conceive of culturally different thought and practice – cultural difference, as it is often referred to – in terms of culturally different action and its associated intentionality. The reasons for this should become clear as the present chapter unfolds. Culturally different action – including conceptually different action – is a species of human action.[1] On analysis, human action turns out to be quite a complex phenomenon. We may, as a start, conceive of an action as that which an agent (or group of agents) does or makes happen – as distinct from that which merely happens to her (or them).[2] An action is a doing rather than a happening. Let me take as my example of a culturally different agent and action in this discussion, the case of an indigenous person engaged in the traditional practice of hunting wild game. We may legitimately suppose that, like many indigenous people throughout the world today, she is using a rifle for this purpose. That person's throwing herself to the ground in order to avoid being seen by the prey she is hunting, is an action, something she does. Her being blown to the ground by a strong wind is something which happens to her. It is not an action. Both doings (actions) and happenings are types of event.[3] An event may be roughly analysed in terms of a metaphysically basic object – in this case, a human agent – undergoing a change in its properties over an interval of time. There are, thus, three key elements of an event: a spatially located object that exists in its own right; a change in the properties of that object; and a temporal interval during which such change takes place.[4]

The indigenous agent throwing herself to the ground and her being blown to the ground are both things that occur: they are both events. Some events – including those referred to here – may be analysed as complex and causally interrelated sets of simpler events. One thing both of the events in question here involve is a bodily event – namely, the body of the agent moving rapidly to the ground. They both

1 Not even cultural incommensurabilists deny this.

2 See Dretske (1988) p. 1, Davis (1994) p. 111.

3 Davidson (1967).

4 Kim (1993) pp. 8–12. There has been a great deal of controversy within philosophical metaphysics as to the nature and interrelationship of events and their components. See Davidson (1969) and (1970b), Kim (1993), chs 1 and 3, Lewis (1986a), Simons (2003). I do not intend to engage with that controversy as it is largely tangential to the concerns of this book.

involve changes in the properties of the agent's body over a short period of time. They involve the having and then the not having of the property of being upright, for example. Both the doing and the happening are, to some extent, bodily events. What distinguishes the two is that the doing – that is, the action – involves certain other phenomena which the non-active happening does not involve. These other phenomena may be conceived of as occurring – at least, to some degree – *inside* the agent.

Specifically, a culturally different action – like any human action – involves *mental phenomena* of a certain kind in a way which a mere happening does not.[5] The bodily event involved in the indigenous agent's action of throwing herself to the ground is something which is conceived of as being predominantly caused by the agent herself rather than by some other phenomenon – such as the wind, say.[6] It is something that the agent herself makes happen. And in this context, the term 'the agent herself' means some aspect of her *mind*; some kind of mental event occurring 'within' her, involving a change in the mental properties possessed by her. What makes the complex event in question an action and not a mere happening is that a component mental event is involved, and involved in a certain way. Without that mental component the phenomenon is not an action. A mental event of a certain kind is a conceptually necessary component of an action. '[T]he very idea of an action…seems to require us to identify some sort of mental component.'[7]

An event characterizable as an action, then, necessarily comprises a bodily event – a movement of some part of the body, say – *and* a certain kind of mental event related to each other in a way we can at this stage conceive of as causal.[8] An action is a causally interrelated *complex* of mental and bodily events. It is a complex event comprising those two simpler types of event. A type of action is individuated or characterized by the types of mental and bodily events involved.[9] The link between these events is both conceptual and ontological. An action is not to be identified solely with one or the other of these events. It is not merely a bodily event, nor is it merely a mental event accompanying a bodily event. Actions are inherently hybrid, *psycho-physical* phenomena. As Colin McGinn points out, they have an internal and an external aspect.[10] There is no action without some

5 Guttenplan (1994b) p. 115.

6 For this reason, we generally hold that there is an element of personal *responsibility* at work in relation to actions which is not at work in relation to mere happenings, including involuntary or reflex behaviour. Lennon (1990) p. 15. See Cane (2002), ch. 2, more broadly, on this point.

7 Guttenplan (1994b) p. 14.

8 Given the problem of causal overdetermination in this sphere, one has to construe the notion of causation here very carefully.

9 Note that different actions may involve the same non-mental event. They differ by virtue of their mental events differing. This becomes an issue in Chapter 4.

10 McGinn 1982 p.86. A series of persuasive arguments have been mounted by philosophers over the years in relation to the deficiencies of conceiving of action solely in terms of one or the other of its constituent parts. See Searle (1983), ch. 3, Davis (1994),

or other bodily event. There is no action without some or other mental event of a certain kind. And there is no action without a characteristic causal relationship between mental and bodily events. An action is the causing of a bodily event by a mental event in a manner to be discussed below. What renders the bodily event involved in the example of the indigenous agent throwing herself to the ground active rather than non-active, is its distinctive causal relationship to a set of action-constituting mental events – her thoughts about what the animal nearby is (that it is her prey, for example), whether it might see her, whether moving to the ground quickly might prevent it seeing her. A bodily event constitutes an element of an action by virtue of it being in such a relationship. A bodily event which does not enjoy such a relationship is not constitutive of an action.[11]

The non-mental constituent of an action need not be conceived of and described *solely* in terms of a bodily event. It may also be conceived of in terms of a set of events in the world external to the body – a set of environmental events – which causally flows from a bodily event.[12] For example, consider a simple action – say, the pulling of the trigger of a rifle by the movement of our indigenous hunter's finger. One the one hand, the agent in question might be conceived of as engaged in the action of moving her finger. Such an action would comprise a mental event (having to do with the agent's finger and the trigger) and the bodily event of the agent's finger moving in a certain way. Alternatively, by altering our conception of the action to make reference to the external causal consequences of the finger moving, we may redescribe it as that of pulling the trigger of a rifle.[13] In this case, the action comprises a mental event, the bodily event of the finger moving *and* the external, non-bodily or environmental event of the trigger moving or the rifle firing, respectively.[14] On such a conception the bodily event and its action correlate (moving the finger) remain largely implicit in the broader description (pulling the trigger).

Dretske (1988) pp. 11–22, Hornsby (1980), chs 1 and 2, for example. I am sympathetic to Dretske's (1988) view that an action is best conceived of not in terms of, say, the *movement* of one's body – a mere bodily event – but rather in terms of *the moving of it* by a mental event– something entirely more complex and far more adequate to our best intuitions about action than any alternatives.

11 The bodily events involved in an action may or may not be publicly observable bodily *movements* and may or may not be causal of some set of external environmental events. For example, the bodily events involved in an agent standing stock still (a so-called negative action) or working out in her head the likely movements of the prey she is hunting (a so-called mental action) do not involve a bodily movement or environmental event perceptible, at least, by an ordinary external observer. See Guttenplan (1994b) pp. 15 and 112 and McGinn (1982) p. 82.

12 Thalberg (1977) pp. 85–112, Hornsby (1980) pp. 29–32.

13 Or, at a greater causal remove, firing a rifle or shooting a prey.

14 The mental event causes the causing of the external environmental event by the bodily event.

Thus, action is properly conceived of as involving not *exclusively* a mental event and a *bodily* event, but rather a mental event and a *non-mental* event – the latter of which may be conceived of either in terms of a bodily event or the causing of an external environmental event by such a bodily event. I will use the term behaviour or *behavioural event* from this point on to refer to the non-mental events which may comprise part of an action. Behaviour, then, can refer to either a bodily event or to the causing of an environmental event by a bodily event. We can speak of the behaviour of moving a finger or the behaviour of pulling a trigger or firing a rifle. Behaviour may or may not have an action-constituting mental cause. We can imagine, for example, a reflex movement of the finger, pulling of a trigger or firing of a rifle. If it has such a cause then the behaviour comprises part of an action. In all cases of behaviour, though, a bodily event necessarily occurs. Such an event is needed to cause any environmental event involved in an action. Action – including culturally different action – may, on this account, be defined as the causing of a behavioural event by a mental event.

We may term actions whose constituent behavioural events are conceived of solely in terms of bodily events (such as a finger moving), as *basic actions*. Actions whose behavioural events are conceived of in terms of the causing of an external environmental event by a bodily event, may be termed *non-basic actions*.[15] Given the definition of an action as the causing of a behavioural event by a mental event, a basic action may be defined as the causing of a bodily event by a mental event and a non-basic action may be defined as the causing of the causing of an environmental event by a bodily event by a mental event. There is no non-basic action without some basic action – no external event constitutive of an action without some bodily event to cause it. A basic action is a conceptually necessary condition of a non-basic action. Non-basic actions may be conceived of as extending some degree along the causal chain that leads from a basic action. They comprehend each member of the set of mentally and bodily caused environmental events which comprise that chain.[16] I will make use of this distinction in the discussion to follow.

The Intentionality of Culturally Different Action

What, then, of the mental dimension of culturally different action? A range of mental properties and their correlative state and event categories are maintainable

15 McGinn (1982) p. 86–8, Ruben (1998) p. 437. See also Thalberg (1977) pp. 85–11, Hornsby (1980) pp. 29–32.

16 The description of an action need not make explicit reference to a bodily event. The same action may be variously described by reference to the various bodily and environmental events which flow from the mental events involved. There are troubling issues in the philosophy of action concerning whether or not we are to speak of there being two actions in the example discussed here – one basic and one non-basic – or merely one action described in two different ways. Anscombe (1963) pp. 37–47, Goldman (1970) p. 10, Davidson (1971), Hornsby (1980) pp. 5–10, Mele (1992) pp. 4–5.

by human agents. These have been argued to include the mental state categories we call beliefs and desires, as well as sensations, emotions, willings and states of awareness or consciousness.[17] It is not clear that all of these categories are necessary in order to provide for the mental component of action.[18] Nonetheless, most philosophers agree that, at the very least, the class of mental phenomena known as *intentional* phenomena must figure amongst the class constitutive of action. That is, actions necessarily comprise some causally interrelated complex of behavioural and *intentional* phenomena. Actions are intentional and may be distinguished from non-intentional, involuntary or reflex bodily events.[19] In order for a set of behavioural events – bodily or bodily-caused environmental – to comprise a part of an action it must be appropriately related to a set of intentional events.

I will have much more to say about the precise nature of intentionality later this chapter. For the time being, though, let me make a few very preliminary, ground-clearing comments. The class of intentional states includes perceptions, beliefs and desires.[20] Such states are traditionally characterized by their being *about* or directed towards some set of possible objects, properties and relations – that is, some actual or counterfactual state of affairs. It is this 'aboutness' or directedness which constitutes their intentionality.[21] An agent is said to perceive *that* a nearby animal she is hunting is alive, to believe *that* the animal is alive and to desire *that* it not be alive. These states of perception, belief and desire are about or are intentionally directed towards a state of affairs involving the animal in question – a state of affairs which may be factual or counterfactual. The state of affairs towards which an intentional state is directed is conventionally termed the content of that state.[22] Like the relationship between an action and a set of intentional states, the relationship between an intentional state and some or other set of content is a conceptual one. It is part of the very idea of an intentional state that it be about some state of affairs, that it have some content.[23] An agent doesn't just believe or desire – she believes that something is the case or desires that something be the case.

---

17 McGinn (1982) pp. 7–11, Guttenplan (1994b) pp. 6–13, Chalmers (1996) pp. 6–22.

18 There is some debate within philosophy as to precisely which types of mental phenomena are necessary elements of action – for example, whether or not *awareness* of either the mental or behavioural phenomena involved in the action is necessary or whether a distinct mental category known as *willing* is involved. McGinn (1982) pp. 84 and 94, Dretske (1988) p. 5, Hornsby (1980), chs 3 and 4, Pettit (1993a) p. 52.

19 Lennon (1990) p. 15.

20 See Searle (1983) p. 4 for a comprehensive list.

21 Searle (1983) p. 4.

22 Braddon-Mitchell and Jackson (1996) p. 176. Pettit (1993a) p. 5.

23 There is no belief that is not a belief *that* some or other state of affairs is, was, might be or might have been the case. There is no desire that is not a desire that some or other state of affairs be the case.

The content of an intentional state has traditionally been conceived of in philosophy as a proposition. Propositions are expressible in language by means of indicative sentences.[24] As a result, intentional states – or propositional attitudes, as they are also called – are linguistically described using indicative sentences (or propositional clauses) in so-called 'that clauses' which express the content of those states.[25] Their content, as well as their attitudinal type (perception, belief, desire, etc.), is what individuates intentional states from each other.[26] Propositions may, in turn, be analysed as comprised of a set of *concepts*.[27] The proposition that 'the animal is alive' is comprised of the concepts 'animal' and 'alive' etc. Thus, an agent may be said to possess not only a given intentional state but also the propositions and concepts informing that state. An intentional state necessarily has propositional content and by virtue of that necessarily has conceptual content. The possession of intentionality – of a mind – entails the possession of a propositional and conceptual scheme. Action, then, may be conceived of as behaviour that is appropriately informed by the conceptual scheme possessed by the agent. I will have more to say about the nature of concepts and conceptual schemes in Chapter 3.

That intentional properties, states and events necessarily figure in the composition of actions follows from the very nature of actions. Consider the nature of the action referred to above, that of the agent throwing herself to the ground in order to avoid being seen by her prey. On reflection, we note that this action is an event which is oriented towards the achievement by the agent of some counterfactual state of affairs, some purpose, goal or end in the world – in this case, that of not being upright or not being seen by her prey.[28] All actions share such an orientation. Actions are inherently oriented towards the realization of some (generally) counterfactual state of affairs in the world by means of some bodily event.[29] They are oriented towards achieving something, towards making a difference to the way the world is by means of behaviour so as to make the

---

24 Such sentences typically say – either truly or falsely – how things are. They indicate a state of affairs. Macdonald and Pettit (1981) p. 5, McGinn (1982) p. 8, Guttenplan (1994a) pp. 486–7.

25 Guttenplan (1994b) p. 29.

26 Lennon (1990) p. 20.

27 As well as a syntax and grammar and so on. Prinz (2002) p. 2.

28 This purpose (as a proposition) will be the content of at least one of the causally relevant intentional states (for example, a desire) involved in the action. Pettit (1993a) p. 18–25, Guttenplan (1994b) pp. 23–4. McGinn (1982) p. 85 maintains that it is not necessary that this purpose be consciously maintained by the agent.

29 Or behavioural event more widely defined. Note that an action may be oriented towards the *maintenance* of some actual state of affairs. This may be construed as a counterfactual state of affairs whereby present relevant conditions (other than temporal) obtain at some future point in time.

world consistent with what we might conceive of as the agent's purpose.[30] They are inherently purposive or teleological in this sense.

But in order to be purposive – in order to be capable of conceiving of and achieving a counterfactual state of affairs by means of some kind of behavioural event – an agent must be able both to *represent* that state of affairs, as well as her actual state of affairs (including her bodily state and environmental context) and to *cause* her body to behave in a manner which might realize that counterfactual state of affairs.[31] She must possess states which are both *representational* of actual and counterfactual states of affairs and *dispositional* of – that is, capable of causing – behaviour in light of those representations. Intentional states are those states of an agent which meet this joint requirement.[32] In physicalist terms, they are a category of higher-order states realized by those physical states of an agent which meet the conditions (or fill the role) of being representational and dispositional as far as her interaction with the world is concerned.[33] They are those physical states which enable an agent to behave purposefully in the world. Holistically clustered in a behaviourally causal intentional complex, intentional states cause an agent's body to behave in a manner which, in general, realizes her purposes. By virtue of their representational and dispositional role, intentional states 'serve to connect an agent with its world'.[34] This connectedness to the world is the hallmark of action.

Intentional states may be classified into different categories on the basis of the specific roles played by those categories within the overall intentional economy of an agent.[35] For the purposes of this book, I will take beliefs and desires to be the categories of intentional states capable of and sufficient for representation and behavioural disposition.[36] I will take them to be the fundamental categories constituting the intentional dimension of action into which all other categories

---

30 Though, as we have seen, not all actions involve behaviour which makes an observable change in the body or environment of the agent, the majority of them do and even those that don't (negative and mental actions) generally operate in conjunction with those that do to serve some purpose ultimately related to maintaining or making an observable difference to the way the world is.

31 By means of a causally related environmental event, if necessary. Of course, the behavioural events involved in the action may or may not actually realize the agent's purpose. Whether they do is an empirical and contingent matter.

32 Intentional states are directed towards states of affairs by either being directly or indirectly caused by (in a representing kind of way) states of affairs or by being causal of behaviour which in turn causes other states of affairs (in a state-of-affairs-realizing sort of way).

33 I will analyse both representation and disposition in terms of a causal relationship between the intentional state and some set of environmental, behavioural and other intentional states.

34 Pettit (1993a) p. 3. Beliefs and desires are 'individuated by their role in mediating an agent's response to her environment'. Lennon (1990) p. 26.

35 Stich (1990) p. 49.

36 'Desires motivate behaviours but beliefs frame them.' Wellman 1990 p. 208.

of intentional state may be analysed.[37] As will, I hope, become apparent, nothing important hinges on my eliding the other categories of intentional states in this manner as far as my overall thesis is concerned. To the extent that other categories of intentional states actually play an independent role in culturally different action, they too must be interpreted and identified by the judge in a manner which is virtually identical to that in which beliefs and desires are interpreted and identified. Beliefs and desires are individuated conceptually and ontologically as the categories they are by the distinctive role they play in actions. That an interrelated complex of beliefs and desires[38] necessarily figures in the constitution of action is a reflection of both the representational and dispositional character of such phenomena and the inherently purposive character of action.

The Rationality of Culturally Different Action

Later in this chapter, I more fully analyse the representative and dispositional character of intentional phenomena in terms of the maintenance of a distinctive causal relationship with environmental input phenomena,[39] behavioural output phenomena,[40] and other intentional phenomena. For the time being, let me just note that in order for intentional phenomena to perform their characteristic role in human action, they must causally interact with each other and with environmental input and behavioural output phenomena according to an overarching set of *regularities* which facilitates the ongoing capacity of the agent to intervene successfully in the world.[41] Agents are beings who 'interact with their environment under the control

37 See Searle (1983) pp. 29–36 on the argument that beliefs and desires are basic to intentionality. Perceptions are representational states which are commonly taken to play a part in the intentional economy of an agent. However, for the sake of simplifying the discussion, I will assume that, in general, a causal regularity exists between an agent perceiving that p and her believing that p. Hence, I will assume that perceptions are comprehended by correlative beliefs. I will assume this notwithstanding the fact that in certain unusual circumstances this regularity may not hold. For example, circumstances may arise where an agent has reason to distrust her perceptual system. Likewise, I will also assume that those intentional categories known as 'willings' or 'intendings' and the like, which are argued by some theorists to provide the dispositional nexus between intentionality and behaviour, are analysable in terms of relevant desires. Searle (1983) p. 29. See McGinn (1982) pp. 94–5 for a contrary view.

38 A behaviourally causal intentional complex.

39 Environmental events which cause intentional events.

40 Behavioural events which are caused by intentional events.

41 A variety of terms have been formulated to describe these regularities. These include habits of inference, rationality, rational regularities and the like. I'll predominantly use the terms 'intentional regularities' and 'rationality'. Pettit (1993a) p. 18 states that these regularities may or may not be associated with 'a structural belief in the corresponding logical principle' which describes them. He uses the term 'habits of inference' to signify these regularities because habits are not necessarily reflected on but are generally largely

of intentional regularities'.[42] These intentional regularities provide to some degree for the effectiveness of the agent's behaviour in realizing the agent's purposes.[43] They enable an agent to realize her purposes – to continue to be an agent – on an ongoing basis.

Intentional regularities may be variously classified. For example, a regularity may exist in relation to the environmental events affecting an agent and her beliefs such that, given certain conditions, the occurrence of a given environmental event causes (with some degree of regularity) a belief in the agent with that event as its content. If the agent's prey is directly in front of the agent, then (assuming other necessary conditions are in place) the agent typically believes that her prey is directly in front of her. Alternatively, a regularity may obtain amongst an agent's beliefs such that, given certain conditions, the occurrence of a certain belief or set of beliefs causes the occurrence of some other specific belief or beliefs. Thus, if the agent believes that if the prey sees her, it will run away and if she also believes that the prey does, in fact, see her, then the agent typically believes that the prey will run away. Another example is that regularity which may exist in relation to certain desires and behaviour such that, given certain conditions, a desire with some specific type of behaviour as its content causes the agent's body to engage in that behaviour. If an agent desires to move her body to the ground, then, assuming the obtaining of other relevant conditions, her body typically moves to the ground. And so on for causal relations between other combinations of environmental, intentional and behavioural phenomena.

Given that intentional phenomena are conceived of as having propositional content, we can conceive of the intentional regularities governing such phenomena in terms of a propositional 'logic' of sorts reflecting the relations that obtain between the propositional content of those phenomena.[44] We can conceive of a set of beliefs and desires issuing in the behavioural event it does by virtue of that set and that outcome being inferentially governed to some degree according to such a

---

automatic or pre-programmed. Lennon (1990) p. 21 agrees, stating that '[t]he possibility of constructing reasoning linking intentional states with one another and with behaviour does not presuppose that whenever an agent acts for reasons she *consciously* rehearses the pattern of argument which we may construct. The reasoning… makes explicit certain conceptual connections between the contents of such states and the description of the action for which they provide the reasons'.

42 Pettit (1993a) p. 11.

43 See Macdonald and Pettit (1981) pp. 60–61. Following Cherniak (1986), I do not want to idealize the capacity of these regularities to further an agent's purposes. Some degree of effectiveness in this regard is required of a being if it is to be an agent, but I do not hold that these regularities necessitate the realization of an agent's purposes in any unrealistically strong sense.

44 I use the term 'logic' loosely here. I want to avoid the implication that agents operate under a strict and idealized form of logic. See Cherniak (1986), ch. 1.

logic.[45] As a result of their propositional nature and their role in the explanation of behaviour and other intentional phenomena, the contents of intentional phenomena may be construed as operating as *reasons* within an inferential matrix.[46] The causal relation between these phenomena may be conceived of as a reason-giving relation. It is because of this construal that the regularities governing intentional phenomena are often conceived of in terms of a concept of rationality.[47]

Given the nature of agents as beings who behave in order to realize their desires, given their beliefs, it is a basic feature of the intentional regularities which govern an agent's beliefs, desires and behaviour that those regularities are such as to maximize the chances[48] that the agent's purposes are realized through her behaviour. That is, it is a conceptually or theoretically necessary feature of the intentional regularities governing agents that they are (and render agents) *practically rational*. A practically rational set of intentional regularities (a practical rationality) regulates the beliefs and desires and behaviour of an agent so as to typically cause the agent to behave in a manner oriented towards satisfying her desires, given her beliefs.[49] Being practically rational means being such that one's desires are (to some agency-sufficient degree) regularly realized by one's behaviour given one's beliefs. Agents qua agents are, at the very least, minimally

45 Hence, these regularities are often termed habits of inference. Davidson (1978) pp. 85–6 states that 'the agent's beliefs and desires provide [the agent] with the premises of an argument'. See also Lennon (1990) p. 21. Though, both Lennon and Davidson hold what are ultimately anti-realist views about the nature of intentional phenomena which differ markedly from my own, aspects of their rationalistic account of intentionality may be usefully incorporated into a physicalist and realist model.

46 Lennon (1990) p. 21 states that 'the intentional content of our intentional states is that feature on which their reason-giving links to each other and to the agent's behaviour depend'. Note that the concept of reason is ambiguous between real phenomena with causal relevance and purely discursive entities which are mere constructs within an interpretive context. Thus, the debate between intentional realists and non-realists. Note that contra Davidson and certain intentional anti-realists I don't equate the causal explanation of an action with its rational justification. Lennon (1990) pp. 37–9.

47 And why rationality is often conceived of in terms of logical consistency. Taylor (1985b) p. 134. By virtue of the fact that intentional phenomena are higher-order phenomena realized by causally efficacious lower-order physical and physically-based phenomena, the reason-giving relation between such phenomena is at the same time both a causal and a logical or conceptual one.

48 A weaker constraint than ensuring the realization of those purposes.

49 Macdonald and Pettit (1981) p. 60, Braddon-Mitchell and Jackson (1996) p. 145. Ascribing practical rationality to an agent involves predicting that she will behave in a way that would satisfy her desires were her beliefs true. 'Your prediction that Jones will step around the hole in the ground is based, say, on your belief that he believes that there is a hole in the ground in front of him and that continuing in a straight line will lead to his falling into the hole, combined with your belief that he does not want [desire] to fall into the hole.' Braddon-Mitchell and Jackson (1996) pp. 145–6.

rational in this sense. Being practically rational to at least a minimally rational degree is constitutive of being an agent.[50]

It is worth noting that the operation of this mode of rationality reflects the fact that beliefs and desires operate collectively to cause behaviour. A practically rational agent behaves in a manner which typically satisfies her desires *given her beliefs*. An agent's behaviour is necessarily caused by an interrelated behaviourally causal *complex* of those desires and those beliefs. Neither a set of beliefs nor a set of desires causes behaviour in an agent independently of a set of the other. Consider the example discussed earlier in which the indigenous hunter throws herself to the ground to avoid being seen by her prey. We can conceive of this behaviour as being motivated at one level by a desire not to be seen by her prey. This desire might have arisen in response to certain beliefs concerning her overall purpose in hunting the prey, the location and perceptive powers of the prey, her own and the prey's physical location, and so on. In order to realize this desire not to be seen, a series of intentional and behavioural events must occur governed by regularities oriented towards or facilitative of the realization of that desire. And so, by virtue of a practically rational regularity governing her, in response to her desire that she not be seen, the agent comes to the belief that 'If I desire not to be seen by the prey, I should move my body to the ground'. By virtue of a further practically rational regularity, this belief causes her to desire that her body move to the ground. And this desire – against the backdrop of the other intentional states mentioned, as part of a behaviourally causal intentional *complex* comprising those other intentional states – causes her body to move to the ground, thus (perhaps) realizing her initial desire not to be seen. It is by virtue of these intentional regularities governing the agent's beliefs, desires and behaviour that given her beliefs the agent is able to realize her desire by moving to the ground. It is by virtue of these practically rational regularities that she is able to act as she does. Without such regularities her behaviour does not comprise action. It is not appropriately oriented towards a purpose.[51]

---

50 That all agents are, at least, minimally rational obtains with conceptual or theoretical necessity (it is a conceptual truth) on this account of agency. Dennett (1978a), ch. 1, Cherniak (1986), ch. 1, Pettit (1993a) pp. 41, 68. Given my physicalistic (and, hence, somewhat Quinean) commitments, I agree with Henderson's (1993) comments at p. 96 that 'there are no good arguments to establish that there is an a priori level of minimal rationality in any but the conceptual sense. (I do not believe that anything is a priori in any other sense.) Recognising such conceptual a priori truths does not conflict with the claim that whatever is so guaranteed about a subject, might, as our theory changes, be found false of the subject understood in the extensional sense. For being a conceptual a priori truth is a matter of the centrality of certain principles to present theory'.

51 'In taking any piece of behaviour as an action we assume that it issues from a desire to achieve a certain outcome and a belief that the course of behaviour in question at least stands a good chance of realising that outcome: we assume … that the event is [practically] rational.' Macdonald and Pettit (1981) p. 27.

Of course, the agent will be more likely to achieve her desired ends if her beliefs – about the location and perceptive powers of the prey, about her own location and, importantly, about the best course of action to take in order to realize her desire – are, to some agency-sufficient degree, true of the world (including her present environmental and bodily situation) and logically sound (both deductively and inductively) in their interrelation.[52] It is only if the agent has an adequate overall view of the way things are and the way things might be that the agent will be in a position to realize her desires.[53] Thus, an agent's practical rationality is effective in the pursuit of her ends only in conjunction with what we may term her *theoretical rationality*. This term describes that feature of the intentional regularities governing the relationship between the environmental situation, perceptions and beliefs of an agent which facilitates the maintenance of an agency-sufficient degree of truth and logical soundness in the beliefs possessed by an agent. Being theoretically rational means being such that one's beliefs are (to some agency-sufficient degree) true and logically sound. An agent can be typically effective in the pursuit of her ends (and thus, be an agent) only if the set of intentional regularities governing her – only if she – is, to some agency-sufficient degree, not only practically rational but also theoretically rational.

Theoretically rational intentional regularities result in an agent being, for example, largely responsive in her belief system to contradictory input from her perceived environment and to logical inconsistencies within that system.[54] In the above example, if the indigenous hunter believes that the prey is not nearby, and that if the prey is not nearby it is safe to come out of her hiding spot, then, if

52 Macdonald and Pettit (1981) p. 60.

53 It is worth noting here that we might expand the concept of theoretical rationality so as to include (or, alternatively, see it as part of a broader mode of rationality – sometimes called attitudinal rationality – which includes) those intentional regularities which also minimize logical contradictions between an agent's *desires* and between her beliefs and desires. On this wider construal, attitudinal rationality implicitly motivates an agent to ensure that her desires are logically consistent with each other and with her beliefs. It motivates her to be responsive to any inconsistencies in this regard. Much of what I have had to say about theoretical rationality above can be applied to the logical relationship between desires and between beliefs and desires. See Macdonald and Pettit (1981), ch. 2.

54 'It would make no sense to ascribe beliefs to an agent without assuming that he was disposed to make moves appropriate to ensure that his beliefs were true...We will not ascribe beliefs of such a kind that we must then admit that the agent seems unresponsive to manifest counterexamples or inconsistencies.' Macdonald and Pettit (1981) p. 12. Theoretical rationality includes deductive rationality (causal regularity) of the kind – if the agent believes that if p then q, and then comes to believe that p, then (to the extent that the agent is theoretically rational) the agent will believe that q. To the extent that she is theoretically rational the agent will not hold logically contradictory beliefs. It also includes inductive rationality of the kind – if the agent has numerous instances of q following on from p, then if she believes that p, she will believe that probably q.

theoretically rational[55], the agent will generally believe that it is safe to come out of her hiding spot.[56] If her environment is as she believes it to be – if her beliefs are relevantly true – then her purpose in acting (to avoid being seen by her prey) may be realized by practically rational behaviour. It is because an agent's body of beliefs are subject to a set of theoretically rational regularities that we may generally characterize beliefs as inherently truth-seeking and bodies of beliefs as (to some agency-sufficient level – perhaps, even largely) true and logically sound.[57] Such regularities may not generate a perfectly true and logically sound system of beliefs – human agents are only human after all – but in a being properly characterizable as an agent they are inherently oriented towards the achievement of some agency-optimal degree of truth and logical soundness given the nature and circumstances of the agent in question. Agents – including culturally different agents – are, therefore, minimally rational in the additional sense that they are governed by an agency-sufficient theoretically rational set of intentional regularities.[58]

Whilst on this point, it is worth flagging for later discussion that we (and, more specifically, a judge) might predict or explain an agent's behaviour with reference to the practically and theoretically rational complex of beliefs and desires which cause that behaviour.[59] Predicting and explaining behaviour is possible by reconstructing the causal or reason-giving links between known or assumed beliefs and desires (the identity of which form part of what I later term a theory of the agent) within the context of a known or assumed practically rational set of regularities (the identity of which form part of what I later term a theory of mind). Likewise, it follows that we may predict or explain an agent's belief with reference to the theoretically rational complex of environmental states, perceptions and other beliefs which ultimately issue in that belief. Predicting and explaining belief is possible by reconstructing the causal or reason-giving links between known or

55 If subject to a theoretically rational set of intentional regularities.

56 The first two beliefs mentioned may be conceived of as reasons for the theoretically rational and conclusive third belief. The relation between beliefs under conditions of theoretical rationality is a reason-giving relation.

57 See Davidson (1974c) and (1975), Macdonald and Pettit (1981) p. 24. Davidson is correct to argue that being part of a body of beliefs which is largely true is a necessary condition for being a belief, though his account of why this is so differs from mine.

58 All agents are minimally rational as a matter of conceptual necessity (given our operative concept of agency here). By regarding each other as agents, 'we regard one another as 'rational and purposive creatures, fitting our beliefs to the world as we perceive it and seeking to obtain what we desire in the light of them'. Lennon (1990) p. 11 quoting Wollheim and Hopkins (1982), Macdonald and Pettit (1981) p. 40. On the question of the nature of conceptual necessity, I agree with Henderson (1993) p. 96, who states that '[r]ecognising such conceptual a priori truths does not conflict with the claim that whatever is so guaranteed about a subject, might, as our theory changes, be found false of the subject understood in the extensional sense. For being a conceptual a priori truth is a matter of the centrality of certain principles to present theory'.

59 I will have more to say about this in Chapters 4 and 5.

assumed beliefs within the context of a known or assumed theoretically rational set of regularities. If asked why an agent behaved the way she did one might make reference to a set of beliefs and desires (and, implicitly, to a set of practically rational regularities regulating those states) saying that they provided the agent's reason for so behaving.[60] This is to say that they caused the agent to behave as she did. Likewise, if asked why an agent believed what she did, one might make reference to a set of other beliefs (and implicitly to a set of theoretically rational regularities), saying that they provided the agent's reason for so believing. Thus, the prediction and explanation of either the beliefs or behaviour of an agent is often construed as a process of rationalizing those beliefs or that behaviour. I will have more to say on these matters when analysing the nature of interpreting – that is, explaining – behaviour in Chapter 5.

With this discussion in hand, we can analyse a simple non-basic action – for example, our indigenous hunter pulling the trigger of a rifle – as an event comprising the causing of a bodily and then external environmental event (the movement of a finger causing the movement of the trigger) by a complex of intentional states.[61] This behaviourally causal complex of intentional states[62], in turn, comprises a set of desires (including the desires to move the finger and pull the trigger) and a set of beliefs (including the beliefs that her finger is in the physical position it is in, that the trigger is in the position it is in, that in order to pull the trigger the agent needs to move her finger in a certain manner). All of these events – intentional and behaviourally – causally interrelate under the governance of an overarching set of theoretically and practically rational regularities.[63] This rationalized causing of the behavioural events by the behaviourally causal intentional complex constitutes the non-basic action of pulling the trigger. This type of action – pulling the trigger of a rifle – is individuated as the type it is by the intentional, bodily and environmental (behavioural) events which constitute it and by the overarching rationality which governs it. A token phenomenon which is constituted in this way – which possesses the properties described here – is and may be identified as a token of the action type pulling the trigger of a rifle.

---

60 See Davidson (1963) and Lennon (1990), for example. 'Your prediction that Jones will step around the hole in the ground is based, say, on your belief that he believes that there is a hole in the ground in front of him and that continuing in a straight line will lead to his falling into the hole, combined with your belief that he does not want [desire] to fall into the hole.' Braddon-Mitchell and Jackson (1996) pp. 145–6.

61 More properly, a non-basic action may be defined as the causing of [the causing of an environmental event by a bodily event] by a complex of intentional states.

62 Throughout this book I will largely refer to this set as a behaviourally causal intentional complex. This complex is comprised of behaviourally causal intentional states.

63 It is important to note at this early stage that the set of intentional states which constitutes a behaviourally causal intentional complex may be quite vast. As we shall see below, this is a function of the holistic nature of intentional states.

The Functional Nature of Intentional Phenomena

What the psychology grounding the discussion so far has presumed is that intentional phenomena exist and may be conceived of as having typical causes and effects.[64] They are phenomena which typically cause behavioural events – that is, bodily events or bodily-caused environmental events. They are phenomena which – through the mediation of an agent's sensory apparatus – are also typically caused by environmental phenomena.[65] And finally, they are phenomena which typically cause and are caused by other intentional phenomena. All of this causal interaction proceeds according to certain regularities describable in terms of practical and theoretical modes of rationality. To be an intentional phenomenon is to be a phenomenon which is by its very nature causally related to or mediating of three categories of phenomena – environmental inputs, intentional inputs and outputs, and behavioural outputs – according to a set of intentional regularities.[66] Intentional phenomena take environmental and intentional inputs and yield intentional and behavioural outputs according to those regularities.[67]

As such, intentional phenomena are phenomena which inherently meet a certain set of conditions – in this case, occupying or filling a characteristic kind of causal-nomic role within a broader system of environmental, intentional and behavioural phenomena.[68] This meeting of such conditions or filling of such a role is definitive of intentional phenomena. The concept of intentionality defines this functional role. Phenomena which are individuated by their filling of a certain causal-nomic role within a larger system of phenomena are *functional* phenomena. Functional phenomena take particular kinds of inputs and yield particular kinds of outputs within a system according to nomic regularities which govern the relationship between those inputs and outputs.[69] They are phenomena which are regularly caused by certain inputs and which regularly cause certain outputs. Intentional phenomena, by virtue of being such, are, therefore, functional phenomena.

64 Braddon-Mitchell and Jackson (1996) p. 39.

65 Eliding for the sake of simplicity the causal role played here by sensory phenomena, I will use the term environmental inputs to describe both the environmental and the sensory phenomena involved in causing an intentional state. I will generally assume that a given environmental input event causes a concomitant sensation of that event. Where the quality of an agent's sensory apparatus is in question I will make specific reference to sensory phenomena.

66 Papineau (1993) p. 56. Likewise, to possess an intentional property or be in an intentional state is to possess a property or be in a state which is so related.

67 Guttenplan (1994b) p. 99.

68 'Something occupies a particular [causal-nomic] role if it causally responds in particular ways to causal inputs with particular kinds of output.' Heil (1998) p. 97.

69 'Functionalism takes mental properties and kinds as functional properties ... specified in terms of their roles as causal intermediaries between sensory inputs and behavioural outputs, and the physicalist form of functionalism takes physical properties as the only potential occupants or realisers of these causal roles.' Kim (1998) p. 19.

Intentional phenomena are characterized as the kind of phenomena they are not by their possession of some or other specific type of physical composition or internal structure (as the natural kind water is, for example) but by their performance of some or other definitive type of causal role or function within a system of things – in this case a system comprising the bodily interaction of an agent with the external world.[70]

For physicalistic naturalism of the kind I advocate, a functional phenomenon exists as a real higher-order phenomenon if it is realized (made real) by a set of physical phenomena – that is, if there is a set of physical phenomena in the world which meets the conditions definitive of that higher-order functional phenomenon. It is by virtue of it filling the role definitive of a functional phenomenon, that a set of physical phenomena *realizes* that functional phenomenon. To meet those conditions or fill that role is to realize the functional phenomenon defined by those conditions or that role. The actual identity of the set of physical phenomena which realize a higher order functional phenomenon is a contingent matter dependent on the laws or causal regularities actually prevailing in the world and is determinable by empirical means.[71] What our best empirical research into this matter tells us is that the set of physical phenomena in the world which meet the conditions definitive of intentional types in humans – the set of physical phenomena which causally mediates between environmental inputs, intentional inputs and outputs, and behavioural outputs according to a set of intentional regularities – is the set of physical phenomena which comprises the states, properties and events of the brain and associated sensory and motor apparatus of human agents. I will term these phenomena, neuro-physical phenomena.

Intentional phenomena are realized by physical phenomena. As such intentional phenomena are existent higher-order phenomena. They exist by virtue of their being realized by physical phenomena – by virtue of there being physical phenomena which meet the conditions defined by the concept of intentional phenomena. Human agents possess an intentional state by virtue of possessing a set of physical states which meets the conditions or plays the causal role definitive of intentional states (specified by the concept of intentionality). They possess intentional states by virtue of possessing a set of physical states which, in fact, causally mediates between the three categories of phenomena mentioned above. Such physical states endow human agents with the capacity to meet the conditions definitive of intentionality. They do all the work in making it the case that intentional phenomena exist, in making it the case that human beings are agents. Intentional phenomena exist in the subordinate or attenuated conceptual

70 Heil (1998) p. 98. Braddon-Mitchell and Jackson (1996) p. 43 state that we can 'distinguish the functional roles specified by the input, output and internal role clauses from what occupies them, and insist that what matters for being in one or another [intentional] state are the roles that are occupied, not what occupies them. Provided the right roles are occupied, it does not matter what occupies them'.

71 Kim (2003) pp. 578–9.

sense that all higher-order phenomena exist. They exist just because there exist physical phenomena which play an intentional role – as defined by our best theory of intentionality – in an agent's interaction with the world. Intentional kinds and properties 'are functional kinds at a higher level of abstraction than physiochemical or biological kinds'.[72] 'To talk of minds and mental operations is to abstract from whatever realises them; it is talk at a higher level ... Talk of minds is merely talk of material systems at a "higher level".'[73]

An agent possesses the intentional property, for example, of believing that there is a fruit on the bush by virtue of possessing a physical (or physically-based) property which is caused by and which causes those environmental, intentional and behavioural inputs and outputs characteristic of believing that there is a fruit on the bush. She does not possess this property by virtue of possessing a physical constitution of some unique 'believing that there is a fruit on the bush' kind.[74] Of course, the physical properties of an agent are not ontologically unimportant. Those properties have to be such as to be able to perform the functional role characteristic of intentional states. An agent believes that there is a fruit on the bush by virtue of being in a physical state which is able to do what a belief that there is a fruit on the bush does. The point that is being made here is that it is *primarily* the functional role of the agent's physical states and not the composition and structure of those states which matters for those states being intentional in character.[75]

Individuating Intentional Phenomena

The functional definition of intentional phenomena *in general* is, as we have just seen, relatively straightforward. Intentional phenomena are generally defined

72 Kim (1998) p. 3.

73 Heil (1998) pp. 90–91. Consistent with the description of higher-order phenomena outlined in the previous chapter, Heil draws a common analogy with the higher-order properties of computers. 'When we discuss computations – the manipulation of symbols in accordance with formal rules – we abstract from the *material nature* of the device performing them. And in so doing, we characterise the [material] behaviour of computing devices at a "higher level".' Heil goes on at p. 114, '... just as in describing the operation of a computing machine at the program level we are describing its *causal structure* in abstraction from its hardware, so in describing mental operations we are describing the causal structure of intelligent agents in abstraction from their biological hardware.'

74 Though it is, of course, possible that there is only one physical constitution in the world which realizes this intentional property.

75 Even if it turns out that there is only one unique physical composition and structure which does or can fill that functional role. It is worth noting here that by virtue of their realization by the physical, there are no non-physical components of intentional phenomena. The intentional is a complex construction and arrangement of the basic ingredients that make up the physical. Braddon-Mitchell and Jackson (1996) p. 13.

as those phenomena which causally mediate between environmental, other intentional and behavioural input and output phenomena according to a set of intentional regularities. However, for *specific* intentional phenomena types – say, the belief that one's prey is nearby or the desire that one not be seen by one's prey – things are more complex. Specific intentional phenomena are such that they are typically caused by specific forms of environmental phenomena, typically cause and are caused by specific kinds of other intentional phenomena and typically cause specific forms of behavioural phenomena – all *provided that* certain relevant background conditions obtain. These conditions most notably involve the simultaneous instantiation of certain other intentional phenomena. As a result, specific intentional phenomena fill a more complex causal-nomic role within a more complex system of environmental, intentional and behavioural phenomena – they meet a more multifaceted set of conditions – than the general category of intentional phenomena discussed above.

For example, consider our indigenous hunter's belief that there is a snake in front of her. This belief is typically caused by the environmental event of there being a snake in front of her – but only provided that certain other beliefs obtain. An example of such an associated background belief is her belief that her sensory faculties are working properly. An agent will not typically believe that there is a snake in front of her in response to the sensory cue that there is if she at the same time believes that her sensory faculties are malfunctioning in some relevant way.[76] An agent's belief that there is a snake in front of her also typically causes a desire in the agent that she move away from the snake – but again, only if certain other associated background intentional states obtain. These other states include, for example, a desire that she not be bitten and a belief that snakes typically bite persons who do not move away from them. If she, in fact, maintains a desire to be bitten or a belief that snakes do not typically bit persons who do not move away from them, then she will not typically desire to move away from the snake in response to a belief that one is in front of her. Again, an agent's belief that there is a snake in front of her typically causes the agent to move her body in a certain snake avoiding manner and not in some other manner. But only in conjunction with other background intentional states including, for example, a desire that she move away from the snake, a belief that moving her body in a certain snake-avoiding manner will realize that agent's desire to move away from the snake, as well as a desire to move her body in that manner.

A belief that there is a snake in front of the agent is a functional state which takes specific environmental and intentional inputs and yields specific intentional and behavioural outputs according to some set of broadly rational intentional regularities – provided that some set of other background intentional conditions obtains. Such a belief is *individuated* – its concept is defined – in terms of a

76 To do so would be theoretically irrational and by definition agents – in general, at least – are not *typically* irrational.

certain sort of pattern of causes and effects.[77] More particularly, it is individuated in terms of three categories of definitional clause reflecting the three categories of phenomena referred to above. These three categories of definitional clause are 'input clauses, which say which environmental conditions typically give rise to which [intentional] states; output clauses, which say which [intentional] states typically give rise to which behavioural responses; and interaction clauses, which say how [intentional] states typically interact' – all in the context of some set of background intentional states.[78] Each distinct intentional phenomenon is individuated by its own characteristic set of such definitional clauses. The three kinds of clauses give the meaning of intentional phenomena terms.[79] The causal functional role of an intentional phenomenon captures our conception of what it is to be that phenomenon.[80] Thus, specific intentional types (and tokens) are ontologically and conceptually individuated or defined with reference to the causes and effects they are conceived of as being typically caused by or causal of within the overall system (agent) in question, against some set of associated background intentional states.[81]

And, of course, the phenomenon which plays the role characteristic of a given intentional phenomenon is a physical – and in humans, at least, a neuro-physical – phenomenon. An individual intentional state is realized by that physical state of the agent which meets the causal functional role definitive of that intentional state. A person believes that there is a snake in front of her not by virtue of being in a state with a certain unique physical structure and composition – though having that structure may be necessary for it to have causal efficacy in the world and for it to play the causal role definitive of a belief that there is a snake in front of the

77 Botterill and Carruthers (1999) p. 9.

78 Braddon-Mitchell and Jackson (1996) p. 40. Braddon-Mitchell and Jackson argue that no vicious circularity obtains here, notwithstanding that intentional states are on this account partly defined in terms of other intentional states. See Braddon-Mitchell and Jackson (1996) pp. 49–52.

79 Heil (1998) p. 103 describes the situation thus, '[t]he possession of any state of mind is characterizable by a conjunction of conditional if-then statements, the antecedents (if clauses) of which include descriptions of inputs *and* specifications of total functional architectures, and whose consequents (then clauses) include outputs (behavioural and other)'. Implicit in such specification is an overarching set of intentional regularities describable in terms of an inferential logic, rationality or theory of agency.

80 Braddon-Mitchell and Jackson (1996) p. 46.

81 Certain early twentieth-century philosophers concerned with the nature of intentional phenomena (for example, Gilbert Ryle (1949)) erred in supposing there to be a simple, one-to-one causal relation between a given intentional phenomenon and a given environmental or behavioural-environmental phenomenon. It is not possible to pair specific individual intentional phenomena with specific behavioural phenomena without reference to other intentional phenomena – a set of background intentional states. See Botterill and Carruthers (1999) pp. 4–6, Heil (1998) pp. 59–66, Braddon-Mitchell and Jackson (1996) pp. 29–40, 151.

agent – but, rather, by virtue of being in a physical state which serves the causal functional role definitive of that belief. This functional role determines the identity of – it individuates – that physical state as a token of the intentional type 'belief that there is a snake in front of the agent'.[82] If an agent is in a physical state which fills the functional role characteristic of a belief that there is a snake in front of the agent, then that agent has a belief that there is a snake in front of her. Any human agent which possesses a neuro-physical state with those functional properties (with that causal role) has that belief. Token intentional states are (ontologically) neuro-physical states. They are typified (conceptually individuated) as the state they are with reference to the role they play in the behavioural interaction of an agent with her environment, past and present.

On analysis, it is evident that an intentional phenomenon – say, a belief that there is a snake in front of the agent – may be typically caused by and causal of a vast number of specific input and output phenomena. All of these typical, causally relevant phenomena, together contribute to the individuation – conceptually and, therefore, ontologically – of the phenomenon in question. The inventory of these phenomena – formulated in terms of a set of definitional clauses describing causal regularities – provides the content of the concept of a belief that there is a snake in front of the agent.[83] Such an inventory may be extensive. Intentional concepts may be quite complex.[84]

A belief that p, for example, may be modelled as that neuro-physical state which meets the following causal-nomic conditions – namely, that:

- it is typically caused by *environmental input* p provided that the set of background intentional states (a, b and c) obtains; and by environmental input q provided that the set of background intentional states (d, e and f) obtains; and by environmental input r…; *and*
- it is typically caused by *intentional input* s provided that the set of background intentional states (g, h and i) obtains; and by intentional input t provided that the set of background intentional states (j, k and l) obtains; and by intentional input u…; *and*
- it typically causes *intentional output* v provided that the set of background intentional states (m, n and o) obtains; and intentional output w provided that the set of background intentional states (p, q and r) obtains; and intentional output x….; *and*

82 Braddon-Mitchell and Jackson (1996) p. 179.

83 This inventory or definition forms part of an interpreter's theory of mind. More on this in Chapter 5.

84 How far back or how far forward in a causal chain is relevant to this individuation is a matter for some community of inquirers to deal with. There is no natural joint at the point at which causation runs out, between those events in a causal chain which are properly causal and those which are not.

- it typically causes *behavioural-environmental output* d provided that the set of background intentional states (s, t and u) obtains; and behavioural-environmental output e provided that the set of background intentional states (v, w and x) obtains; and behavioural-environmental output f ....

Any phenomenon which meets this complex set of conditions is a belief that p. This complex definition serves as the content of the concept of the belief in question. It holds as a conceptual truth for some relevant conceptual community. The contents of this definition are determined by that community. The belief in question maintains these causal relations as a matter of analytical necessity within that community. As a conceptual truth it is knowable by virtue of knowing the content or meaning of the concept in question, by acquiring the concept of the intentional state in question.[85] We will explore further in the next chapter how such knowledge is acquired by human agents.

A given physical token or type can meet a variety of conditions or play a variety of causal-nomic roles within a system of things. Picking up on a point made in the previous chapter, the same piece of glass can serve as a doorstop, weapon, item of modern art or paperweight. The set of conditions or role which make it a paperweight – and which make any higher-order functional phenomenon the phenomenon it is – is determined by the thought and practice of some set of agents, some conceptual community who in response to their cognitive contact with the physical realizers of the higher-order phenomenon, note the conditions it meets or role it plays and find that role important enough to generate a higher-order functional concept about.[86] And so it is with intentional states. The fact that it is a physical phenomenon's tripartite causal relation with environmental and intentional inputs and intentional and behavioural outputs which individuates that phenomenon as an intentional phenomenon is a fact which arises out of the conceptualizing practices of some authoritative community of agents – for my purposes, the community of physicalist and functionalist theorists of mind. It is a fact that I will, as a functionalist, take as a given for the purposes of this discussion.

Similarly, the fact that it is this or that set of environmental and intentional inputs and intentional and behavioural outputs which individuates a physical phenomenon as the intentional phenomenon it is – say, a belief that there is a fruit on the bush – is also a function of the conceptualizing practices of some community of agents – for my purposes, my common sense community or 'folk', as well as the community of philosophers who accord authority to that folk in these matters.[87] Though two physical states which, in fact, meet different total

85 Kim (2003) pp. 571–2.

86 See Kim (1998) pp. 104–5, 110.

87 The identity of the actual parameters of my folk is an open question and one I am in no position to determine – nor need I for my purposes. There are interesting philosophical questions to be had about which of the many propositions about intentional regularities a community holds should be taken as definitive of intentional concepts. David

functional conditions are ontologically different intentional states, a conceptual community may include them under the same concept to the extent that they share the same functional specification. In some contexts it just does not matter that they ontologically distinct at the margins of their causal relations with other phenomena. They may be classified as the same states. The concept of an intentional state specifies the set of conditions a physical state has to meet in order to be conceptualized or judged a member of that intentional type. A conceptual community selects some set of the total functional specification of an intentional state as the content of its concept of that state. The set selected will reflect and serve that community's conceptual purposes and will take its place within that community's body of concepts and theories about the world (and other discourses).

It follows from the preceding discussion about the functional nature of intentional phenomena that they are, as an ontological matter, *holistic* phenomena.[88] That is, they exist qua intentional phenomena only within a causally interrelated network of inputs and outputs and necessary background condition, only within a causally interrelated world (environmental and bodily) and a mind. They exist only on the condition that (at least) some set of the various other phenomena – environmental, intentional and behavioural – which feature in their individuating conditions and with which they maintain causal relations exist. What individuates a given intentional state (makes a physical state that intentional state) is the set of causal relations which that physical state enjoys with phenomena of the three classes mentioned. What is ontologically necessary for that physical state to enjoy such causal relations and be the intentional state it is – that is, what is ontologically necessary for the intentional state in question to exist – is the existence of at least some set of those other phenomena. So, a set of environmental states (some part of the world), a set of intentional states (a mind) and a set of behavioural states (a behavioural repertoire) must exist for a given intentional state or a set of intentional states to exist. It follows from this ontological point that when ascribing a set of intentional states to an agent one is implicitly asserting the existence of the holistic existence conditions of that state and that agent's causal interaction with some set of those conditions. The existence of higher-order phenomena which are holistic in nature is, then, quite compatible with a naturalistic ontology.

It is worth mentioning here that the fact that a given intentional state – say, a belief that there is a snake in front of the agent – is individuated by its causal relations with a set of environmental, intentional and behavioural phenomena and is holistically dependent on that set of phenomena does not entail that all of those phenomena – including all of the individuating background *intentional*

Lewis (1972) recommends that we select our causal propositions from those which are *most central* among the relevant community's opinions about the various intentional states. These comprise those publicly expressible *platitudes* about intentional state roles which are both known and known to be known within the community in question.

88 See Fodor and Lepore (1992), esp. ch. 1 and Davidson (1970a) and (1974a). By extension, minds, conceptual schemes, actions and ways of life are also holistic phenomena.

states – play any part in causing any of the behaviour which that belief might cause as part of a behaviourally causal intentional complex. They do not. It should be clear, for example, that the behavioural output states which individuate a belief cannot and do not play a role in causing any of the behavioural states that belief typically causes. As a matter of conceptual or theoretical necessity, a behavioural state is caused by a complex of intentional states not other behavioural states. So too, those individuating environmental input states or other intentional states which do not actually obtain in the action situation in question cannot be causal of behaviour in that situation. Only those that do obtain in the actual situation could be said to be causal as far as the behaviour in question is concerned. The key role played by most of the phenomena which feature in the individuating definition of a behaviourally causal intentional state is conceptual and ontological, not causal.

This is not to say that *none* of those phenomena which feature in the causal relations individuating of a behaviourally causal intentional state are causal. Some of them will be, as a matter of conceptual or theoretical necessity. Some set of the environmental and intentional phenomena which feature in the individuating definition of a behaviourally causal intentional state may be properly taken to play a causal role in relation to behaviour caused by that state. That they do play a causal role in conjunction with the behaviourally causal intentional state is why they figure in the individuating definition of that state in the first place. The point I am making here is that some, though not all, of the phenomena which conceptually individuate or which are holistically necessary for the existence of a behaviourally causal intentional state need feature as behaviourally causal in any action implicating that state.[89] The existence of a behaviourally causal intentional state *presupposes* an individuating and holistically necessary set of phenomena but does not render all of the members of that set behaviourally causal. The collectively causal nature of intentional phenomena (as far as behaviour is concerned) should be distinguished, therefore, from the conceptually individuated and holistic nature of those phenomena.

Whilst on this issue of the collectively causal nature of intentional phenomena, it is clear that by virtue of the holistic nature of such phenomena the number of intentional states involved in causing a given piece of behaviour will necessarily be quite vast. That is, any given token behaviour will be caused by a complex of intentional states which constitutes some significant part or vector of an agent's overall intentional scheme. Consider the example, mentioned above of the agent

89 It is the behaviourally causal intentional complex which is realized by the neuro-physical state which causes a given instance of behaviour. Causally efficacious neuro-physical states realize behaviourally causal intentional *complexes* and not merely individual intentional states because individual states don't cause behaviour in isolation from each other. Further, given the nature of properties, states and events it is not the case that some part of a causally efficacious neuro-physical state can be identified with a part of behaviourally causal intentional complex – a given belief, say. See Braddon-Mitchell and Jackson (1996) p. 189.

engaged in a certain kind of snake-avoiding behaviour. We have seen that such behaviour may be typically caused by a belief that there is a snake in front of the agent. However, the behaviour will be caused by this belief only if the agent also maintains certain other intentional states – for example, a desire that she move away from the snake, a belief that moving her body in the snake-avoiding manner in question will realize that agent's desire to move away from the snake, and a desire to move her body in that manner, and so on. The list of intentional states associated with the initial belief in causing the behaviour in question may be quite substantial. This is because for each of the intentional states listed a series of other intentional states are implicated.

For example, the agent will only possess a desire to move away from the snake if she at the same time possesses a set of beliefs about what snakes are, and what movement is and what movement can affect vis-à-vis snakes. The belief that moving her body in the snake-avoiding manner in question will realize the agent's desire to move away from the snake, in turn implicates as a necessary condition of its possession by the agent a series of other beliefs about bodies and her body, desires and the realization of desires, and so on. And for each of these implicated beliefs a series of other beliefs may be implicated. Given the holistic nature of intentional states, the possession of a given set of intentional states entails the possession of a numerous set of associated intentional states. Possession of an intentional state entails possession of some theoretically significant part of a mind. Given their necessary implication with what we might reasonably suppose to be a behaviourally causal set of intentional states – the belief that there is a snake in front of the agent, the desire to move away from the snake, the belief that moving her body in the snake-avoiding manner in question will realize that desire, and so on – we may plausibly take all of this extended set of intentional states to be behaviourally causal, to comprise the behaviourally causal intentional complex.

In fact, only some relatively circumscribed set of this larger complex need draw the attention of any theorist, interpreter or other interested party in any given practical context. Though the web of intentional phenomena causally implicated in any given effect may, *in principle*, be drawn quite extensively (this is a feature of causation and causation-related practice at large), much of that web may be of little practical use in the vast majority of those circumstances in which inquirers are called to think about causation and identify causal antecedents. The property of being causal in a given circumstance is a higher-order property possessed by a phenomenon. What is causal in a given situation or whether a given phenomenon is causal in that situation is a conceptual matter. This is to say that it is a matter of some or other human practice given some or other practical ends. And so, though a vast range of intentional states may, in principle, be causally linked to a given token or type of behaviour, *in practice* – specifically in our explanatory or interpretive practice – only a certain sub-set of those states will be causally significant. That is, we can distinguish as a conceptual matter between the in-principle, total set of intentional causal antecedents for a kind of behaviour and those that are explanatorily or otherwise practically relevant to an agent or set of agents. We can distinguish between what I will term the behaviourally causal intentional complex and the more practically circumscribed behaviourally explanatory intentional complex.[90] This latter complex forms a subset of the former. Those members of the behaviourally causal intentional complex which are not members of the behaviourally explanatory intentional complex – those intentional states which serve as a causal background for behaviourally explanatory states – may be termed behaviourally relevant background intentional states.[91] Though, on the face of it, the taxonomy engaged in here may seem rather mechanical and gratuitous, it will, in fact, serve us well in making sense of the judicial interpretation of testimonial action later on in this book.

Ideally, having made a place in the physicalist ontology for the behavioural and intentional components of action, then, I should complete my physicalistic theorizing of action by making a similar place for the causal relations which my model of action posits as obtaining between those components. Likewise, a complete functionalist account of intentional phenomena also demands an explanation of the nature of the causal relation which obtains between intentional phenomena and the various phenomena – environmental, intentional and behavioural – which individuate those intentional phenomena. Such discussion would take me well outside the parameters of a book such as this. Nonetheless, two key interrelated problems present themselves for physicalists here. The first is explaining how, given their metaphysical status and nature, intentional phenomena can play a causal role at all in relation to behavioural (and other) phenomena. The second is addressing what appears to be a case of causal over-determination in relation to the causing of behaviour (or other set of action-based relata) if *both* the intentional and physical causes of behaviour are conceived of as metaphysically distinct.[92] Though I will not defend it in any detail here, my overall position is that a realizationist-functionalist of intentional phenomena is able to ground an account of the causal nature of intentional phenomena far more cogently and in a manner which avoids more theoretical pitfalls than any other account of intentional phenomena.[93] On the realizationist-functionalist approach adopted here, I am, then, able to make a plausible place for action and its components within the physicalist schema.

---

90 Each complex containing, respectively, behaviourally causal intentional states and behaviourally explanatory intentional states.

91 Each of the members of the behaviourally explanatory intentional complex features as a background intentional state in the causal relations individuating each other member of that complex.

92 Any account of intentionality which posits intentional phenomena as so metaphysically autonomous as to be causally distinct from those physical phenomena which sufficiently cause behavioural events faces the problem of causal overdetermination. The only way for a physicalist to avoid overdetermination without taking the problematic epiphenomenalist path, is to assign an ontological status to the intentional realm which does not entail causal independence. Realization physicalism assigns such a status. See Kim's excellent defence of realizationism in this regard in Kim (1998).

93 Again, see Kim (1998) and Melnyk (2003) on this.

Complex Action

With this general model of action in place let me now make some comments about the kinds of culturally different action which generally become the subject of legal proceedings – complex actions. Our focus in exploring the general nature of action up until this point has been on simple basic and non-basic actions. Culturally different ways of life are comprised of a vast set of such actions performed over some period of time by the individual agents who make up the minority group.[94] Thus, a culturally different way of life is comprised of the rationally governed set of behavioural and intentional events constitutive of each of the basic or non-basic actions making up that way of life. However, in making a legal claim for the recognition and protection of some or other aspect of their culture, culturally different groups do not generally represent that culture in terms of such basic actions. Rather, the subject of a cultural minority's legal claim is represented and formally recognized and protected at a higher level of generality and complexity than this. The action of moving one's finger or pulling a trigger is not the explicit subject of a claim. It is more complex actions such as hunting – which comprehend these simpler basic and non-basic actions – which are made the explicit subject of a legal claim. Let me pursue this issue here.

An individual agent may perform a simple basic or non-basic action such as moving her finger or pulling a trigger. However, such events may comprise part of a more complex series of events which may also be conceived of as an action performed by an individual agent. Such complex individual actions (as I shall term them) are characterized as the actions they are by the identity of the simpler actions which comprise them and by the temporal, causal and semantic relationships which exists *between* those simpler actions. For example, the simple basic action of moving her finger or the simple non-basic action of pulling a trigger or firing at a prey (which both comprehend that basic action) may be part of a series of simple basic and non-basic actions which constitute the complex individual action of hunting. Hunting may be analysed (quite crudely for our purposes) in terms of a temporally ordered and causally interrelated series of simpler component actions such as looking for prey, following the prey, hiding from the prey, shooting the prey, carrying the prey's carcass back to camp, and so on. Each of these component actions may be to some degree complex in itself and further analysable in terms of a temporally ordered set of even simpler actions, down to a set of non-basic and, ultimately, basic actions. Shooting the prey, for example, may be analysable in terms of the simpler non-basic actions of raising the rifle to the shoulders, pointing the rifle in the direction of the prey, sighting the prey through the rifle-sight, pulling the trigger, firing at the prey and lowering the rifle. And, of course, for each of these simple non-basic actions a set of constitutive basic actions (such as moving the arm or finger in a certain way) may be identified.

94 The relevant period of time may be held to be over a number of generations of the group's members or within some significant time span of a given generation of members.

The key point here is that the complex individual action of hunting is characterized or individuated as that action by the identities of its component actions (complex and simple), as well as by the temporal and causal interrelationships of those component actions. It possesses the intentional and behavioural and internal structural (causal) properties of each of its component simple actions, together with the temporal and causal structural-interrelational properties of its component actions. Hunting, for example, is characterized not merely by the properties or identity of the component simpler actions mentioned above, but also by the temporal order in which they are performed. Hunting has certain characteristic temporal properties. Its component actions have characteristic temporal properties vis-à-vis each other – structural-interrelational properties, as I am terming them. The looking, following, shooting and carrying back to camp must take place (roughly) in that order in order for hunting to be undertaken.[95] Carrying the prey back to camp and *then* hiding from it and shooting it does not constitute hunting the prey but, rather, some other form of complex action. Note also that these component actions may bear a *causal* relation to each other, often comprehended by the temporal relationship. The component action of carrying of the carcass back to camp occurs after the shooting of the prey *because* of the shooting of the prey. This component action maintains a causal relation with the earlier action as well as a temporal one. The two component actions may be conceived of as having causal structural-interrelational properties as well as temporal ones. However, a requisite temporal relation may exist between two actions without their being any significant causal relation between them. The carrying of prey back to camp must temporally follow the looking for prey in an exercise of hunting but it is not (except in a tenuous and insignificant sense) *caused* by the looking for prey.

As far as the intentional phenomena comprising a complex individual action are concerned, they will reflect the identity of the various simpler component actions of the complex action. However, it is worth noting that some significant number of those component actions may be characterized as being oriented towards the realization of some state of affairs we might identify as the characteristic purpose (or set of purposes) of the complex series as a whole. That is, a complex individual action may be characterized by its overarching purpose, a purpose reflected in the propositional content of some set of its component simpler actions. It is the relationship of all the various component actions to this defining purpose (directly by involving the proposition comprising this purpose as part of their propositional content or indirectly through their relationship to directly related component actions) which renders those actions part of a complex action known as hunting and not an independent set with unrelated ends.

So, hunting, for example, may be individuated as such by its orientation towards the realization of the state of affairs or purpose of obtaining of the carcass of some prey for consumption. Its component actions may be analysed as also

95 Of course, things are more complex than this, with some repetition of various component actions likely in a real life hunting exercise.

oriented towards this purpose at some level, as being intentionally informed to some significant extent by a desire to realize this purpose, to obtain a carcass for consumption. Thus, in relation to hunting, the action of looking for prey is not performed out of zoological interest, following the prey is not performed with the purpose of getting some exercise, shooting it is not performed with the purpose of testing the rifle. They are all performed with the overarching purpose of obtaining its carcass for consumption. This is not to say that component actions cannot at the same time have more immediate purposes – the agent may run this way rather than that with the immediate purpose of not being seen by the prey, for example. Rather, it is to say that any more immediate purposes are believed and desired by the agent to serve the ultimate purpose of that complex action of which the relevant simple action is a part.

It is worth noting that complex individual actions may be conceived of at different levels of generality, defined with reference to sets of conditions descriptive of more or less types of simpler action. Hunting is defined more generally than hunting with a rifle or hunting kangaroo with a rifle or hunting kangaroo on foot with a rifle. It comprehends a wider range of component action combinations than do those more narrowly specified complex actions. No matter how generally or precisely they are defined, the conditions necessary and sufficient for being a complex action may be met by a *range* of different component actions and by a range of temporal relations between them and not some unique set with some unique temporal relationship. That is, complex actions may be, within certain conceptually circumscribed limits, multiply realizable. There is no unique set of component actions which constitutes hunting, for example. Two agents may both be engaged in the complex action of hunting despite performing different component actions. One may be running after the prey on foot and occasionally hiding behind trees to avoid being seen. The other may be pursuing the prey in a vehicle without any attempt to hide his presence. Even with two agents pursuing the prey on foot, the one might have occasion to hide behind trees quite frequently and the other not hide at all. Nor is there any unique temporal order of things – though there may be a range of acceptable orders.[96] Given the conditions definitive of hunting, both sets of component actions may realize the complex action of hunting despite their differences.[97]

Thus, a complex individual action such as hunting is analysable to varying degrees of simplicity and basicity in terms of a purposive, temporally ordered and causally related set of actions – including non-basic and basic actions – performed by an individual agent over some period of time. It comprehends all those actions

96 For example, an agent who fired their rifle before spotting the prey would not properly be considered to have engaged in the complex action of hunting. Likewise, if she pulled the trigger and then raised the gun to her shoulder and sighted, she would not be properly engaged in the action of shooting the prey.

97 A similar analysis may be done of any action that is not basic. The non-basic action of pulling the trigger of a rifle may be realized by a range of different basic finger movements.

that it is analysable into. Reference to a complex individual action implicitly refers to that range of simpler actions which do or may constitute it. Further, it is identifiable as the action it is by reference to its components and their structural-interrelational properties. For each of the non-basic and basic actions involved, a constitutive set of behavioural events (bodily or bodily-caused environmental) and intentional events obtains, all under the governance of some set of intentional regularities. And so, a complex individual action is constituted and structured by a temporally ordered and causally interrelated set of behavioural and intentional events interacting with each other under a governing set of regularities.[98] It consists of a temporally patterned set of rationalized 'causings' of behavioural events by behaviourally causal intentional complexes. It is characterized or individuated by those events and by the temporal and causal relationship between them. A token phenomenon (or set of phenomena) which is constituted in the way characteristic of hunting – which possesses the intentional, behavioural and structural-interrelational properties described by the concept of hunting – is and may be identified as a token of the action type hunting. And at the heart of this complex action, as with all actions, is a characteristic counterfactual purpose or goal comprehended by the intentional content of the action which the agent seeks to realize through the behavioural events constituting the component actions.

Complex individual actions, such as hunting animals or gathering resources or teaching children the ways of the group, may be performed at a given time by an individual agent.[99] Additionally, though, certain complex individual actions may be performed simultaneously by a group of agents, enabling us to attribute the action to that group as a whole.[100] On the one hand, the members of the group may each be engaged in the same type of complex action, but with their own individual and even differing purposes. For example, a group of agents may each be engaged in the complex action of picking fruit from a grove of bushes, each of them with their own distinct (though similar) purpose of obtaining fruit for their *own* individual consumption. In such a situation there is no shared group-oriented purpose and, therefore, the agents act not *as a group* in any unified sense but rather as a set of independent individuals engaged in a contingently collective performance of the complex individual action in question. Picking fruit

98 A complex action comprises a series of changes in the intentional and behavioural properties of an agent over time linked by an overarching purpose ascribable to the agent.

99 Miller (2001).

100 Of course, in some contexts we might also be justified in attributing an action to a culturally different group when only some of the members of that group perform the action. That is, the group may be taken in a sense to maintain all of those actions performed by some set of its membership. Thus, if a select group of indigenous elders, for instance, engages in certain ritual acts, we might for some theoretical purpose or other attribute those acts to the group as a whole The group may be said to engage in such ritual acts by virtue of the actions of the members – the elders – in question. Such acts may be said to comprise part of the way of life of the group.

solely for one's own consumption is fundamentally an individual action even if performed simultaneously with others.[101] Its performance by more than one agent simultaneously is irrelevant to its identity as the action it is. It is not a group action in the sense of the agents in question sharing some common or group purpose.[102]

On the other hand, each of the agents simultaneously involved in the complex individual action of picking fruit may do so with a shared or common purpose – say, that of obtaining fruit for consumption by the group at large. In both our examples, the agents involved share to some degree the intentional, behavioural and other properties characteristic of the complex individual action of picking fruit. However, in the second case they each maintain a common purpose in the form of shared desire to obtain fruit for the group. We can conceive of them as acting *as a group* rather than as a set of distinct individuals. For this reason we may conceive of the collective phenomenon in question as a complex *group action*. In such case, no significant coordination is required of the individuals in the group, other than in the minimal sense of not getting in each other's way or not picking fruit from a bush that has already been harvested, and so on. What each of the agents individually does is not significantly informed by or dependent on what others in the group are actually doing. The actions of the various agents are not interdependent in any significant sense.[103] They each merely each perform the same complex individual action over roughly the same period of time with the same end in mind. Each agent is capable of performing the component individual action of picking fruit independently of any of the others doing so.

I will term this kind of group action a *collective action*. Picking fruit for the group constitutes a collective action where the purpose informing constituent individual complex actions is shared by the relevant agents and where those actions are performed simultaneously but without significant coordination of the agents performing the action. Collective actions lack significant semantic relations between their complex individual action components.[104] Collective actions are individuated as the type of collective actions they are not merely by the properties of the complex individual action type being performed by the group (those properties referred to above) but also by the fact of the distribution of the performance of the complex action across multiple members of the group.[105] Collective actions

101 One might quibble with this point and argue that an overarching and, perhaps, unconscious purpose of providing nourishment for the group at large is indeed being served. If so, then the collective action in question takes on the qualities of a group action per the discussion to follow.

102 We might refer to such a phenomenon as a simultaneous set of complex individual actions.

103 Miller (2001) p. 6.

104 I will have more to say on this below.

105 A collective action comprises a series of changes in the intentional and behavioural properties of a group of agents over time linked by an overarching purpose ascribable to those agents.

possess the intentional, behavioural, temporal and causal properties of complex individual actions together with group-distributive properties.

Other complex group actions, though, are such that they involve a significant degree of coordination or cooperation between the members of the performing group in the sense that what any given member does at a given point in time is significantly informed by and dependent on what other members are actually thinking and doing at that time. The complex individual actions of individual agents which serve as the components of such an action are to a significant degree semantically related to – 'about', if you like – the actions of other agents. The component individual complex actions of such group actions are semantically interrelated in a manner characteristic of the action type in question. Such actions are inherently collaborative. A degree of deliberate and potentially highly complex coordination must be engaged in by the agents performing the action in question. I will term such a complex group action a *joint action*[106] and distinguish it from the uncoordinated complex group action that is, for example, the collective picking of fruit.

An example of such an action is a group ritual involving a number of agents performing some set of complex individual actions in a coordinated manner and with a shared purpose at or over some point or period of time.[107] One agent might perform the complex individual action of chanting some part of a ritual song, another might simultaneously be engaged in dancing, another in playing a musical instrument, and so on. What differentiates this action from a collective action is that the various agents involved in its performance consciously coordinate their own component actions with the component actions of others. Joint actions are far more collaborative than collective actions in this sense. They involve component individual actions which have characteristic semantic relations with other component individual actions, which are significantly about other component individual actions. The component individual actions of a given type of joint action possess not merely a characteristic set of intentional, behavioural, temporal, causal and group-distributive properties[108] but also a characteristic set of semantic structural-interrelational properties. Some of the component actions of a

106 See Searle (1990), Gilbert (1989) and Bratman (1992).

107 Joint actions need not be comprised of different types of complex individual action but may involve group members simultaneously performing the same type of complex individual action – for example, chanting a ritual song in unison is a joint action rather than a collective action because the individual chanters consciously coordinate their own actions closely with those of others.

108 Certain joint actions may be defined with reference to specific categories of agent performing specific categories of complex individual action. For example, ritual x may be characterized by the fact that elderly males (and no other category of group agent) perform the singing component or perform all components of the joint action. A group of younger males or females performing the same individual actions in the same temporal order and so on may not count as being a token of ritual x because the action does not possess the requisite group-distributive properties.

joint action characteristically possess the property of being the intentional object of other actions. This property is not comprehended by their own intentional properties.

Actions are intentional phenomena. They are inherently directed towards or about certain states of affairs. One kind of state of affairs which an action may be directed towards is that involving other actions. An action may be directed towards another action. For example, pursuing a line of discussion famously developed by H.L.A. Hart,[109] an agent may engage in action of a kind we might describe as the adopting of a critical-reflective attitude towards the action of another agent. He might perform the simple action of uttering the words 'that's good' in response to another agent hunting in a certain area. Alternatively, he might utter the words 'that's bad' and engage in series of simple or complex actions involving threatening, chasing and assaulting that other agent either individually, collectively or jointly. Critical-reflective actions are characterized by their being informed by a category of concepts (or intentional propositional content) we might also term critical-reflective or normative; concepts such as good, bad, should, ought, right, wrong and the like. Further, critical-reflective actions may take the form of simple or complex individual actions, collective actions or joint actions. A critical-reflective action may be an individual simple or complex action performed regularly by some set of agents. Where a set of agents simultaneously engage in a simple or complex critical-reflective action with a shared purpose – say, permitting or preventing hunting by the agent in question – then that action may be said to take the form of a collective critical-reflective action. And where the critical-reflective action is a complex one performed by a group and involving a significant degree of coordination amongst the set of agents involved – say, the capture of the agent involved in the proscribed hunting and the bringing him before a group of elders for ritual punishment – we may conceive of it as a joint critical-reflective action we might term legally sanctioning the offender.

Where it is the case that within a group some set of the group members *regularly* engage in critical-reflective action of some kind or other towards some other kind of action – say, the action of hunting in a certain area by certain agents – we may be justified in asserting the existence of a category of action known as a *social rule* within the group. Where a rule-sufficient number of agents engages with rule-sufficient regularity in critical-reflective – or to take Hart's term, secondary – actions (simple or complex, individual, collective or joint) directed towards hunting or any other (primary) action then a social rule (and, potentially, a *right*) exists amongst that group.[110] A social rule, then, is a set of interrelated complex individual actions, possessing rule-characteristic intentional, behavioural, temporal, causal and semantic properties, which are performed with rule-characteristic regularity and which are rule-characteristically distributed across a group of agents. Within a group of agents, specific rule types are characterized by the intentional, behavioural

109 Hart (1961).

110 Hart (1961), ch. 5.

and structural-interrelational properties of the primary and secondary actions comprising them, including in some cases the specific distribution of those actions across the group (or some wider) membership. This point about social rules is of some importance to the discussion in the next chapter. In determining whether or not a social rule maintained by an indigenous group constitutes a component of legally recognizable element of indigenous land title, for example, a judge must come to know to some practically adequate degree the intentional, behavioural and structural-interrelational properties of some practically adequate set of the primary and secondary actions comprising that rule.

Finally, to clarify a point made at the outset of this discussion on complex actions, given the potentially vast number of simple action types which culturally different group might want to have recognized and protected at law and given the fact that many of these serve as components of more complex and more generally described actions, the set of actions a cultural minority bring into issue in a legal proceeding will normally be described in relevant legal documents and conceived of by all throughout the legal hearing and, ultimately, identified in a judicial decision or determination in as general a form as will comprehend all those simple actions. And so, rather than seeking to claim and prove and determine on an individual basis the discrete simple action types of running, hiding, raising a rifle to the shoulder, sighting a prey and pulling a trigger (or the myriad basic actions which might comprise these), it is the more complex and general action type of hunting, whether as an individual, collective or joint action, which would serve as the explicit object of legal proceedings – in an indigenous land title claim, say. The action type of hunting comprehends a range of combinations of simpler action types – non-basic and basic.[111] It is hunting which explicitly serves as a claimant action type and its constituent simpler actions are rendered claimant action types only implicitly. Also implicit in the concepts of the general and complex actions which comprise the claimant set is the set of intentional and behavioural events and properties and the governing regularities which constitute each of those simpler actions, as well as the temporal order and personal distribution which characterize those general and complex actions as the actions they are.

111 That is, all those basic and non-basic action combinations which meet the conditions for being the complex action of hunting.

Chapter 3
Indigenous Land Title: A Case Study

Introduction

Before exploring in detail the nature and limits of the judicial understanding of culturally different actions, it is important to clarify the nature of the legal framework within which judicial efforts at such understanding take place. We must gain a working grasp of the nature of both the conceptual and practical context within which the problematic of judicial understanding under conditions of cultural difference is located. As mentioned in the introductory chapter, I propose to take as a paradigm example of the judicial understanding of cultural difference the law and process involved in an indigenous land title determination hearing[1] across a representative number of common law jurisdictions, including the United States, Canada, Australia and New Zealand. By virtue of their shared origins in the English common law of colonization, classical Euro-international law, and the groundbreaking early nineteenth-century Indian title jurisprudence of Chief Justice John Marshall of the US Supreme Court, the present day indigenous land title law of these jurisdictions shares a significant enough degree of doctrinal and procedural content to justify treating them generically as far as the issues here are concerned.[2]

The first part of this chapter explores the nature of the concept of indigenous land title – or, more correctly, the nature of the judicial conception of indigenous land title. It is this conception which conditions the interpretive and other actions of the judge and other relevant agents throughout the hearing process across the various jurisdictions and which, ultimately, determines the outcome of an indigenous land title claim in those jurisdictions. It is for this reason that I commence this chapter with a discussion of the concept of indigenous land title rather than

1 By this I mean a full hearing before an authorized judge into whether a claim for indigenous land rights will be formally recognized (determined) by the state.

2 This is not to deny the differences in indigenous land title law which exist between the various jurisdictions. Those differences, however, in no way affect the course of the analysis and argument to follow. See Bartlett (2000) pp. 3–9, 109. The shared origins and contemporary overlap of the law in the various jurisdictions is evident in a reading of the foundational cases within those jurisdictions. See, most importantly, *Johnson v McIntosh* (1823) 21 US 8 Wheat 543; 5 L Ed 681 (US); *Calder v A-G (British Columbia)* (1973) 34 DLR (3d) 145 (Canada); *Mabo v Queensland (No. 2)* (1992) 175 CLR 1 (Australia) (hereafter, referred to as the Mabo case); *R v Symonds* (1847) NZPCC 387 and *Ngati Apa v Attorney General* [2003] 3 NZLR 643 (New Zealand).

proceed directly with an account of the indigenous land title process. Everything which goes on in that process is informed by that concept. What goes on in that process cannot be properly understood without a prior grasp of the nature of that concept. The second part of this chapter, though, does provide an overview of the indigenous land title determination hearing process. It identifies the various types of cognitive, interpretive and adjudicative activities which the judge is called upon to perform and the various kinds of evidence, argument and explanation which the judge is called upon to interpret or otherwise cognitively appropriate over the course of a hearing, as well as the locations within the hearing process where those judicial activities occur. By doing so it also articulates the rationale of judicial efforts at understanding and interpreting evidence of indigenous actions. With information in hand about the nature of the procedural and conceptual context within which a judge is called upon to interpret evidence of indigenous actions, understand those actions and make a determination of whether or not they are indigenous land title, it is intended that the legal and practical relevance of the substantially philosophical chapters to follow may be better appreciated.

The Judicial Conception of Indigenous Land Title

A determination of indigenous land title is intended to protect, to some degree, some or all of the way of life of indigenous people from interference by the actions and artefacts of non-indigenous agents. It does so by providing successful indigenous claimant groups with a set of legally enforceable rights to perform certain legally recognized actions upon a legally delimited area of land or waters free (to some extent, at least) from non-indigenous interference. It is oriented towards providing a basis for a preventative or punitive legal response in response to such interference. An analogy might be made here with the freehold title to land which many people in common law jurisdictions possess under their respective property law in relation to their homes. Such title gives the possessor a legally enforceable right to perform a range of actions on the land in question – say, build a house on the land, sleep, cook and watch TV in the house, plant a garden and play in it – largely without interference from others. If interference is threatened, the resources of the legal system may be called upon to prevent that interference. If interference occurs, compensation may be ordered, those interfering may be punished. The title provides legal protection for a range of actions which constitute some part of the way of life of the landowner. In order to receive a grant of such title in relation to an area of land a legal process must be engaged in. So too, it is thought, with indigenous land title.[3]

An indigenous group which seeks legal protection for their way of life by way of an indigenous land title determination (hereafter, a claimant group), must

3 Whether the indigenous land title process is in fact capable of providing the recognition and protection it aspires to is, of course, an issue this book seeks to address.

lodge a formal application for a determination of indigenous land title with an appropriate court. This application may be referred to as an indigenous land title claim. Further, we may refer to that part of their way of life for which a claimant group seeks protection as a claimant set of actions and a member of that set as a claimant action.[4] A claimant set of actions may comprise the whole or some part of a claimant group's way of life, depending upon the intentions of that claimant group. The purpose of such an application is to obtain a positive determination of indigenous land title from an authoritative judge over the course of a legal hearing.[5] A positive determination of indigenous land title is a legally formalized and enforceable decision or order by a judge that, amongst other things, indigenous land title exists in relation to a particular area of land or waters and is held by the claimant group.

This decision, in turn, may be glossed in terms of a belief and formal assertion on the part of a judge that some or all of the claimant set of actions *is* indigenous land title – that the claimant group maintain[6] as part of their way of life a set of actions which has the properties described by the judge's operative concept of indigenous land title.[7] Only that set of indigenous actions – that portion of the claimant group's way of life – which actually has the properties described by the judge's operative concept of indigenous land title[8] and which, in the course of a determination hearing, is proved by the claimant group and is believed by the judge to have those properties may properly receive legal recognition and protection under indigenous land title law.

In formulating a concept of indigenous land title for application to a claimant set of actions, the presiding judge relies upon a series of beliefs about relevant phenomena – including most importantly the meaning of relevant statutes and case law relating to the concept of indigenous land title. For example, in Australia indigenous land title is statutorily defined as,

> the communal, group or individual rights and interests of [indigenous people] in relation to land or waters, where:

4 It is by virtue of indigenous land title claimants being indigenous and culturally different agents that a claimant action, set of actions, way of life, concept or conceptual scheme may be referred to as an indigenous or culturally different action, set of actions, way of life, and so on.

5 Hereafter, referred to as 'the judge' or 'a judge'. I will assume for the purposes of this book that such a judge is a non-indigenous agent of normal sensory, cognitive and rational capacity who acts only on the basis of legally valid rules and reasons.

6 That is, some set of the members of the group have performed, do perform and will continue to perform those actions with a legally sufficient degree of regularity.

7 I use this term to designate the concept of indigenous land title which the judge holds and relies upon at the point in the hearing at which she determines whether or not the claimant set of actions is indigenous land title.

8 Which we will assume for the purposes of this book to be a legally valid concept of indigenous land title. See the discussion below on the meaning of this term.

> (a) the rights and interests are possessed under the traditional laws acknowledged, and the traditional customs observed, by the [indigenous people]; and
> (b) the [indigenous people], by those laws and customs, have a connection with the land or waters; and
> (c) the rights and interests are recognised by the common law of Australia.[9]

Indigenous land title is defined in most common law jurisdictions roughly along these lines as a set of indigenous, traditional, legal-customary rights and interests in relation to some area of land or waters.[10] In addition, these rights and interests provide their holders with a legally specified connection to that area and are compatible with certain norms of the common law of the jurisdiction in question. The written terms of a jurisdiction's legal definition provide its judges with a basis for conceptualizing indigenous land title. The judge's beliefs about the meaning of those terms fundamentally inform the judge's operative concept of indigenous land title. The relevant legal terms are interpreted by the judge as signifying a set of criterial properties which the claimant set of actions must possess if it is to merit a positive determination of indigenous land title. Key terms in the definition – 'rights and interests', 'in relation to land or waters', 'traditional', and so on – signify different properties or sets of properties in this respect. Claimant sets of action which possess the properties described by the terms of this definition, as far as the judge interprets it, are eligible for recognition by that judge as indigenous land title.[11] Claimant sets of actions which do not possess those properties are not eligible and will not receive from that judge a positive determination of indigenous land title.

In interpreting the terms of the common law definition and in developing and adopting an operative and legally valid concept of indigenous land title, the presiding judge does not act in a vacuum but, rather, on the basis of her beliefs

9 Native Title Act 1993 (Cth) s.223(1).

10 This definition is a statutory expression of an earlier common law definition of indigenous land title operative throughout the common law world and articulated in seminal cases such as *Johnson v McIntosh* (1823) 21 US 8 Wheat 543; 5 L Ed 681 (US); *Calder v A-G (British Columbia)* (1973) 34 DLR (3d) 145 (Canada); the Mabo case (Australia); and *R v Symonds* (1847) NZPCC 387 (New Zealand). The Privy Council has also adopted this common law definition in a number of cases concerning various of the former African colonies of Great Britain, including *Amodu Tijani v Secretary, Southern Nigeria* [1921] 2 AC 399. Whilst it is true that Canadian law adopts a notion of indigenous title which is oriented more towards indigenous *culture* than indigenous law, nothing hinges on this as far as the discussion to follow is concerned. See *Delgamuukw v British Columbia* [1997] 3 SCR 1010 at para. 114 (hereafter referred to as the Delgamuukw case). I will use the terms 'common law' and 'legal' definition to refer to this largely shared definition of indigenous land title across the common law jurisdictions.

11 Assuming other necessary conditions for recognition (such as the non-extinguishment of title by the state) are met.

about the semantically relevant interpretive and other practices of a range of other agents in relation to the common law definition, including fellow judges (the most important of which are those comprising authoritative majorities of the ultimate court of appeal). To the extent that the judge's interpretation of the common law definition and conception of indigenous land title is informed by the beliefs and practices of other authoritative agents, including other judges, we can conceive of the judge as being a member of an interpretive or conceptual community as far as the content of the concept of indigenous land title is concerned. Further, to the extent that a significant part of the beliefs of indigenous land title judges to do with indigenous land title are or are reasonably capable of being *shared* by those judges at some point in time, we can speak of there being at that point in time a collective and authoritative judicial conception of the concept of indigenous land title and of the properties described by that concept.[12] We can speak of a given judge possessing what I will term a legally valid concept of indigenous land title – a concept possessed or reasonably likely to be possessed by a legally authoritative conceptual community – and relying upon such concept as her operative concept of indigenous land title at the moment of determination.[13]

The semantic view adopted in this book is consistent with a range of philosophical perspectives – including the physicalist perspective outlined in the next chapter – according to which the meaning of a signifier or the content of a concept is not a transcendent 'given' in the sense of existing or occurring

12 One need only look to the significant degree of uniformity of judicial practice within the indigenous land title system in the various jurisdictions (from the trial courts to the ultimate courts of appeal), as well as to the existence and effectiveness of those institutional mechanisms put in place to ensure to ensure such uniformity (various channels of communication between judges, including appeal mechanisms) to be persuaded of the existence of a widely and substantially shared concept of indigenous land title. The existence within the Australian and Canadian judiciaries of peripheral disagreement in relation to certain of the content of the concept of indigenous land title does not significantly detract from my point. See Bartlett (2004) pp. 157–9, Perry and Lloyd (2003) p. 22 and the Delgamuukw case on this. In adopting this position, I implicitly reject radically indeterminist theses about the capacity of written rules to influence the actions of judges. See Hart (1961) ch. 7, Fish (1989), MacCormick (1990) and Rosenfeld (1992).

13 One useful way we might conceive of the idea of a legally valid concept of indigenous land title is as a concept which a majority of the members of the jurisdiction's validity-determining, ultimate court of appeal actually hold or might reasonably be persuaded to hold. My use here of the term 'legally valid' is informed by Hart (1961). For the purposes of this book, I will use the term 'concept of indigenous land title' to refer to a legally valid concept of indigenous land title and the term 'judge' to generically refer to a judge who possesses a legally valid concept of indigenous land title as her operative concept of such title. By this theoretical device I hope to render this book an inquiry into the interpretive capacities and limits, not of specific, individual and idiosyncratic judges, but of the judiciary as a whole – and, potentially, of the legal system at large.

prior to or independently of some or other set of human actions.[14] Rather, the meaning of a signifier or content of a concept – in this case, the meaning of the written terms of the legal definition or the content of the concept of indigenous land title – emerges out of the acts of interpretation and other actions associated with that signifier or concept performed by some or other set of agents within a given natural and practical context.[15] The meaning of an act, utterance or written set of terms or the content of a concept is localized to and is contingent upon the semantically relevant thoughts and practices of a set of agents I have been referring to as a conceptual community. In the context of a discussion about the conceptual and interpretive capacity of indigenous land title judges, the agents which most importantly matter as far as the meaning of the terms of the legal definition of indigenous land title are concerned – that is, as far as the content of the concept of indigenous land title goes – are the conceptual community of authoritative judges – trial judges at first instance, and appeal court judges through to the ultimate court of appeal. This is because it is those judges who, under the indigenous land title regime, are given the role of determining whether or not any claimant set of actions possesses the properties referred to by the legal definition of indigenous land title.[16] To anticipate discussion in the next chapter, indigenous land title is a functional phenomenon, the individuating conditions, definition or conceptual contents of which are determined by the practices of an authoritative conceptual community.

This practical and social dimension of the concept of indigenous land title gives it both a contingent stability over time, as well as a capacity for change. Its stability enables us to speak of there being a legally valid concept of indigenous land title describing a given set of properties at or over a given point or period of time.[17] It enables us to speak of the content of the concept in a relatively determinate manner. Its capacity for change – the semantic dynamism of the concept of indigenous land title – admits of the possibility of the concept being modified by a judge or set of judges over the course of a hearing or set of hearings in response to evidence and argument – specifically, in relation to culturally different indigenous actions not described by any existing concept of indigenous land title.[18] This dual nature of

14 In the sense maintained by those critiqued by Quine (1953b). See Berger and Luckman (1967), Barnes (1995) pp. 104–12, Margolis (1999), Bruner et al. (1999) on the socially constructed nature of concepts.

15 Smith (1968).

16 Of course, judicial interpretations of the legal definition and their consequent conceptualizations of indigenous land title are themselves informed by the semantically relevant practices of wider communities of agents – including, for example, the 'ordinary language' or 'common sense' public or 'folk'.

17 Patton (1996) pp. 159–60.

18 Connolly (2005). A classic example of such a conceptual shift is that which occurred between the 1919 Privy Council case of *Re Southern Rhodesia* [1919] AC 211 (in which it was held that the concept of indigenous land title describes the property of being non-nomadic) and the 1921 case of *Amodu Tijani v Secretary, Southern Nigeria* [1921] 2

the judicial conception of indigenous land title is fundamental to its role within the determination hearing process and within this book.[19]

Whilst on this issue of the dynamism of the concept of indigenous land title, it is worth emphasizing the important point just made that an indigenous action for which a judge possesses virtually no concept at the commencement of a determination hearing – that is, a significantly conceptually different indigenous action as far as the judge is concerned – will not be adequately described by any concept of indigenous land title that judge might possess at the commencement of the hearing. Were her concept of indigenous land title to do so, that would entail her possessing some practically adequate part of the concept of that action. As will become clear in Chapter 4, this is because possessing a description of a phenomenon constitutes possessing some part of the concept of that phenomenon. One of the consequences of the radical cultural incommensurability thesis, if it were true, would be that necessarily no legally valid concept of indigenous land title would describe a claimant set of actions. This is because to be a legally valid concept of indigenous land title is to be possessed by some set of judges but, on the incommensurabilist schema, no concept possessed by any such judges can describe a claimant set of actions.[20]

Thus, not only must a judge acquire a practically adequate[21] concept of a culturally different indigenous action in order to properly evaluate the comprehension of that action by her standing concept of indigenous land title at any given point in time but she must acquire a practically adequate concept of that action also in order to determine whether or not her standing concept of indigenous land title might be supplemented or otherwise altered so as to comprehend or describe that action in manner which satisfies what she believes to be the operative legal norms regulating such conceptual change.[22] That is, she not only needs to

---

AC 399, (in which it the property of being non-nomadic was no longer held to be part of the concept of indigenous land title). The dynamic nature of judicial concepts of indigenous land title enables us to conceive of a judge being persuaded by argument over the course of a determination hearing to change the content of the concept of indigenous land title she holds at the commencement of that hearing (her standing concept of indigenous land title) and adopt an alternative set of content as her operative concept of indigenous land title prior to the moment of determination.

19 There will be, of course, normative constraints upon the degree to which a judge might reasonably alter her existing concept of indigenous land title in this way. See for example, Brennan J's comments in the Mabo case at p. 29 about the 'skeleton of principle which gives the body of our law its shape and internal consistency' at work in the common law of indigenous land title in Australia.

20 My rebuttal of the radical cultural incommensurability thesis in Chapter 6 enables me to also rebut the incommensurabilist idea that necessarily no legally valid concept of indigenous land title describes any claimant set of actions.

21 That is, adequate to the proper performance of her adjudicative purposes.

22 These norms are also the product of the actions of some set of authoritative norm-constituting agents. I will have more to say on the nature of norms below.

understand an indigenous action in order to evaluate whether or not it is indigenous land title as she understands indigenous land title, but she needs to understand an indigenous action in order to decide whether and how to create, through her authoritative judicial actions and reasoning, an altered concept of indigenous land title descriptive of that action which might serve as a legally valid concept for other judges in the future. Throughout the following discussion, I will explain the need for a judge to understand an indigenous action to a practically adequate degree with reference to the fact that such understanding serves as a necessary condition for the proper evaluation of whether that action is described by a legally valid concept of indigenous land title. In doing so, it is my intention not merely to implicate the relationship between such understanding and evaluation but also the fact that the judicial understanding of a conceptually different indigenous action is a necessary condition of that judge being able to consider reforming her standing concept of indigenous land title and establishing a new legally valid concept of indigenous land title (which she would then acknowledge describes the indigenous action in question).[23]

Notwithstanding its dynamism over time due to changes in judicial practice, what has remained constant since the dawn of indigenous land title, and what we may reasonably take for granted as a constant as far as future judicial practice is concerned, is that the terms of the various common law jurisdiction's legal definition of indigenous land title denote a set of *actions* performed by an indigenous group, and not some other set of phenomena.[24] Further, the concept of indigenous land title denotes not just *any* set of indigenous actions but a set of actions whose members are not only performed with sufficient regularity but are intentionally (including conceptually) and behaviourally constituted, as well as causally and otherwise collectively or structurally interrelated, in a characteristic manner. That is, the judicial conception of indigenous land title – the concept of indigenous land title – describes a set of indigenous actions with characteristic

23 As I discuss below, an important part of this judicial concept-reforming process involves counsel for the claimant group presenting explanatory submissions about the content of a concept of indigenous land title which describes conceptually different indigenous actions – a concept which I term below, the claimant group's operative concept of indigenous land title – and argumentative submissions that the adoption of such concept by the judge is compatible with authoritative legal norms regulating and determining the limits of validity of judicial concept formation within the indigenous land title sphere.

24 That indigenous land title is fundamentally a set of actions rather than mere non-intentionalized behaviour is reflected in the view of Justice Toohey in the Mabo case at pp. 187–8 who states that an indigenous physical presence on land must have a 'connection with or *meaning* in relation to a society's economic, cultural or religious life'. That is, a mere behavioural presence must be informed by a meaningful complex of intentional states. Even Canadian indigenous title law with its emphasis on prior occupation rather than traditional law demands an intentional dimension. See the Delgamuukw case at paras 114–18 and the case of *Hamlet of Baker Lake v Minister of Indian Affairs and Northern Development* (1980) 107 DLR (3d) 513.

intentional, behavioural, structural-interrelational and other properties. It is this category of phenomena which the indigenous land title judiciary throughout the common law world collectively understands their shared legal definition of indigenous land title as describing. It is this category of phenomena which properly merit the recognition and protection associated with a positive determination of indigenous land title. That this is so may be seen more clearly if we analyse the contemporary practice of indigenous land title judges in relation to the terms of the common law definition.

Upon analysis of current judicial interpretive practice it is apparent that the most important component of the legal definition as far as the judiciary is concerned is the term 'rights and interests'. Indigenous land title is, for the judiciary, most fundamentally a set of indigenous rights and interests, a set of rights and interests maintained by some indigenous group. It is a set of rights and interests which also has the properties described by the other terms of the definition – being legal or customary, traditional, in relation to land and waters, and the rest. The indigenous land title judiciary in most jurisdictions has interpreted the term 'rights and interests' in a manner informed by the legal theory of the English jurist, H.L.A. Hart.[25] On this theory, rights and interests are phenomena which subsist within a set of social rules or norms. For Hart, a social rule exists within a group of agents to the extent that amongst some rule-sufficient proportion of that group certain actions are performed with some rule-sufficient degree of regularity. For heuristic purposes I shall call these actions primary actions. In addition, some rule-sufficient proportion of the group must, with some rule-sufficient regularity, adopt a *critical reflective attitude* towards – must possess a characteristic set of beliefs and desires about – the performance of those primary actions and perform certain actions – secondary actions – informed by that attitude with some rule-sufficient regularity.[26] That is, they must maintain a critical-reflective set of beliefs and

25 Most importantly, Hart (1961) pp. 54–7. The most explicit appropriation of Hart by the Australian judiciary occurs in the High Court of Australia case of *Members of the Yorta Yorta Aboriginal Community v State of Victoria* (2002) 214 CLR 422 (hereafter referred to as the Yorta Yorta case) at pp. 442–3. There is evidence of it also in judicial comments in the important Canadian cases of *R v Van der Peet* [1996] 2 SCR 507 (hereafter referred to as the Van der Peet case) and the Delgamuukw case. Hart's theory is broadly consistent with the views of contemporary theorists of conventions, norms and rules such as Ullmann-Margalit (1977), Raz (1984 and 1990), Tuomela (1984), Searle (1995), and Miller (2001).

26 Hart (1961) p. 57. Thus, the distinction made by Hart (1961) p. 9–10 and the indigenous land title judiciary between, on the one hand, social habits as sets comprising merely primary actions and, on the other, rules where this additional critical-intentional and critical-active dimension exists. Hart (1961) p. 56. Justice Nicholson in the Australian case of *Daniels v State of Western Australia* [2003] FCA 666 at para. 304 reflects the wider judicial appropriation of Hart in stating that the evidence tendered in that case indicated that the various primary actions (which he rather misleadingly termed 'observable behaviours') performed by the claimant group 'are more than social habits and [have] about them the quality of being a social rule in that some at least (and indeed a considerable number) of

desires *about* the performance of the primary actions and this must be displayed to some rule-sufficient extent in their behaviour.[27] Critical reflective beliefs and desires include those which are informed by normative concepts such as ought, should, right, wrong, good, bad and the like.

Critical-reflective or secondary actions include thinking that the performance of some primary action by another agent is right or wrong, verbally or otherwise commending or encouraging or physically punishing that agent for the performance of that action, verbally justifying one's secondary actions by reference to the rightness or wrongness of the performance of the primary action, as well as a range of others.

> What is necessary [for a rule to exist] is that there should be a critical reflective attitude to certain patterns of behaviour as a common standard, and that this should display itself in criticism (including self-criticism), demands for conformity, and in acknowledgments that such criticism and demands are justified, all of which find their characteristic expression in the normative terminology of 'ought', 'must' and 'should', 'right' and 'wrong'. These are the crucial features which distinguish social rules from mere group habits ...[28]

Rights and interests are conceived of by Hart and much of the indigenous land title judiciary across the common law world as existing only in the context of a set of social rules.[29] They constitute a sub-species of rule. For example, a right to hunt in a given geographical area exists in a group where some right-sufficient proportion of the group (right-holders) engage in the primary action[30] of hunting (as of right) in that area with some right-sufficient degree of regularity and, at the

---

the first applicants group look upon the behaviour in question as a general standard to be followed by the group as a whole'. The judge goes on to explicitly quote Hart (1961).

27 These secondary actions are informed by intentional states which are (broadly) about the primary actions, which have the primary actions as their reference (part of their content).

28 Hart (1961) p. 57.

29 'If there is to be this right ... there must ... have been somewhere in the society a general social practice more complex than any that can be described in terms of habit of obedience: there must have been the acceptance of the *rule*.' Hart (1961) pp. 54–5. The Australian High Court adopted a similar view in the Yorta Yorta case at p. 441 when it stated that 'When it is recognised that the subject matter of the inquiry is rights and interests (in fact rights and interests in relation to land or waters) it is clear that the laws or customs in which those rights or interests *find their origins* must be laws or customs having a normative content and deriving, therefore, from a body of norms or normative system ...'. The majority judgement in the Canadian case of Van der Peet also reflects this view.

30 It is not a necessary condition of an action being performed as of right that the agent knows that the action is being performed as of right. What renders the action performed as of right is the set of secondary actions performed by the right-constituting sub-group of agents.

same time, some right-sufficient proportion of the group (right-regarders)[31] engage with some right-sufficient degree of regularity in critical-reflective secondary – that is, rights-constituting – actions in relation to instances of those primary actions by both right-holders and non-right holders.[32] Such secondary, rights-constituting actions may include condoning, encouraging or (intentionally) not interfering with the performance of hunting by right-holders, verbally criticizing, physically interfering with or punishing after the fact the performance of hunting by those who are *not* right-holders, justifying these actions by means of normatively phrased reasons, for example ('I criticized him because he should not have been hunting there. It was wrong. He had no right to do so'), and teaching youngsters in the group to do likewise.[33] These secondary actions subsist within a complex discursive relationship with each other and with relevant primary actions. They are characterized by their critical-reflective intentional and behavioural content and by their temporal, causal and semantic relation to relevant primary actions.

It can be seen that on this model a right (and similarly, an interest) is a complex of semantically and causally interrelated actions distributed across and performed with some degree of regularity by some proportion of the membership of a group.[34] Some of these actions – namely, the secondary actions – have rights-characteristic conceptual and intentional properties, which Hart and the judiciary conceive of in terms of the possession of a characteristic critical-reflective or normative content and a temporal-causal and semantic relation to relevant primary actions. Such actions are informed by normative concepts and are prone to be caused by (and, therefore, temporally follow) relevant primary actions, as well as to be semantically 'about' those primary actions. Likewise, primary actions, whilst not possessing any right-specific conceptual or intentional content, have a temporal-causal and semantic relation with secondary actions in that they are prone to cause (and, therefore, temporally precede) certain secondary actions, as well as serve as the intentional object of those secondary actions.

In order to be properly recognized as indigenous land title by a judge, a claimant set of actions must (as a necessary but not sufficient condition) comprise a set of such complexes. It must comprise one or more right or interest. This

31 Becker (1977) pp. 8–9. The class of right-regarders may include some or all of the right-holders who may hold such an attitude to their own actions as of right (Hart's 'self-criticism'). Hart (1961) p. 56.

32 Secondary actions may themselves be performable as of right and, hence, take the additional role of primary actions in the context of another rule to do with them. One might have the right to criticize the breach of another right. Thus, certain actions may have a dual status as both primary and secondary depending on the context.

33 Members of a rule-bound community take the rule as their guide and the breach of the rule as their 'reason and justification' for criticizing or punishing offenders. Hart (1961) p. 10.

34 Recall the discussion in Chapter 2 in which I argued that rules and rights may be conceived of as kinds of complex action comprised of simpler primary and secondary actions.

is what indigenous land title is for the judiciary. As a necessary, though not sufficient condition of comprising such title, claimant set of actions must possess the intentional, behavioural and structural-interrelational (temporal, causal and semantic) properties inherent in this notion of a right or interest. It must be comprised of a set of primary actions performed as of right and a set of secondary actions which by virtue of their critical-reflective intentional and behavioural content and semantic and temporal-causal interrelationship with relevant primary actions and other secondary actions, confer rightness on primary actions. And, in addition, of course, these actions must be performed by a requisite proportion of group members with a requisite degree of regularity.[35] In order for an *individual* indigenous action to be recognized and protected as indigenous land title it must be a member of such a set. It must be a primary or secondary action subsisting within such a system of actions and possessing the intentional, behavioural, structural-interrelational and other[36] properties characteristic of such an action.

In addition to possessing the properties characteristic of a set of rights and interests, the claimant set of actions must also possess the properties held by the judiciary to be described by the legal definitional terms 'traditional', 'in relation to land and waters', 'recognized by the common law of the jurisdiction', and so on.[37] Without going into a detailed analysis here, the effect of these terms, as consistently interpreted by the judiciary, is to require further intentional and behavioural properties to be possessed by the claimant set of actions. For example, the definitional term 'in relation to land and waters' is presently held in common law courts to require of the claimant set of actions both an intentional and a behavioural relation to various physical or geographical phenomena. The definitional term 'traditional' is presently held by the judiciary to describe a similarity requirement on the intentional and behavioural properties of the present-day claimant set of actions and any correlative pre-colonial actions maintained by the claimant group's forebears prior to colonization.[38] Finally, as an example, the definitional

35 For simplicity's sake I will from this point on include these structural properties of the concept of rights and interests under the rubric of intentional properties. The judicial identification of the existence of such structural properties (being performed by a requisite proportion of group members, being performed with a requisite degree of regularity, being performed in the right causal order) in a claimant set of actions requires the judge to interpret the members of that set or evidence of or argument about that set or both.

36 The proportionality and regularity requirements are not interrelational properties of the set of actions in question. They are discrete properties of that set.

37 Only the three terms mentioned here have been taken by the indigenous land title judiciary to impose any additional *intentional* requirements to the claimant set of actions than are imposed by the term 'rights and interests'. The other key term in the statutory definition – 'connection' – has not been conceived of by the judiciary as describing any intentional properties, only behavioural ones (physical presence), and so will not be considered here. See Bartlett (2004) pp. 110–21 and Perry and Lloyd (2003) pp. 21–4 and 764–6 on the Australian case law on this.

38 Connolly (2005).

term 'recognized by the common law' presently imposes a requirement that the intentional and behavioural content of members of the claimant set of actions not be inconsistent with certain non-indigenous legal (common law) norms within the jurisdiction in question.[39] Their being inconsistent or not with such common law norms will be a product of their intentional and behavioural properties. In order to be adjudged indigenous land title, the intentional and behavioural properties of indigenous actions must fall into the category of properties consistent with these norms.

In evaluating whether or not a claimant set of actions is indigenous land title the judge evaluates whether that set of actions possesses the intentional, behavioural and other properties described by the statutory terms 'rights and interests', 'traditional', 'in relation to land and waters', and so on (as those terms are interpreted by the judge). Amongst these categories of properties, it is the intentional properties described by the concept of indigenous land title which are most problematic as far as this book is concerned. The content given to the concept of indigenous land title by contemporary judges demands that any action constituting indigenous land title possess a characteristic set of intentional properties. In order for a judge to evaluate whether or not an indigenous action is an indigenous land title action – whether or not it possesses intentional properties which are characteristic of indigenous land title actions – the judge must possess a concept of the intentional properties of that indigenous action. This is to say that she must *understand* the intentional properties of that indigenous action. Such understanding together with an understanding of the other categories of properties of an indigenous action is a necessary element of understanding the indigenous action at large. Such understanding, though, is precisely what the incommensurabilist theorists mentioned in Chapter 1 deny judges can achieve.

The Indigenous Land Title Determination Hearing

Throughout the pre-hearing process, the claimant group *claim* to maintain a set of actions which is indigenous land title according to a legally valid concept of indigenous land title. That is, they claim to maintain a set of actions, the intentional, behavioural and structural-interrelational properties of which are described by

39 The claimant set of actions must not be 'antithetical to the fundamental tenets of the common law' (the Yorta Yorta case at p. 453). The roots of this doctrine throughout the common law world lie in the old English case, *The Case of Tanistry* (96) (1608) Davis 28 (80 ER 516). An historical example of an indigenous practice which failed the test for non-indigenous recognition on this ground was the Indian practice of suttee (the ritual burning alive of a widow with her dead husband) which was forbidden by English colonial law in 1829 on the ground that it was malum in se or contrary to public policy. See Allen (1964) p. 503. Practices such as infanticide and senilicide might also be refused recognition on this basis.

such a concept. Within the hearing process the claimant group are required to *prove* – that is, cause the judge to believe – on the balance of probabilities that they do, in fact, maintain such a set of actions, that they hold indigenous land title. Throughout the hearing, the onus lies with the claimant group to persuade the judge that the group maintains on the claim area a set of actions that are described by a legally valid concept of indigenous land title. The claimant set of actions must not merely *be* indigenous land title but must be *proved* by the claimant group to be indigenous land title. The claimant group must act in a manner which facilitates the judge's *knowing* that the claimant set is indigenous land title.

Judicial knowledge that the claimant group maintain a set of actions that are described by a legally valid concept of indigenous land title may be analysed in terms of three elements or phases. First, the judge must possess, to some practically adequate degree, knowledge that the claimant group maintain with sufficient regularity over a sufficient period of time some or other set of actions on the claim area.[40] Secondly, the judge must possess, to some practically adequate degree, knowledge of the intentional, behavioural and structural-interrelational properties of the actions maintained on the claim area. This is to say that she must possess to some practically adequate degree concepts of those indigenous actions. She must understand those actions to some practically adequate degree. Finally, the judge must, to a practically adequate degree, be in possession of knowledge that a set of actions with such properties is described by a legally valid concept of indigenous land title. The onus lies with the claimant group to ensure that by the time the judge makes her determination of indigenous land title, she is in possession of the requisite degree of knowledge of each of these things. The claimants meet this evidential onus by providing the judge with suitable evidence, explanation and argument about these things over the course of the hearing.

In order to know that the claimant group maintain some or other set of actions on the claimant area with the requisite degree of regularity, the judge must be provided with and must cognitively appropriate sound evidence that they do.[41] That is, the claimant group must, at some stage over the course of the hearing, *evidence* the actions they want recognized and protected. They may do this by providing witnesses or documents which reliably testify to the fact of such maintenance or by leading evidence of members of the group actually performing actions on the claim area (from which, together with other relevant evidence, the judge might

40 By 'practically adequate degree' here, I mean to a degree sufficient to enable her to make a proper determination of indigenous land title. I will generally use the term 'practically adequate' in the discussion to follow to refer to that *degree* of knowledge or concept possession, or to that *set* of concepts or intentional states and so on, necessary to enable a judge to properly perform her various cognitive, interpretive and adjudicative functions.

41 This process of cognitive appropriation involves not merely understanding the evidence but assigning it some probative value with reference to the claim at large.

infer to the maintenance of those actions), or by some combination of these.[42] Given that much of the evidence that a set of actions is maintained will, at the same time, constitute evidence of the properties of that set of actions, evidence led in pursuit of this phase of judicial knowledge is largely coincident with evidence led in pursuance of the second phase of judicial knowledge mentioned above.

As far as that second phase is concerned, in order to know the intentional, behavioural and structural-interrelational properties of those indigenous actions which are evidenced by a claimant group with a view to evaluating their description by a legally valid concept of indigenous land title – that is, in order to understand those actions to a practically adequate degree – the judge must possess to some practically adequate degree concepts of those properties constituting the action.[43] A judge cannot possess a true belief that an evidenced indigenous action possesses the property x without possessing some practically adequate concept of property x. As we saw in Chapter 2, this stands as a conceptual truth about the possession of beliefs. How, for example, could one know that an apple possesses the properties of being red, spherical and edible without possessing concepts of those properties? How could one possess the concept of (that is, understand) 'apple' without possessing some set of the concepts of its properties? Possession of concepts of the properties of indigenous actions is a necessary condition of knowledge of the properties of those actions. It is a necessary – though not sufficient – condition of understanding those actions.[44] Understanding an indigenous action requires an understanding of some set of the properties of that action.

Where the judge does not adequately possess to a practically adequate degree a set of concepts of the properties of an indigenous action at the commencement of the hearing – that is, where an indigenous action is, to some degree, conceptually different as far as the judge is concerned, where the judge does not understand the action to a practically adequate degree – she must acquire a practically adequate

42 In addition to group members actually performing an indigenous action on the claim area, representations (audio or visual) of actions actually being performed on the claim area might be tendered. I will use the terms performative and representational real evidence of (the behavioural properties of) an indigenous action, respectively, to describe these forms of evidence. Any such evidence will normally need to be supplemented by oral or written testimony about the maintenance of actions on the claim area (including that the action is performed by the group with the legally requisite degree of regularity) as well as about the authenticity of such evidence and other legally relevant matters. Ligertwood (1988) pp. 278–81 and Heydon (2000) p. 47.

43 Additionally, of course, she must also know *that* those actions possess the properties in question. Possessing a concept or set of concepts to a practically adequate degree in this context involves possessing sufficient of the content of a concept or sufficient concepts in the set as would enable the identification of the actions in question.

44 We will see in Chapter 4 that in addition to the mere possession of a set of concepts of the properties of an action, further *knowledge that* those concepts are components of the concept of the action in question is required in order to possess a concept of or understand that action.

set of such concepts over the course of the hearing. The indigenous land title judge comes to understand a conceptually different indigenous action by a process of concept acquisition. She acquires the relevant concepts by being provided over the course of the hearing with sufficient sound evidence (and explanatory submissions) about the content of the concepts of the properties of the indigenous action – which is to say, about the properties of the indigenous action, about the action – as would rectify the deficiency. The onus lies with the claimant group to provide this evidence and explanation so as to enable the judge to acquire the relevant concepts and understand the indigenous action in question to the degree necessary for her to properly perform her ultimate determinative function.

Relevant evidence here predominantly takes the form of oral or written testimony about the contents of the property concepts in question – about the intentional, behavioural and structural-interrelational properties of actions of the type in question. Simply put, this is to say that it takes the form of testimony about the nature (properties) of the indigenous actions under claim. This might be supplemented by performative or representational real evidence of that action,[45] as well as real evidence of other phenomena implicated in the concepts of the properties of that action. Of course, in order to take epistemic advantage of that evidence and those submissions the judge must successfully *interpret* or otherwise cognitively appropriate those sources of information.[46] In Chapter 5 I will explore the nature of such interpretation and cognitive appropriation in detail and in Chapter 6 I will explore the limits of the judicial capacity to do so.

Finally, knowing the intentional, behavioural and other properties of the actions actually maintained by the indigenous group on the claimant area, the judge must go on to evaluate whether or not those actions are described by a legally valid concept of indigenous land title. In order to know that a set of indigenous actions are so described – in order to properly make a positive determination of indigenous land title – the judge must possess as her own operative concept a legally valid concept of indigenous land title which actually describes that set of actions. This is to say that she must possess as her own operative concept the claimant group's operative

45 Or, more correctly, of its behavioural properties. Real evidence of intentional properties is not a possibility, as we shall see in Chapter 4. Intentional properties are inferred from behavioural properties which may be evidenced by real evidence. I will have more to say about such things in Chapter 4.

46 Real evidence of environmental or bodily phenomena implicated in the concept of an indigenous action may, depending upon the purpose for which it is being tendered, require only observation and not interpretation for it to be adequately cognitively appropriated by the judge. Such evidence is always supplementary to testimonial evidence and performative evidence which serve as the dominant sources of information about the concept of an indigenous action. Thus, the primary means by which a judge comes to acquire a concept of and understand an indigenous action is by interpreting testimonial evidence about that concept (and, to a lesser degree performative or representational evidence of the behavioural component of that action). I will have more to say about this in Chapter 5.

concept of indigenous land title.[47] Where the judge does not at the commencement of the hearing already possess such a concept of indigenous land title, she comes to possess such a concept by virtue of being provided with, interpreting and accepting both oral or written explanatory submissions from claimant counsel about the content of that concept, as well as oral or written argumentative submissions about its legal validity (with reference to authoritative legal norms regulating and determining the validity of judicial concept formation within the indigenous land title sphere), over the course of the hearing.[48] As mentioned earlier in this chapter, in order to be able to properly engage with such explanatory and argumentative submissions and decide whether or not to alter her existing concept of indigenous land title so as to comprehend conceptually different indigenous actions (within the constraints of the norms of legal validity), the judge must possess practically adequate concepts of those actions. She acquires such concepts by the means just discussed.

The identity and amount of evidence and the nature and amount of explanation and argument offered by the claimants throughout the hearing process will reflect their evaluation of what is required to enable the judge to adequately understand (know the properties of) the claimant set of actions,[49] be satisfied of its maintenance on the claim area and properly determine its comprehension by or subsumption under a legally valid concept of indigenous land title. In order to meet their evidential burden in this regard, they need only provide enough evidence and submissions to enable the judge to do these things. If they do not meet this burden their claim will fail. Likewise, the judge doesn't need to cognitively appropriate *all* of the evidence and argument provided to her but merely enough of that evidence and argument as will enable her to properly perform her tripartite cognitive task.

Though the onus is on the claimant group to provide whatever evidence, explanation and argument is necessary to enable the judge to understand the claimant set of actions, the judge is not an entirely passive agent in all of this. Notwithstanding the actions of the claimant group and other parties in providing evidence and submissions, in order to be able to effectively understand the judge must herself act – to some degree, at least – so as to come to the knowledge required of her, so as to acquire true beliefs about the concepts of evidenced indigenous action and their properties. The parties in their provision of evidence and submissions bring the judge into epistemic contact with evidentiary tokens of the indigenous actions or other epistemically informative phenomena (the utterances and artefacts which constitute oral and written testimonial evidence

47 Which, because we are assuming the claimant group to be rational, we may assume describes the claimant set of actions.

48 In addition to submissions about the content of the claimants' operative concept of indigenous land title, the claimants will also lead argumentative submissions that the judge should adopt that concept as her own.

49 Which is to say what is required to enable the judge to acquire a practically adequate set of the concepts of relevant properties of the claimant set of actions.

and submissions, for example). However, the judge herself needs to be active in behaving effectively (given her role) in relation to and in cognitively making sense of relevant phenomena provided by the parties. She needs to effectively observe and cognitively grasp the nature and significance of demonstrations of claimant behaviour, viewings of geographic locales, and objects tendered as real evidence. She needs to act so as to best interpret the meaning of claimant behaviour, the testimony of witnesses, informative documents and the submissions of counsel. Her capacity to do so will be a function of the nature of the epistemic conditions which obtain over the course of the determination hearing, including the legal norms regulating her actions in relation to evidence.[50]

For the benefit of readers unfamiliar with legal process, let me briefly outline the normal order of events within the determination hearing process.[51] First, the claimants, through their counsel, present their opening submissions in which they summarize and explain both the matters in controversy between the parties[52] and the evidence and argument which will be put forward by them over the course of the hearing in relation to the existence of indigenous land title. It is at this point that they will flag with the judge the concept of indigenous land title they wish her to adopt as her operative concept.[53] They then lead their evidence in support of their claim that they maintain a set of actions which is indigenous land title and, if called upon, may explain the nature and role of that evidence within the claimant case.[54] This phase of proceedings may involve the claimants leading evidence about the concepts of conceptually different indigenous actions with the aim of enabling the judge to understand those actions. The other parties to the claim may cross-examine claimant witnesses and otherwise explore, test and challenge any of the evidence of the claimants. Following this, the other parties commence the presentation of their case challenging some or other aspect of the claimant case. They may give opening submissions also, outlining the nature of their opposition to the claim and the evidence to be led by them.[55] They too may then lead evidence in support of their case which may be tested and challenged by the claimant counsel in cross-examination. Finally, the other parties and then the claimant group

50 I will have more to say about this in Chapters 6 and 7.

51 See Heydon (2000) ch. 9 and Cairns (1996) pp. 568–85.

52 For example, whether the claimant group maintain any actions on the claim area or whether any such actions are described by a legally valid concept of indigenous land title.

53 Additionally, such argument will have been flagged in various trial documents and pre-hearing proceedings. Ligertwood (1988) p. 149.

54 Including how it is related to other evidence led by the claimants and what its relevance is to the issues at stake in the hearing.

55 Note the possibility of the other parties arguing after the close of the claimants' evidence that the claimants have not proved their case to the required standard – that is, that the claimants have not provided evidence capable of establishing the material facts upon which the claim is based (a no case submission). Alternatively, the other parties might not lead any evidence, in which case the claimants proceed directly to give their closing submissions before the other parties do.

may make closing submissions summarizing and explaining the cases presented, identifying the weaknesses in the opposing cases and making whatever arguments have to be made to establish their respective positions, including arguments about the concept of indigenous land title the judge should adopt and the probative value or weight to be given to the evidence led.

After all of this, the judge retires to consider the evidence, explanation and argument presented by the parties and to reach a decision as to whether and to what extent the claim has been proved.[56] If the judge chooses to make a determination, that determination generally takes the form of a formal written order confirming or denying the existence of indigenous land title in the claim area.[57] If positive, such order will commonly include a description of the nature and extent of the indigenous land title rights and interests which exist there, the identity of the persons holding those rights and interests and the relationship between those rights and interests and any non-indigenous rights and interests in the area.[58] The core content of such an order will usually be advised to the parties at a later proceeding convened specifically for that purpose and, thereafter, becomes part of the public record. The effect of such a determination at non-indigenous law is to give the rights identified in the determination – the rights comprising the claimant group's indigenous land title – the status of rights at non-indigenous law. It is to render them rights which the non-indigenous legal system may enforce and protect to the extent prescribed in the determination order.

Determining Indigenous Land Title

To conclude this chapter, let me illuminate the preceding discussion with a description of a simple scenario involving a claimant group who hunt in a certain area and who are concerned to protect that practice by way of an indigenous land title determination from future interference.[59] In order to keep the discussion manageable, I will assume that their practice of hunting is performed as of right

56 Given the complexity of indigenous land title cases, the judge will generally not provide an immediate judgement. There is generally no jury in an indigenous land title determination hearing anywhere in the common law world. Questions of fact and law are decided solely by the presiding judge.

57 If the judge is not satisfied that the evidence and argument provided by the parties are sufficient for her to decide one way or the other whether indigenous land title exists in the claim area, the judge may refrain from making a determination at all, in which case the legal status quo continues in relation to the indigenous group's way of life within the claim area. See Perry and Lloyd (2003) p. 771 on this. Generally speaking, a non-determination is preferable to a negative determination for a claimant group.

58 See, for example, the (Australian) Native Title Act (Cth) s.225.

59 I will have cause later in the book to consider an example of a conceptually different indigenous action but for now will consider an action which is not conceptually different as far as a non-indigenous judge is concerned.

according to the concept of indigenous land title presently adopted by the judiciary and outlined above, and that this right to hunt constitutes the entirety of the claimant set of actions. That is, the claimant set of actions comprises the primary action of hunting and a series of right-constituting secondary actions – approving of hunting in the claim area by right-holding members of the group, criticizing non-right holders for hunting there, and so on. My aim at this point is merely to broadly illustrate the epistemic and interpretive demands which the indigenous land title determination process might place on a judge as far as indigenous actions are concerned, not to explore in any detail issues of conceptual difference and the judicial understanding. These will be dealt with in later chapters.

In order to succeed at hearing, the group must establish to the satisfaction of the judge that they perform the practice of hunting as of indigenous land title right – that is, they must prove that they perform with some legally sufficient degree of regularity the primary action of hunting within the context of a set of rights-constituting secondary actions and that those actions are traditional, are in relation to land and waters, are compatible with common law norms, and so on. This requires of them that they lead sufficient evidence and make sufficient submissions as would enable the judge to know to a practically adequate degree the properties of each of the indigenous actions – primary and secondary – constituting the claimant set. In order to know this, the judge needs to possess to a practically adequate degree a concept of each of those properties – a concept of the properties of the action of hunting, of the action of approving of hunting in the claim area by right-holding members of the group, of the action of criticizing non-right holders for hunting there, and so on. She needs to understand each of these actions to a practically adequate degree. Were the judge to lack a concept of some or all of the properties of indigenous actions, it would be incumbent upon the claimant group to lead whatever real or testimonial evidence and make whatever explanatory submissions about the properties of those actions and the content of their concepts as would be sufficient to enable the judge to acquire those concepts.

And so, were the judge not to possess a concept of any of the properties of hunting – that is, were she not to possess a concept of hunting – relevant evidence in this regard might comprise the enactment for the judge's benefit of hunting on the claimant area (the court being relocated to the claimant area for this purpose). Whilst there, the judge might be called upon to observe the behavioural properties of the action, the nature of the landscape or the existence and behaviour of the wildlife being hunted. The group might instead or in addition lead photographic or video evidence which represents group members hunting in the claim area or engaging in rights-constituting secondary actions in relation to that hunting. On such a basis the judge might come to know the behavioural properties of the indigenous action of hunting and perhaps, by interpretive inference from that knowledge, come to know its intentional properties. Alternatively, the claimant group might lead oral testimonial evidence from members of the group or non-indigenous anthropological experts explaining the intentional, behavioural or other properties of the action of hunting with reference to concepts the judge already possesses – running, chasing, throwing, killing, animal, etc. In order to facilitate the knowledge sought, interpretation by the judge of the utterances constituting such testimony would be required.

At any stage throughout the evidentiary process, the group (through its counsel) might be called upon to explain the nature of a given token of evidence, the role it plays within the claim, its relationship to other evidence, its relevance to the question of whether the claimant set is indigenous land title, and so on. This too would require interpretation of its meaning by the judge. In all cases, the purpose of tendering and admitting such evidence and making such submissions is to provide the judge with sufficient information about or knowledge of (the concepts of) the intentional, behavioural and other relevant properties of the claimant set of actions or of phenomena explanatorily related to those properties, as would allow her to understand and properly evaluate the extent to which that set of actions is described by her operative concept of indigenous land title. In coming to know the properties of indigenous actions – this is an action termed 'hunting' with properties a, b and c; this is an action termed 'sanctioning non-right holders for hunting in the claim area' with properties j, k and l; this is an action termed 'educating children about the right to hunt' with properties x, y and z;, and so on – the judge is involved in a process of understanding those actions. That process involves the judge cognitively appropriating real evidence and interpreting testimonial evidence of and submissions about (the concepts of) those actions: about their intentional, behavioural and other relevant properties. It involves the judge coming to know the meaning and conceptual significance of that evidence and those submissions.

In addition to proving the properties of the actions comprising the claimant set (by providing evidence, explanation and argument sufficient to enable the judge to adequately know the properties of the members of that set), the claimant group must also prove that the set is performed with legally sufficient regularity. They do so by means of a sufficiently probative set of evidence and submissions to this effect. Following this, they must go on to argue that the identified and maintained set is described by a legally valid concept of indigenous land title. If successful in this and if certain other matters are favourably addressed,[60] then they may obtain a determination of indigenous land title from the judge. To the extent that the indigenous land title determination is respected and enforced by non-indigenous agents, the hunting (and secondary right-constituting) practices of the indigenous group will have received some degree of legal protection from non-indigenous interference.

The judge's key aim in a determination hearing is to properly evaluate whether the claimant set of actions is described by a legally valid concept of indigenous land title. In order to ascertain this, she needs to understand the claimant set of actions to a practically adequate degree. In order to do this she needs to be provided with evidence of and submissions about (the concepts of) the members of that set;

60 If extinguishment of indigenous land title by the state is not proven, for example.

about the intentional, behavioural and other relevant properties of the members of that set. Further, she needs to interpret or otherwise cognitively appropriate this evidence and these submissions to some practically adequate degree. The rest of this book is devoted to exploring her capacity to do so and, thus, to understand indigenous actions under conditions of conceptual difference.

Chapter 4

The Judicial Understanding of Culturally Different Action

Understanding Culturally Different Action

In many areas of law – particularly, as we have just seen, in matters to do with cultural minority rights claims – judges are called upon to take notice of and reason about culturally different actions with reference to some or other legal concept or standard or norm implicating the intentional, behavioural and structural-interrelational (causal, temporal, semantic and group-distributive) properties of a set of actions. In order for a judge to properly determine whether or not an action is an action which meets or is described by the criterial set of properties inherent in the legal concept in question, she must know to a practically adequate degree what the intentional, behavioural, and structural-interrelational properties of that action actually are. She must understand that action.[1] Knowing the various properties of an action to some practically adequate degree is just what understanding an action is. But in order to know the properties of an action – in order to understand that action – the judge must possess, to a practically adequate degree, concepts of those properties and must know that that action possesses those properties.[2] These two conditions (conceptual and epistemic) are together necessary and sufficient for the understanding of an action type. Further, the former serves as a necessary condition for the latter. One cannot know (or even merely believe) that an action possesses a set of properties x, y and z unless one possesses the concepts x, y and z. Possessing to a practically adequate degree concepts of the properties of an action is a necessary condition of understanding that action and properly evaluating its legal status.

---

1 Knowing to a practically adequate degree the intentional, behavioural and structural-interrelational properties possessed by a culturally different action type entails possessing to a practically adequate degree a concept of that action type. And possessing to a practically adequate degree a concept of that action type is what understanding that action, on my construal, entails.

2 This knowledge is, of course, conditional upon possession of the property concepts. Further, when I refer to understanding an action or knowing or possessing a concept *to some or other degree* I am referring to knowing or possessing some or other part of the definition or description comprising the concept of that action. I will have more to say on this later in this chapter.

Recall that in Chapter 2 I noted that the propositional content of intentional states may be analysed in terms of a set of concepts. The proposition that 'the animal is alive' is comprised of the concepts 'animal' and 'alive' etc. An agent may be said to possess not only a given intentional state but also the propositions and concepts informing that state. Culturally different agents by virtue of their very agency possess a scheme of concepts which inform (the propositional content of) their various intentional states. I have been terming these, culturally different concepts. A culturally different concept is defined here as any concept possessed by a culturally different agent. We may reasonably assume (and it is not disputed by cultural incommensurability theorists – indeed, it may be entailed by their position) that culturally different agents are able to understand their own and each other's actions. They, therefore, possess concepts of what are – from the judge's perspective, at least – culturally different actions, and of the various component properties of those actions – intentional, behavioural and structural-interrelational. As such, concepts of culturally different actions, concepts of the various intentional, behavioural and structural-interrelational properties of such actions and concepts of all the environmental and bodily phenomena which feature in the individuating causal relations of and which are holistically necessary for the existence of the intentional states of culturally different agents are, on our definition, components of the conceptual schemes of culturally different agents. This point is crucial for the discussion to follow.

We saw in Chapter 2 that an intentional property is a neuro-physical property of the agent in question which performs a functional role in the behavioural interaction of that agent with his external environment. More precisely it is a neuro-physical property which causally mediates between environmental, other intentional and behavioural input and output properties according to a set of intentional regularities. As such it is ontologically and conceptually individuated as the property it is with reference to the set of environmental and intentional input phenomena and intentional and behavioural output phenomena it typically maintains causal relations with, as well as to a set of associated background intentional phenomena. Thus, the concept of an intentional property is analysable in terms of a set of component concepts – sub-concepts, if you will – of environmental, behavioural and other intentional phenomena, as well as a concept of causal relatedness. Given the holistic nature of intentional properties, the set of component sub-concepts comprising the concept of an intentional property may be quite vast. Indeed, given that a substantial number of intentional properties are implicated in each and every action, the number of component concepts implicated in a single action may be so numerous as to encompass a significant part of a conceptual scheme.[3] Nonetheless,

3 Possessing a concept of an intentional property, in the sense of knowing its functional description, involves knowing a substantial set of propositions about the causal relations which typically obtain between the world, mind and body of some set of agents. It involves possessing a theory of mind about some set of agents. I will have more to say about this in the Chapter 5.

as components of concepts uncontroversially possessed by culturally different agents, all of these component concepts are also culturally different concepts. In order, then, for a judge to possess to a practically adequate degree concepts of the intentional properties of culturally different actions (as she is required to do if she wishes to properly make a determination of indigenous land title, say), she must possess to a practically adequate degree a substantial set of culturally different concepts.[4]

The same goes in relation to concepts of the behavioural and structural-interrelational properties of culturally different actions. In order to know to a practically adequate degree the behavioural properties of a culturally different action type the judge must possess to a practically adequate degree concepts of those behavioural properties. Again, we saw in Chapter 2 that a behavioural property is individuated as the property it is with reference to a set of causally related bodily and (for non-basic actions) environmental phenomena. Thus, the concept of a behavioural property is analysable in terms of a set of concepts of ordinarily observable, macroscopic bodily and (for non-basic actions) environmental phenomena, together with a concept of causal relatedness. As components of concepts possessed by culturally different agents, all of these concepts are also culturally different concepts (although it may turn out that a judge possesses them also). In order, then, for a judge to possess to a practically adequate degree concepts of the behavioural properties of culturally different actions, she must again possess a set of culturally different concepts.[5] Further, in order to know to a practically adequate degree the *structural-interrelational* properties of a complex culturally different action type (a joint action or social rule, for example), the judge must possess to a practically adequate degree concepts of the various elements of those properties elaborated in Chapter 2 – temporal relatedness, causal relatedness, semantic relatedness[6] and group-distribution. Given the possession of concepts

---

4 One can possess the concept of an intentional property to a greater or lesser degree depending upon the proportion of the total definition or total functional specification of that property one knows or possesses. The set of sub-concepts whose possession is sufficient to possess a given intentional concept or complex will be termed a possession-sufficient set of sub-concepts. I will have more to say on this below.

5 It is worth noting here, in addition, that given the holistic nature of actions, in order to possess a concept of the environmental element of a behavioural property, the judge must possess a concept of the action's intentional properties. Per Quine (1960), one cannot determine which bit of the world comprises the environmental element of an action without a holistic knowledge of the intentional profile (properties) causing the behaviour in question. And, as we have just seen, in order to possess a concept of any such intentional properties the judge must possess a practically adequate set of culturally different concepts.

6 Recalling that the semantic properties of a complex culturally different action have to do with that action (or its component actions) being the intentional object of another culturally different action, knowing the semantic properties of a complex culturally different action requires the judge to know the intentional properties of that other action. Therefore, possessing a concept of the semantic properties of a culturally different action necessarily

of these things by culturally different agents able to understand their own actions and their various properties, these too are culturally different concepts. Hence, in order to know to a practically adequate degree the intentional, behavioural and structural-interrelational properties of a culturally different action type – in order to understand or possess a concept of the action simple or complex – the judge must possess to a practically adequate degree a substantial set of culturally different concepts. We may conceive of these component culturally different concepts as sub-concepts of the concept of the action type. They make up the content of the concept of the action.

Let me illustrate this discussion by considering the simple, non-basic action of the indigenous hunter from Chapter 2 pulling the trigger of a rifle. This action is analysable as the causing of the behaviour of pulling the trigger of a rifle by a complex of intentional properties which we can, for our purposes here, crudely conceive of as comprising the properties of desiring to pull the trigger, believing that by moving the finger thus the trigger will be pulled and desiring to move the finger thus.[7] The behavioural property of pulling the trigger of a rifle is a non-basic behavioural property comprising the property of the agent's finger moving in a certain way[8] causing the event of the trigger of a rifle moving in a certain way. It comprises the bodily property of the finger moving and the bodily-caused environmental event of the trigger of a rifle moving in a certain way and the causal relation between these. The concept of this behavioural property is crudely analysable in terms of the bodily sub-concept of 'finger' and the environmental sub-concepts of 'trigger' and 'rifle', together with concepts of 'movement', 'causation', and the like. Given the functional and, therefore, holistic nature of certain environmental phenomena implicated in a behavioural property, the possession of certain such sub-concepts may involve the possession of some possession-sufficient set of other concepts. Possessing the concept of the functional concept 'trigger', for example, involves possessing a description or theory of what kind of thing a trigger is. And possession of such a theory necessarily involves the possession of some set of the concepts of those things involved in that theory – concepts such as 'catch', 'release', 'hammer' and 'gun-lock', for example.[9] And even possession of these may entail the possession of some further set of the concepts which individuate them – those concepts which individuate or constitute the concept of 'catch', for example. Thus, possessing a concept of the behavioural

involves possessing a concept of the intentional properties of some other culturally different action. And this, as we have seen, involves possessing a set of culturally different concepts.

7 We will take these intentional states to comprise the behaviourally causal intentional complex as far as the present discussion goes.

8 Or, more correctly, one of a certain range of ways. This constitutes the basic behavioural element of the action.

9 I'm drawing here on the *Oxford English Dictionary Online* definition of trigger for a simple description of the concept.

component of the action in question entails the possession of some possession-sufficient set of bodily, environmental and other concepts.[10]

Likewise, the intentional property of desiring that the trigger be pulled is that physical property which meets the set of causal-functional conditions – environmental, behavioural (bodily-environmental) and intentional – individuative of that property. The concept of that desire is constituted by the set of concepts comprising the tripartite description of those conditions. Possession of that concept entails possessing some possession-sufficient set of those sub-concepts. It involves possession of some set of the concepts of individuating environmental and intentional input phenomena and intentional and behavioural output phenomena and of the causal relations between these. And for each of the individuating intentional concepts of this desire a further range of environmental, intentional and bodily concepts are invoked, some set of which must also be possessed in order to ground possession of the concept of the desire in question. Further, to this set of concepts must be added those that are implicated in the other intentional properties constituting the behaviourally causal intentional complex – the believing that by moving the finger thus the trigger will be pulled and the desiring to move the finger thus.

Overall, possession of the concepts of the various behaviourally causal intentional properties involved in the action entails possession of some possession-sufficient set of a very large set of concepts of individuating environmental, bodily, intentional and other phenomena – a possession-sufficient set of concepts.[11] In adding these to those required to possess a concept of the behavioural component of the action in question, one ends up with an even more numerous set of bodily, environmental, intentional and other concepts, possession of some subset of which is necessary for the possession of the concept of the action in question. And, of course, for a *complex* action one must add to the set of component concepts, concepts of any of those structural-interrelational properties discussed in Chapter 4 which are not implicated in the concepts of component simple actions. For a culturally different action – simple or complex – all of the concepts implicated in the concept of that action and its properties are, as I have argued, culturally different concepts. These concepts may be conceived of as component sub-concepts of the concept of the culturally different action in question and may comprise a vast set.

Now, it is, at least, conceivable at this stage of our discussion that the judge may, at the commencement of the legal hearing, possess some or all of the culturally different concepts she needs to possess in order to perform her various functions.[12] However, where the judge does *not* possess a practically adequate set

10 These concepts comprise component sub-concepts of the concept of the action in question.

11 And of course, in most real-life cases the behaviourally causal intentional complex constituting an action comprises far more behaviourally causal intentional states than I have allowed for here in this example.

12 This proposition is denied, of course, by conceptual incommensurabilists.

of culturally different concepts at the commencement of the legal hearing – that is, where a degree of *conceptual* difference relevantly obtains[13] – she must acquire a practically adequate set of those concepts over the course of the hearing if she is to come to an understanding of relevant culturally different actions. Under conditions of conceptual difference, understanding is possible only by means of a process of concept acquisition on the part of the judge. Before turning to the specific ways by which a judge might acquire an acquirable concept over the course of a legal hearing, let me make some general points about the nature of the acquisition of concepts by judges.

The Possession and Acquisition of Concepts

Concepts and their Possession

In Chapter 2, I mentioned that a concept is a component of the propositional content of an intentional state.[14] Consider an intentional state type which occasionally arises in Australian indigenous land title matters and which we may, for the sake of clarifying the discussion, take as a paradigm of judicial understanding and concept acquisition – the belief that there is ochre in the ground.[15] This belief is comprised of a set of concepts, including those of 'ochre' and 'ground', syntactically related to each other within the propositional content of the belief. Prinz captures this fundamental point about concepts in his statement that '... concepts are constituents of thoughts ... concepts are to thoughts as words are to sentences'.[16] An intentional state is a (conceptualized) phenomenon individuated as the state it is with reference to its causal-functional role in the behavioural interaction of an agent with its environment. A concept is, therefore, a component of such a phenomenon – which is to say that it is itself a functional phenomenon individuated as the concept it is with reference to its causal-functional role in the behavioural interaction of an agent with its environment. To possess (be in) an intentional state is to possess the concepts comprising that state. To possess a concept is to possess an intentional state – a belief or a desire – whose propositional

13 Conceptual difference may be construed here in terms of an agent not possessing some set of the sub-conceptual content of a concept possessed by another agent.

14 It is useful at this point, prior to engaging in a discussion of the nature of concepts, to note Georges Rey's comment that, '[t]he notion of a concept, like the related notion of meaning, lies at the heart of some of the most difficult and unresolved issues in philosophy and psychology' (Rey (1994) p. 185).

15 Ochre is an important natural resource for many of Australia's indigenous people and is utilized by them in a range of cultural practices.

16 Prinz (2002) p. 2. Lynch (1997) p. 418, likewise states that 'concepts are whatever composes the propositional content of our assertions and beliefs'. See also Papineau (1978) p. 136.

content is informed by that concept. It is to possess a physical state which serves a characteristic (concept containing) causal-functional role in the interaction of an agent with its environment.

A judge may possess the concept of ochre by virtue of possessing the belief that there is ochre in the ground. In functionalist terms, this is to say that she may possess the concept of ochre by virtue of being in a physical state which plays a 'belief that there is ochre in the ground' causal-functional role in the behavioural interaction of the judge with her environment. More fully, though, she possesses the concept of ochre by virtue of being in a physical state which plays any of the causal-functional roles characteristic of intentional states containing the concept of ochre, whose propositional content includes or is informed by that concept. Of course, as we saw in Chapter 2, to possess a belief that there is ochre in the ground a judge must at the same time possess a range of other intentional states which feature as background intentional states in the individuating set of causal relations of that belief, some of which states will also be informed by the concept of ochre. Thus, a judge possesses the concept of ochre by virtue of possessing a *set* of intentional states informed by that concept. This fact reflects the holistic nature of intentional states and of concepts.

By virtue of the embeddedness of concepts in intentional states and of intentional states in actions, concepts have a practical dimension. The possession of a given concept manifests itself in a characteristic range of actions. Lynch states that 'to have or grasp a concept involves *being able to use it* when asserting or believing. To have the concept of a tree is to be able to pick out trees from non-trees, to make judgments about trees and to be capable of understanding at least some of the consequences of such judgments'.[17] A judge possesses the concept of ochre, for example, by being able (or disposed) to engage in actions informed by intentional states containing the concept of ochre – by being able to dig for ochre, by being disposed to point to ochre when asked where the ochre is, by being able to testify that ochre is a yellow powder, and so on. A judge manifests her possession of the concept by actually engaging in these actions (or by at least possessing a disposition to do so).

This practical dimension of concepts may be made sense of by tapping into another key feature of concepts: namely, that a concept is theorisable not merely as a component of an intentional state but also as a description or *definition* specifying the essential conditions (individually necessary and jointly sufficient) which a phenomenon must meet for membership of the class of phenomena comprehended by or referred to by the concept – possessing a certain set of properties, for example.[18] That this should be so follows from our discussion in

17 Lynch (1997) p. 418 (emphasis added).

18 A significant body of critique has been levelled against definitionalist theories of concepts on a variety of grounds. See Laurence and Margolis (1999) for a good overview of these criticisms. For the response of conceptual definitionalists to these criticisms, see Jackendoff (1983), Pinker (1989), Peacocke (1992) and Rey (1983 and 1985), for

Chapter 2 about what functional phenomena (including concepts) are. Consider a simple example of a paperweight. A paperweight is an object which (actually or potentially) keeps loose paper in place. A token object is a paperweight – a member of the type we call paperweight – if it meets this condition. It is conceptualisable as a paperweight by the relevant conceptual community – that is, it is comprehended under their concept of paperweight – by virtue of meeting this condition. This set of conditions may be taken to constitute the concept of paperweight. And because this set of conditions may be construed as a definition, the concept of paperweight may be construed as a definition – in this case the definition 'an object which (actually or potentially) keeps loose paper in place'. We can perform a similar analysis upon the concept of ochre, understood as comprehending all of those token phenomena which meet the condition (or possesses the property) of being a yellow powder found in the ground and used (by Australian indigenous people, for example) for ceremonial purposes.

To possess the concept of ochre is to possess a description or definition of the conditions an object must meet in order to be ochre. This definition is possessed as part of the propositional content of some or other intentional state. Thus, *one way* we can theorize possessing a concept is in terms of maintaining an intentional state whose propositional content is analysable into some possession-sufficient part of the total definition which constitutes the concept. An example of such an intentional state is a belief whose propositional content takes definitional form and contains some possession-sufficient part of the total definition which constitutes the concept – say, the belief that 'ochre is a yellow powder found in the ground and used for ceremonial purposes'.[19] Such a belief does not comprise the concept of ochre, nor does the proposition contained in that belief that 'ochre is a yellow powder found in the ground and used for ceremonial purposes' comprise the concept. Rather, the concept of ochre is the definitional component of these two things – namely, the description 'a yellow powder found in the ground and used for ceremonial purposes'. Possessing this definition may be conceived of as grounding a practical capacity to act in a concept-of ochre-possessing manner in

---

example. I do not intend to engage here in a sustained defence of the definitionalist theory of concepts other than to say that within the constraints of a project such as this, the definitionalist approach to concepts provides a credible and a manageable account of a very complicated and controversial subject matter. As Laurence and Margolis (1999) p. 10 state, a definitionalist theory of concepts 'has powerful explanatory resources, offering unified accounts of concept acquisition, categorisation, epistemic justification, analytic entailment, and reference determination, all which flow directly from its basic commitments'. The main rivals of definitionalism – for example, the prototype theory of concepts (see Rosch and Mervis (1975)) – are, arguably, even more vulnerable to critique.

19 We can analyse this proposition more precisely as maintaining the fact or state of affairs that 'in my linguistic community the signifier "ochre" is conventionally taken to signify a yellow powder found in the ground and used for ceremonial purposes' or 'in my linguistic community, the phenomenon we conventionally refer to as "ochre" exists and is a yellow powder found in the ground and used for ceremonial purposes', or some such.

the world, in a capacity to distinguish between ochre and other things, for example, in one's day to day activities.[20]

We may conceive of the *total definition* comprising a concept as describing the complete set of individually necessary and jointly sufficient conditions a phenomenon must meet in order to be a member of the class referred to by the concept.[21] We may conceive of these conditions as naturally determined (in the case of natural kind higher-order concepts) or determined by the practices of some conceptual community (in the case of functional higher-order concepts).[22] This point alerts us to the fact that a concept may be conceived of as being possessed to a greater or lesser degree by an agent such as a judge, depending upon the proportion of the total definition (above the possession-sufficient minimum) possessed by that judge (by virtue of her intentional states). A judge who, for example, believes that ochre is a yellow powder *found in the ground* may be said to possess the concept of ochre to a greater degree than a judge who believes merely that ochre is a yellow powder. Conceiving of a concept in terms of a definition is one way we can make sense of a judge's capacity to distinguish between those phenomena described by the definition and those that are not, to act towards the former in manner informed by a belief that they are ochre and towards the latter in a manner informed by a belief that they are not ochre, and so on. The more of the definition a judge possesses the more discriminating she may be in her actions involving the concept, in her use of the concept.

The definitional nature of concepts points us to another feature of concepts – namely, that concepts are decomposable into those other concepts which feature in their constitutive definition.[23] They are decomposable into other concepts I have been terming 'sub-concepts'. The sub-concepts of a concept may be conceived of as referring to the necessary and sufficient conditions or properties described by the total definition of the concept. Concepts are, therefore, analysable in terms of their component sub-concepts and the characteristic syntactic relationship which exists between those sub-concepts.[24] These sub-concepts and the syntactic relationship between them constitute the *content* of the concept. The concept of ochre (I will term it a primary concept because it is our primary subject of concern at this point) is constituted by the sub-concepts (let me term them secondary

20 Lynch (1997) p. 418.

21 Laurence and Margolis (1999) p. 9.

22 I do not intend to go into the numerous vexed issues concerning the notion of the total content of a concept.

23 A wide range of philosophers have adopted this view of concepts, including such notables as Locke (1975) and Carnap (1959). In light of the holistic nature of concepts, unlike Locke and Carnap, I do not hold to the view that all concepts are ultimately decomposable into some set of primitive sensory concepts. See Katz (1972) and Clark (1973).

24 Rey (1983) and (1994), Laurence and Margolis (1999) pp. 8–14, Prinz (2002) pp. 32–48. As syntactically structured phenomena, concepts resemble in certain respects the propositional contents of intentional states.

concepts[25]) of yellow, powder, and the like, syntactically related to each other in a manner characteristic or constitutive of the concept of ochre. The content of the concept of ochre may be analysed as comprising these sub-concepts and the characteristic syntactic relation between them.[26] And, of course, each of these secondary concepts may themselves be analysed in terms of a further set of characteristically syntactically related sub-concepts (tertiary concepts vis a vis the primary concept of ochre) – powder, for example, as finely grained solid matter, or some such. And these tertiary concepts, too, may be analysable in terms of other lower-order sub-concepts.[27]

A concept, therefore, may be comprised of and may be analysed in terms of a large set of sub-conceptual (secondary, tertiary, and so on) concepts, syntactically related to each other in a highly complex manner. The sub-conceptual content of a given primary concept may extend to some significant part of the total conceptual scheme possessed by a judge. As we saw above with our example of the simple, non-basic action of pulling the trigger of a rifle, the concept of an action is analysable in terms of a set of component sub-concepts of its properties – behavioural, intentional and structural-interrelational – each of which may be further analysed, generating a vast set of component sub-concepts. This set comprises the sub-conceptual content of the concept of the action in question. The actual boundaries of a concept's set of sub-conceptual content may be difficult to determine, even if a total definition comprising that concept were determinable. Concepts subsist as holistic phenomena within a web of other concepts. Their content comprises this web of characteristically related concepts. The holistic nature of concepts reflects the holistic nature of intentional states of which concepts serve as components.

If we consider again the simple definitional belief that ochre is a yellow powder found in the ground and used for ceremonial purposes (the propositional content of which contains some part of a concept of ochre), we see that it is individuated by a set of causal relations with environmental, intentional and behavioural phenomena linked within a theory of mind to a set of background intentional states, which in this case might include, say, a definitional belief that powder is a fine-grained solid (the content of which contains some part of a concept of powder). In the simple

25 Secondary concepts are a category of the sub-concepts of a primary concept.

26 The syntactic relation here is important. The concept of car analyses out as comprised of sub-concepts of four, wheel and vehicle which are syntactically related in terms of a four-wheeled vehicle and not a four-vehicled wheel.

27 I do not wish to imply by my use of the terms primary and secondary and the like that the sub-concepts of ochre are, in any absolute sense, more foundational than that concept. The relationship between concepts and sub-concepts is not a hierarchical one in any absolute sense. It arises as a conventional and contextual matter out of the act of considering the content or relationship with other concepts of a given concept – in this case ochre. I prefer the non-foundationalist metaphor of a web of interrelated concepts rather than that of a pyramid or some such in thinking about the relationship between concepts and sub-concepts. Quine (1953b), Katz (1972), Clark (1973), and Laurence and Margolis (1999) pp. 18–21.

example set up here, holding the former belief entails holding the latter, as well as other definitional background beliefs (and their conceptual contents) to do with phenomena such as the ground, finding, ceremonies, and the like. This is to say that possessing the concept of ochre as I have defined it above entails possessing the concept of powder, as well as the other sub-concepts of ochre. And possessing the concept of powder entails possessing some set of the sub-concepts of that concept (fine, grain, solid, and the like). Possessing the concept of ochre, then, necessitates possessing such relatively lower-level concepts because possessing intentional states informed by the concept of ochre necessitates possessing intentional states informed by such relatively lower-level concepts.

The amount of the total definition constituting a concept which must be possessed by a judge in order for that judge to be justifiably considered in possession of that concept – that is, what constitutes a possession-sufficient part or degree of a total definition – is, ultimately, a conventional matter determinable by the thought and practices of some or other authoritative conceptual and interpretive community, generally with reference to some set of practical ends.[28] It may not be the case that a judge must possess as part of the propositional content of her intentional states the *whole* of the total definition constituting a concept in order to be adjudged to be in possession of that concept. A judge may possess merely some part of that total definition. As long as that part is sufficient to justify the ascription to her by an authoritative conceptual and interpretive community of an intentional state containing the concept in question, we may consider her in possession of that concept to some less than full but nonetheless possession-sufficient degree.[29]

I take it as a matter of theoretical necessity[30], though, that in order to possess a concept a judge must, *at the very least*, possess a definition or description of a *set* of conditions which are individually necessary *and* jointly sufficient for

28 See Margolis (1999), for example.

29 In addition to maintaining a general base level standard of sufficient possession of a concept, a conceptual community (including some part of a community) may also maintain certain context-relative standards of possession. A distinction may be made within such a community between bare possession of a concept and a *practically adequate* possession of that concept, in light of some specific set of practical ends or some specific context of use. Whether possessing the concept of ochre to a bare possession-sufficient degree constitutes possessing it to a *practically adequate* degree will depend for a conceptual community upon the nature of the practice or practices for which possession of the concept is required. Practically adequate possession is a contextual matter. For example, possessing no more than a set of intentional states informed by the definition 'yellow powder' may constitute a practically adequate possession of the concept of ochre for the purpose of visually distinguishing a sample of ochre from a sample of charcoal but not for the purpose of explaining the chemical composition of ochre to a class of science undergraduates.

30 That is, given the terms of my theory of concepts or as a convention of my theoretical community.

membership of the class of phenomena comprehended by the concept.[31] This entails the possession of concepts of at least two such conditions. If one condition was necessary and sufficient for being a member of a conceptual class then there would be no distinction between the concept of that condition and the concept of that class. For example, if being yellow was a necessary and sufficient condition of being ochre, there would be no distinction between the concept of yellow and that of ochre or between their possession by an agent. The concept of ochre could be applied to describe, for example, the same things as the concept of yellow. Possessing a concept of merely one of the necessary conditions for membership of a kind does not constitute possessing a description or definition of that kind.

This is to say that in order to sufficiently possess a concept an agent must possess, at the very least, more than one of the sub-concepts of that concept. A sub-concept of a concept is, by definition, not that concept. The concept of yellow is not the concept of ochre. To possess merely a single sub-concept of ochre (say, the sub-concept of yellow) is to possess merely that sub-concept (yellow) and not the concept (ochre). With at least more than one of the sub-concepts of a concept possessed, an agent is, at least, in the running to be adjudged in possession of a concept by a rational conceptual and interpretive community. Additionally, though, in order to possess a concept it is not enough to merely possess some unrelated multiple set of its sub-concepts. To possess a description, it is not enough to possess a syntactically unrelated set of concepts. A description comprises a *syntactically related* set of concepts. Ochre is properly described as a yellow powder found in the ground and used for ceremonial purposes and not as a grounded ceremony used for powdered yellow. So too, a concept comprises a syntactically related and not a random set of sub-concepts. Only the possession of an appropriately related set of sub-concepts will justify ascribing possession of a primary concept to an agent. In order to possess the concept of ochre, an agent must, for example, possess intentional states informed by the definition 'yellow powder' and not merely possess the concepts of yellow or powder as unrelated or misrelated components of other non-ochre informed intentional states.

In light of this discussion, we can analyse the possession of a primary concept as involving the possession of some possession-sufficient set of the sub-concepts of the concept together with knowledge *that they are* sub-conceptual components of that primary concept and, finally, knowledge *of* the characteristic syntactic relation they maintain with each other within the definition or description which

31 Beyond this, authoritative communal practice may vary as to the extent of the total definition which must be possessed in order to adjudge an agent in possession of the concept defined. A point, though, may be reached at which the amount of the total definition possessed by a judge (via her intentional states) may be considered so sparse by communal standards as to render that judge insufficiently in possession of the concept in question by those standards.

constitutes the primary concept.[32] And so, we can conceive of a judge possessing the concept of ochre to a bare possession-sufficient degree (or to some practically adequate degree) by virtue of her possessing, for example, the sub-concepts of yellow and powder, knowing that these concepts are sub-conceptual components of the concept of ochre and knowing the syntactic relation they bear to each other (yellow powder, not powdered yellow). By virtue of it comprising these kinds of knowledge, concept possession by an agent is an epistemic or theoretical state of affairs as well as a practical one.

A judge can possess the concept of ochre to a greater or lesser degree above the possession-sufficient minimum by virtue of possessing a greater or lesser number of its component sub-concepts, together with the requisite knowledge of their componency and syntactic relationship. So, a judge can possess a relatively sparse concept of ochre by virtue of her possessing to some degree the sub-concepts of yellow and powder (by possessing some set of the sub-conceptual content of those two concepts and knowledge of those sub-concepts' componency and relationship) together with knowledge that those two sub-concepts comprise part of the concept of ochre and knowledge that those two sub-concepts are syntactically related in a 'yellow powder' manner. Alternatively, a judge can possess a richer concept of ochre by virtue of her possessing to some degree the sub-concepts of yellow, powder, found, in, ground, ceremony and use together with knowledge that these are sub-concepts of the concept of ochre, and knowledge of their syntactic relation within that concept (yellow powder found in the ground and used for ceremonies).

As implied earlier, possessing some set of the sub-concepts of a primary concept without possessing knowledge that they are sub-concepts of that primary concept and knowledge of their syntactic relation is, as a theoretical matter, not sufficient to constitute possession of the primary concept. A judge cannot be said to possess a definition to any degree merely by possessing the component sub-concepts of the definition without any idea that they comprise part of the definition or how they are related to each other within that definition. A set of syntactically unconnected concepts does not constitute a definition. A judge may possess the concepts yellow and powder but without knowing that they are sub-concepts of the primary concept of ochre or without knowing their syntactic relation within that concept, she cannot be said to sufficiently possess any part of the definition comprising the concept of ochre, she cannot be said to possess the concept of ochre to a possession-sufficient degree.

32 I will assume here that the possession of a single secondary sub-concept will not be taken as sufficient to constitute possession of a primary concept. It follows from this that a concept may not be possessed by virtue of one or more of these three conditions not obtaining – that is, where the judge does not possess some possession-sufficient set of the sub-concepts of the concept, or does not possess knowledge that those sub-concepts are sub-conceptual components of the primary concept or does not possess knowledge of the characteristic syntactic relation those sub-concepts maintain with each other within the definition which constitutes the primary concept.

Intentional states and, therefore, their conceptual content may be consciously or unconsciously (explicitly or implicitly) possessed by a judge.[33] That is, their possession need not be the subject of conscious reflection on the part of an agent possessing them. Though I have been analysing the possession of a concept in terms of possession or knowledge of a definition comprising some set of sub-concepts syntactically related to each other in a characteristic manner, knowledge of this definition – of its sub-conceptual content and the syntactic relationship between that content – need not be the subject of conscious reflection by the agent. A concept may be conceived of as being tacitly possessed, without the judge possessing that concept being able to explicitly articulate the definition constitutive of that concept or expressly identify its component sub-concepts and their semantic relationships. The possession of a concept by a judge arises out of the fact that her thought and action are able to be or are, in fact, informed by intentional states containing all or some part of the content of that concept, whether or not the judge in question is aware at any point of the identity of those intentional states or concepts or able to give an explicit account of them. This is a reflection of the practical dimension of concept possession mentioned above. Possession of a concept involves being able or disposed to engage in behaviour caused by intentional states including that concept and whose complete intentional explanation includes that concept. I will have more to say about this notion of implicit knowledge in the next chapter.[34]

The Judicial Acquisition of Concepts

A judge possesses a concept at or over a given point or period of time by virtue of possessing at or over that time an intentional state – for example, a definitional belief that ochre is a yellow powder – whose propositional content contains some definitional part of the total definition constituting the concept. As we saw in Chapter 2, a definitional belief, like any belief, is a neuro-physical state of a judge which maintains a distinctive causal-functional relationship with the external world, with other intentional states maintained by the judge and with a behavioural repertoire. It is a neuro-physical state which both is typically caused by a distinctive individuating range of environmental and intentional inputs,

33 Braddon-Mitchell and Jackson (1996) p. 146. Botterill and Carruthers (1999) p. 79. I follow up this point on tacit knowledge in my discussion of the theorizing practices of interpretive agents in Chapter 5.

34 We shall see in Chapter 5 that a judge – indeed, any interpretive agent – may tacitly possess and apply a set of beliefs constitutive of a theory of mind. So too, she may tacitly possess and apply the concepts comprising those beliefs and that theory. Whilst on this point, it is also worth noting that an agent does not need to associate the signifier 'ochre' (or any other signifier or sign) with the concept of ochre in order to possess that concept. The attachment of a signifier to a concept is an action (of thought) associated with possession of that concept.

given the obtaining of certain associated background intentional states *and* which typically causes a distinctive range of intentional and behavioural outputs, *given* the obtaining of certain associated background intentional states. A judge possesses a definitional belief by virtue of being in the requisite physical state. And, typically, she is in the requisite physical state by virtue of having been subject to the causal influence of *at least one* of the members of the set of individuating environmental or intentional inputs which typically cause that state in that agent, whilst *at the same time* possessing the background intentional states relevantly associated with that input. Something needs to have caused the physical state that is the belief in question. That something will typically be one of the phenomena identified in the total functional definition of the belief as typically causal of the belief. These phenomena fall into two categories – environmental events (which in the legal context we may identify with the various forms of evidence or submissions about a concept made available to a judge) and intentional events (which in the legal context we may conceive of as comprising the elements of a process of reasoning on the part of a judge).[35]

A belief that ochre is a yellow powder is a physical state which, amongst other things is typically caused by the environmental event of there being ochre in front of the agent, but only given the possession by the agent of a series of associated background intentional states, including the belief that the agent's sensory apparatus is working correctly, the belief that powder is a fine-grained solid, and so on. Given the possession of these background intentional states and the presence of ochre in front of the agent, it follows by virtue of a non-strict intentional regularity of the kind discussed in Chapter 2 that that agent will believe that ochre is a yellow powder. But, of course, the agent will only possess the background intentional states associated with this belief if the agent has previously been subject to the causal influence of at least one of the members of the set of individuating environmental or intentional inputs which typically cause each of those background states, whilst at the same time possessing the background intentional states relevantly associated with those inputs. And likewise for the background states involved in the causing of these background states. If she has not been subject to the relevant causal influences she will not possess the relevant intentional states and concepts.

What emerges from this complex picture is that in order for a judge to possess the definitional belief and component concept in question, not only must the judge possess a substantial number of other associated intentional states and concepts (concepts are holistic) but the judge must have been in appropriate causal relations with a substantial set of possession-relevant environmental and intentional phenomena over the course of her life generative of such associated states. This is consistent with the point made in Chapter 2 that it is a general principle inherent in the theory of mind possessed by most agents (and adopted by this book) that a subject agent who has not been in appropriate causal relations with any of the

35 Recall that in Chapter 2 we effaced perceptual events from our analysis.

environmental or intentional inputs typically causal of a given belief or of the background intentional states associated with the causing of that given belief by such inputs will, typically, not possess such belief. Likewise, it also is a general principle inherent in most theories of mind that a subject agent who *has* been in appropriate causal relations with at least one of the environmental or intentional inputs typically causal of a given belief and of each of the background intentional states associated with the causing of that given belief by such inputs (and so on) will, typically, possess such belief.[36]

In order to possess the definitional belief and concept in question this causal contact with environmental and intentional phenomena over time cannot have been in any temporal order whatsoever. Rather it must have taken place in an order which enabled the judge to acquire the background intentional states (primary background intentional states) necessary for the possession of the belief in response to a given environmental or intentional input. The possession of those primary background states must have arisen prior to being subject to that input. And the possession of the secondary background states associated with the causing of each of those primary background states must have arisen prior to being subject to the input which caused those primary background states. Likewise, for the tertiary background states associated with the causing of the secondary background states, and so on.

To illustrate, if we consider the acquisition of a philosophical concept – say, the definitional belief that physicalism is an a posteriori metaphysical doctrine – it is clear that mere causal contact with an utterance to this effect will not bring about such a belief unless one already possesses a series of other beliefs about the nature of the physical, the a posteriori, and metaphysical doctrines. Such beliefs themselves will not be acquirable by an agent unless that agent has previously acquired other beliefs about the kinds of things implicated in these concepts – about entities, properties, relations, sensory experience, and so on. These are themselves complex concepts, the possession of which will require the agent to have acquired a range of more basic philosophical and common sense concepts. All of this is just to say that in belief acquisition as in many other things, you have to learn to walk in order to learn to run. This is not to deny, of course, that a potentially vast range of different temporal orderings of the agent's causal contact with relevant environmental and intentional phenomena may be compatible with the agent's ultimately possessing the belief in question. One may acquire the concept of physicalism early in life or later, for example, and by one of a range of philosophical curricula. The key point here is that it is not the case that 'anything goes' temporally as far as concept acquisition is concerned. There may, though, be many ways leading to the acquisition of a given concept or intentional state.[37]

36 As we shall see in Chapter 5, this point is consistent with the important role which an interpreter's justified beliefs about the subject agent's environmental and intentional history play in the interpretive process.

37 More on this point below.

The judge's acquisition of a concept is caused by and is explained by the fact that the judge has, over the course of her life, come into appropriate causal contact with a series of environmental events and has been subject to a series of intentional events in a temporal order which have both established a requisite set of background intentional states and been ultimately causal of the occurrence of a belief (or other intentional state) containing the concept.[38] One way to usefully – though, rather metaphorically – think about what is a highly complex set of conditions for the acquisition of a concept is in terms of the judge having taken a distinctive (though not unique) concept-possessing environmental and intentional *trajectory* through time and space. It is the taking of this trajectory which may be considered to have forged her intentional profile at large, including her possession of any definitional belief or concept in question. A judge acquires a definitional belief (and, indeed, any intentional state informed by the concept in question) by taking one of the range of such trajectories which lead to possession of that belief (or other intentional state). At a certain point along the agent's environmental and intentional trajectory, when sufficient associated background intentional states have been put in place and when an appropriate environmental or intentional event occurs, the judge acquires the definitional belief in question.

This is to say that at a point in the judge's intentional development, when some possession-sufficient set of the sub-concepts of the primary concept in question have been acquired, the judge is able to gain knowledge *that* those sub-concepts are sub-concepts of that primary concept as well as knowledge of *what* their syntactic relation is in response to some relevant environmental or intentional event. She is able to acquire that primary concept. At that point, a possession-sufficient set of the sub-conceptual content of the concept in question is maintained by the judge and the judge may be considered 'ripe' for the acquisition of the concept or belief.[39] At a given point in time, depending upon the course of her causal engagement with the world and her intentional development,[40] a judge may acquire a concept instantly upon being subject to the causal influence of a particular environmental or intentional event.[41] With the relevant sub-concepts in place, the occurrence of a particular environmental or intentional event may trigger a cognitive or conceptual response in which those sub-concepts are recognized as components of the primary concept and their syntactic relation within that concept known.

---

38 Clark (1973).

39 This approach to concept acquisition is consistent with Wellman's (1990) account of, what he terms, conceptual engendering. At p. 318, he states '[i]n this process [of conceptual engendering], an early achieved concept or distinction engenders or makes possible later conceptual progeny'.

40 Depending upon her possession of relevant background intentional states.

41 One of the set of such events which will be causal of the definitional belief (possession of the concept) in question, given the possession of those background intentional states.

Where, for example, a judge possesses some set of the sub-concepts of ochre (yellow and powder, say) but not knowledge of their componency or syntactic relation within the concept of ochre then the judge may acquire knowledge of those things (assuming the judge possesses the relevant generic concepts for such knowledge)[42] by a variety of means. She may observe some actual ochre or a suitable visual representation of ochre (a photograph, say) and, by virtue of that observation, come to know that it is a yellow powder. In response to such observation she may come to know that the concept of ochre is comprised of the sub-concepts of yellow and powder, and know the syntactic relation between those sub-concepts (yellow powder not powdered yellow). Alternatively, she may observe and interpret the behavioural component of a testimonial action[43] or signifying component of an artefact (the marks comprising a written document, say) asserting that ochre is a yellow powder or that the content of the concept of ochre is 'yellow powder' and come to believe the proposition asserted. Finally, on the basis of some set of beliefs and desires she possesses, she might reason to a conclusion that ochre is yellow powder or that the concept of ochre is constituted by the sub-concepts of yellow and ochre syntactically related in a 'yellow powder' kind of way. That is, an intentional event may be causal of the definitional belief that ochre is a yellow powder, say, given the possession of certain associated background intentional states.

In all cases she acquires the concept of ochre by the epistemic means mentioned only on the condition that she already possesses some possession-sufficient set of the sub-concepts of the concept of ochre. Given her possession of the sub-concepts of yellow and powder, the judge, like any other agent, may come to possess the concept of ochre by virtue of coming into appropriate causal contact with actual or representational or testimonial *evidence* (construed in a broad non-legal sense) or with a train of reasoning to do with that concept. Given her beliefs about the content of the sub-concepts of yellow and powder (given her possession of these sub-concepts) and given certain other background intentional states possessed by her, the environmental events implicated in such evidence or the intentional events implicated in such reasoning typically cause – and may, in fact, cause – a belief in her that ochre is yellow powder (or some other ochre-informed intentional state). They may cause the judge to acquire or possess the concept of ochre. This point is worth labouring because it is vital to the rest of my argument.

Where the judge does not possess a possession-sufficient number of the sub-concepts of ochre – in our simple example, does not possess the concept of powder, say – then she has to acquire a possession-sufficient number of those sub-concepts before she can acquire the concept of ochre. And she acquires a sub-concept of ochre by the same kinds of means by which she acquires the concept of ochre. That is, by means of evidence or a process of reasoning which causes her to possess

42 We may assume that she does as she is capable of acquiring concepts which are not culturally different for her.

43 For example, the oral testimony of a witness or explanatory submission of counsel.

such sub-concepts, against the background of a set of other intentional states – including, for example, beliefs about the content of some possession-sufficient set of the sub-concepts of these secondary sub-concepts (tertiary sub-concepts of the concept of ochre). For example, she may acquire the sub-concept of powder by means of testimonial evidence about that sub-concept – by interpreting and accepting an utterance asserting that powder is a finely-grained substance.[44] Where the judge does not possess sufficient of the tertiary sub-concepts as would enable possession of a secondary concept (she doesn't possess concepts of fine or grain), she must acquire those tertiary concepts by means of evidence or reasoning about those tertiary concepts.

And so on, into the sub-conceptual 'depths' of the concept of ochre,[45] building up a possession of the content of that primary concept, sub-concept by sub-concept; gradually acquiring that primary concept by her cognitive and interpretive efforts in response to real, representational and testimonial evidence and reasoning about its content until such time as she possesses sufficient of its sub-concepts and sufficient knowledge of their syntactic relations as would constitute a practically adequate possession of the concept of ochre, given her purposes. This building up may be achieved by any one of a range of combinations of real, representational and testimonial evidence and streams of reasoning in any one of a range of temporal orders, reflecting the range of trajectories available for acquiring a concept or possessing an intentional state. Of course, it should not be supposed from this simple description of things that the judge's way into possession of the concept of ochre must proceed by way of an item of evidence or a line of reasoning correlating to one and only one unpossessed sub-concept, that the evidence she encounters or conclusions she reaches about sub-conceptual matters must necessarily present themselves to her in some atomistic and linear manner. Rather, the judge may simultaneously gain knowledge of a number of sub-concepts of the primary concept upon coming into appropriate causal contact with a single environmental (evidential) event or piece of testimony or concluding belief, depending upon her intentional profile at that time.

In order for the judge to be able to build up a primary concept in this manner from some or other sub-conceptual base, sufficient relevant evidence has to exist and (by some means or other) come within the sensory range of and be cognitively appropriated or conceptualized by the judge. In order to cognitively appropriate any such evidence the judge has to possess a capacity and motivation to do so. Alternatively or additionally, given a sufficient sub-conceptual base, the judge must possess a capacity and motivation to engage in the kind of reasoning which will lead to the acquisition of the primary concept in question.[46] Further, in relation

---

44 With knowledge in place about the concept of powder, the judge may then go on to acquire the concept of ochre on the basis of the kind of evidence about that concept mentioned above.

45 Or, to shift metaphors, across the sub-conceptual web of the concept of ochre.

46 Including interpretive reasoning of the kind to be discussed in Chapter 5.

to both evidence and reasoning, the external environmental conditions surrounding the judge must be such as to effectively enable the judge to cognitively appropriate relevant evidence and do the requisite reasoning. We can conceive of these factors to do with judicial concept acquisition in terms of a set of *epistemic conditions* obtaining (or not) in relation to a judge or set of judges and a concept or set of concepts. In order for a judge to be able to acquire a concept she does not at some relevant time adequately possess (given her possession at that time of, at least, some set of the sub-conceptual content of that concept), epistemic conditions conducive to the acquisition of that concept must obtain in relation to that judge. The judge must think and act acquisitively under a set of epistemic conditions which are conducive to the acquisition of that concept.[47]

Following through our analysis here, we can categorize the epistemic conditions affecting the judicial acquisition of a concept – including a culturally different concept – in terms of either the internal capacities of the judge or the external circumstances surrounding the judge. From a physicalist point of view, both categories of epistemic conditions comprise physically realized phenomena whose nature and effect on judicial concept acquisition is, in principle, knowable on the basis of scientifically sound empirical-cum-interpretive inquiry. As far as internal capacities go, the judge must, for example, possess sensory apparatus which will enable her to sense appropriate relevant evidence provided to her about the concept under acquisition. She must possess cognitive apparatus enabling her to effectively conceptualize what she senses by way of evidence. She must possess behavioural apparatus and a behavioural repertoire which will enable her to behave in a concept acquisitive manner in relation to evidence of that concept – which will enable her to locate and manipulate such evidence in a manner conducive to her acquiring the concept. Alternatively or additionally, the judge must be able to reason effectively from premises to conclusions about concepts under acquisition.[48] Judicial concept acquisition depends on the amount and nature of the reasoning about the concept in question a judge is willing and able to engage in over the course of the hearing. She must possess a capacity to reason effectively in this regard.

This is all to say that the judge must possess a range of theoretical and practical skills – understood in terms of the possession of functional sensory, cognitive and behavioural apparatus, appropriate intentional states (beliefs and desires) and

---

47 I want to distinguish here between the existence and nature of the sub-conceptual base possessed by the judge (or, if you like, the existence and degree of conceptual difference obtaining between her and the indigenous concept under acquisition), on the one hand, and the epistemic conditions obtaining in relation to her, on the other, by which I mean those other circumstances or phenomena relevant to her capacity to acquire that concept (examples of which are mentioned here).

48 Again, particularly in relation to the premises and conclusions constituting the various theories utilized in the process of interpreting testimonial evidence about culturally different concepts. More on this in Chapter 5.

an effective behavioural repertoire – in relation to the cognitive appropriation of evidence of and the carrying out of reasoning about those concepts she seeks to acquire. Concept acquisition is not a passive affair. It is a complex form of action oriented towards understanding[49] which has both a theoretical and a practical dimension. The judge must be in possession of those skills which will enable her to engage in such action. She needs a certain know-how in relation to the complex action of concept acquisition. Some knowledge-sufficient set of her beliefs about the acquisition process and its subject matter must be true. She must also be in possession of appropriate and sufficient (and sufficiently strong) desires as would motivate her to locate, manipulate and cognize (pay attention to) relevant evidence to a sufficient degree and to pursue the amount and kinds of reasoning required to acquire the concepts in question.[50]

As far as external circumstances relevant to the judicial acquisition of concepts go, this is most importantly a matter of the amount and quality of evidence relevant to concept acquisition which is both in principle and in fact available and provided to the judge for her sensory and cognitive appropriation. It is also a matter of the external assistance available to her, in principle and in fact, in locating, manipulating and cognitively appropriating relevant evidence or engaging in relevant reasoning. Also important here is the time available to the judge to access evidence or engage in reasoning, including any externally imposed time limits. Another key category of external factors involves the environmental conditions affecting the judge's sensation and cognition of evidence or the conduct of her reasoning. These conditions include such things as available light, distance and line of sight in relation to the judge and the evidence, as well as background noise and other auditory conditions, and so on. They also include the availability and provision of external technological phenomena such as amplification, computers, vehicles, binoculars, and so on, by which the judge's own sensory, behavioural and reasoning capacities may be supplemented or improved.

So, for example, in order for a judge to acquire the concept of ochre, given her possession of the sub-concepts of yellow and powder, enough of the right kind of evidence must be provided to her. A token of ochre, or a visual representation of ochre, or oral testimony about the nature of ochre – and not some conceptually irrelevant piece of evidence – must be provided to her. These together with the concepts possessed may be sufficient to cause her to acquire the concept of ochre. Of course, if the causing of the possession of the concept is to follow her sensory and cognitive apparatus must be functioning in a manner which enables the provision of such evidence to cause the relevant ochre-informed intentional state. If the judge's sensory apparatus is not functioning effectively or if environmental conditions are such that the judge cannot see the token ochre or hear the testimony,

49 That is, informed by beliefs and desires about the concept in question and its acquisition (including the very process of acquisition).

50 The judge may not have the requisite desire to acquire the concept or it may not be stronger than her desire to do something else.

then the tendering of that evidence will not cause the acquisition of the concept. Likewise, if a malfunction in her cognitive functioning prevents the sensation of the token ochre causing a belief about what is sensed the concept will not be acquired. So too, if the judge does not pay attention to what is shown to her, or hurriedly misperceives it.

Again, assuming possession of requisite sub-concepts and beliefs, if the judge's cognitive faculties are malfunctioning in a manner which prevents her from engaging properly in the kind of reasoning which might lead to the acquisition of a concept, that concept will not be acquired by that means. If the judge is unable to make the inference from the beliefs that there are powders of all colours in the world and that yellow is a colour to the conclusion that there is yellow powder in the world, then she will not be able to acquire the concept of ochre (simply defined) by this means. And if the judge simply does not have enough time available to her for concept acquisition – say, by virtue of the norms regulating the length of the evidence-tendering phase of the hearing – or if she desires not to spend enough time, she will not be in a position to acquire the concept in question. Given a specific sub-conceptual base in the possession of the judge, her capacity to acquire a concept informed by that base will depend upon the nature of the kinds of epistemic condition described here.

The process of judicial concept acquisition outlined here resembles the process by which the judge acquired virtually all of the concepts she presently possesses. It also resembles the way in which culturally different agents themselves acquired the culturally different concepts the judge might seek to acquire – which is to say, by an empirical and interpretive engagement with acquisitively relevant aspects of the world (including the actions of culturally different agents) and by a process of reasoning which take place within the context of possessing a background intentional profile relevantly similar to that of the culturally different agents as far as the acquisition of the culturally different concepts in question is concerned. This is to say that the judicial acquisition of culturally different concepts – if it is at all possible – takes place by a process of enculturation into the world and a way of life of the culturally different group in question; a process resembling in important respects the process of enculturation which the members of that group themselves pursued in coming to possess the concepts in question. The idea of being subject to or engaging in a process of enculturation comprises an alternative way of conceiving of the process of concept acquisition to that elaborated above under the description of taking an environmental-intentional trajectory through space and time.

Again, this is not to say that in acquiring a culturally different concept the judge must pursue precisely the same process of enculturation – the same trajectory – as that pursued by any of the members of the culturally different group. As was touched upon above, given the range of causal relations which individuate an intentional state, causal relations with any one of a range of sets of environmental and intentional phenomena are capable of causing the definitional belief or other intentional state in question to be possessed by the agent. Further, for each of the associated background intentional states which figure in each of the causal relations with an environmental or intentional input, a range of inputs are causal. And the same goes throughout the intentional web involved here. The number of environmental-intentional trajectories leading to a given intentional state may be substantial. Any one of this range of trajectories is capable of causing an agent to possess that state. This feature of concept acquisition explains how a significant number of agents with different life experiences can, nevertheless, be said to possess the same intentional state or concept.

So, for example, a judge or culturally different agent may come to maintain a definitional belief about ochre by virtue of having come into the right kind of causal contact with the environmental event (in legal terms, real evidence) of there being ochre in front of her, whilst possessing certain background beliefs about the reliability of her sensory system, about the definitions of some set of ochre's sub-concepts, and so on. Each of these background beliefs may have been acquired in response to other earlier environmental events, and likewise for the background beliefs involved in those earlier environmental causings. Alternatively, though, a judge or culturally different agent may come to maintain the definitional belief about ochre not by coming in direct causal contact with ochre but by virtue of having been in causal contact with the intentional event of desiring to believe what a perceived and interpreted testifying agent believes – namely, that ochre is a yellow powder – whilst at the same time possessing a range of associated background intentional states to do with the interpreted content of that witness's mind. Many of these background intentional states may themselves have been caused, not by environmental events, but by other intentional states over the course of the judge's or culturally different agent's intentional development, as may many of the background intentional states implicated in the causing of this former set of background intentional states, and so on. The point here is that the same definitional belief or concept may be acquired by similar or by quite different environmental-intentional trajectories.

This leads us to the question of the relationship between a judge's degree of possession of a concept and the degree of work or amount of action required of her to acquire that concept. At a given point in a judge's life, when a significant set of concepts are possessed by her – including a possession-sufficient set of the sub-conceptual content of the concept in question[51] – and when her epistemic conditions at that point enable a relevant environmental or intentional input to exert appropriate causal effect upon her, that judge may instantly acquire the concept in question in response to that input. She may acquire the concept in question instantly by virtue of this dual set of pre-requisites for concept acquisition – possession of an adequate sub-conceptual base and the obtaining of conducive epistemic conditions – being in place at that point in time. At that point in time,

51 Which, drawing on our discussion in Chapter 2, we can conceive of in terms of a sufficient set of the background intentional states associated with the causing of a definitional belief about the concept.

with that sub-conceptual base in place and under those conditions, virtually no concept-acquisitive work will be required of the judge in order for her to acquire the concept in question. Of course, this dual set of pre-requisites for concept acquisition will be in place only if the judge has undergone one of the range of complex, ordered sets of causal relations with the world which causes those pre-requisites to be in place at the moment in question; only if she has taken one of the numerous environmental-intentional trajectories which are causal of the concept in question.

Alternatively, at a given point in a judge's life, when, by virtue of her environmental and intentional history up to that point, sufficient background intentional states associated with the intentional state containing the concept in question are *not* possessed by her or when her epistemic conditions at that point do not enable a relevant environmental or intentional input to exert appropriate causal effect upon her, the judge may have to engage in a significant degree of concept-acquisitive work in order to acquire an acquisition-sufficient sub-conceptual base or come into appropriate causal contact with a relevant environmental or intentional input. Though the judge may have come some way along a trajectory that leads to the possession of a concept, more cognitive engagement with the world and intentional development may need to take place in order for her to possess the concept at all or to the degree in question. She may have to work hard at pursuing a trajectory which will lead to the possession of the concept in question. She may have to perform a significant number of acquisition-oriented actions locating, manipulating and cognizing relevant evidence and engaging in relevant reasoning in regard to each of the sub-conceptual elements of the concept under acquisition. She may need to exert a substantial degree of concept-acquisitive effort in acquiring and synthesizing those sub-concepts she does not possess in order to build up to some practically adequate degree the primary concept she does not possess.

What emerges here is a general proposition along the lines that the less sub-conceptual content of a culturally different concept a judge possesses at a given point in time (the more the degree of conceptual difference which obtains between the judge and the concept), the more cognitive and interpretive work she will have to perform in response to evidence about that concept and the more reasoning about that she will have to engage in in order to constructively acquire that concept. Likewise, the *more* sub-conceptual content of the concept a judge possesses at the relevant time (the less the degree of conceptual difference which obtains between the judge and the concept), the less evidence she may be required to come into contact with and cognitively appropriate and the less reasoning she may have to engage in in order to construct the concept. The less overall effort she will have to engage in to acquire the concept. In either case, the more conducive to concept acquisition her epistemic conditions are the greater her chances are in succeeding in that task. In light of this we can imagine a situation of judicial concept acquisition in which the degree of sub-conceptual content of a culturally different concept possessed by a judge conspires with the obtaining of non-conducive epistemic conditions to produce a situation in which the judge is unable to perform the acquisitive work required of her. We can imagine a situation in which a culturally different concept or set of such concepts is not acquirable by a judge or set of judges – at least whilst that degree of sub-conceptual content is possessed or those epistemic conditions obtain. The plausibility of such a situation obtaining in a physicalistic world (a situation, by the way, argued for by the radical conceptual incommensurabilists) is something I will have more to say about in Chapter 6.

Cultural Difference as Conceptual Difference

In light of this discussion of concepts and their acquisition, we can not only accept the theoretical possibility of conceptual difference obtaining between a judge and a claimant, witness or other agent but also explain the existence of such difference. As mentioned in Chapter 1, conceptual difference obtains between a judge and a culturally different agent – or between the conceptual schemes of these agents – when the scheme of concepts possessed by the judge does not include some set of the concepts possessed by the culturally different agent.[52] It obtains when the content of the judge's conceptual scheme differs to some degree from the content of the culturally different agent's scheme, and vice versa. In more overtly physicalistic terms, this is to say that it obtains when the judge does not possess physical states which play the same intentional-functional role as certain of the physical states possessed by the culturally different agent. Where conceptual difference obtains between a judge and culturally different agent in relation to a given concept, the culturally different agent will possess a physical state which is typically caused by one of the members of the characteristic concept-individuating set of environmental or intentional inputs, given the possession of associated background intentional states and which typically causes one of the members of the concept-individuating set of intentional or environmental outputs, given the possession of associated background intentional states and the judge will not possess such a physical state.

One reason the judge may not possess a concept is because she (unlike the culturally different agent in question) has, at no stage, been subject to the causal influence of at least one of the members of the set of individuating environmental or intentional inputs which typically cause that concept in that agent, *whilst at the same time* possessing the background intentional states relevantly associated with that input. That is, she may not possess the concept in question because she has not been subject to the causal influence of at least one of the members of the set of individuating environmental or intentional inputs which typically cause that concept *or* because, though she has been subject to the causal influence of one such input, she did not at that time possess sufficient of the background intentional

52 Rescher (1980) p. 333.

states associated with that input as would cause the possession of the concept (which is to say that she did not possess sufficient of the sub-conceptual content of the concept in question) or because both of these states of affairs has obtained. This second mentioned mode of judicial deficiency may be explained by the fact that the judge has at no stage been subject to the causal influence of at least one of the members of the set of individuating environmental or intentional inputs which typically cause each of those requisite background states, whilst at the same time possessing the background intentional states relevantly associated with those inputs. And so on. Of course, in order to explain the *difference* between the judge and culturally different agent in respect of this concept it must be the case that the culturally different agent *has* been subject to at least one of the requisite inputs and has possessed the associated background intentional states for that input.

This is to say that conceptual difference between two agents or two sets of agents is explicable with reference to the environmental and intentional influences those two agents or sets of agents have been subject to over the course of their lives and to the temporal order of those influences. It is explicable with reference to the fact of those agents having taken different environmental and intentional trajectories over the course of their lives, trajectories different enough to lead to the one possessing a concept which the other does not possess.[53] For example, one key source of conceptual difference lies in differences in the environmental inputs which two agents have been causally subject to over the course of their lives. Two agents may have been raised in and may, at the relevant time, still inhabit quite different natural and social environments. A culturally different agent, for example, may possess the concept of ochre, say, by virtue of having taken one of the many available environmental-intentional trajectories which lead to the possession of that concept. He may have been in the right kind of causal contact with ochre at some point in time whilst at that point in time possessing one of the sets of background intentional states associated with the causing of a belief that ochre is a yellow powder by that environmental input.

The judge, on the other hand, may not, over the course of her life, have come into appropriate causal contact with ochre or with any other environmental or intentional input causal of possession of the concept of ochre,[54] even though she may have possessed the background intentional states (sub-concepts of ochre) associated with such inputs. In purely conceptual terms, she may possess the sub-concepts of ochre but not have come into causal relations with an environmental

53 It is for this reason that we may conceive of each individual as possessing her own distinct conceptual scheme – though there may be sufficient similarities between individual schemes to enable us to speak of shared or group-specific schemes. Of course, mere difference in trajectory does not entail difference in concepts possessed because the same concept may come to be possessed by different trajectories. I will have more to say on this below and in Chapter 6.

54 In legal terms, she may not have come into appropriate contact with real evidence of ochre or with testimonial or performative evidence about ochre.

or intentional event which brings about knowledge that those sub-concepts are syntactically interrelated in a primary concept and knowledge of that syntactic relation. Alternatively, the judge may have come into appropriate causal contact with one or more of the causal inputs for the concept in question but not possessed the requisite background intentional states at the time she did so. Until such time as the judge comes into causal relations with some causally effective input phenomenon whilst at the same time possessing associated background intentional states, the judge will not possess a concept of ochre and the situation of conceptual difference which obtains as far as the judge is concerned in relation to this concept and to any scheme of concepts containing it or agent possessing it will continue.

In this scenario, the environmental-intentional trajectories of the judge and culturally different agent differ in a certain respect. As a result of this difference, the culturally different agent possesses the concept of ochre and the judge does not. This, in turn, entails that the conceptual schemes of the two agents differ in this respect. The one scheme contains a concept which the other does not contain. The more the environmental-intentional trajectories taken by the judge and culturally different agent relevantly differ, the more the one may[55] possess concepts not possessed by the other, the more their conceptual schemes may differ. Agents and schemes may be conceptually different to a greater or lesser degree depending upon the number of concepts they do not hold in common. The greater the number of culturally different concepts not possessed by the judge, the greater the degree of conceptual difference between her and the culturally different agent, between her scheme and the culturally different agent's. The degree of conceptual difference is a function of the degree to which the two agents have taken different environmental and intentional trajectories over the course of their lives. Differences in the natural and social environments in which the two agents have lived are important in this respect. The actual 'amount' or degree of such conceptual difference will depend upon the number of concepts which are not held in common by the two agents in question at some point in time.[56] Of course, given that different trajectories may lead to possession of the same concept not all differences in the trajectories taken by two agents generate conceptual difference. A difference in the concepts possessed by two agents entails that those agents have taken different environmental-intentional trajectories in respect of those concepts. However, as has been mentioned, a difference in the trajectories taken

55 There is no entailment here. Different trajectories do not necessarily lead to the possession of different concepts. As mentioned above, the one concept may be acquired by means of different trajectories.

56 One has to be careful in attempting to quantify conceptual difference given their holistic nature. The number of concepts in a conceptual scheme may be indeterminable. Nonetheless, we can still make some sense of the idea that two agents differ to greater or lesser degrees in the concepts they maintain with reference to the kinds of actions which comprise their way of life, for example.

by them does not entail that they possess different concepts. Some differences in trajectories taken will generate conceptual difference and some will not.

Extending our use of the notion of conceptual difference, culturally different concepts, intentional states and actions may also be conceived of as being conceptually different to a greater or lesser degree as far as the judge is concerned. The greater the number of conceptually different sub-concepts (sub-concepts not possessed by the judge) informing a culturally different concept as far as the judge is concerned, the greater the degree to which that concept is conceptually different as far as that judge is concerned. Likewise, the greater the number of conceptually different concepts informing the propositional content of a culturally different agent's intentional states as far as the judge is concerned, the greater the degree to which those states are conceptually different as far as that judge is concerned. Finally, the greater the number of intentional states informing a culturally different action which the judge does not possess concepts for (and, by extension, the greater the number of concepts comprising the propositional content of each of those states which are not possessed by the judge), the greater the degree to which that action is conceptually different as far as the judge is concerned.

On the issue of conceptually different concepts, it is worth emphasizing here the point made towards the close of the previous section – namely, that the degree of conceptual difference which exists between a culturally different concept and a judge is a factor affecting the ability of that judge to acquire that concept. By degree of conceptual difference here, I mean the amount and identity of the sub-conceptual content of the culturally different concept which the judge already possesses and the amount and identity of the sub-conceptual content she needs to acquire in order to acquire the concept in question. The more of the sub-conceptual content of a given concept a judge possesses at a given point in time, the less sub-conceptual content that judge needs to acquire. This is to say that the less the degree of conceptual difference which obtains between a judge and a concept, the further along a trajectory for acquiring that concept she will be and the less concept acquisitive work she needs to engage in. The less sub-conceptual content the agent needs to acquire, the less appropriate environmental inputs (evidence) will need to be provided to her and cognitively processed by her and the less reasoning (including interpretive reasoning of the kind to be discussed in Chapter 5) will need to be performed by her. The less the degree of conceptual difference between the judge and the culturally different concept, the better the judge's overall acquisitive situation will be vis-à-vis that concept.

And of course, the greater the degree of conceptual difference between the judge and the indigenous concept, the more sub-concepts of that primary concept will need to be acquired by the judge in order to acquire that primary concept.[57] Because these sub-concepts can only be acquired in response to environmental and intentional inputs (evidence and reasoning) the greater the degree of conceptual

57 The greater the number of concept-causing conditions which need to be put in place to enable possession of the culturally different concepts in question.

difference, the greater the number of concept-causing conditions which will need to be put in place: the greater the amount of evidence which needs to be provided to and cognitively processed by the judge and the greater the amount of reasoning which will need to be engaged in by her. Concept acquisition under conditions of conceptual difference (to any degree) is potentially more time consuming and cognitively demanding than concept acquisition under conditions of conceptual similarity. Conceptual difference worsens the judge's overall epistemic situation, it puts a greater concept-acquisitive burden on her (and on the parties charged with supplying her with evidence). Under certain epistemic conditions – where for example, the judge's cognitive skills are deficient, or where adequate evidence simply cannot be provided to her in the time available – the degree of conceptual difference which obtains between a judge and culturally different concept may be so great that a judge may not be able to meet that burden. She may not be able to acquire the culturally different concept in question whilst those conditions obtain. Given the degree of conceptual difference which obtains, other more optimal conditions might be necessary in order to enable her acquisition of the concept in question.[58]

On the physicalist-functionalist model of intentionality and understanding adopted in this book, it is *possible*, then, that some set of judges (including all judges) and some set of culturally different agents (including all such agents) have taken environmental and intentional trajectories which not only differ but which differ in a manner which results in the set of culturally different agents possessing concepts not possessed by the set of judges. It is theoretically possible that some or other degree of conceptual difference obtains between any or all judges and culturally different agents. It is possible that an indigenous land title judge, for example, will not possess to any possession-sufficient degree, nor to any practically adequate degree, *some* set of the concepts possessed either by claimant indigenous agents or witnesses testifying about indigenous concepts and actions and that some set of the intentional states and actions of those agents will be conceptually different as far as the judge is concerned (and, of course, vice versa). This proposition, at least, is shared by cultural incommensurabilists and myself.[59]

It does not follow, though, from the mere claim that some or other degree of conceptual difference is theoretically possible that some or other degree of conceptual difference between a judge and culturally different agent is a theoretically *necessary* state of affairs. The approach taken here so far does not *entail* that a judge and a culturally different agent take conceptual trajectories which are so different as to generate the acquisition of different concepts. It does not entail that a judge and culturally different agent cannot take trajectories which

58 I will come back to this discussion in Chapter 6.

59 What is not shared is the proposition that it is possible (let alone necessary) that a judge possess none of the concepts possessed by a culturally different agent. I will have more to say on this in Chapter 6.

are similar enough to generate an identical set of concepts.[60] It is possible on the view outlined here for two sets of agents, including a set of judges and a set of culturally different agents to take identical environmental-intentional trajectories (or even different trajectories) which result in those sets of agents possessing globally identical conceptual schemes – though, given the way the world actually is, the obtaining of any such identity of trajectory or scheme is extremely unlikely. The theoretical possibility of conceptual difference which subsists within the physicalist-functionalist theory of concepts, intentionality and understanding adopted here is a *contingent* one. Because some or other degree of conceptual difference between some or all judges and culturally different agents is possible within the theoretical framework outlined here, it follows that it is not necessary that no conceptual difference obtains between those classes of agent. That is, global conceptual identity between judges and indigenous agents is not necessitated by the physicalist-functionalist picture of things.[61] And, as I shall argue in Chapter 6, nor is global conceptual difference between such agents.

Conclusion

Conceptual difference, to the extent that it is possible, is contingently so. Whether conceptual difference actually obtains between a set of judges and a set of culturally different agents, what the extent of any such difference actually is and in relation to which concepts it obtains in a given case or set of cases are contingent (not necessary) matters dependent upon the environmental-intentional trajectories of the agents in question. The existence, extent and identity of any conceptual difference between a judge and a culturally different agent depend on how the world has relevantly been for the agents in question. Where relevant differences have existed in the natural and social environments of those agents over the course of their lives and in the development of their conceptual schemes and worldviews, then conceptual difference will exist to the extent of those differences. Where no such relevant differences have existed, then conceptual difference will not exist (and, depending on your definition of cultural difference, no cultural difference either). This much follows from what we have seen so far. Whether any specific degree of conceptual difference is theoretically *impossible*, however, is an issue I will explore in Chapter 6 when I critically engage with the radical cultural

60 In order for the approach taken here to entail such, an additional premise would have to be added to do with the impossibility of the two kinds of agent in question possessing the same innate conceptual base. As we shall see in Chapter 6, no such premise is viable within the physicalist-functionalist schema adopted in this book.

61 This proposition is contrary to the radical conceptual *identity* thesis maintained by the interpretationist school of thought is to be discussed in the next chapter. This school of thought asserts the necessity of conceptual identity (or something near enough to identity) between all agents. See, for example, Davidson (1973, 1974b, 1974c) and Child (1994).

incommensurability thesis in pursuit of knowledge of the maximal degree of conceptual difference possible between a judge and culturally different agent. With this description of the judicial understanding of culturally different action in place and our noting of the link under conditions of conceptual difference between any such understanding and the acquisition of culturally different concepts, let me now turn to an account of the primary way in which the judicial acquisition of concepts takes place (as a general matter) over the course of a legal hearing – namely, by the judicial interpretation of testimonial action. It is after such an account has been elaborated that we can fully comprehend both the nature and limits of judicial understanding in the legal sphere.

Chapter 5

Judicial Understanding and the Interpretation of Evidence

Testimonial Evidence and the Judicial Acquisition of Concepts

We saw in the previous chapter that, as a general matter, the acquisition of a concept by a judge proceeds by means of the judge coming into appropriate causal – that is, sensory and cognitive – relations with some practically adequate set of relevant environmental or intentional phenomena, given the possession of relevant background intentional states. We can conceive of any such environmental phenomena in terms of evidence of or about how the world relevantly is, which the judge accesses of her own accord or which is provided to her by other agents, or which she otherwise comes into appropriate causal contact. We can conceive of any such intentional phenomena in terms of the elements (including the conclusion) of a process of reasoning on the part of the judge. Put simply, a judge acquires a concept by means of the sensory-cognitive appropriation of evidence to do with (the sub-conceptual content and syntactic structure of) that concept, as well as by means of reasoning about that evidence or otherwise about that concept. This evidence can take a variety of forms including actual tokens of relevant environmental phenomena; audio, visual and other representations of such phenomena; and oral or written testimony about the nature of such phenomena or otherwise about the concept in question (its sub-conceptual content and syntactic structure).[1] One way or another, the judge must come into causal contact with and cognitively appropriate some practically adequate set of such evidence and, additionally or alternatively, must engage in some practically adequate set of relevant reasoning if she is to acquire a concept to a practically adequate degree.

Of the three categories of evidence about concepts generally available to and relied upon by a judge over the course of a legal hearing – real, representational and testimonial – the most common, the most important and the most theoretically challenging is testimonial evidence. Though testimonial evidence can take oral

---

1 As has been mentioned, such testimony may be taken to encompass not merely the testimony of witnesses (testimonial evidence, properly termed) but also explanatory submissions by counsel about the nature of relevant phenomena or the content of relevant concepts. Most of what I have to say below about the judicial interpretation of witness testimony applies to the interpretation of counsel submissions.

or written form, it is on oral testimony that the following discussion will focus.[2] Testimonial evidence may be presented either as independent evidence about the content of a concept under acquisition or as evidence supplementary to real and representational evidence about the content of such a concept. Real evidence of a set of environmental phenomena implicated in a concept is – in practice, if not of necessity – of little use to a judge in acquiring that concept without some supplementary testimony on the part of some or other testifying agent as to the identity (at least) of those aspects of such phenomena relevant to the concept in question. Under conditions of conceptual difference, the sensory and cognitive engagement of a judge with a token set of environmental phenomena – a set of natural or artefactual objects, a geographic location – needs to be guided by an testifying agent (a witness or counsel) so as to enable the judge to make cognitive contact with the appropriate property or object or relation or other element of the set of phenomena actually being evidenced and not some irrelevant aspect of that set.

So too, with representational evidence – audio, visual or other kind – of some conceptually relevant set of environmental phenomena. Some agent needs to testify as to what aspect of the inevitably complex representation evidenced should command the judge's attention and comprehension as far as acquiring a concept is concerned. Real and representational evidence is, as a rule, tendered in legal proceedings in conjunction with testimonial evidence about that real and representational evidence (and about the phenomena evidenced by that real and representational evidence). As either an independent cause of a judge acquiring a concept or as supplementary to a real or representational cause, testimonial evidence is central to judicial concept acquisition and the understanding of action within the legal process. For this reason testimonial evidence will command our attention in the discussion to follow.

The Interpretation of Testimonial Evidence

The mere presentation of testimonial evidence about the content of a concept to a judge is not a sufficient condition[3] for the judge's acquisition of the concept in question. Its mere tendering during a hearing is not sufficient for the judge to be caused to possess an intentional state informed by the concept in question. In addition, the judge must cognitively appropriate that testimonial evidence in a

2 I justify this focus on the grounds that oral testimony is more common in indigenous land title hearings than written testimony and that the tendering of written testimonial evidence at hearing generally requires the tendering of some supplementary oral testimony by a witness about that written evidence. In any event, given the ontological relation which exists between written texts and actions (written texts are the artefacts of actions), much of what I have to say about the interpretation of oral testimonial evidence (a form of action) could be reworked to apply to the interpretation of written testimonial evidence. Hence, nothing of significance is lost by maintaining the proposed focus.

3 Nor, strictly, is it a necessary condition.

manner which causes her to possess an intentional state informed by that concept.[4] This cognitive appropriation of testimonial evidence may be termed interpretation. Thus, it is a necessary condition of the judge utilizing testimonial evidence in the task of concept acquisition that she interpret that evidence. In order to acquire a concept over the course of a hearing, the judge must (as a general rule) interpret testimonial evidence about that concept.[5] Adequately grasping the nature of the judicial interpretation of testimonial evidence is, therefore, fundamental to adequately grasping the nature of judicial concept acquisition and understanding, both generally and within a context involving cultural difference. It is for this reason that I engage in the discussion here. In providing a thoroughly argued basis for asserting the existence of a set of concepts shared to some degree by all interpretive agents, the discussion here assists us in theorizing the limits of conceptual difference and concept acquisition in the next chapter.

If we think about the very nature of oral testimonial action – our key focus here – we can gain insight into the nature of the interpretation of such action. Oral testimonial evidence comprises a set of utterances. As such it constitutes a set of actions performed by some or other agent. In order to enable us to better integrate our discussion of testimonial evidence with the preceding themes of this book and with the philosophical literature on interpretation, I propose to refer to oral testimonial evidence from this point in terms of a set of *testimonial actions* performed by testimonial agents (witnesses or counsel). Our interest here is, therefore, in the judicial interpretation of testimonial actions.[6] As a kind of action, a

4 She must cognitively appropriate the testimonial evidence to a practically adequate degree (given her overarching ends).

5 The more conceptual difference which exists between the scheme of the judge and a culturally different agent, the more likely testimonial evidence must be interpreted by the judge in order to acquire that agent's concept. Culturally different agents themselves could not have built up their conceptual schemes from infancy (a developmental state involving significant conceptual difference vis-à-vis other conceptually more developed agents within the culture) without testimonial assistance from other agents. This point will become clearer in Chapter 6. It is worth noting here that in denying the judicial acquisition of culturally different concepts, the radical cultural incommensurability thesis denies the capacity of a judge to successfully interpret testimonial evidence about culturally different concepts. Indeed, the radical cultural incommensurability thesis is committed to the inability of a judge to cognitively appropriate to any practically adequate degree *any* category of evidence about culturally different concepts – real, representational or testimonial.

6 In the context of an indigenous land title determination hearing, a testimonial agent might be – conceivably, at least – a member of the claimant group or some other indigenous or non-indigenous witness (or counsel) with relevant knowledge about any concepts in question. Whilst on the issue of actions tendered in evidence, another important kind of such action at an indigenous land title hearing is, what I term, performative evidential action. This kind of evidence comprises actual token performances of claimant indigenous actions by some set of claimant agents at some point in the hearing for the benefit of the judge's understanding of those actions. As a form of action, performative evidential action

testimonial action comprises the causing of a behavioural event by a behaviourally causal intentional complex. It is constituted by a testimonial behavioural event and a causally related set of testimonial intentional events, some set of which may be taken as explanatory of that behavioural event or otherwise useful to her given her practical purposes. This is to say that some set of the behaviourally causal intentional complex comprising a testimonial action is classifiable as a behaviourally explanatory intentional complex for judicial purposes, whilst the remainder is classifiable as a behaviourally relevant background intentional complex.

More specifically, we can define oral testimonial action about the content of a concept as action that is tendered by a party to the hearing and which is performed by a bona fide and knowledgeable testimonial agent[7] with the purpose of causing the judge (by her observing and interpreting its behavioural component) to acquire some part of the content of that concept (including a practically adequate part). We can analyse this purpose in terms of the possession of a desire on the part of the testimonial agent to cause the judge to possess an intentional state containing some part of the content of the concept in question – for example, to possess a practically adequate definitional belief about the content of that concept.[8] Such a desire is a necessary component of any testimonial action of the kind involved here. Of course, as we saw in Chapter 2, any such desire will necessarily obtain in conjunction with a series of other behaviourally causal intentional states, some of set of which will be behaviourally explanatory and will enable the judge to achieve her interpretive end – the acquisition of the concept that testimony is about. This is to say that some set of the behaviourally causal intentional states implicated in the testimonial action will contain as part of their propositional content some part of the concept in question.

Consider for example, the case of a witness who testifies about the content of the concept of ochre in order to cause the acquisition of that concept by a judge who does not at the commencement of the witness's evidence possess that concept. In the course of his testimony, such a witness might, for example, assertively utter a sentence which implicitly or explicitly conveys information about the sub-conceptual content and syntactic structure of the concept of ochre (that is, about the properties of the kind of substance ochre is). For example, he might utter the sentence 'ochre is a yellow powder found in the ground and used for ceremonial purposes' with the purpose or desire of causing the judge to believe the proposition contained in this sentence and as a result acquire some part of the concept of ochre

---

is also cognitively appropriated by the judge (if it is at all, of course) by means of a process of interpretation virtually identical to the process described below by which she interprets oral testimony. Thus, virtually all of what I have to say below about the interpretation of testimonial action applies to performative evidential action.

7 I will focus on such an agent – the norm – in order to keep the discussion manageable.

8 For example, the belief that ochre is a yellow powder found in the ground and used for ceremonial purposes.

(perhaps, a practically adequate part). If adequately interpreted, the utterance will convey information to the judge about the sub-conceptual content and syntactic structure of the concept of ochre.

This testimonial action comprises the behavioural event of a certain manipulation of the vocal apparatus of the witness, as well as a set of behaviourally causal intentional events which we may simply construe for the time being in terms of a *belief* that ochre is a yellow powder found in the ground and used for ceremonial purposes, a *desire* that the judge possess an intentional state containing some part of the content of the concept of ochre, a *belief* that by manipulating one's vocal apparatus in a certain way this desire will be realized (the judge will possess such an intentional state) and a *desire* to behave in that way. In the case of such an utterance, the definition which the witness intends to impart to the judge ('a yellow powder found in the ground and used for ceremonial purposes') may be conceived of as being 'located' within the complex of behaviourally causal intentional events comprising the testimonial action as the propositional content of at least one of those events. That is, the concept of ochre may be conceived of as being located in the first of the beliefs just mentioned. That belief contains the concept of ochre. That belief will form part of the behaviourally explanatory intentional complex here, that complex comprising those behaviourally causal interpretive states which enable the judge to realize her interpretive purposes in the situation in question.[9]

Now, if the judge can come to know the identity of this belief to a practically adequate degree – that is, if she can come to possess a practically adequate true belief about the propositional content of this belief – the judge will have come to possess that propositional content as part of her belief, and in doing so will have acquired the concept of ochre contained within it.[10] If she can come to believe that 'the witness believes that ochre is a yellow powder found in the ground and used for ceremonial purposes', the judge will have acquired the definition and, hence, the concept of ochre. She will possess an intentional state informed by the definition or concept of ochre. Her acquisition of the concept will have been a consequence of the uttering of the sentence in question by the testimonial agent. The question for us concerns how the judge comes to possess such a belief in response to a testimonial action of this kind. The answer is by a process of interpretation of that action.

---

9 Evidence about a concept is necessarily informed by some part of the sub-conceptual content of that concept. If a concept cannot be acquired to any degree – that is, if its sub-conceptual content cannot be acquired – then evidence about that concept cannot be interpreted to a practically adequate degree because any such interpretation requires the possession of some part of the sub-conceptual content of that concept.

10 She need not believe that proposition to be true, of course, and so doesn't 'know' the proposition in this stronger sense. I am not concerned at this stage with this additional phase of her response to the utterance. Whether she believes the proposition contained in it or not, by identifying that proposition she possesses the concept contained in it.

The Nature of Interpretation

The mere utterance by the witness of the sentence in question (the mere performing of the testimonial action in question) is necessary but not sufficient to realize that utterance's purpose – namely, the possession by the judge of the belief that ochre is a yellow powder found in the ground and used for ceremonial purposes. It is necessary but not sufficient for the acquisition of the concept of ochre by the judge. In order to realize its purpose, the utterance must actually cause (solely or jointly) the judge to possess a belief about the witness's belief which contains the definitional proposition and concept in question. It can only do so if an additional necessary condition obtains – that is, if the judge herself acts so as to come to knowledge of the identity of the propositional content of the witness's belief in which that definitional proposition and concept subsists. It can only do so, if the judge acts interpretively in relation to the utterance. The judge can only acquire the concept of ochre in response to the testimonial action in question if she interprets that action to a practically adequate degree, given her overall interpretive purpose.[11]

We can make sense of knowing the identity of an intentional state such as the witness's ochre-belief in the example here by recalling what such a state is. It is a behaviourally causal component of a testimonial action. It is a state which, together with other behaviourally causal intentional states, causes the behavioural component of such an action. Thus, identifying that state involves identifying some part of the intentional cause of the behavioural component of that action, some part of that action's behaviourally causal intentional complex. This is to say that interpretive action can be conceived of as a type of action oriented towards the identification of some interpretively relevant part of the total intentional cause of the behavioural component of another action – a part of the behaviourally causal intentional complex of that other action I have been referring to as the behaviourally explanatory intentional complex.[12] Interpretive action is action oriented towards (or informed by a desire to do with) realizing a specific purpose – namely, knowing the identity of some interpretively relevant part of the intentional cause of the behaviour under interpretation.

Interpretive relevance here is a function of the judge's overall purpose or desires in engaging with the testimonial action in the first place. In the case of our ochre utterance, the judge's purpose in interpretively engaging with that utterance is to

---

11 In our example here, that purpose is to acquire some part of the concept of ochre.

12 Henderson (1993) p. 1. Braddon-Mitchell and Jackson (1996) p. 256. 'In interpretation one seeks to find others explicable in their beliefs, desires and actions'. Henderson (1993) p. 115. In addition to speaking of the interpretation of *behaviour*, we can also speak more broadly of the interpretation of an *action* (the explanation of the behavioural component of that action with reference to its intentional component), and the interpretation of an *agent* as involving (the explanation in intentional terms of any behaviour that agent is engaged in).

identify one or more of those behaviourally causal intentional states possessed by the testimonial agent which contain the definition of ochre. Thus, within the context of our present example, the behaviourally explanatory intentional complex which the judge seeks to identify includes the belief that ochre is a yellow powder found in the ground and used for ceremonial purposes. *Interpretation* is the successful identification of some interpretively relevant part of the intentional cause of an agent's behaviour, given the interpreter's purposes. *Interpretive action* involves acting with a view to achieving such identification. Engaging in interpretive action towards a testimonial action about a concept may, if successful, result in the judge acquiring some part of that concept and coming to a better understanding of any action implicating that concept.

To the extent that identifying the cause of something is a form of explanation of that thing, we can properly conceive of interpretive action as a form of explanatory action and interpretation as a form of explanation.[13] Interpretation is the explaining of the behaviour of an agent in intentional terms – a making sense of behaviour from a cognitive and theoretical perspective which Dennett terms 'the intentional stance'.[14] It is the explaining of behaviour from a point of view which tacitly (at least) conceives of behaviour as the causal product of a functionally characterized and nomically governed set of intentional events.[15] An adequate explanation of a phenomenon does not always require the identification of each and every other phenomenon which might be causally traced to the phenomenon in question. Adequate explanation is context- or purpose-dependent. It is a function of the

13 So-called causal explanation. See Dray (1957), Winch (1958), Hempel (1965), Davidson (1963), von Wright (1971) and Turner (1980).

14 Dennett (1987) ch. 2. The nature of this stance is reflected in Braddon-Mitchell and Jackson's (1996) p. 145 comment that 'we can make successful predictions about the behaviour of ... people. We make them by noting patterns in behavioural response, patterns that we can latch on to independently of knowing in detail what is going on inside the complex machines ... Most of us know little about the internal wiring, but all we need to know to make the prediction is the regularity that we observe "from the outside"'. Though I differ quite importantly from Dennett on the metaphysics of intentionality – I am a realist about intentionality whilst Dennett is a non-realist instrumentalist (see Dennett 1987) – his notion of the intentional stance remains a useful one if realistically remodelled. The model of human interaction with the environment which emerges from this stance (on my terms) may be analysed as constituting an intentional redescription or higher-order conceptualization of the non-observed, base physical phenomena which realize that interaction – a process we have discussed in Chapter 2. As a result of it constituting a higher-order conceptualization of physical phenomena, the intentional stance is capable of tracking to a significant extent the physical phenomena which realize its objects. It is for this reason that it is capable of providing a degree of predictive and explanatory success adequate to the various day-to-day purposes of human beings.

15 'According to functionalism, psychological knowledge will always be of states with a certain role, characterised in terms of how they are produced and of their effects on both other such states and behaviour.' Botterill and Carruthers (1999) p. 9.

inquirer's particular ends or purposes in engaging in explanatory action in the first place. It is for this reason that in interpreting testimonial behaviour a judge will not be concerned to expressly identify each and every member of the behaviourally causal intentional complex involved with that behaviour. Rather, she will be concerned to identify a behaviourally explanatory subset of that complex containing sufficient intentional states as will enable her to realize her interpretive purpose of acquiring the concept she needs to acquire in order to perform her determinative or other formal functions.

This interpretive or intentional stance is informed (even if implicitly) by the physicalist-functionalist theory of agency, action and intentionality outlined earlier in this book.[16] In light of the ontological continuity of intentional and behavioural phenomena with the physical and higher-order natural and social world, we can conceive of interpretation as methodologically continuous with physicalistic philosophy and with the natural and social sciences – both expert and folk.[17] Scientific and philosophical psychology serve as more systematic and explicit versions of the largely unconscious and less precise theorizing carried out in the everyday folk psychological sphere.[18] Interpretation of the kind engaged in by judges has a place in the physicalistic scheme of things. It is for this reason that, in practice, interpretation may be usefully informed by relevant propositions of our scientific and common-sense knowledge of the world at large. Indeed, one of the advantages of adopting a physicalistic approach to interpretation is that it can make good sense of the articulation of our interpretations of others with our

16 Given the functional status of action and intentionality, interpretation constitutes a physicalistically legitimate mode of explanation along the lines elaborated in Chapter 1. I will pursue an argument to this effect below.

17 Macdonald and Pettit (1981) p. 81, Henderson (1993) pp. 1, 13.

18 Stich (1996). The reason why both folk practice and scientific psychology and physicalist philosophy share the same basic physicalist-functionalist approach to the behavioural interaction of humans (and other beings) with their environment is because this approach is a successful one by all our folk and scientific theoretical and practical indicators of success. This approach works in explaining how and why things relevantly are and in predicting how things relevantly will be in both everyday and expert contexts. It is a view of human beings and their interactions with each other and the world which is consistent with and supported by an ever-increasing body of empirical evidence discovered and theoretically synthesized by the sciences of socio-biology, developmental and cognitive psychology, linguistics, anthropology, and the like. See Nichols and Stich (2003) pp. 2–9 for references here. See also Astington (1996) and Botterill (1996). Though most human groups do not expressly articulate the nature of their interpretive practices in terms of a physicalist-functionalist theory of things, there is good scientific and philosophical reason to think that that theory does, in fact, describe the nature of that practice universally. See Wellman (1990) ch. 4, Carruthers and Smith (1996) p. 3 and Botterill and Carruthers (1999) pp. 31–8.

scientific and common-sense knowledge of things in a way that non-physicalist approaches cannot.[19]

And, of course, such methodological monism is precisely what would be expected from a physicalistic account of interpretation.[20] As a physicalistically legitimate mode of explanation not fundamentally different from the form of explanation employed in the natural and social sciences, we might expect interpretation to be subject to the same set of methodological constraints as applies in those fields – constraints such as a sensitivity to relevant evidence or experience (especially disconfirming evidence or experience), logical consistency with other beliefs and theories held about the world, and a sensitivity to changes in those other beliefs and theories, to name a key few.[21] The methodological constraints which operate on interpretation are not unique, notwithstanding the arguments of methodological separatists such as Davidson and others who hold that the 'logic of explanation (and testing) in the human sciences is fundamentally different from what we employ in natural sciences'.[22] This feature of interpretation will become clearer below as we make sense of things in greater detail.

Put very simply, the judicial interpretation of testimonial behaviour at hearing – like all interpretation – proceeds by way of a largely inferential cognitive and theoretical process we can analytically reconstruct as having two key phases. The first, relatively straightforward phase involves the identification of the testimonial agent as an agent and his behaviour as just that, an intentionally caused component of an action and not a reflex or other mere happening. This proceeds on the basis of a general theory of agency possessed by the judge.[23] The second, more complex phase of the interpretive process – and the one which will serve as the focus for most of the discussion to follow – involves a process of *inference* from what is believed or assumed by the judge to be the case about the present behavioural outputs, environmental inputs and behaviourally relevant background intentional states and governing intentional regularities or rationality class of the testimonial agent (a set of judicial beliefs we may conceive of as comprising part

---

19 By virtue of the latter conceiving of interpretation and its subject matter dualistically as a fundamentally, metaphysically distinct mode of knowing and class of phenomena.

20 I shall go on later in this chapter to reiterate an earlier construal of the set of beliefs informing everyday interpretive action as a folk psychology continuous with much of philosophical and scientific psychology and quite at home within the physicalistic worldview. It follows from this point that interpretive explanations of behaviour are reducible to physical or other higher-order explanations of behaviour in the sense outlined in Chapter 1.

21 Henderson (1993) p. 13.

22 Henderson (1993) p. 1. Winch (1958), Davidson (1970a and 1974a) and McDowell (1985) are examples of methodological separatists. Davidson bases his view on the fact that interpretation is necessarily charitable in a way scientific explanation is not. This feature of interpretation is claimed to be a function of the distinctively holistic nature of its subject matter – intentional phenomena.

23 The content of which is along the lines set out in Chapter 2 of this book.

of the judge's theory of the testimonial agent[24]) to what is not yet the subject of belief by her – the identity of the behaviourally explanatory intentional complex involved in the testimonial action in question.[25] This process of inference takes place within the context of a further set of beliefs maintained by the judge about the causal regularities which typically obtain between the behavioural outputs, environmental inputs and intentional states of some set of human agents, a set of beliefs we may conceive of as the judge's theory of mind.[26]

In order to interpret the behaviour of a testimonial agent, the judge must possess and apply to that agent a theory of agency, a theory of mind and a theory of the testimonial agent and must infer to the best conclusion she can about the identity of the behaviourally explanatory intentional cause of that behaviour on the basis of those theories.[27] In our ochre example, it is in the set of behaviourally explanatory intentional states that the definition of the concept of ochre is to be 'found'. Finally, any conclusions reached by the judge about the identity of the behaviourally explanatory intentional complex at work in an action under interpretation as a result of this process of inference (as well as any beliefs or assumptions made about the agent's behaviourally relevant background intentional states) remain – like all explanatory hypotheses – provisional or hypothetical, in the sense that they are subject to ongoing confirmation or disconfirmation and remain vulnerable to

24 Together with beliefs about interpretively relevant past environmental inputs and behavioural outputs and about the rationality class the testimonial agent is a member of. I have more to say on this below.

25 If the judge knew by some direct (say, perceptual) means the identity of the behaviourally explanatory intentional states involved in the testimonial action there would be no need for her to engage in any process of interpretive inference to the identity of those states.

26 Conceiving of the interpretation of action n terms of the possession and application of a set of theories of things rather than in some other terms is not uncontroversial. See the longstanding and ongoing debates between simulation theorists and theory theorists of interpretation. See Davies and Stone (1995) and Carruthers and Smith (1996) for a useful collection of essays on this debate. Gordon (1986), Heal (1986), Goldman (1989) are important texts advocating the cause of simulation theory. Notwithstanding the efforts of such advocates, I would argue that the theory-theory approach to interpretation is the most empirically plausible of the physicalistically legitimate higher-order theories of interpretation presently on offer. The contemporary philosophical roots of the theory-theory approach to interpretation may be traced to Lewis (1966 and 1972) and to important articles by Dennett (1978b) and Harman (1978).

27 The first two kinds of theory mentioned here are general theories, descriptive of all or some significant set of agents. They may be analysed as dialectically interrelated components of a more comprehensive general theory we may term the judge's general psychology. To the extent that the judge's general psychology is part of the general theory of agency and mind shared by her interpretive community or folk, we may conceive of her general psychology as comprising some part of a folk psychology. The third kind of theory mentioned above is not a general theory but a descriptive account of certain interpretively relevant properties of a specific agent – the one under interpretation.

revision in the face of any further justified beliefs about the testimonial agent the judge might acquire, whether by way of further relevant evidence or reasoning about that agent.[28]

Ascribing Agency

The first phase of the interpretive process involves the judge ascribing agency to the testimonial agent and activity (the quality of being part of an action) to her testimonial behaviour. As mentioned, it involves her properly recognizing the testimonial agent as an agent and not some other kind of being and the behaviour of that agent as the intentionally caused component of an action and not a reflexive bodily state or other mere happening.[29] This phase proceeds by means of the judge evaluating the nature of the evidential situation confronting her (which we might simply construe as comprising a human being located within and interacting with an environmental context whilst being subject to certain bodily events) with reference to her beliefs about the general nature of agency and action; about what agents and actions, in general, are. I shall term the propositional content of the set of beliefs which the judge relies upon in such a situation as the judge's theory of agency.[30] Such a theory describes the general nature of agents and actions along the lines outlined in Chapter 2.[31] On the basis of her theory of agency, the judge forms a belief as to whether or not the evidential situation confronting her involves an agent performing an action, calling for further interpretive action on her part. If the evidential situation is described by her theory of agency, the reasonable judge will be justified in ascribing (and will, to the extent that she is reasonable, in fact, ascribe) agency to the subject in question and behavioural status to relevant bodily states of that subject. If the situation is not so described, she will not be so justified and will not, to the extent that she is reasonable, ascribe agency and action to the subject.[32] In addition to this, the judge relies upon her theory of agency to make a

28 As we shall see, so too do the hypothesized intentional propositions of the theory of the testimonial agent adopted by the judge.

29 One way we may conceived of this phase of things is in terms of the judge initial adopting of Dennett's (1987) intentional stance towards the testimonial agent and his behaviour. There are also resonances between the notion of agency ascription offered here and the notion advocated in certain hermeneutic schools of thought to do with interpreters coming to the interpretation of an agent with a pre-understanding of that agent. See Thompson (1981), Taylor (1985c) and Gadamer (1989), for example.

30 Botterill and Carruthers (1999) p. 78, Botterill (1996).

31 Which, as I mentioned there, is itself based on a universal folk psychology of agents.

32 To ascribe agency to a subject is to recognize that subject as described by one's theory of what an agent is. To ascribe activity to the behaviour of an agent is to recognize that behaviour as described by one's theory of what an action (including its behavioural component) is. To the extent that her ascriptions are correct (which entails to the extent that her theory of agency is true), the judge will have correctly identified the subject as agent

range of other inferences about the behaviour and intentional profile of the agent encountered by her.[33]

At the heart of my account of agency ascription lies the following proposition – namely, that in ascribing agency, all interpretive agents (including judges) possess and interpretively rely upon to some significant degree the same partially innate, partially learned, largely true, physicalist-functionalist theory of agency.[34] Let me, at this point, attempt to justify this proposition by justifying its various elements. First, that all interpretive agents (including the judge) possess and apply a *theory* of agency in ascribing agency and action to agents and their behaviour, rather than ascribe agency by some alternative, non-theoretical means (intuition, simulation, or the like) follows from the terms of the physicalist-functionalist account of agency, action and concept acquisition offered in this book.[35] To the extent that that account is true (and I maintain that it is true), the proposition in question is true. Recall the point made in Chapter 4 that to recognize something as the kind of thing it is is to evaluate the properties of that thing with reference to the properties described by the definition or concept of that kind. To properly identify an evidential situation as involving an agent is to evaluate the properties of that situation with reference to the properties described by a definition of agency. An interpreter must possess and apply a definition of agency in order to evaluate a subject being as an agent, in order to properly ascribe (or not) agency to that subject. As we saw in Chapter 2, agency is a complex phenomenon and so the definition or description of agency is, in turn, quite elaborate. It constitutes a concept we can rightfully re-describe as a *theory* of agency.[36] Thus, in identifying a subject as an agent – in properly

---

and the event as action. It hardly needs to be stated that if the subject under consideration by the judge is not an agent then any bodily event it is subject to will not constitute behaviour and will not be explicable by reference to any intentional cause. Further, though, even if the subject before an interpreter is identified as an agent, if the bodily event it is subject to is not behavioural but merely a reflex or the like, then, again, that event (and any environmental event caused by it) will not be explicable with reference to any intentional cause.

33 The nature of these inferences and the full interpretive role of a theory of agency will become clearer as this chapter unfolds.

34 Namely, that outlined in Chapter 2.

35 This proposition follows from the physicalist-functionalist theory of things and if that theory is true (and we have good reason to think that it is) then this proposition is true. Of course, though this proposition is necessarily true as a theoretical matter (that is, though the state of affairs described obtains as a matter of theoretical necessity) within the context of the physicalist-functionalist account of things offered in this book, it is not, *logically* true or necessarily the case that all interpretive agents possess a theory of agency. That these things are true is – logically, at least – a *contingent* matter. Like physicalist-functionalism itself, all of the elements of the proposition asserted here may (logically) be false.

36 As part of the overall psychology we use in interpreting others, the various propositions inherent in a concept of agency have 'just the sort of cognitive economy which is distinctive of theories – unifying, integrating and helping to explain a diverse body of data'. Botterill and Carruthers (1999) p. 78. Botterill (1996) p. 110 states that

ascribing agency to that subject – an interpreter must possess and apply a theory of agency. This follows as a matter of theoretical necessity from the terms of the physicalist-functionalist account of things elaborated in this book. If that account is true then so is this proposition.

Within a naturalistic schema, the theoretical necessity of a state of affairs entails the empirical fact of that state of affairs – assuming, of course, that the theory in question is true.[37] Consistent with it being a theoretical truth within a naturalistic schema and consistent with the physicalist-functionalist theory of things in question being true, it comes as no surprise to find that the proposition that in ascribing agency, all interpretive agents possess and interpretively rely upon a theory of agency (and not some other means) is, in fact, supported by empirical evidence that that is the case.[38] Such empirical evidence lends support not only to the proposition in question, but also to the physicalist-functionalist account of things advocated here within which it is articulated. The physicalist-functionalist theory of agency, action and intentionality advocated here is, in this respect, compatible with the empirical evidence and with our best science on agents and their actions. We are justified in adopting the physicalist-functionalist account at large. We are justified as a theoretical matter and as an empirical matter in accepting the so-called 'theory-theory' of agency ascription which flows from it.[39]

In Chapter 1, I argued against adopting a non-physicalist account of things in making sense of the world – including, agency and action. No such account can find any place within the physicalistic system of knowledge. It can find no support in our best science. It follows from that argument that we should not adopt an account of the ascription of agency rooted in a non-physicalist account of things – for example, an account which posits the deployment by an interpreter of some non-physicalistic, non-functionalist, non-theoretical *intuition* about agency.[40] Further, though, even within a broadly physicalist account of things, we should reject any account of agency ascription which is not optimally compatible with the physicalist-functionalist view offered here. An account of agency ascription which is most compatible with physicalist-functionalism (and by virtue of that, with our best science and empirical evidence) should be preferred to one that is not. For

theories are 'information-bearing systems which yield explanations and predictions, which support counterfactual projection, which may postulate unobservables and may implicitly define concepts, and which achieve cognitive economy by integration of information under a small number of general principles'. The concept of agency described in Chapter 2 meets this set of criteria.

37 Of course, within such a schema, the empirical fact of a state of affairs does not entail the theoretical necessity of that state of affairs because a range of alternative empirical facts may be consistent with the theory in question.

38 Premack and Woodruff (1978), Wimmer and Perner (1983), Wellman (1990), Gopnik (1993 and 1996), Astington (1996), Botterill (1996).

39 Wellman (1990) pp. 94–8.

40 A means which certain cultural incommensurabilists seem to be committed to, as we shall see in the next chapter.

that reason, we should reject the most popular alternative account of interpretation and agency ascription presently advocated by theorists – the so-called simulation theory of interpretation. Though, arguably compatible with physicalism per se, this account does not follow from and is not compatible with the physicalist-*functionalist* account of agency, action and intentionality argued for here.[41] Nor, as a result, is it compatible with our best science and empirical evidence on the subject.[42]

Additionally, simulation theory suffers a number of independent theoretical flaws which should encourage us to rule it out of contention as a plausible theory of agency ascription and of interpretation, at large.[43] I do not intend to engage in a sustained critique of simulationism here. I merely direct the reader to the arguments offered by a number of theorists that a simulation theory bereft of functionalist and theory-theory content cannot provide a credible account of intentionality and interpretation.[44] Ultimately, as physicalists and functionalists, we are most justified in adopting a theory-theory approach to interpretation and the ascription of agency.[45] We are justified in accepting the proposition that all

---

41 For example, theory-theory is more consistent than simulation theory with the epistemic and methodological monism of physicalism according to which all phenomena in the world are predicted and explained by the one theoretical means. Given that simulation theorists do not deny the role of theorizing in making sense of other aspects of the world, theorizing has a better claim than simulation as the means by which we explain and predict (interpret) the behaviour of ourselves and others.

42 See Davies and Stone (1995) and Carruthers and Smith (1996) for a useful collection of essays on this issue. Notable essays include Carruthers (1996), Nichols et al. (1996) and Perner (1996). See also Nichols and Stich (2003).

43 Botterill (1996) and Stone and Davies (1996). Botterill and Carruthers (1999) p. 81 argue that 'theory-theory not only furnishes us with a philosophical account of what conceptions of mental state types are: according to theory-theory it is also the folk psychological theory which supplies the ordinary mindreader with those very conceptions. Simulationism, cannot very well just borrow this functionalist account, according to which such states as belief, desire, hope and fear are understood in terms of their general causal interactions with other mental states, characteristic stimuli, intentions and subsequent behaviour. Simulationism has to give up on the functionalist account of how we understand concepts in the vocabulary of propositional attitudes and intentional states – because such an account effectively involves implicit grasp of a theory. This looks like a serious gap unless the simulationist can come up with an equally plausible account of how we might conceptualise the propositional attitudes'. It is worth noting that the flaws in simulation theory provide further reason to accept a physicalist-functionalist account of agency and action rather than some non-functionalist account.

44 See, again, Davies and Stone (1995) and Carruthers and Smith (1996).

45 Even if it turns out that agency ascription and interpretation are *partly* theoretical and *partly* simulationist – as some have argued (e.g. Stich and Nichols (2003)) – the argument I offer in Chapter 6 about the limits of conceptual difference largely stands. My descriptive account here is, in proper physicalistic spirit, always open to empirical and theoretical counterargument and revision.

interpretive agents (including judges) possess and apply a theory of agency in ascribing agency and action to agents and their behaviour.

Returning to our original complex proposition, we are also justified in holding that the theory of agency possessed by all interpretive agents is *largely true*.[46] Again, this follows from the terms of the physicalist-functionalist account of things according to which an agent is a being whose action-relevant beliefs are largely true.[47] To the extent that an agent is an interpretive agent, his interpretation relevant beliefs are largely true. It is theoretically necessary on this account of things that interpretive agents possess a largely true theory of agency – that is, a theory of agency true enough to enable interpretive agents to get agency ascription right to whatever extent justifies us in conceiving of them as interpretive agents. In addition, of course, there is sound empirical evidence of the widespread success of interpretive agents in ascribing agency and action to each other.[48] As a matter of fact, they generally get such ascription right. That the theory they rely upon in ascribing agency is largely true is the best explanation for such success.[49] As Kathleen Lennon argues, 'the presuppositions on which such [interpretive] explanations rest are likely to be true, and provide an instructive insight into our mode of responding to our environment'.[50] These presuppositions constitute a theory of agency.

In addition to this, empirical evidence also points to the *innateness* in physiologically normal human beings of some significant part of a theory of agency.[51]

---

46 That is, true enough to render them capable of ascribing agency with degree of success capable of individuating them as interpretive agents by reference to our best concept of such agents – which is to say, capable of justifying the ascription of the concept of interpretive agent to them. This is not an uncontroversial point. Some have argued that the folk theory of agency, as well as the associated folk theory of mind to be discussed below, is or may be largely false despite its interpretive success. See Churchland (1981) and Stich (1983) chs 10 and 11.

47 It is by virtue of his beliefs being largely true that his actions are largely successful in realizing his desires, given those beliefs.

48 Wellman (1990), Gopnik and Wellman (1992), Gopnik (1993 and 1996), Astington (1996) and Botterill (1996).

49 Astington et al. (1988) p. 3. Of course, there is more to interpretive success than merely possessing a largely true theory of agency. The interpretive agent must (as a matter of theoretical necessity) possess a cognitive capacity to successfully apply his largely true theory of agency to evidential situations that confront him from time to time – that is, a capacity to soundly reason from theory and beliefs about the evidential situation to conclusion about the agency and activity of that situation. An interpretive agent's theory of agency may contain some propositions which are not true. That agent may also on occasion fail to apply that theory properly to the evidential situation confronting him or may fail to reason soundly to a conclusion about agency or activity.

50 Lennon (1990) pp. 11–12.

51 Either possessed in some prototypical form at infancy or emerging in early childhood out of an innate neurophysiological mechanism by virtue of some combination of neurophysiological development and learning (via environmental, including social,

That is, humans possess, by virtue of the physical structure of their neural systems, a genetically grounded realization base for the set of beliefs which comprise the innate part of a theory of agency. Botterill and Carruthers, for example, rely on sound empirical findings in developmental psychology in arguing that a theory of agency comprises part of the normal, native, cognitive endowment of humans and enables them to recognize certain other beings – especially, other humans – as agents.[52] Nichols and Stich similarly argue on the basis of scientific findings in developmental psychology that physiologically normal humans are innately programmed to ascribe agency on the basis of certain visual and other cues.[53] Scientific evidence of developmental rigidity in the capacity of human children to identify agents and actions points to the fact that some part of a theory of agency is innate to all humans and that interpretive development, generally, within humans involves a genetically controlled process of theoretical maturation.[54]

This is not to say, though, that interpretive agents cannot supplement and refine their innate theory of agency (and their interpretive skills) over the course of their lives by a process of individual learning in response to their direct experience of other agents or by a process of socialization into the potentially more sophisticated and practically adequate folk theoretical agency beliefs of their conceptual community or by adopting the relevant findings of philosophical or scientific psychology in this regard. Clearly they can. Nichols and Stich, for example, point to sound empirical evidence that whilst there is an innate interpretive capacity whose developmental staging is the same across cultures, it is surrounded by a variable body of cultural accretions and concepts.[55] This points to the possibility of individual interpretive agents having better or worse interpretive capacities than other agents, including at the level of agency and action ascription.

---

cognitive input). I need not take sides in this issue. See Leslie (1991), Gopnik and Melzoff (1993), Baron-Cohen (1995), Gopnik (1996), Segal (1996) and Nichols and Stich (2003). The fact that the theory of agency is innate does not entail that it is true as a matter of logical (or even theoretical) necessity. It does not entail that it is true a priori in any strong sense of this notion. We might make sense of such theory in terms of a weak notion of the a priori along the lines pioneered by Quine (1953b) and refined by Henderson (1993) and others. That is, as central to all of the systems of beliefs about the world (worldviews) maintained by interpretive agents but always vulnerable to revision or rejection in the face of significant enough empirical evidence or changes in the system of beliefs about the world in which it is logically situated.

52 Botterill and Carruthers (1999) pp. 78–9, 94.

53 Nichols and Stich (2003) pp. 96–7.

54 Astington et al. (1988) p. 14 and Gopnik (1996). These and other theorists (Wellman (1990), Avis and Harris (1991), Botterill (1996), Astington (1996)) point to evidence that all children achieve the same ability to utilize a theory of agency at much the same age, independent of differences of intelligence and social input.

55 Nichols and Stich (2003) pp. 3–4 and pp. 206–9. See also Miller (1984), Gopnik (1996) p. 171, Astington (1996) p. 186, Lillard (1998) and Nisbett et al. (2001).

If follows from the empirical evidence of innateness just mentioned, together with additional empirical evidence in neuro-science that there are no relevant differences in the neuro-physical (realizer) properties of interpretive agents or racial or cultural classes of interpretive agent, that all interpretive agents (including judges) possess largely the *same* innate theory of agency.[56] As far as the non-innate part of a theory of agency goes, an increasing body of social scientific evidence points to a significant part of that part also being universally shared by interpretive agents by virtue of a universally endured process of learning and socialization.[57] Indeed, if we accept that the non-innate part of an agent's theory of agency is largely true, and if we accept as a theoretical matter (arising out of the terms of the physicalistic metaphysics and method we are relying on here) that there is only *one* true theory of agency, we are led to conclude that the content of some part of the non-innate part of the theory of agency possessed by interpretive agents is shared by all of them.[58] Indeed, if we accept the theoretical premise that there is only one true theory of agency (or of anything for that matter), as well as the premise that the theory of agency possessed by all interpretive agents is true in both its innate and learned elements, then the universal sharedness of *both* the innate and the learned elements of that theory on the part of interpretive agents follows as a logical matter.

We can make explanatory sense of this idea in sound physicalistic terms by stepping back a little and informing our consideration of things by the relevant findings of the best of the biological, sociological and psychological sciences. If we accept the evidence and arguments offered in those sciences of the general functionality of neuro-physical evolutionary process over time, of the social transmission of knowledge across generations and of the epistemic development of the individual over the course of his life, and if we accept the evolutionary, socially and psychological *value* of successful interpretive practice, we might expect a true rather than untrue propositions of a theory of agency to be biologically and socially transmitted to generations of interpretive agents and to be learned by individual agents over the course of their lives. And to the extent that there is only *one* true theory to be transmitted or learned, we might expect the *same* true theory to be transmitted to or learned by all interpretive agents. Thus, it is consistent with all we know about the way the world is as physicalists – with our best science

56 Wellman (1990), Botterill and Carruthers (1999) pp. 79–80. If their relevant neuro-physiological properties are the same, their higher order beliefs and possessed theories are the same. This follows from the supervenience of beliefs and possessed theories on relevant neuro-physiological properties (a relationship comprehended by that of realization).

57 Astington et al. (1988), Gopnik (1996), Wellman (1998), Nichols and Stich (2003).

58 It is possible (and indeed, evidence of different levels of agency ascription skill in individuals supports it being a fact) that given individuals and groups of agents may possess non-innate elements of a theory of agency not possessed by other individuals and groups. That is, theories of agency may differ from each other around the edges.

– to think that a single theory of agency is possessed by all interpretive agents – including culturally different ones.

And as far as the actual content of that core, universally shared theory of agency goes, there is good reason to believe that it takes the form of the *physicalist-functionalist* theory of agency, action and intentionality outlined earlier in this book. That is, the theory of agency shared by all interpretive agents is a physicalist-functionalist one along the lines elaborated in Chapter 2.[59] Again, this follows as both a theoretical-logical and an empirical matter. As far as the empirical evidence goes, not only do the findings of developmental psychology point to the innate possession of a theory of agency *per se*, but those findings indicate that the content of that theory takes the form of a physicalist-functionalist psychology.[60] Botterill and Carruthers, for example, point to evidence that by virtue of their innate properties, humans cannot help but think about each other in terms of beliefs, desires and a governing rationality – that is, in the terms of a physicalistic-functionalist theory of agency. They point to a body of empirical evidence which supports the proposition that normal humans are physiologically *programmed* to think about and act towards others (as well as themselves) not only theoretically but physicalist-functionalist theoretically – that is, in terms of the various phenomena outlined in Chapter 2 of this book.

Additionally, as a theoretical matter, it follows from the propositions maintained by physicalist-functionalists that all interpretive agents possess the same theory of agency, that that theory is largely true, that there is only one true theory of agency; and that the one true theory of agency is the physicalist-functionalist theory of agency, that all interpretive agents, therefore, possess the physicalist-functionalist theory of agency.[61] This interrelated set of propositions collaborates not merely to justify the conclusion just reached but also to justify the general proposition stated at the commencement of this present discussion that in ascribing agency, all interpretive agents (including judges) possess and interpretively rely upon the same partially innate, partially socialized, largely true, physicalist-functionalist theory of agency.

The physicalist-functionalist theory of agency relied upon by interpretive agents is comprised of a range of propositions and component concepts, specifically

59 There is an issue here as to whether the folk theory of agency is as true and complete as the philosophical and scientific theory of agency and whether it is better thought of as comprising some practically adequate part (as far as day to day interpretive practice is concerned) of that more true and complete theory of agency. Recall our discussion in Chapter 4 to do with the partial possession of concepts and the failure to possess a concept to a practically adequate degree.

60 Premack and Woodruff (1978), Wimmer and Perner (1983), Wellman (1990), Gopnik (1996), Botterill (1996), Nichols and Stich (2003).

61 Botterill and Carruthers (1999) p. 9 state that '[a]ccording to functionalism, psychological knowledge will always be of states with a certain role, characterised in terms of how they are produced and of their effects on both other such states and behaviour'.

those of the physicalist-functionalist theory of agency elaborated in this book. It comprises propositions such as 'an agent is a being which behaviourally interacts with its environment in a manner caused by intentional states under the governance of a set of intentional regularities' and 'an action is the causing of a behavioural event by a complex of intentional events'.[62] It comprises concepts such as those of agent, action, intentional state, belief, desire, environmental input, behavioural output, causation, and the like. These concepts, in turn analyse out into a set of constituent sub-concepts (mentioned throughout this book), rendering possession of a theory of agency entailing of possession of a substantial scheme of agency-related concepts.[63] Thus, it follows from the complex proposition about theories of agency justified above that all interpretive agents (including judges and testimonial agents) *qua interpretive agents* possess and interpretively rely upon a partially innate, partially learned, physicalist-functionalist set of agency-related concepts – a set of concepts I will term universal agency concepts. It is because interpretive agents possess a practically adequate set of such concepts – concepts that adequately define the phenomena in question for interpretive purposes – that they are able to correctly identify agents and actions as such and go on to successfully predict and explain the behaviour of those agents and actions in their interpretive practice. It is because they possess a set of such concepts that they are interpretive agents.[64]

I have analysed in some detail the justification for the complex proposition asserted above not only in order to shed some light on the agency ascription phase of the interpretive process but also because this proposition and various of its justificatory elements are of great importance in the discussion about the limits of conceptual difference which is to follow in the next chapter. As an incidental – though not unimportant – matter, it not to be supposed by all this talk of theorizing on the part of interpretive agents that they need *expressly or consciously* hold the tenets of the physicalist-functionalist theory of agency universally possessed by

---

62 Wellman (1990) pp. 3–4 conceives of the theory of agency possessed by all interpretively normal human beings as comprising certain core propositions, including that there is a mental realm or mind associated with agents, that an agent's mind is distinct from his behaviour and external environment (there is a physical realm distinct from the mental realm), that mind causes behaviour and is caused by events in the external environment, that beliefs and desires exist and perform distinctive roles within the realm of mind, and so on.

63 An agency-related conceptual scheme.

64 Of course, as we saw in the previous chapter it is possible that interpretive agents possess a range of concepts in addition to these universal agency concepts which are not universally shared. It is also worth noting here that the possession of such concepts is a pre-condition of being an agent capable of interpretation but not of being an agent *per se*. Animal agents not capable of interpreting each other's behaviour need not possess these concepts as a theoretical necessity. They need only possess some or other set of concepts capable of rendering them able to rationally interact with their environment. No entailments as to conceptual content possessed flows from this condition of basic agency.

them. It is plain that most such agents do not. If called upon, most interpretive agents would not be able to articulate the content of the theory of agency they are purported here to possess to any or any epistemically adequate degree. This is not a problem for our analysis, though. We can make quite plausible sense of the idea of interpretive agents possessing a complex theory of agency and utilizing it in their engagement with the world without expressly or consciously doing so. That is, it is quite plausible to hold that they possess and apply the universal theory of agency in their interpretive practice tacitly, unconsciously or automatically.[65] There is nothing uniquely problematic about their doing so. The possession of a number of human cognitive capacities may be conceived of in terms of the tacit possession and application of a set of beliefs about the way things are in the world, the contents of which are systematic enough to justify description as a theory.

Human grammatical skills, for example, may be plausibly conceived of in terms of the possession and application of a theory of how to speak and write correctly – that is, a grammar comprising a systematic scheme of grammatical propositions. An agent may be able to speak grammatically and recognize grammatical utterances in others and yet not (and not be able to) consciously call to mind the propositions of the grammar she relies upon as she does so or even be able to give an explicit account of those propositions if asked. We need not deny that she possesses a theory of grammar (grammatical knowledge) on that basis. So too, an agent may be able to identify others as agents and yet not consciously call to mind or be able to give an explicit account of the psychological propositions about agency upon which she relies in doing so.[66] Nonetheless, both capacities here may be made sense of in terms of a tacit process of theorizing. They may plausibly be conceived of in terms of acting on the basis of some complex, interrelated and largely true set of beliefs about how things relevantly are.

Braddon-Mitchell and Jackson nicely capture this aspect of the interpretive process at large (including the ascription of agency phase) in their noting that,

> we have a rich and complex implicit knowledge (along with our explicit knowledge) of the interconnections between our mental states and their inputs and outputs. What reveals our implicit knowledge in the case of grammar is our ability to classify sentences as grammatical or ungrammatical. What reveals our implicit knowledge in the case of the mind is our ability to predict and explain behaviour in circumstances by means of mental states … the fact that we can make the predictions shows that we have cottoned on to the crucial regularities – otherwise, our predictive capacities would be a miracle. They show we have an implicit mastery of a detailed, complex scheme that interconnects inputs, outputs and mental states … Perhaps one day the [scheme] will be made fully explicit – what there is waiting to be elucidated will be elucidated … [It] is

65 Braddon-Mitchell and Jackson (1996) p. 146, Botterill (1996) p. 113, and Nichols and Stich (2003) ch. 3.

66 Which is not to say that she could not do so if asked.

> not something anyone can yet write down, but it exists to be written down in theory.[67]

Ascribing agency and activity, then, involves the judge recognizing the testimonial agent to some practically adequate degree as a being which is subject to bodily events, certain of which are caused by – and which may, therefore, be explained with reference to – a complex of intentional events under the governance of some or other minimally rational set of regularities which result in that agent, in general, possessing largely true beliefs and largely succeeding in realizing her desires given her beliefs. As Macdonald and Pettit state, '[i]n taking any piece of behaviour as an action we assume that it issues from a desire to achieve a certain outcome and a belief that the course of behaviour in question at least stands a good chance of realising that outcome: we assume ... that the event is [practically] rational'.[68] Ascribing agency involves believing the subject to be a being whose behaviour can be made sense of in terms of a rationalized belief-desire psychology (a theory of mind), whose beliefs are largely true and logically consistent and whose desires are largely appropriate and non-contradictory, given her beliefs.[69] And it involves subsequently acting towards that being on that basis. Such ascription imposes, as a matter of theoretical necessity, a requirement of minimal rationality upon the agent which, as we shall see below, reduces the number of plausible candidate behaviourally causal intentional complexes which might be posited to explain his behaviour.[70] It does not follow from an ascription of minimal rationality to testimonial agent that that agent be governed by any *particular* set of intentional regularities. Only that he be governed by some or other set of regularities which meets the minimal standards of rationality implicated in the universal theory of agency possessed by the judge.[71]

---

67 Braddon-Mitchell and Jackson (1996) pp. 56–8.

68 Macdonald and Pettit (1981) p. 27. In interpreting behaviour, 'we are concerned with ascribing to the agent a complex of beliefs and desires such that granted that complex the action is [practically] rational; it is an event which the [agent] believed would bring about or at least make more likely a state of affairs that he desired ...'. Ibid. p. 11.

69 Macdonald and Pettit (1981) p. 24, Pettit (1993) p. 235, Lennon (1990) ch. 1. Being part of a body of beliefs which is largely true is constitutive of being a belief. To the extent that governance by a set of intentional regularities or rationality is necessarily ascribed to an agent, this phase of the interpretive process may be conceived of as one involving the rationalization of the agent and her interaction with the world (including her behaviour).

70 This reduction of interpretive options takes place, as we shall see, through the mediation of the judge's theory of mind which (for a theoretically rational judge, at least) will reflect the constraints of the judge's theory of agency.

71 These standards may be conceived of as being weakly a priori in the sense that they are central to the judge's theory of agency but are not immune from revision or rejection in the face of significant discrepant experience or shifts in the judge's system of beliefs about the world at large. Henderson (1993) pp. 95–6.

In the context of a legal hearing, the correct ascription of agency and activity to the bodily events of a testimonial witness will generally (and, of course, contingently in a given situation) not pose a problem for the judge, even under conditions of significant conceptual difference. Agency will be readily and correctly ascribed to such a witness as a matter of course. The circumstances of the hearing will dictate this.[72] Of course, whether she can go on to successfully interpret the behaviour of the testimonial agent is another matter. More is required for that than the mere ascription of agency. A descriptively adequate theory of mind must be possessed and applied by the judge, together with knowledge of the actual environmental, behavioural and intentional properties of the witness or claimant under interpretation – that is, a descriptively adequate theory of the testimonial agent.

Developing and Deploying a Theory of Mind

As mentioned, the second, phase of the interpretive process is analysable as involving a complex process of inference[73] on the part of the judge from what is believed or assumed by the judge to be the case about the present behavioural outputs, environmental inputs and behaviourally relevant background intentional states and governing rationality of the testimonial agent – a set of beliefs we may conceive of as comprising the judge's theory of the testimonial agent – to a belief about what is not yet the subject of belief by her – namely, the identity of the behaviourally explanatory intentional complex causing that agent's testimonial behaviour.[74] This process of inference takes place within the context of a further set of beliefs maintained by the judge about the causal regularities which typically obtain between the environmental inputs, behavioural outputs and intentional states of some set of human agents (conceivably, at least, at this stage, including

72 Even cultural incommensurabilists could not seriously deny a judicial capacity to, at the very least, ascribe agency within this context. Certainly, in order to maintain the radical cultural incommensurability thesis, one would need to maintain such a capacity. It is a premise of the thesis that culturally different people are *agents* and not mere objects, for example. On what basis, then, could incommensurabilists deny such a capacity to a judicial member of their own cultural group? This phase of judicial interpretive practice, then, occurs relatively unproblematically in practice.

73 A number of theorists, including Botterill and Carruthers (1999) p. 9 and Heil (1998) p. 92 have conceived of this process of inference as a form of inference to the best explanation or as a mode of reverse engineering.

74 Recall that if the judge knew the identity of the behaviourally explanatory intentional states involved in the testimonial action there would be no need for her to engage in any process of interpretive inference to the identity of those states. Further, the judge's theory of the testimonial agent may include propositions describing interpretively relevant past environmental inputs and behavioural outputs (and intentional states for that matter). See below on this last point.

the testimonial agent in question) – a set of beliefs we may conceive of as the judge's theory of mind.

We can analyse this phase of the interpretive process as comprising four component sub-phases. The first comprises the development and application to the testimonial agent of a theory of mind. The second comprises the development and deployment by the judge of a theory of the testimonial agent under interpretation. The third involves the judge inferring within the theoretical parameters of these two theories to a provisionally held belief about the identity of the behaviourally explanatory intentional complex at work in the testimonial action under interpretation and the final phase involves the testing and revision of the various propositions involved in this process – whether they be those about the identity of the behaviourally explanatory complex or those about the behaviourally relevant background intentional profile[75] of the testimonial agent – in the face of any further justified beliefs about the testimonial agent which might be subsequently acquired by the judge. Let me consider the first of these sub-phases now.

An interpretive agent is an agent who possesses concepts of some set of the intentional states possessed by some set of human agents. An agent would not be an interpretive agent – that is, an agent capable of interpreting the behaviour of some set of human agents – without possessing such concepts. How could she identify an intentional cause of some or other behaviour – interpret that behaviour – without a concept of that intentional cause? We have seen in Chapter 2 that intentional states are individuated by the set of causal relations they typically enjoy with environmental inputs, behavioural outputs and other intentional states, against the background of a set of other intentional states.[76] Concepts of intentional states are complex physicalist-functionalist definitions constituted by a proposition (or set of propositions) describing the set of causal relations which individuate those states.[77] Thus, by virtue of possessing a set of concepts of intentional states, an interpretive agent such as a judge necessarily possesses a set of beliefs about some set of the causal relations which typically obtain between the environmental and intentional inputs and intentional and behavioural outputs of some set[78] of human agents. She possesses a set of beliefs with physicalist-functionalist propositional content.

Again, given the systematic, unifying and explanatory nature of the propositional content of such beliefs, we can construe their possession by an

75 'Behaviourally relevant background intentional profile' here means the agent's behaviourally relevant background intentional complex together with the set of intentional regularities the agent is subject to (that is, his rationality class).

76 They are individuated by the typical causal-functional role they play within a system of environmental and intentional inputs and intentional and behavioural outputs.

77 A concept of an intentional state comprises a description of the tripartite causal-functional set of relations which that state typically enjoys with environmental, behavioural and other intentional phenomena.

78 Conceivably, at this stage, the total set of human agents.

interpretive agent in terms of the possession of a *theory* of the relevant causal relations which obtain in relation to some set of human agents, a theory I will term a theory of mind.[79] Many other theorists agree with this characterization. Kathleen Lennon, for example, argues that the set of propositions informing the beliefs relied upon by judges in interpreting behaviour 'has the status of a causal explanatory theory; for it employs a system of conceptualization of reality which generates laws and generally leads to successful predictions and retrodictions'.[80] Likewise, Botterill and Carruthers point out that,

> our psychological knowledge of others [is] on a par with theoretical knowledge in two respects. Firstly, the functional roles assigned to various mental states depend upon systematic relations between such states and their characteristic causes and effects. So it seems that we have a common-sense theory of mind, or a folk psychology which implicitly defines ordinary psychological concepts. Secondly, the application of that theory is justified in the way that theories usually are, namely by success in prediction and explanation.[81]

Given the nature of its propositional content, the theory of mind possessed by an interpretive agent is of a physicalist-functionalist kind. Consistent with the theoretical necessity just outlined of interpretive agents possessing a physicalist-functionalist theory of mind as part of their interpretive apparatus, is a body of empirical evidence in developmental psychology and other related disciplines to this effect.[82] Such evidence adds to the set of physicalistically sound reasons available for believing that interpretation proceeds by means of a theoretical procedure involving in part the possession and deployment of such a theory of mind.[83]

---

79 Botterill and Carruthers (1999) p. 78. As mentioned above, the judge's theory of mind comprises part of the judge's general psychology. I have already argued in the Chapter 2 that the regularities which obtain in the intentional realm, though not exceptionless and law-like, are regular enough to ground workable predictions and explanations of thought and behaviour and are, hence, sufficient to ground a workable theory.

80 Lennon (1990) p. 12. See also Braddon-Mitchell and Jackson (1996) p. 256.

81 Botterill and Carruthers (1999) pp. 9–10. Again, Botterill (1996) p. 110 defines theories as 'information-bearing systems which yield explanations and predictions, which support counterfactual projection, which may postulate unobservables and may implicitly define concepts, and which achieve cognitive economy by integration of information under a small number of general principles'. A judge's general psychology, comprising a theory of agency and a theory of mind, meets this set of criteria.

82 Gopnik and Wellman (1992), Astington (1996), Botterill (1996), Gopnik (1996), Nichols and Stich (2003) p. 212.

83 It is worth noting here that the theoretical relationship between a theory of mind and a set of intentional state concepts is a dialectic one. Possession of a set of intentional state concepts entails the possession of a theory of mind. Equally, though, possession of a theory of mind entails the possession of a set of intentional state concepts – namely, those

A judge's theory of mind is analysable as containing a set of propositions describing, at various levels of generality, the causal relations that typically exist between the environmental inputs, intentional states and behavioural outputs of *some set* of human agents. It may include propositions such as 'for all normal agents, the environmental event of there being ochre in front of the agent, typically causes the belief that there is ochre in front of the agent, provided certain other intentional states x, y, and z obtain', or 'for all normal agents, the desire to dig ochre out of the ground typically causes the agent to engage in ochre digging behaviour, provided that certain other intentional states p, q and r obtain', and so on.[84] The judge's overall set of theory of mind propositions may (conceivably, at least, at this stage) contain general propositions which describe some set of the intentional regularities which *all* agents are subject to, kind-specific propositions which describe some set of the intentional regularities which some or other *group or kind* of agents is subject to, and idiosyncratic provisions which describe some set of the intentional regularities which some specific idiosyncratic agent is subject to.[85] In her interpretive practice, the reasonable judge will rely upon those theory of mind propositions which she has reason to believe apply to the testimonial agent in the evidential situation in question. We can conceive of the judge working out which set of theory of mind propositions actually apply to the testimonial agent in question – general, kind-specific or idiosyncratic – in terms of her identifying that agent's rationality class. Such identification takes place at the 'theorizing the testimonial agent' phase of the interpretive process described below.[86]

To take up our ochre testimony example, a judge's theory of mind might be conceived of as including, say, the theoretical proposition that for all normal testimonial agents, the environmental event of the performance of an utterance by another agent within the hearing range of the testimonial agent which in the testimonial agent's linguistic community signifies, 'Please tell the judge what x

---

intentional states which feature in that theory. Botterill and Carruthers (1999) p. 10 state that 'we have a common-sense theory of mind, or a folk psychology which implicitly defines ordinary psychological concepts'. Possession of a theory of mind and a set of intentional state concepts also entails possession of a set of concepts about the environmental and bodily phenomena which feature in those concepts and that theory. Possession of a theory of mind – being an interpretive agent- therefore involves being in possession of a substantial and multi-varied set of concepts. To be an interpretive agent is to possess a potentially vast and complex conceptual scheme. It is to inhabit a world.

84 Where x, y and z etc. stand for some or other set of background intentional states.

85 For example, the proposition 'for this specific (and idiosyncratic) agent, the environmental event of there being ochre in front of the agent, typically causes the belief that there is charcoal in front of the agent, provided certain other intentional states x, y, and z obtain'. See Davidson (1986b) on this last point.

86 For the sake of simplicity, I will tend to focus the following discussion on general theory of mind propositions. Nothing important hinges on this at this stage.

is',[87] typically causes a desire in that testimonial agent to perform an utterance which in that agent's linguistic community signifies what he believes to be the definition of x, *provided that* the testimonial agent desires to cause the judge to possess a true belief about the identity of the agent's (belief about the) definition of x and believes that this desire can be realized by performing an utterance which in the agent's linguistic community signifies what he believes to be the definition of x, and provided that the testimonial agent possesses some further set of behaviourally relevant background intentional states (a, b, c ...). The judge's theory of mind may also include the theoretical proposition that for all normal testimonial agents, the desire in that testimonial agent to perform an utterance which in the agent's linguistic community signifies what he believes to be the definition of x typically causes the behavioural event of the agent performing an utterance 'y' which signifies in the agent's linguistic community what the agent believes to be the definition of x, *provided that* the testimonial agent believes that x is whatever the utterance 'y' signifies in his linguistic community, and believes that the utterance 'y' signifies in the agent's linguistic community the definition of x, and believes that by performing the utterance 'y' he will typically realize the desire to perform an utterance which in the agent's linguistic community signifies what he believes to be the definition of x, and provided that the testimonial agent possesses some further set of behaviourally relevant background intentional states (d, e, f ...).[88]

In interpreting a witness's testimonial behaviour in uttering 'a yellow powder which is found in the ground and which is used for ceremonial purposes' in response to the environmental event of counsel uttering 'Please tell the judge what [ochre] is',[89] the judge might call upon a set of theoretical propositions contained in her theory of mind, including the two propositions mentioned above, to infer from her beliefs about the observed environmental and behavioural events together with certain other beliefs she holds or is prepared to assume about the agent's behaviourally relevant background intentional profile – in this case, say, beliefs or assumptions that the agent possesses the behaviourally relevant background intentional states (a, b, c, d, e, f ...) mentioned above – to infer to the possession by the agent of a set of behaviourally explanatory intentional states involved in the action, including the belief and desires mentioned above. This set will include the belief that that [ochre] is whatever the utterance 'a yellow powder which is found in the ground and which is used for ceremonial purposes' signifies in the agent's linguistic community. Coupled with her knowledge of what the utterance, in fact,

87 Where x stands for a vocal signifier which in the agent's linguistic community signifies some phenomenon x.

88 Note that the judge's theory of mind cannot possess a concept or definition of ochre where she does not possess that concept.

89 Where [ochre] is conceived of by the judge at this stage as merely a vocal signifier which in the agent's linguistic community signifies some phenomenon of which the judge has, as yet (in our hypothetical scenario), no concept.

signifies in the agent's linguistic community, the judge may infer to a belief that the agent believes that ochre is a yellow powder which is found in the ground and which is used for ceremonial purposes. By inferring to this behaviourally explanatory complex of intentional states (including, most importantly the concept-containing belief in question), the judge successfully interprets the testimonial behaviour. She identifies its intentional explanation given her purposes.

And by doing so, she comes to possess the concept of ochre if she didn't already possess it. By doing so, she overcomes conceptual difference in this regard. Thus, the judge's theory of mind provides an inferential matrix for making intentional sense of observed or otherwise cognitively accessed behaviour within an observed or otherwise cognitively accessed environmental context, against the background of a set of beliefs about the intentional states possessed by the testimonial agent. It is important to note that this theory is utilized in interpreting the behaviour of a testimonial agent only in conjunction with a theory of the environmental, behavioural and behaviourally relevant background intentional profile of that agent (the judge's theory of the testimonial agent), the nature of which I will have more to say about below. Further, for much the same reasons as those rehearsed above in relation to the possession and deployment of a theory of agency, it is no objection to the account offered here about a theory of mind that such theory is not consciously possessed and deployed. The theoretical machinations involved in this phase of the interpretive process may, again, be quite plausibly understood as tacit ones.

The content of a judge's theory of mind is a product of both her own cognitive development in the face of her individual experience of the interaction of agents with the world and that of the community of interpretive agents into which she is born and subsequently socialized.[90] The theory of mind maintained by a folk or individual is a function of the environmental-intentional trajectory of that folk or individual through space and time along the lines discussed in the previous chapter. As with a theory of agency, there is scientific evidence arising out of neuro-physiology and developmental psychology to support the contention that neuro-physiologically normal humans have an innate capacity to acquire, develop and apply some or other theory of mind in making sense of themselves and others and that they are innately programmed to, in fact, do so in the face of their interaction with the world.[91] There is, though, no compelling empirical or other

90 Lewis (1972), Wellman (1990, 1995 and 1998), Harris (1995), Astington (1996), Gopnik (1996), Carruthers and Smith (1996) p. 5, Lillard (1997).

91 Evidence of developmental rigidity across all cultures – that is, a genetically controlled process of maturation – in the development and deployment of a theory of mind backs this up. Wellman (1990), Leslie (1991), Gopnik and Melzoff (1993), Baron-Cohen (1995), and Nichols and Stich (2003) ch. 3.

reason (at present, at least) to believe that any of the *actual propositions* informing a theory of mind are innate.[92]

Rather, the empirical evidence suggests that the propositional content of theories of mind emerges as a result of an individual agent's experiential and cognitive engagement post-natally with human agents interacting with some part of the world including her socialization by such engagement into the theory of mind (and the concomitant scheme of intentional state concepts) historically acquired and developed and presently possessed by her interpretive and conceptual community or 'folk'.[93] And this is entirely consistent with the theoretical account of beliefs and their acquisition offered in this book. Human agents are born and socialized into a community of agents which may be conceived of as an entity existing and acting temporally and spatially so as to acquire, develop and transmit to its members a set of beliefs about the intentional regularities governing the behavioural interaction with the world of that community's members and other agents that community has relevantly encountered over its history. Over the course of their lives as members of such communities, individual agents acquire some part of their community's folk theory of mind as they develop an ability to make sense of and predict the behaviour of themselves and other agents. This process takes place as part of their overall cognitive development.

As Macdonald and Pettit point out, a folk psychological theory in both its theory of agency and theory of mind aspects,

> is something which each of us picks up in developing competence at accounting for actions, both our own and those of other people. The conception is not appropriated in the way in which we typically learn bits of theory: the initiate is not given a set of axioms about the antecedents of action, nor is he told any particular story about the workings of the mind. What happens rather is that he is introduced to the use of various concepts by means of which action is explained. He learns when it is appropriate to regard a piece of behaviour as action proper, and not just a reflex, what sorts of questions it is then in order to consider, and how he may make a case for one answer rather than another. In learning these things he picks up concepts such as those of intention, desire, decision, perception, judgment, belief and a host of associates. The development of skill at applying those concepts, and at using them in the exploration of action, means initiation into the orthodox conception of agents.[94]

---

92 Except at a level of generality which might render certain putative propositions of a theory of mind more properly classifiable as propositions of the innate theory of agency. Of course, were evidence in support of the innateness of the propositions of a theory of mind to come to light at some point in the future, that would only support my theoretical argument about the limits of conceptual difference.

93 See Astington (1996) for an interesting discussion of the mechanics of this process.

94 Macdonald and Pettit (1981) p. 58.

Thus, there is no need for a judge to develop her own theory of mind from scratch on the basis of her own cognitive engagement with agents in the world. Over time, she can appropriate the accumulated psychological wisdom of her folk. Additionally, though, over the course of her life she is able to supplement and refine her received folk theory of mind and develop a more comprehensive theory and an improved interpretive competence, by means of her own individual cognitive and interpretive encounters with agents acting in the world, as well as with theories of these things. That she can do so reflects an innate capacity on her part in this regard. One should not lose sight of the importance of this individualized mode of theory of mind construction, especially in the context of a discussion about the capacity of individual judges to acquire culturally different concepts.

Though her theory of mind will be generally true and largely comprehensive of those agents she and her folk habitually come in contact with, it does not follow from anything said so far that a judge is assured (as a matter of logical or even theoretical necessity) of possessing an interpretively adequate theory of mind for a given testimonial agent. Some set of the theory of mind propositions she relies upon in interpreting the testimonial agent may be false or may be not applicable to (may not be true of) the testimonial agent in question.[95] Alternatively, her theory of mind may not be comprehensive enough – it may not include propositions which describe the regularities which actually govern the testimonial action under interpretation. This is consistent with the points just made about the acquisition and development of a theory of mind, both communally and individually. The theory of mind maintained by a folk or individual is a function of the environmental-intentional trajectory of that folk or individual through space and time along the lines discussed in the previous chapter. As a result, the contents of a folk or individual theory of mind are inevitably limited by the nature and limits of that trajectory. A folk theory of mind arises as a theoretical response on the part of a community of interpretive agents to that limited set of the behavioural interactions of agents with their environment which the folk in question have come into cognitive contact with historically, both within and outside their community.

Because both individuals and communities of agents can and do differ in their experiential engagement with and theorizing about the world and the interaction of agents with that world, the propositional content of their theories of mind can and do differ between individuals and communities to a degree which reflects the degree of difference in their respective engagement with and making sense of their part of the world over time. That is, the members of one conceptual community (or members within a community) may possess theoretical beliefs about certain intentional regularities and may, therefore, possess certain intentional state concepts which members of another group do not possess.[96]

95 Though it may be applicable to or true of some other agent or set of agents.

96 Judges as a class may differ from other classes of agents within their conceptual communities in relation to the contents of the theory of mind and intentional conceptual scheme they possess and, as a result, may possess a capacity to interpret behaviour not

Though all interpretive agents possess some or other theory of mind, they do not necessarily possess the same theory of mind, nor do they necessarily possess different theories of mind. Such difference can be explained – indeed, it is to be expected – in light of the account of concept and belief acquisition outlined in the previous chapter. It is an empirically-interpretively determinable matter as to the degree to which the intentional concepts and propositions of a theory of mind are shared across communities (including universally shared) and what the identity of any such shared concepts and propositions might be. Any intellectually responsible theorist of these things must acknowledge Noam Chomsky's warning that '... in invoking folk psychology we have to be careful to observe the practice of serious ethnoscience, distinguishing parochial and culture-bound notions from the elements of 'folk theories' that are a common human endowment, grounded in our nature'.[97]

That an interpretive agent's theory of mind is *largely true* follows from the general ongoing success which interpretive agents have had historically and which they presently have in predicting and explaining the behaviour of others and themselves.[98] Folk and individual theories of mind are largely true – they (largely) accurately describe the intentional regularities human agents are subject to – because as a matter of fact they have been hypothesized, refined and confirmed through experience by communities and individuals over time with the aim of being largely true, as all largely true theories of things are.[99] As a result, there is reason to believe that a folk or individual theory of mind constitutes a higher order theory of things which broadly reflects the lower-order and physical causal regularities which exist between the lower-order and physical states of an agent's body, brain and world. But it does not follow from any of this that a given theory of mind – folk or individual – is either completely or necessarily true or comprehensive of all actual or possible intentional regularities which may obtain in the world. Like all broadly successful empirically-based theories of things it may be in error to some

possessed by those others. Further, within the community of indigenous land title judges, certain individuals may possess concepts of and maintain theoretical propositions about intentional phenomena which are not possessed by other judges and may hold an interpretive advantage as a result.

97 Chomsky (1994) p. 155. To the extent that a conceptual community is individuated as such on the basis of some significantly shared set of concepts and beliefs amongst its members, there will be a limit to how much those members can differ in regard to the set of concepts and beliefs they possess. Each member of a conceptual community may be taken to possess some (membership-sufficient) part of the conceptual scheme and worldview ascribable to the community at large.

98 Again, eliminativists such as Churchland (1979, 1981 and 1986) and one incarnation of Stich (1983), as well as certain interpretationists such as Dennett (1987) and Davidson (1970a) and (1974a) deny the truth of theory of mind propositions in the sense of accurately representing real phenomena.

99 Lennon (1990) pp. 11–12. Fodor (1974 and 1987) and Papineau (1993) pp. 65–8 agree with Lennon.

degree or limited in scope with reference to our best scientific knowledge about agents and the world – though, as a conceptual matter, it cannot be not so false or limited as to render an interpretive agent possessing such a theory so interpretively unsuccessful as to no longer qualify as an interpretive agent.[100] It is possible at a given point in time that an interpretive agent, including a judge, does not possess in her theory of mind a description of an intentional regularity knowledge of which is necessary for her to interpret a given testimonial or other action. In order to interpret such action, the judge must acquire knowledge of such regularity. She does so, as we have seen, by means of cognitively appropriating evidence (including further interpretable testimonial evidence) about that regularity.[101]

Although there is no strong empirical or other reason (at present, at least) to believe that any of the *actual propositions* informing a theory of mind are innate, there reason to believe that certain of the *conceptual* content of a theory of mind is innate – namely, the conceptual content inherent in the theory of agency which structures and informs each and every theory of mind. Though not all theories of mind need include the same set of environmental or intentional or bodily concepts – they need not and might not all include the concept of ochre, say[102] – they necessarily include, as a conceptual matter, certain concepts implicated in the very idea of their being a theory of mind. Recall what a theory of mind is. It is, as a conceptual matter, a set of propositions which describe the causal regularities which typically obtain between the environmental inputs, behavioural outputs and intentional states of human agents. Examples, include, say the proposition that for all agents, the environmental input event of there being ochre in front of the agent typically causes the belief that there is ochre in front of the agent, provided that the agent possesses some specific set of background intentional states (say, the belief

100 Flaws in folk and individual theories of mind have been identified by scientific psychological study. See Churchland (1979, 1981 and 1994), Stich (1983) and (1996) Chapters 2 and 3. Such flaws have grounded eliminativist calls for the abandonment of such theories of mind in favour of more precise and correct scientific theories of the regularities governing human behaviour. Despite the risk of error and consistent with the ontologically and epistemologically tolerant kind of physicalism I outlined in Chapter 1, I reject the wholesale scepticism of eliminativists such as Paul Churchland in relation to the truth and theoretical or practical value of folk and individual theories of mind. I agree with Kathleen Lennon (1990) p. 11 that 'reason-giving explanations form the basis of our everyday interaction with other people. They provide a model of understanding ourselves which is fundamental to both our view of ourselves and our view of others ... To reject such a model of understanding seems scarcely intelligible, indeed self-defeating'.

101 More on this below.

102 For the reasons set out in the previous chapter in regard to concept acquisition. The failure of an agent's or community's theory of mind to include a concept of ochre, for example, may be explained with reference to fact that that agent or community presently inhabits (and historically has inhabited) an environment which includes neither ochre nor any representation of or testimony about ochre and has not engaged in any kind of reasoning about the sub-concepts of ochre which might cause the possession of the concept of ochre.

that his sensory apparatus is functioning properly and so on) or the proposition that for all agents, the desire that ochre be dug out of the ground typically causes the behavioural output event of the agent digging ochre out of the ground, provided that the agent also possesses some specific set of background intentional states (say, the belief that by performing the bodily event associated with digging the desire in question might be realized). Though propositions such as these do not share all their concepts in common, they do share a certain set of their concepts in common. These include the concepts of agent, environmental input event, behavioural output event, intentional state, belief, desire, causation, and so on – concepts I have identified in the previous section as universal agency concepts.

Though the specific identity of the various environmental, intentional[103] and behavioural (bodily-environmental) concepts implicated in a theory of mind may differ from theory to theory, depending upon the environmental-intentional trajectories of the agents or sets of agents who possess the theories in question, what is common to all such theories (because they are theories of mind and not some other kind of thing) is some set of the set of universal agency concepts mentioned in the previous section of this chapter. Human theories of mind, though not necessarily sharing their propositional contents and many of their concepts (environmental, intentional and bodily concepts, for example), are all informed by a set of universal agency concepts, by some part of the universal theory of agency. There is, then, as a matter of theoretical necessity and empirical fact, a universally shared dimension to all of the different theories of mind which interpretive agents possess. It is this conceptual dimension which individuates those various theories as theories of mind.

This is to say that theories of mind are informed by and are articulated within an overarching theory of what an agent and an action are. A judge's theory of mind will necessarily be informed by the conceptual constraints of her theory of agency.[104] Further, by virtue of the fact that that theory of agency is vulnerable to empirical counterevidence and changes in the judge's overall body of theory about the world (phenomena which feed into the development of her theory of mind as well), it is also true to say that a judge's theory of mind will inform the judge's theory of agency. The two kinds of theory are dialectically interrelated.[105] A theory

---

103 By intentional concept here I mean concepts such as the concept of the belief that there is ochre in the ground, or the concept of the desire that the judge believe the utterance of the sentence "ochre is a yellow powder." I do not mean the general concept of belief or desire or intentional state which is universally possessed by all interpretive agents.

104 To the extent that a true theory of agency implicates a minimal rationality in all agents, a true theory of mind (grounded in such a theory of agency) will also in its propositional content reflect and be constrained by (to some weak a priori or analytical degree) the minimal rationality requirement governing agents. The minimal rationality implicated in a theory of agency conditions the development of the propositional contents of a theory of mind.

105 Indeed, there is a close relationship between *all three* of the theory types involved in interpretive action.

of mind, by its very nature, describes with some degree of accuracy the intentional regularities governing a certain kind of phenomenon – namely, agents. And agents are precisely the kind of phenomena comprehensively described by a theory of agency. Similarly, ascribing agency to an agent pursuant to a theory of agency involves believing that the behaviour of that agent can be predicted and explained on the basis of an account of some set of the intentional regularities governing human agents – that is, a theory of mind. A theory of agency foreshadows a theory of mind in this sense. Both kinds of theory are analysable as integrated with or components of what we might conceive of as a grand theory of the nature of agents and their governing intentional regularities – a true and complete general psychology, if you like – some part of which is possessed by interpretive agents. Indeed, our analytic distinguishing between these two kinds of theory – agency and mind – may be recognized as a theoretical conceit engaged in for heuristic reasons.[106]

Inferring to the Intentional Cause of Behaviour

The possession and application of both a theory of agency and a theory of mind are jointly necessary but not sufficient conditions for acquiring knowledge of the propositional content of the complex of intentional states which causes testimonial behaviour about a concept. In addition to these, the judge must possess and theoretically deploy some set of true beliefs about the present behaviour of the testimonial agent, the environmental situation of that agent and the behaviourally relevant background intentional profile of that agent at the time of interpretation. By 'profile' here, I mean both the agent's interpretively relevant background intentional states[107], *and* the mode of rationality (general, kind-specific or idiosyncratic) which, within the constraints of minimal rationality, governs the agent in the situation in question. Having ascribed agency to the testimonial agent, and with a comprehensive enough theory of mind in hand identifying which environmental or intentional events typically cause which intentional events and which intentional events typically cause which intentional or behavioural events in a set of human agents which includes the testimonial agent, and with a comprehensive enough set of beliefs about the behaviourally relevant background

106 As alluded to earlier in this chapter, if we generalize enough from specific propositions of a theory of mind, we reach a set of propositions which might find a place within a theory of agency – a theory of what an agent is. At a certain point an abstract proposition of a theory of mind may constitute a proposition of a theory of agency. In this sense we might conceive of certain of the propositions implicit in a theory of mind as being innate or universally socialized.

107 Recall that we are referring here to intentional states that are not behaviourally explanatory in the direct sense outlined in Chapter 2 but, rather, serve as background states to behaviourally explanatory states.

intentional profile[108] of the testimonial agent, the judge may be in a position to successfully infer from an observed and believed behavioural output of the testimonial agent (the bodily event comprising his utterance) within an observed and believed environmental context to the behaviourally explanatory intentional cause of that behavioural output. She may be able to identify that set of intentional states of the testimonial agent which contains the concept she needs to acquire.[109]

We can conceive of the propositions the judge maintains in relation to the present environmental inputs, behavioural outputs and behaviourally relevant background intentional profile of the testimonial agent as components of a theory of that agent. Additionally, to the extent that they are interpretively relevant (in the sense that they provide a basis from which to infer, within the context of a theory of mind, to present intentional properties) a theory of the testimonial agent may also comprise some set of propositions about *past* environmental, behavioural and intentional properties of that agent.[110] Some of the propositions of this theory may be believed by the judge – some justifiably – and, as we shall see, some may be hypothetically *assumed* by her for interpretive purposes. The kinds of propositions a theory of the testimonial agent might contain include propositions such as, 'the testimonial agent is presently subject to the environmental event of their being an utterance of the kind "Please tell the judge what ochre is" within normal hearing range", "the testimonial agent presently believes that her hearing apparatus is functioning normally", "the testimonial agent is presently subject to the behavioural event of uttering a sentence of the kind "Ochre is a yellow powder found in the ground and used for ceremonial purposes", "the testimonial agent is presently subject to the general set of intentional regularities which all human agents are subject to (a general governing rationality) in environmental and behavioural situations such as this one"', and so on.[111]

108 By this profile here I mean intentional complex and governing rationality.

109 Note my use of the term 'may' here. The judge is not assured (as a matter of logical or theoretical necessity) of possessing an interpretively adequate theory of mind. Some set of the theory of mind propositions she relies upon in interpreting the testimonial agent may be false (as we shall see, her theory of mind need only be *largely* true, not entirely true). Alternatively, her theory of mind may not include propositions which describe the regularities which actually govern the testimonial action under interpretation. I will have more to say on this latter risk below.

110 An interpretively adequate theory of the testimonial agent may or may not contain propositions about past environmental, intentional, behavioural and rational properties of that agent. It may be interpretively adequate solely on the basis of propositions about present properties.

111 Though the propositional content of a theory of the testimonial agent is not innate but rather acquired through empirical and interpretive engagement with the world and socialization into a folk psychology, there is sound scientific evidence to support the view that the capacity to acquire, develop and deploy such a theory is innate and shows developmental rigidity. Wellman (1990), Botterill and Carruthers (1999) ch. 3, Nichols and Stich (2003) ch. 2.

It is only in conjunction with such a set of propositions that the judge can utilize her theory of mind in reaching a conclusion about the behaviourally causal intentional complex at work in the testimonial action under interpretation. Though a judge's theory of mind identifies some set of the regularities which operate in the realm of human action – it tells the judge, for example, that *if* a testimonial agent is subject to the environmental event of the utterance by another agent within the hearing range of the sentence, 'Please tell the judge what ochre is', then that testimonial agent will typically desire to perform an utterance which signifies what he believes to be the definition of ochre, assuming certain other intentional conditions obtain – it does not provide the judge with propositions about the environmental inputs, behavioural outputs and intentional states which *actually* furnish the mind and world of the testimonial agent under interpretation. It does not, for example, inform the judge that there is or is not an utterance of the kind mentioned in hearing range of the agent under interpretation. A true theory of the testimonial agent is what does this. And without the knowledge provided by such a theory the judge cannot use her theory of mind to successfully identify the behaviourally causal intentional complex at work in the testimonial action in question here.

This can be seen by analysing the inferential phase of the interpretive process in syllogistic terms along (roughly) the following lines. The judge's theory of mind provides her with propositions of the kind 'if present environmental input p, and present behavioural output q and present behaviourally relevant background intentional profile r, then (typically) present behaviourally explanatory intentional complex s'. By itself such proposition does not enable the judge to justifiably conclude that behaviourally explanatory intentional complex s typically obtains in the situation confronting her. She needs to possess the further proposition 'p and q and r' in order to do so. She needs to justifiably believe as part of her theory of the testimonial agent that the present environmental input, behavioural output and behaviourally relevant background intentional profile p, q and r actually obtain. To the extent that the propositions in question – that is, those of both her theory of mind and theory of the testimonial agent – are true or, at least, justified and her reasoning sound, her conclusion as to the identity of the behaviourally explanatory intentional complex will also be true or justified.[112]

That the judge's initial theory of the testimonial agent will – and, indeed, must – include a description of the present behavioural output of that agent to get the interpretive process up and running should be clear. In order to successfully interpret the behaviour of the testimonial agent, the judge must know the identity of that behaviour to some interpretively adequate degree. Without a belief about the identity of the behaviour of the testimonial agent there is nothing for the

112 Of course, given the fallibility of all of her beliefs, the judge must hold her interpretive conclusion provisionally and subject it to a degree of ongoing scrutiny in the face of further justified beliefs she might acquire about the testimonial agent or relevant aspects of the world at large.

judge to interpretively act upon. In relation to the legal context under discussion, that behaviour will comprise the bodily event of a vocal utterance, the meaning (intentional cause) of which, of course, remains to be identified by the judge. The judge's initial theory of the testimonial agent will also include a description of some set of the present environmental inputs of that agent at the time he is giving his evidence. These inputs will comprise some set of the events or states constituting the hearing environment (whether it be in court or outside it), including those events constituting the utterances of questioning counsel. Given that there is no good reason to doubt as a general matter the capacity of a judge to possess true beliefs about the identity of the bodily outputs comprising oral testimony or the environmental inputs the testimonial agent is subject to, I intend to take for granted the possession by the judge of justified beliefs about these phenomena. The important theoretical concerns lie elsewhere.

Specifically, they lie with the judge's knowledge or justified beliefs about the identity of the behaviourally relevant background intentional profile of the testimonial agent. Knowledge of the testimonial agent's environmental inputs and behavioural outputs – even together with the possession of an adequately descriptive theory of mind – is not sufficient for the judge to successfully infer to the unknown behaviourally causal intentional complex at work in the testimonial action. This is because environmental inputs and behavioural outputs underdetermine the identity of the behaviourally causal intentional complex at work in an action. As Braddon-Mitchell and Jackson point out,

> [t]he functional roles definitive of distinct psychological states can share particular inputs and outputs. There is substantial overlap in the definitive inputs and outputs for distinct psychological states. The desire for nourishment is different from the desire for gustatory pleasure, but often they mediate between exactly the same inputs and outputs. Both result in the sight of Brie being followed by the consumption of Brie. [113]

Within any theory of mind, more than one behaviourally causal intentional complex may be compatible with any given combination of environmental inputs

113 Braddon-Mitchell and Jackson (1996) p. 258. Macdonald and Pettit (1981) p. 11 similarly point out in relation to behavioural outputs that 'a given piece of behaviour, or even a pattern of pieces, may be associated with any of a number of mental states: it may be taken to issue from this set of beliefs or that, for example, depending on what desires are ascribed to the agent'. Quine's (1960) point about there being multiple translation manuals for a language is just the point that there are multiple intentional complexes associated with (or intentional explanations of) any given piece of behaviour. The translation of an utterance or language is a form of the ascription of a set of behaviourally explanatory intentional states to an agent or set of agents. Unlike myself, Quine moves from epistemological underdetermination in the mental sphere to ontological indeterminacy, holding that there *is* no unique intentional cause (meaning) to an action. See, on this, Quine (1960) ch. 2, Hookway (1988) pp. 136–9, Hylton (2004) and Kirk (2004).

and behavioural outputs. Additionally, no theory of mind is complete, no theory of mind describes all of the (actual and possible) intentional regularities human beings are or might be subject to. Thus, for any given set of environmental inputs and behavioural outputs, a range of intentional complexes and their component states – some not even described by the theory of mind in question – may serve as plausible candidates for identification as behaviourally causal. In order to identify the behaviourally causal intentional complex operative in any interpretive situation, the judge must possess an interpretively adequate set of true beliefs about the behaviourally relevant background intentional profile of the testimonial agent.[114] She must use these in conjunction with her knowledge of environmental inputs and behavioural outputs in order to more determinatively infer (within the context of a theory of mind) to the identity of the intentional complex which is explanatorily causal of the testimonial behaviour in question.

The question at this point, though, is how the judge comes to hold true or justified beliefs about the behaviourally relevant background intentional profile of the testimonial agent. Unlike the environmental inputs and behavioural outputs which the testimonial agent is subject to at the time of interpretive engagement, these are not readily observable. Like the behaviourally explanatory intentional complex itself – indeed, like any set of intentional states – their identity is knowable only inferentially along the lines elaborated here. This is to say that the identity of the testimonial agent's behaviourally relevant background intentional profile is itself knowable only by a process of interpretation. Now it may be the case that the judge possesses knowledge of some part of the behaviourally relevant background intentional profile of the testimonial agent by virtue of her having had interpretive contact with that agent prior to that agent giving evidence at hearing. That agent might be an expert witness, say, who has been called to testify before the judge on a number of previous occasions. On those occasions the judge may have successfully interpreted that agent's testimonial actions and come to certain (true) conclusions about that agent's behaviourally causal beliefs and desires, including his background beliefs and desires. But, of course, this only raises the question of how the judge was able to acquire knowledge of those intentional states on those previous occasions, given her need to know as a prior matter the agent's behaviourally relevant background intentional profile at that time. Alternatively, and more commonly, the judge may have had no prior interpretive contact with the testimonial agent and must interpretively engage with him in an epistemically austere interpretive environment, involving no more than knowledge of the agent's agency, environmental inputs and behavioural outputs. This is the situation which Quine, Davidson and others have described as that of

114 In order to justifiably identify such complex, the judge must possess an interpretively adequate set of justified beliefs about the behaviourally relevant background intentional profile of the agent.

radical translation or radical interpretation.[115] In either case, whatever the nature of the judge's interpretive experience of the testimonial agent, the philosophical problem remains of addressing what appears to be a vicious circularity within interpretive practice. The problem remains of explaining interpretation under conditions of epistemic austerity.

The way out of this theoretical bind is to note the operation of an interrelated pair of interpretive principles which, as a general matter, guide the interpretive practice of agents. Knowledge of these principles may be conceived of as comprising part of an interpretive agent's overall psychological knowledge.[116] Put very simply, the overarching principle which should guide a judge or any interpretive agent in the interpretive task is that of explanatory reasonableness.[117] That is, in order to maximize the chances of interpretive success, the judge should believe or assume about the testimonial agent whatever is most reasonable in light of the aims of the interpretive process – explaining in intentional terms the cause of the testimonial agent's behaviour – and the judge's justified beliefs about other interpretively relevant matters, including agents generally and the world at large. The judge should not come to beliefs or make assumptions about the testimonial agent which make no sense given all that the judge justifiably believes about that agent, agents in general and the world at large.

As has been mentioned, interpretation is a species of higher-order explanation. As such, it is subject to the constraints all explanation is subject to, the most important and overarching being that of explanatory reasonableness.[118] The propositions comprising one's explanation of any matter – including the behaviour of an agent – must be consistent both with relevant empirical evidence[119] and with other relevant beliefs comprising one's system of knowledge. This is to say that all of the propositions of one's theory or explanation of things must be open to

---

115 Quine (1960) and Davidson (1973). Of course, there are important differences between these two philosophical concepts.

116 Again, this knowledge may be tacitly possessed by interpretive agents. Further, there is good scientific evidence of an innate capacity on the part of normal interpretive agents to develop, refine (by personal experience and socialization) and deploy such knowledge. Wellman (1990), Botterill and Carruthers (1999) ch. 3, Nichols and Stich (2003) ch. 2.

117 Henderson (1993) p. 57. Both Grandy's (1973) 'principle of humanity' and Henderson's 'principle of explicability' are comprehended by this principle. Grandy's principle of humanity 'instructs us to prefer the interpretation that makes the utterance explainable'. Grandy (1973) p. 445. 'The principle of explicability counsels us to so interpret as to construe people as doing explicable things, in view of their beliefs and desires, and as believing and desiring explicable things in view of their other beliefs and desires and their training… The adequacy of an interpretation turns on the explicability of what is attributed to those interpreted'. Henderson (1993) pp. 5–6.

118 Classic accounts of this point of view include Nagel (1961), Hempel (1965) ch. 12 and (1966), Popper (1968).

119 Which is to say, one's justified beliefs about that evidence.

revision in the face of contradictory empirical evidence and relevant changes in one's overall system of knowledge, including within the theory or explanation in question. In the context of interpretation, this is to say that each of one's beliefs about any of the behaviourally causal intentional profile of an agent must be consistent with one's beliefs about the past, present and future environmental inputs and behavioural outputs of that agent, with one's other beliefs about the behaviourally causal intentional profile of that agent, with one's theory of agency and mind and with one's best theories about the world at large. In positing a set of behaviourally relevant background intentional states, the judge should posit those states it is most reasonable to posit, all relevant things considered. It is only by this means that she can get the interpretive process underway and maximize her chances of interpretive success.[120]

Where the judge lacks sufficient justified beliefs about the behaviourally relevant background intentional profile of the testimonial agent as would enable her to identify the behaviourally explanatory intentional complex involved in a testimonial action with an explanatorily adequate degree of certainty[121] and where some such profile needs to be posited in order to get the interpretive project up and running, what explanatory reasonableness calls for is that the judge reasonably and provisionally *assume* an intentional profile on the part of that agent with a view to testing those assumptions (and, for that matter, any beliefs she holds about the agent's intentional profile) against further beliefs she might acquire about the agent over the course of the hearing. The judge must supplement her initial content-sparse theory of the testimonial agent with a set of assumed and provisional propositions about that agent sufficient for her to pursue the interpretive task. The judge must establish what many theorists have described as an interpretive 'bridgehead' into the intentional profile of the testimonial agent.[122] It is only by doing so that the judge can break through the explanatory impasse which obtains under conditions of epistemic austerity – and, indeed, often under epistemically richer conditions – in relation to the testimonial agent.

Of course, if the judge happens to hold beliefs about the behaviourally relevant background intentional states and governing rationality of the testimonial agent, the judge should rely upon those beliefs as best she can to infer to a behaviourally explanatory intentional complex within her theory of mind.[123] But to the extent

---

120 Grandy (1973) pp. 449–50.

121 Where the judge's theory of the testimonial agent is interpretively inadequate in this respect.

122 Hollis (1970) pp. 214–15, Lukes (1982) p. 271. Henderson (1993) p. 36 describes this in terms of 'an entering wedge into the language and actions of those we seek to interpret'. This bridgehead comprises the set of intentional states the interpreter hypothesizes at the commencement of the interpretive encounter as possessed by the interpretee.

123 These may include beliefs about some part of the behaviourally explanatory intentional complex (though, of course, not all of it) as well as other interpretively relevant intentional states.

that her beliefs are not adequate to the interpretive task, the judge should make whatever reasonable assumptions she can. The judge should rely as best she can on what she justifiably believes to be the case about the intentional states and governing rationality of the testimonial agent and reasonably assume whatever else about those states and that rationality is required to enable her to reach a provisional conclusion about the behaviourally explanatory intentional complex at work in the action. This is the basic methodological constraint which operates upon interpreters, in general – to hold reasonable beliefs and to make reasonable assumptions about the agent under interpretation.[124] The more the judge believes about the intentional profile of the testimonial agent – that is, the less a situation of epistemic austerity obtains – the less the judge needs to assume about the agent. Conversely, the less she believes about that profile – that is, the more a situation of epistemic austerity obtains – the more she needs to assume in order to facilitate interpretation. Assumption is demanded when justified belief runs out.[125]

The judge should not make assumptions about the testimonial agent which are logically inconsistent all that the judge justifiably believes about that agent, agents in general and the world at large. The reasonableness of the judge's conclusion about the behaviourally explanatory intentional complex will be a function of the reasonableness of the judge's assumptions about the agents' behaviourally relevant background intentional profile. Though I am reconstructing the interpretive process here in terms of a two stage procedure of assuming a behaviourally relevant background intentional profile and then inferring to a behaviourally explanatory intentional complex within the constraints of a theory of mind, given the logical relationship between the two sets of intentional states, we might just as plausibly construe the process in terms of the judge assuming both a behaviourally relevant background intentional profile and a behaviourally explanatory intentional complex consistent with that profile, with a view to testing all or any elements of this behaviourally causal intentional profile in the later fine tuning phase of the interpretive process.

As far as the content of those assumptions goes, what reason calls for under conditions of epistemic austerity is that the judge assume behaviourally relevant background intentional profile identical to her own, subject to any relevant differences in that profile she justifiably believes obtain in relation to the testimonial agent.[126] Under such conditions – while and to the extent that these conditions prevail – the judge is subject to the so-called methodological 'principle of charity'

124 Quine (1960), Grandy (1973), Davidson (1973 and 1974c), Lewis (1974) and Lukes (1982).

125 It is for this reason that the need for making assumptions (including charitable assumptions) is most compelling at the early stages of an interpretive encounter than at later stages.

126 This latter clause enables an interpreter to include in their theory of the testimonial agent any differences in intentional profile the interpreter has reason to believe obtains in relation to that agent.

in her assuming of an intentional profile vis-à-vis the testimonial agent.[127] In order to pursue the interpretive process, the judge has to start somewhere; she has to make some set of assumptions about the intentional profile of the testimonial agent. As Braddon-Mitchell and Jackson point out, 'it is better to start from somewhere we find plausible than from somewhere we find implausible, and plausibility here must in some way come back to the interpreter's own perspective on matters. We inevitably regard what we ourselves think as not hopelessly implausible – otherwise we would not think it'.[128] Given the general truth, appropriateness and rationality of her own intentional profile the judge is justified in presuming – at least to start with – that the testimonial agent holds largely true and rational beliefs, largely appropriate desires given his beliefs and largely behaves rationally in light of his beliefs and desires, *by the judge's own lights*.[129]

Not only that but, all things being equal, it is better to start from somewhere we are familiar with than somewhere we are not. Constructing and ascribing to the testimonial agent a necessarily[130] vast set of intentional states would be an unrealistic task for any interpretive agent, let alone a judge acting under the practical constraints of the legal process. Far easier would it be, and potentially just as effective, to apply to the testimonial agent a ready-made intentional profile which the judge has knowledge of and which, moreover is compatible with her theory of mind – namely, her own (adjusted for known differences). The finite means available to a judge (or any interpreter) in interpreting others in situations of limited knowledge, thus, require her to be egocentric – and, hence, ethnocentric – to some degree in her starting hypotheses.[131] It requires her to be charitable.[132]

---

127 Quine (1960), Grandy (1973), Davidson (1973 and 1974c), Lewis (1974), McGinn (1977). There is some evidence that human beings are innately programmed to be charitable in conditions of limited knowledge about other agents. Nichols and Stich (2003) pp. 106–7. In our testimonial example, the principle of charity might counsel a interpretively rational judge to provisionally assume an intentional profile on the part of the testimonial agent according to which when subject to the environmental event of an utterance involving a request to tell the judge what ochre is, that agent believes that he should do so and believes that by operating his vocal apparatus in an "ochre is a yellow powder" kind of way he can achieve his desire to do so, and so on.

128 Braddon-Mitchell and Jackson (1996) p. 147. Grandy (1973) p. 443, too, points out the reasonableness of the interpreter using his own set of intentional states as an assumptive model in interpretation under conditions of epistemic austerity.

129 Though what degree of overlap exists between the two largely true and appropriate set of beliefs and desires remains to be seen in each case. Pettit (1993) pp. 234–8.

130 By virtue of the holistic nature of intentional states. Henderson (1993) pp. 26, 39.

131 Pettit (1993) pp. 234–8.

132 Again, there are resonances between Anglophonic philosophy's discussion of charity in interpretation and the hermeneutic views of continental philosophers such as Gadamer who states, for example, at (1989) p. 566 that 'understanding can only succeed on the basis of an original agreement'. See Lampert (1997) on this.

Charity, however, is not to be pursued at all costs. On the account of interpretation offered here, the principle of charity is subordinate to and, in the right circumstances, merely serves the ends of the primary interpretive principle of explanatory reasonableness. The principle of charity is fundamentally a pragmatic principle – justified primarily on the basis that it facilitates the judge's explanatory aims under epistemically austere interpretive conditions.[133] Justifying the principle of charity on pragmatic grounds, does not entail that any assumptions of intentional identity or similarity are, in fact, true.[134] An assumption of similarity, though pragmatically justified, may not be empirically justified.[135] It is entirely consistent with a pragmatic adoption of a charitable set of assumptions that some set of those assumptions be false and be found to be false or otherwise unjustified by the judge as further beliefs about the testimonial agent are acquired by her over the course of the hearing. Though, as a matter of psychological fact they may be very powerful, theoretically, at least, charitable assumptions remain at all times provisional. They are not fixed in any strong a priori manner as certain so-called interpretationist theorists have argued.[136] They may or may not reflect the way things are in relation to the testimonial agent's intentional profile. Any similarity which an interpreter must find 'is a function of present theory and not a function of some special constraint'.[137] The principle of charity may be justified on pragmatic grounds but not – at least, on the account of agency and intentionality adopted in this book – on conceptual grounds.[138] Charity is not justified as an ongoing

133 Grandy (1973) p. 443, Lukes (1982) pp. 264, 272–5, Root (1986) p. 287.

134 'Whether our simulation of the other person is successful will depend heavily on the similarity of his belief-desire network to our own'. Grandy (1973) p. 443. See also McGinn (1977) p. 525.

135 Hempel (1962) p. 12, Follesdal (1982) p. 303.

136 Such theorists have been argued to include Davidson and Dennett. See Child (1994) ch. 1, for a detailed discussion of interpretationist approaches. See also McGinn (1977), Lukes (1982), Root (1986) and Henderson (1993). It is not clear that Davidson's commitment to charity as a matter of *ongoing* interpretive necessity is as strong as some of his critics (for example, McGinn) maintain. There are indications in both his early and later writings that he holds the view that although charity is a necessary *starting* point in a situation of radical interpretation, it is not a position which must be maintained at all costs, as further information about the interpretee is acquired. See, for example, Davidson's comment in (1974a) that although 'the basic strategy must be to assume that by and large a speaker we do not yet understand is consistent and correct in his beliefs – according to our own standards, of course … once the [interpretive] project is underway, it is possible, and indeed necessary, to *allow some slack for error or differences* of opinion'. (my emphasis). See also Davidson (1974b p. 152, 1974c p. 196 and 1986 pp. 103–4). Lukes (1982) pp. 262–4, Root (1986) pp. 286–7 and Henderson (1993) pp. 34–6 concur on this point.

137 Henderson (1993) p. 112. '… the proper way of conceiving of whatever minimal rationality requirement there is, is to conceive of it as resting on the structure of present theory, not on a fundamental principle of charity.' Ibid. p. 113.

138 Henderson (1993) pp. 26–34.

methodological principle on conceptual grounds (or any other grounds) because, as we saw in the previous chapter and as I will argue in the next, a substantial degree of conceptual difference between the judge and a testimonial agent is theoretically possible. Under conditions of epistemic austerity, the judge is in no position to know whether and to what extent conceptual difference obtains. In such a situation, the most reasonable course for the judge to take is to adopt the principle of charity solely on pragmatic grounds and be willing to abandon any charitable assumptions in the face of justified beliefs contradicting those assumptions as they arise.[139]

Under conditions of epistemic austerity, effective interpretation requires the judge to be charitable but, above all, *reasonable* in her assumed ascriptions of an intentional profile to the testimonial agent. Charitable assumptions should be abandoned as the judge comes to hold justified beliefs contradicting them. Equally, they may be maintained as the judge comes to hold justified beliefs consistent with those assumptions. Justification for adopting the principle of charity as an interpretive guide gives way as the judge acquires more and more justified beliefs about the intentional profile of the testimonial agent.[140] This is because the need to make any assumptions at all about that profile dissipates as the judge acquires justified beliefs about it. Because conditions of epistemic austerity in regard to a testimonial agent generally coincide with the early stages of the interpretive process, the principle of charity is generally most justified and constraining at that early stage and generally less justified and constraining at later stages of the process as the judge's relation to the testimonial agent become epistemically richer.[141]

The principle of charity continues to be justified as long as and to the extent that epistemic austerity obtains. It is a methodological principle, the justification of which is variable and not fixed, depending entirely upon the epistemic situation of the interpreter vis-à-vis the interpretee. To hold it otherwise is to render an interpreter vulnerable to interpretive error, particularly in a situation where the

139 This approach avoids the concerns of some theorists (for example, Levinas (1969), Derrida (1992), Cornell (1992) pp. 155–69, Motha (1998), Smith (1997)) that interpretive practice is inherently 'violent' towards conceptually different agents because it necessarily construes those agents in the terms of the interpreter's conceptual scheme and not in terms of their own scheme.

140 Grandy (1973) p. 444, Lukes (1982) p. 264.

141 Henderson (1993) pp. 41, 104. Henderson states that 'the principle of charity allows us to develop provisional interpretive schemes [theories of testimonial agents] that can serve as the basis for further inquiry, although not necessarily further charitable work ...To continue to pursue charitable interpretation in the later stages of interpretation would be to forget the preparatory role of charity in developing first-approximation schemes as provisional bases from which to construct refined interpretive schemes'. Henderson (1993) pp. 51 and 56. Quine (1970) agrees that as the interpretive process proceeds and as difference begins to emerge the maintenance of charity becomes less justified. Henderson (1993) pp. 43–7.

interpretee is not relevantly identical to the interpreter in intentional profile.[142] The judge's commitment to explanatory reasonableness, on the other hand, is not limited to any particular stage of the interpretive process. It applies from the moment of commencement of the interpretive encounter until its completion in a satisfactory explanation of the behaviour in question. The more the judge justifiably believes about the testimonial agent, the more the judge can and should rely on those beliefs in formulating an intentional profile for the testimonial agent and in reaching a satisfactory judgement about the behaviourally explanatory intentional complex at work in the testimonial action. This account of the role in interpretation of the principles of charity and explanatory reasonableness is that which is most consistent with the theoretical standards inherent in the epistemically monistic physicalism espoused in this book.

Fine Tuning the Theory of the Testimonial Agent

Of course, merely making a set of assumptions about the testimonial agent does not guarantee that they are correct, no matter how reasonable those assumptions might be.[143] They are, after all, merely provisionally held hypotheses whose reasonableness in the circumstances may be largely pragmatic. In order to achieve an explanatorily adequate degree of certainty about the intentional cause of the testimonial behaviour, the judge must subject all her assumptions about any or all of the agent's behaviourally relevant background intentional profile, together with any provisional conclusions she may have reached on the basis of those assumptions about the identity of any or all of the behaviourally explanatory intentional complex involved in the action[144] to the test of theoretical compatibility with all further justified beliefs about the agent's intentional profile or related matters she might acquire over the course of the hearing – whether by way of evidence or argument.[145] The judge's assumptions about the intentional profile – including the behaviourally explanatory intentional complex – of the agent may or may not be borne out in light of those further beliefs. They may or may not

142 Drawing partly on Donnellan (1966), Grandy (1973) pp. 445–7 gives a set of examples in which 'the invocation of charity as the primary constraint [on interpretation] leads to incorrect results'.

143 They are certainly not necessarily true as certain interpretationists might argue. Davidson (1974a and 1974b), Dennett (1987), Child (1994) ch. 1.

144 Inferentially reached on the basis of her assumptions or beliefs about the intentional profile of the testimonial agent, her beliefs about the environmental inputs and behavioural outputs of the agent, and relevant propositions from her theory of mind.

145 Henderson (1993) pp. 40, 48, 62–3. It is possible that the judge might acquire subsequent justified beliefs about the intentional profile of the testimonial agent or related matters outside the hearing process – say, by watching TV or speaking to knowledgeable persons in the intervals between evidence. I do not intend to discuss this possibility. In any event, much of what I have to say about the acquisition of further beliefs about the testimonial agent during the hearing proper will be relevant to extra-curricular beliefs.

find a place in the judge's web of relevant beliefs and theories about the agent and the world at large. All assumptions must be held provisionally, must remain open to revision or rejection in light of any contradictory evidence or changes in her system of knowledge which might subsequently arise and must, in fact, be actively tested in the light of the judge's further experience of the agent or of other relevant evidence or argument until such time as the judge is satisfied of their truth or justification. At that point she might reasonably act upon them and, if they are true, succeed in her interpretive project.[146]

To the extent that her subsequent justified beliefs about the testimonial agent are logically inconsistent with any of her assumptions – or for that matter any of her beliefs – about that agent, the judge must be prepared to abandon those assumptions and beliefs and make any changes to her theory of the testimonial agent which are required in order to maintain logical consistency in that theory.[147] To the extent that subsequent justified beliefs are consistent with her assumptions or existing beliefs, she may consider those assumptions and beliefs more secure, less provisional and more worthy of maintenance on her part. In any event, the judge must maintain the whole of her theory of the testimonial agent in a largely provisional and fallibilistic manner, as is proper with any theoretically explanatory endeavour[148], and be prepared to fine tune – abandon or amend – any part of it in response to any confirming or falsifying beliefs she might acquire as the interpretive process proceeds.[149] Only in this way has the judge any reasonable chance of successfully interpreting the testimonial behaviour in question. The interpretive process, like all explanatory enterprise, is highly dynamic.

The judge may – in principle, at least – acquire further justified beliefs about the intentional profile of the testimonial agent by a number of evidential means. Testimonial evidence in general comprises an ongoing series of utterances, each of which may have a distinctive intentional cause or meaning, and each of which may be independently interpreted. In seeking further justified beliefs about the intentional profile informing a given utterance in the series, the judge may rely on her interpretations of earlier or later utterances in the series or, indeed, of any beliefs about the agent's intentional profile arising out of her interpretive engagement with those utterances at that earlier or later stage. Of course, the judge

146 I emphasize that, at this stage, the discussion must be about the *in principle* acquisition of interpretively relevant beliefs by the judge over the course of a legal hearing because we have yet to determine whether and to what extent the epistemic conditions which actually obtain in such a hearing will, *in fact*, permit the judge to acquire such beliefs.

147 All within the weak a priori constraints imposed by the judge's theory of agency.

148 Here we see the continuity of interpretation with other modes of theoretical explanation per our physicalistic premises.

149 Again, any fine tuning will be constrained to some degree by the content of her theory of agency. As we shall see, though, neither theory remains fixed in any strong a priori sense and the provisions of the judge's theory of the testimonial agent may cause her to make changes to her theory of agency.

may be interpretively proactive here. Subsequent utterances by the testimonial agent may be in direct response to the judge asking questions of the agent with the very purpose of clarifying the intentional cause or meaning of an earlier remark. Beliefs arising out of such earlier or subsequent interpretive engagement on the judge's part may not result in any certainty about the agent's intentional profile in relation to the utterance in question but they may enable the judge to reduce her set of candidate intentional profiles or component states to some helpful degree as far as the utterance in question is concerned. She may be able to interpretively 'triangulate' between her interpretive attempts in relation to a series of utterances by the testimonial agent in order to hone in on an increasingly justified set of beliefs about that agent's intentional profile. Similarly, she may rely on earlier or later interpretations of other kinds of behaviour in environmental context which the agent has engaged in. For example, a testimonial agent may make testimonial utterances whilst at the same time handling an item of real evidence (a relevant object of some kind) or whilst moving over or pointing out some geographical feature he is testifying about. These actions, to the extent that they are interpretable and interpreted may give the judge some further clue as to that agent's intentional profile in relation to a given utterance under interpretation.

This process might be refined so as to take the form of making a series of predictions about the subsequent behaviour of the testimonial agent on the basis of an hypothesized intentional profile (including behaviourally causal complex) and then passively observing or even provoking behaviour on the part of the agent in order to test those predictions. To the extent that the subsequent behaviour is consistent with the prediction and with the original hypothesis that prediction is consistent with, that hypothesis may be further (though not necessarily conclusively) confirmed. To the extent that that behaviour is inconsistent with the prediction and original hypothesis, that hypothesis may be called into question and replaced with another one more consistent with the subsequent interpretation and other justified beliefs. The judge might continue doing this, utilizing some part of the set of candidate intentional profiles and states available to her, rapidly running alternative hypotheses and gradually zeroing in on the most justified member of that set as far as she is concerned. By running and testing alternative hypotheses on an ongoing basis the judge might build up a better, more justified hypothesis about the behaviourally relevant background intentional profile and behaviourally explanatory intentional complex at work in the testimonial action.

And, of course – at least, in principle – the judge might rely upon the utterances of *other* testimonial agents testifying about the intentional profile of the original testimonial agent (or about the intentional profile of the group of agents the testimonial agent is a member of or of agents in general)[150] in gaining justified beliefs about that profile. Such testimony might be directly about the operative

150 'Providing us an understanding of what is said and done is not the task of an interpretive scheme [theory of the testimonial agent] alone. Rather, understanding is the job of an interpretive scheme and sociological and psychological theories. It is this combination

intentional profile of the testimonial agent at the time he performed the testimonial action in question or it might be about the past environmental inputs, behavioural outputs, intentional states and governing intentional regularities of the testimonial agent from which the judge might, within the context of her theory of mind, infer to aspects of the target intentional profile of the testimonial agent along the lines just mentioned. An anthropologist giving her account of the meaning of earlier testimonial evidence given by an indigenous agent is a conceivable (at least) example of this in the indigenous land title context. Of course, to the extent that the judge is not able to adequately interpret those utterances, they will be of no assistance to her.[151]

This raises an important question to do with those situations in which the propositional content of the behaviourally explanatory intentional states of the testimonial agent are themselves informed by concepts which the judge does not possess and which she needs to possess in order to adequately interpret that agent's evidence and acquire the original target concept. Recall our earlier example of the judge seeking to acquire the concept of ochre. In order for the judge to acquire that concept she must interpret or otherwise cognitively appropriate evidence about that concept sufficient to cause her to acquire knowledge of its sub-conceptual content and syntactic structure. Our focus earlier was on oral testimonial evidence about the concept of ochre – specifically, a testimonial utterance of the kind "a yellow powder found in the ground and used for ceremonial purposes." in response to a question by counsel. In our discussion there, the judge was able to acquire the concept of ochre by interpreting the witness's utterance in light of her theory of mind (including the two propositions mentioned above) and her knowledge of what the sentence uttered by the witness signified within that agent's linguistic community.

But she was only able to interpret the utterance and come to a belief that the witness believed that "ochre is a yellow powder found in the ground and used for ceremonial purposes' because she already possessed the various concepts implicated in that definition – yellow, powder, ground and the rest. It was her possession of these sub-concepts of ochre which enabled her to draw the interpretive conclusion in question and acquire the concept of ochre.[152] Her interpretive and linguistic

---

of theoretical and descriptive resources that allows us to account for the behaviour or our subjects, and that can be empirically adequate.' Henderson (1993) p. 66.

151 I will have more to say on this eventuality below. It is worth noting here that the process of judicial interpretation of testimonial action outlined here differs from that described by traditional philosophical discussion in that on the model outlined here the judge may rely upon a range of sources of information about the original testimonial action (including the testimony of others) whilst under traditional philosophical models the paradigm interpreter is restricted solely to further observation of subsequent actions on the part of the interpretee. For example, Quine (1960), Hollis (1970), Davidson (1973), Lukes (1982). Additionally, other forms of evidence – real or performative – may also assist the judge in this regard.

152 No belief without possession of the concepts comprising the propositional content of that belief.

efforts provided her with knowledge that these concepts comprised sub-concepts of the concept of ochre and with knowledge of the syntactic relationship of these sub-concepts within that concept. This, so far, is consistent with the discussion in the previous chapter that in order to acquire a concept an agent must, inter alia, possess some possession-sufficient set of the sub-concepts of that concept. The acquisition of concepts proceeds from an intentional space which is already informed by a distinctive set of concepts. Necessarily, a concept is acquired against a background of *some* distinctive set of conceptual sub-content, together, of course, with cognitive engagement with some set of environmental or other intentional events which are causal of possession of that concept.[153] Where, however, the judge does not possess some possession-sufficient set of the sub-concepts of ochre – say, where she does not possess the concept of powder[154] – she will not be able to acquire a belief implicating the definition mentioned here – or at least not an adequate part of that definition – for her practical purposes. Neither her theory of mind nor her theory of the testimonial agent will adequately contain the concept of powder and so she will not be able to rely on those theories to infer to an interpretively adequate belief about the intentional states of the testimonial agent which contain that concept. Hence, she will not – whilst her conceptual deficiency obtains – be able to acquire practically adequate knowledge of the concept of ochre.

The judge rectifies this conceptual deficiency in relation to the concept of powder by the same means she rectifies her deficiency in relation to the concept of ochre – namely, by interpreting or cognitively appropriating and reasoning about evidence (real, performative, testimonial) about the concept of powder, its sub-conceptual content (fine, grained, solid, etc.) and its syntactic structure.[155] She interprets further testimonial evidence which we can conceive of as being aimed at clarifying the meaning of the original utterance in simpler terms – that is, in terms of concepts the judge possesses. And if testimonial evidence offered to her *in this regard* is relevantly informed by concepts she does not possess, she must interpret and cognitively engage with other evidence about *those* concepts until she reaches some level or vector of the sub-conceptual content of ochre that she *does* possess. At that point, the judge may then start to acquire – by constructing it sub-concept by sub-concept – the concept of ochre, in a manner analogous to the way the testimonial agent himself originally acquired the concept. This constructing of the concept may be achieved by any one of a range of combinations of appropriations of evidence and processes of reasoning in any one of a range of temporal orders, reflecting the range of trajectories available for acquiring a concept.

153 I will argue below that this proposition is central enough to the physicalist-functionalist account of things upon which this book is based as to constitute a component of that account's possibility-defining theory of things.

154 I will assume for the sake of the argument that the concept of powder is a necessary member of all possession-sufficient sets of the sub-concepts of ochre.

155 This evidence may be provided by the testimonial agent in question or by some other testimonial agent.

The judge proceeds as best she can in the epistemic conditions which obtain at hearing to acquire the concept of ochre, sub-concept by sub-concept, by testimonial or other evidential means over the course of the hearing.[156] The less of the sub-conceptual content of the concept of ochre she possesses at the commencement of the hearing – that is, the more conceptually different that concept is as far as she is concerned – the more of that sub-conceptual content she will have to acquire over the course of the hearing, the more concept acquisitive (interpretive and cognitive) work she will have to do over the course of the hearing in order to acquire that concept.[157] And, conversely, the more of the sub-conceptual content of the concept of ochre she possesses, the less interpretive effort will be required of her over the course of the hearing. This is merely to repeat in an interpretive context a number of points made in the previous chapter about concept acquisition and conceptual difference.[158]

The judicial interpretive process of hypothesizing behaviourally relevant background intentional profiles, reaching hypothetical conclusions about behaviourally explanatory intentional states on the basis of such hypotheses, acquiring further beliefs by the means mentioned and testing those hypotheses against those beliefs, revising any or all of them if necessary and then repeating the process, continues as long as the constraints imposed both generally and by the determination hearing process allow, and as long as the judge, thinking and acting within those constraints, desires it to continue, given her interpretive and wider judicial purposes. The reasonable and conscientious judge will, within those constraints, seek to continue the process of acquiring beliefs about a given testimonial agent until she possesses enough beliefs to enable her to justifiably identify those behaviourally explanatory intentional states which might provide her with useful information about the target concept. Within those constraints, she will continue to engage in interpretive action in relation to a given testimonial

156 Here, real evidence of ochre itself or of a powder or a yellow object and so on, may be of use to her.

157 Of course, if it turns out that the judge and the testimonial agent share no sub-concepts at all in common – that is, if it turns out that a global conceptual difference necessarily or even possibly obtains – then the judge will not be able to interpret evidence about any concept that agent might testify to. If a concept cannot be acquired to any degree – that is, if its sub-conceptual content cannot be acquired – then evidence about that concept cannot be interpreted to a practically adequate degree because any such interpretation requires the possession of some part of the sub-conceptual content of that concept. Interpretive success depends upon some degree of conceptual shared ground. More on this in the next chapter.

158 It is ultimately the responsibility of the parties to provide the judge with evidence about concepts and, where necessary, evidence about the evidence about concepts. Of course, the judge may, within the constraints of the norms regulating her actions within the hearing process, be proactive by, for example, asking clarificatory questions of witnesses, asking the parties to provide her with evidence she can understand and which will enable her to acquire any interpretively relevant concepts she does not possess.

action until she justifiably believes that she has acquired all the useful information about the target concept that testimonial action has to offer her. Overall, within the constraints operative upon her within the determination hearing process, the judge will continue interpreting the set of testimonial actions led by the relevant party about a given target concept until such time as she believes that she has acquired sufficient justified beliefs about that concept to enable her to adequately perform her judicial functions.[159] She will continue interpreting testimonial actions in this manner in relation to all of the concepts which the parties provide evidence about over the course of the hearing.[160]

A key point which emerges from this discussion is that the more the judge justifiably believes about the past, present and future environmental inputs, behavioural outputs and intentional states of the testimonial agent either directly or via inference within a theoretical framework, the better placed she is to justifiably eliminate implausible ascriptions of intentional states to the agent and hone in on the most plausible ones. The more beliefs she has about the testimonial agent prior to the hearing the better placed she will be to succeed in her interpretations of that agent over the course of the hearing. No matter what her pre-hearing epistemic situation, the more interpretively relevant beliefs about the testimonial agent she is able to acquire over the course of the hearing, the better placed she will be interpretively, the more able she will be to construct an interpretively adequate theory of the testimonial agent and reach a justified – perhaps, even true – conclusion about the behaviourally explanatory cause of the testimonial behaviour in question. And the more conducive the conditions under which the judge thinks and acts are to the acquiring of such beliefs, the greater her chances at succeeding in interpreting testimonial evidence and performing those judicial roles dependent upon such interpretation. An interpretive environment which facilitates the acquisition of such beliefs by the judge and the development on her part of an interpretively relevant theory of the testimonial agent will be an environment which facilitates the judge's capacity to interpret testimonial actions. In the indigenous land title context, it will be an interpretive environment which facilitates the capacity of the judge to go on from that interpretation to understand and legally recognize the indigenous actions those testimonial actions are about.[161]

Of course, notwithstanding her confidence that she has adequately interpreted the testimonial action – that she possesses sufficient beliefs about the intentional

159 Which in the indigenous land title context involves understanding the indigenous action the concept relates to in order to properly evaluate that action's compatibility with a legally valid concept of indigenous land title.

160 Of course, a key element of the constraints which apply to the judge in these respects is the evidence tendering actions of the parties and the amount of evidence about concepts they provide the judge. The judge can only do her best interpretively with what she receives by way of evidence from the parties.

161 I will have more to say on this issue of interpretively conducive epistemic conditions in the next chapter.

profile of the testimonial agent to justify a conclusion about the behaviourally explanatory intentional complex at work in that action – this confidence may be misplaced. She may not, in fact, possess enough justified beliefs about the intentional profile of the testimonial agent to reach a justified conclusion about the behaviourally explanatory intentional complex at work in his utterance. The judge may not have had cognitive access to behaviourally causal intentional states by virtue of deficiencies in her theory of mind. Her theory of mind may need supplementing by evidential and argumentative means in order to acquire knowledge of regularities involving such states. Behaviourally causal intentional states may have been erroneously eliminated by the judge from her considerations by virtue of some theoretical error on her part or by virtue of some flaw in the evidence she relied upon in formulating her candidate intentional complexes. And, of course, even if her conclusion about the behaviourally causal intentional complex at work in the testimonial action is *justified* as far as she is concerned or as far as some other standard of justification is concerned, it might still be false, for a range of reasons. Judicial interpretive action is not guaranteed of success. Like all human epistemic activity it is a fallible exercise.[162]

Another possible outcome of the interpretive process is that the judge may not at any stage of that process think herself justified in identifying a behaviourally explanatory intentional complex in relation to a testimonial action. At the point at which the judge considers herself bound to reach a conclusion about that complex, she may recognize that *cannot justifiably do so*, that she just does not adequately understand the testimonial agent's evidence. She may consider herself at that point to be at an interpretive dead end with still too many candidate intentional complexes to choose in the face of testing. The process of interpretation may fail, then not merely because it results in an unjustified or incorrect ascription of a behaviourally explanatory intentional complex but also because it results in no ascription at all. If the judge believes that she is not justified in identifying the intentional component of the testimonial action, she will not rely upon that evidence to inform her beliefs about the content of the content of the concept that testimonial action is about. In the context of an indigenous land title determination hearing, if overall, the judge is unable to interpret sufficient testimonial actions as would ground a justified belief in the content of an indigenous concept, then she will not be able to justifiably rely on such belief to evaluate the compatibility of a relevant indigenous action with a legally valid concept of indigenous land title. She will be stymied in her judicial function in this regard. The claimants will not have succeeded in meeting the onus placed upon them by the rules of the determination hearing process, an onus requiring them to enable the judge by way of evidence and submissions to reach a justified conclusion as to whether or not

162 By virtue of the non-closed nature of the intentional realm, it may not be a physical state characterizable as a set of intentional states which actually causes the behaviour in question but rather some other non-intentionally characterizable physical cause.

the indigenous action in question is an indigenous land title action. Their claim will fail in regard to that action.

One final important point here. Whatever the actual content of the judge's theory of the testimonial agent, to the extent that the judge is theoretically rational, that theory will be logically compatible with, as well as informed by, some part of the conceptual content of her theories of agency and mind. Consider, for example, the various propositions implicated in the theory of the evidential agent mentioned above. All of them are variously informed by concepts such as agent, intentional state, environmental input event, behavioural output event, intentional regularity, and the like. A theory of the testimonial agent, though not possessed of universal propositional content – testimonial agents differ in their environmental, behavioural and intentional profiles both between themselves and individually over time – *is* comprised in no small part of some set of the universal agency concepts mentioned earlier in this chapter. Again, this is to be expected given that such a theory constitutes a theory of some or other agent and their behavioural interaction with the world. All agents, by virtue of being agents, possess agency defining properties. A theory of a given agent will contain concepts of those properties. By virtue of its conceptual relationship with a theory of agency and a theory of mind, a theory of a testimonial agent may be seen as just as much a part of a comprehensive psychology of human beings as those other theories.

Conclusion

The aim of this chapter was to provide a naturalistically sound account of the judicial acquisition of concepts by evidential means. If culturally different concepts (including conceptually different concepts) are a species of concepts in general (as I have argued in the previous chapter) and if they are, in principle, acquirable by judges then this chapter has, I would argue, achieved its aim and by doing so has enabled us to better grasp the nature of the judicial understanding of culturally different action (one of the aims of this book). If it turns out, though, that culturally different concepts are, as a matter of theoretical necessity, not acquirable by judges – that is, if it turns out that the radical cultural incommensurability thesis is correct – then this chapter has done little more than provide insight into the judicial acquisition of concepts subsisting within her own culture and we are no wiser as to the nature of the judicial acquisition of culturally different concepts or the judicial understanding of culturally different actions. The value of the discussion in this chapter to the overall ends of this book, then, hinges on the plausibility of the radical cultural incommensurability thesis which I have yet to engage with directly. It is time to do so now and in the process cast some light, not merely on the nature but also on the *limits* of the judicial understanding of culturally different action.

Chapter 6
The Limits of Cultural Incommensurability

The Radical Cultural Incommensurability Thesis

With a general naturalistic model of the judicial understanding of action, the judicial acquisition of concepts and the judicial interpretation of testimonial evidence in hand, I want to explore now the (natural) limits of these modes of judicial activity by pursuing a systematic critique of the radical cultural incommensurability thesis outlined in Chapter 1. Recall that my purpose in doing so is not to critically engage with the views of any particular theorist or theorists. It does not matter to my project here whether, as a matter of fact, any theorist actually subscribes to the precise terms of the thesis in question. Nor does it matter that the thesis is, by virtue of its extremity, plainly implausible, as many might think. My purpose in engaging with the thesis in the manner I do is to provide a framework for a more general inquiry into and identification of the extent to which the conceptual scheme of a culturally different agent might differ from that of a judge (the limits of cultural difference) and the extent to which a judge might be incapacitated from acquiring or understanding those culturally different concepts she does not possess (the limits of judicial concept acquisition and understanding). Of course, any such identification on my part might then be used to critically explore and evaluate the views of any actual cultural incommensurabilist – including any of those mentioned in Chapter 1. However, I do not intend to do so in the discussion to follow.

To reiterate, the radical cultural incommensurability thesis maintains that as a matter of theoretical necessity no judge possesses or is able to acquire any culturally different concept. This is to say that there is no theoretically possible world in which any judge possesses or acquires any culturally different concept or that the possession or acquisition by a judge of a culturally different concept is theoretically impossible. The incommensurability invoked by the thesis is *necessary* in that it is alleged to obtain in all theoretically possible worlds and, therefore, under all theoretically possible epistemic conditions. No circumstances are possible – internal or external to the judge – under which a judge possesses or acquires a culturally different concept. The thesis is *general* in that it applies to all judges and all culturally different agents and associated groups. And it is *global* in that it obtains for all culturally different concepts, together with the propositions, intentional states, and actions informed by those concepts. The scheme of concepts maintained by judges and the scheme maintained by culturally different agents have no conceptual content in common right down to the basic conceptual categories which might be argued to structure the very experience of the world maintained by these agents and nothing can be done by a judge to enable those schemes to have any content in common, no matter what relevant circumstances that judge might find herself in.[1]

In the context of interpreting evidence of and understanding culturally different actions, the thesis holds that judges do not possess and cannot acquire concepts of any of the environmental or bodily or intentional phenomena which feature in culturally different actions or of the causal relations which obtain between these various phenomena within the culturally different scheme of things, or of the structural-interrelational properties of complex culturally different actions. Those agents effectively inhabit radically different worlds. Hence, the interpretation of testimonial evidence about culturally different actions, the understanding of culturally different actions and the proper recognition and protection of such actions by a judge – all of which demand the possession by the judge of those culturally different concepts informing the intentional states comprising those actions – are also all theoretically impossible.[2] The radical cultural incommensurability thesis implicates not merely conceptual difference and a conceptual-acquisitive

1 It follows from this notion of the respective agents inhabiting radically different worlds that not only are judges not in possession of and unable to acquire culturally different concepts but culturally different agents are not in possession of and are unable to acquire any of the concepts possessed by the judge and other members of her culture. This element of the radical cultural incommensurability thesis raises important questions about the very participation of culturally different agents in the legal process. As a dominant societal institution thoroughly informed by dominant societal concepts possessed by the judge, if the legal process is entirely conceptually opaque to culturally different agents one might reasonably ask what it would be that would possibly motivate those agents to engage with that process in the manner that they do.

2 The same goes, incidentally, for the judicial interpretation of *performative* evidential action and the cognitive appropriation of *real* evidence about culturally different concepts and actions. Performative evidential action is, after all, just another form of action informed by culturally different concepts. Further, a practically adequate cognitive appropriation of real evidence of relevant environmental and bodily phenomena semantically and ontologically implicated in culturally different concepts and actions along the lines outlined previously also requires the judicial possession of some set of culturally different concepts. Without some knowledge of the worldview of the culturally different agents in question, (involving necessarily the possession of some set of cognitively useful culturally different concepts), the judge will not be in a position to know *which aspects* of those environmental or bodily phenomena actually figure in or are relevant to the properties of the intentional states comprising the action in question. This is because those aspects will necessarily be the subject of concepts – culturally different concepts – which the judge does not possess. This is basically Quine's (1960) 'gavagai' point. With our ochre example, the judge might, for example, take the conceptually relevant properties of the observed real evidence of ochre to be its surface area and weight (two properties, let us suppose, she possesses concepts of) and might suppose that ochre is defined in terms of a phenomenon possessing that surface area and weight – that the concept of ochre comprehends all phenomena of that area and weight, no matter what their colour or other properties.

incapacity but also a radical interpretive and epistemic incapacity on the part of judges.

In exploring the plausibility of the radical cultural incommensurability thesis, I will be adopting the physicalist-functionalist account of intentionality, action and interpretation, outlined in previous chapters as my possibility-defining theory of things. This is to say that I define theoretical possibility and necessity with reference to the set of possible worlds in which that account of things is true. In seeking to delimit the boundaries of cross-cultural difference and cognitive capacity I am concerned to inquire in this chapter into whether, given what I have said about intentionality, cultural difference and understanding, it could be the case that a radical cultural incommensurability obtains between a judge and those culturally different agents participating in a legal hearing. Is it theoretically necessary – or even possible – I want to know, that no judge possesses or is able to acquire any culturally different concept? And if a global general difference and incapacity is neither necessary nor possible, then what kind and degree of difference and incapacity *is* possible from the naturalistic perspective adopted throughout this book?

As has been mentioned, radical cultural incommensurability may be analysed as having two interrelated aspects – that of radical conceptual difference and that of a radical incapacity in relation to concept acquisition.[3] Within the terms of the thesis in question, the latter is entailed by the former. It is an analytic truth that concept acquisition entails concept possession. To acquire a concept is to come to possess it. By the logical principle of *modus tollens*, according to which the negation of the consequent of a conditional entails the negation of the antecedent, the proposition that necessarily no judge possesses any culturally different concept entails the proposition that necessarily no judge acquires any culturally different concept. This is to say that radical (necessary, general, global) conceptual difference logically entails radical concept-acquisitive incapacity.[4] In pursuing an inquiry into the plausibility of the radical cultural incommensurability thesis at large, the inquirer might usefully approach the issues by means of a consideration

3 Bar-on (1994) p. 157. The dialectic at work in the radical cultural incommensurability thesis reflects the two aspects of concept acquisition mentioned in Chapter 4 – the degree of conceptual difference obtaining at the commencement of the interpretive encounter and the epistemic conditions obtaining over the course of that encounter.

4 The entailment here is consistent with the proposition arising out of our analysis of the process of concept acquisition in the previous two chapters that the lack of an adequate sub-conceptual base on the part of a judge (such as obtains in a situation of radical conceptual difference between a judge and a culturally different agent), will disable the acquisition by the judge of concepts possessed by that other agent. Strictly speaking, the inclusion of the concept acquisition clause of my formulation of the radical cultural incommensurability thesis here is logically redundant. It might simply be phrased 'as a matter of theoretical necessity no judge possesses any culturally different concept'. Nonetheless, there is significant theoretical benefit to be gained, I think, by explicitly distinguishing between and discussing the two aspects of the thesis and I will continue to do so.

of the plausibility of *either* or both of its two component aspects obtaining. If the obtaining of either or both of these two aspects is implausible from the physicalist-functionalist point of view adopted here then the incommensurabilist thesis at large will be rendered implausible from that point of view.

In the discussion to follow, I adopt this strategy, exploring the plausibility of each of the two elements of the thesis – radical conceptual difference and radical concept-acquisitive incapacity – in turn. It is worth noting here that notwithstanding the entailment of the latter by the former, the rebuttal of the former does not entail the rebuttal of the latter. Thus, if it were to be established in the discussion to follow (in the second part of this chapter) that the radical conceptual *difference* aspect of the thesis is implausible, it would nevertheless remain logically conceivable, at least, that a radical concept-acquisitive incapacity obtains in relation to non-shared culturally different concepts by virtue of some other reason unrelated to conceptual difference – for example, by virtue of the epistemic conditions which necessarily obtain for the judge over the course of the hearing process.[5] In exploring the plausibility of the radical cultural incommensurability thesis at large, then, it is incumbent upon me to explore the plausibility of the claim that a judicial concept-acquisitive incapacity is theoretically necessary *independently* of any claim asserting radical conceptual difference. I follow up my obligation in this regard in the third part of this chapter. My ultimate conclusion in this chapter is that *neither* the assertion of radical conceptual difference nor that of any radical concept-acquisitive incapacity is plausible from the physicalist-functionalist point of view.

The Limits of Conceptual Difference

One obvious way to think physicalistically about the limits of conceptual difference is in terms of the account of the physical realization of intentional states and their conceptual content offered in Chapters 1, 2 and 4. Recall that what it is to possess a given concept is to possess one or more of a range of intentional states containing that concept. Further, what it is to be in any such intentional state is no more than to be in some neuro-physical state which meets a distinctively individuating set of intentional-functional conditions within a more complex system of agency (incorporating a causal web of environmental, other intentional, and behavioural states) along the lines outlined in Chapter 2.[6] It is solely by virtue of meeting that set of conditions that a neuro-physical state realizes the intentional

5 That is, the proposition that 'if radical conceptual difference then radical concept acquisitive incapacity' does not logically entail the conclusion 'no radical concept acquisitive incapacity' from the premise 'no radical conceptual difference' – that is, it does not follow from 'if x then y' and 'not x' that 'not y'.

6 That is, it a neuro-physical state which is caused by such and such environmental or intentional inputs, given such and such background intentional states, and which causes

state (and, therefore the concept) in question. We saw in Chapter 2 that two neuro-physical states which are identical as far as the intentional-functional roles they play are concerned, necessarily realize identical intentional states – and, hence, identical concepts – in the agents in which those states are located. Because it is theoretically possible on the physicalist-functionalist account of things argued previously for any or all judges and any or all culturally different agents to possess neuro-physical states fulfilling identical intentional-functional roles within broader neuro-physical systems – and how could it not be? – it is theoretically possible for such agents to possess identical (that is, shared) intentional states and concepts. There is nothing in the physicalist-functionalist picture of things which would rule out a neuro-physical state possessed by a judge and one possessed by a culturally different agent both being such as to be typically caused by the same set of environmental and intentional inputs and typically causing of the same set of intentional and behavioural outputs, given some set of background intentional states – as a possibility, at least. No aspect of that picture of things is inconsistent with such a situation obtaining. And if it is theoretically *possible* for such agents to possess such neuro-physical states in common, then it is not theoretically *necessary* that such agents do not possess such states, as well as the concepts those states realize, in common.

For it to be necessarily the case within the physicalist-functionalist paradigm that judges and culturally different agents possess no concepts in common, it would have to be necessarily the case that such agents possess no concept-realizing neuro-physical states of similar functional role in common. But no tenet of physicalist-functionalism necessitates this state of affairs. Hence, conceptual identity or similarity of some degree or other between the conceptual schemes of any or all judges and any or all culturally different agent is theoretically possible on the physicalist-functionalist approach. Indeed, by virtue of the fact that a range of degrees of functional role similarity in concept-realizing neuro-physical states, up to and including global role identity, is possible between any judge and any culturally different agent, a range of degrees of shared concepts or conceptual scheme similarity, up to and including global conceptual scheme identity, are possible on that approach. Consequently, on this basis the radical conceptual difference thesis which demands the impossibility of any degree of conceptual similarity between judge and culturally different agent is rendered implausible within the physicalist-functionalist schema.

This line of argument is a strong rebuttal of any assertion of the *necessity* of global and general conceptual difference from within a physicalist-functionalist account of things. However, it does not rule out the theoretical *possibility* of such difference obtaining. There is, though, a sound physicalist-functionalist argument which does so – which establishes not only that global general conceptual difference is not theoretically *necessary*, but that it is not theoretically *possible*.

such and such intentional and behavioural outputs, given such and such background intentional states.

The roots of this argument are to be found in the discussion in the previous chapter about the nature and preconditions of interpretive agency. There I argued in some detail the proposition that by virtue of being able to interpret the behaviour of themselves and other agents, all interpretive agents possess some interpretively adequate part of a tripartite psychology (comprising theories of agency, mind and specific agents) which is necessarily informed in part by a core set of agency concepts – concepts such as agent, intentional state, belief, desire, environmental input, behavioural output, causation and the like. The possession of this set of concepts by interpretive agents may be explained on our model by reference to physicalistically sound evidence that some part of the set are innate and some part is the result of a significantly shared process of socialization (through appropriately interacting with other agents from birth) into effective interpretive agency. Whatever, the explanation, it follows from the terms of the physicalist-functionalist account of things adopted here that a set of agency concepts exists which is possessed to some degree or other by all interpretive agents no matter what their environmental-intentional trajectories through life, no matter what their race or culture.[7] As physical-functionalists, we have good reason to accept this proposition as true. It follows from the terms of the terms of the physicalist-functionalist approach offered here and is, in any event, supported by sound evidence.[8]

However, we can go further and argue that the possession by all interpretive agents – all judges and culturally different agents – of this shared set of agency concepts is so central to the physicalist-functionalist theory of agency, intentionality and interpretation elaborated here as to constitute a possibility-defining component of that theory.[9] If we accept such argument (and, in light of the discussion in the

7 Because I have earlier defined culturally different concepts as those that are possessed by culturally different agents (and that are *not* possessed by judges and other dominant societal agents) and because I do not want to switch definitions midstream, I will continue to refer to the shared set of agency concepts (and any other shared concepts) as culturally different concepts even though their necessary possession by judges and other agents within her culture makes this ascription somewhat problematic.

8 Within my physicalist-functionalist schema, empirically sound evidence of universal agency concepts only rebuts the proposition that global conceptual difference is theoretically necessary. It does not rebut the proposition that global conceptual difference is theoretically possible. This is because an empirical truth is not a theoretically necessary truth for theorists of this bent. It reflects the way the actual world is but not the way all theoretically possible worlds are.

9 Lewis (1986), Poland (1994) pp. 266–83, Braddon-Mitchell and Jackson (1996) pp. 17–26, Post (1987) pp. 170–73, Divers (2002). There can be degrees of centrality here in relation to specific theoretical components of a grand theory of things such as physicalist-functionalism. The account of concept acquisition articulated in Chapter 4 might be judged less central to physicalist-functionalism than, say, the account of interpretive agency articulated in Chapter 5. By virtue of this, the former might be judged less possibility-defining or more weakly a priori in Henderson's terms.

preceding chapters, I would urge that we should) then it follows that it is not theoretically possible for any judge and any culturally different agent (let alone all judges and all such agents) *qua interpretive agents* to be globally conceptually different, to hold no concepts in common. On the physicalist-functionalist account of things offered here, it is theoretically *necessary* that all judges and all culturally different agents possess some interpretively adequate set of this shared set of agency concepts, as well as some set of the sub-conceptual content of those concepts in common.[10] Judges and other agents can differ in regard to a whole range of other concepts possessed by them – environmental, bodily, intentional, and so on – but not in regard to this set.

Not only is the radical conceptual difference thesis – the thesis that global general conceptual difference is *necessary* – not plausible within our theoretical schema, but the thesis that global general conceptual difference is *possible* is not plausible either. It is not theoretically possible that any or all judges share no concepts in common with any or all culturally different agents.[11] Global general conceptual difference is theoretically impossible.[12] Of course, it is wise to remember here that the physicalist-functionalist account of things offered in this book is itself contingently and not necessarily true, as a logical or metaphysical matter.[13] It may be false within the broader modal realms of logical or metaphysical possibility. Thus, the proposition in question here is neither logically nor metaphysically true, nor is it possibility-defining within those broader modal realms. It is merely theoretically true, given physicalist-functionalism. Of course, an opposing theorist might want to deny the parameters of possibility established here and argue a case from an alternative metaphysical or even logical perspective. I will have something to say about this below.[14]

---

10 Of course, as we saw in the Chapters 4 and 5, it is possible that interpretive agents possess a range of concepts in addition to these shared agency concepts which are not shared. Further, Chapter 5 made clear that this set of shared agency concepts is not sufficient in itself to engender a practically adequate understanding of a culturally different action or a practically adequate interpretation of a testimonial action about a culturally different action. Other non-necessarily-shared concepts are also required.

11 Thus, a *general* global conceptual difference obtaining between all judges and all culturally different agents does not obtain.

12 This is not to say that global conceptual difference is not possible in relation to the conceptual schemes of two *non-interpretive* agents or between the schemes of an interpretive and a non-interpretive agent. Some non-interpretive agents may, then, be globally different as far as a judge is concerned but not any culturally different agent.

13 Lewis (1983) p. 362, Post (1987) p. 187, Poland (1994) p. 266.

14 In order to salvage their view, advocates of a radical conceptual difference in this sphere would have to adopt a non-physicalist-functionalist theory of interpretive agency. More broadly, they would have to adopt a theory of agency which did not involve defining an interpretive agent in terms of the possession of some (necessarily shared) set of concepts. One strategy such incommensurabilists might adopt here – which appears to have been adopted by some of the cultural incommensurabilists mentioned in Chapter 1 (see Motha

Apart from providing a strong critique of the radical cultural incommensurability thesis the argument offered here also provides us with a sense of where the limits of conceptual difference between judges and culturally different agents might be set. That point is – at this stage, at least – as much difference as is compatible with the necessarily shared possession of some interpretively adequate set of agency concepts. Two interpretive agents – a judge and a culturally different agent – may conceptually differ to whatever degree is compatible with them both possessing such a set of agency concepts. It is theoretically possible – again, at this stage – that they possess no concepts in common other than these. The theoretically possible upper limit of conceptual difference between judges and culturally different agents, the maximal possible degree of conceptual difference which may obtain between a judge and such agents (at this stage of my argument, at least), is not global difference but, rather, global difference less the necessarily shared set of agency concepts.

Though I do not intend to engage in a detailed analysis of the content of the necessarily shared set of agency concepts (indeed, a full inventory may be beyond the capacity of any theorist), there is reason to believe that the extent of those concepts and their sub-conceptual content is not theoretically insignificant – at least, in the context of a discussion about global conceptual difference. A sustained analysis of any one of the agency concepts mentioned above would identify a substantial set of other concepts extending right down into the set of basic categorial concepts which, arguably, structure our very perception of the world.[15] The single agency concept of causation, for example, calls up a series of metaphysical concepts – those of object, time, relation, change, and so on. The total conceptual content of the universal psychology may comprise a web of concepts constituting a theoretically significant proportion of the overall scheme of concepts possessed by an agent. By use of the term 'theoretically significant' here I do not mean to imply that the necessarily shared set of agency concepts constitutes a relatively large proportion of the total set of concepts possessed by an interpretive agent. Rather, I mean that it is significant enough in size to cogently rebut the radical conceptual difference thesis. This is to be expected given the holistic nature of all concepts.

Notwithstanding that the set of necessarily shared agency concepts comprises a theoretically significant proportion of the overall scheme of concepts possessed by an interpretive agent, that set may still comprise a relatively small proportion of the total set of conceptual content possessed by an agent. It is not necessarily so significant as to render the conceptual identity thesis of the interpretationists

(1998) pp. 88–9 and Pether (1998) p. 118) – is to conceive of interpretive agency along metaphysically dualist and, roughly, Kantian lines in terms of the maintenance of a scheme-content dichotomy. As has been persuasively argued by Davidson (1974c), though, such strategy cannot escape an irresolvable slide into either contradiction or vacuity.

15 If certain Kantian-like strands of the science and philosophy of human perception are right. See Goldman (1986) ch. 9.

true as a theoretical matter. Whilst on my account the judge necessarily possesses *some* of the concepts possessed by a culturally different agent, she does not necessarily possess all or most of them. The mere possession by her of the set of necessarily shared agency concepts does not, for example, *entail* the possession of any specific set of the other conceptual content which might feature in a theory of mind or subject agent maintained by a culturally different agent. It does not entail the possession by her of a concept of any of the environmental or behavioural phenomena which feature directly or indirectly[16] in the individuating causal relations of the intentional states of a culturally different agent. It does not entail the possession by her of concepts of any element of such agent's world, other than those elements general to agency and intentionality. This state of affairs leaves open the theoretical possibility of a substantial proportion of a culturally different conceptual scheme – a vast set of culturally different concepts – remaining outside the judge's conceptual ken at a given point in time. The rebuttal of the radical conceptual difference thesis mounted here is compatible with the theoretical possibility of a substantial degree of conceptual difference obtaining between a judge and a culturally different agent at a given point in time – enough conceptual difference, I would argue, to provide for the politico-ethical concerns motivating much of the critique of the legal system by cultural incommensurabilists.[17] We might supplement the line of argument elaborated so far by reflecting upon the initial stages of conceptual scheme acquisition by agents in general, including interpretive agents. Consider the question of how human infants acquire concepts following birth in response to their sensory and behavioural engagement with the world. On the account of concept acquisition outlined in Chapter 4 – an account I want to argue is so central to physicalist-functionalism as to form part of the physicalist-functionalist possibility-defining theory of things – a concept is acquired by an agent only on the condition that some set of the sub-conceptual content of that concept is possessed by that agent. This set of sub-conceptual content serves as part of the background set of intentional states associated with an agent being caused to hold an intentional state containing the (primary) concept by some or other environmental or intentional input. If this is the case, then it must also be the case that human infants acquire concepts in response to their initial sensory experiences of the world (their initial environmental inputs, whether in the womb or after birth) by means of some set of pre-experiential concepts – that is, by means of an innate concept-acquisitive conceptual repertoire.

It is entailed, then, by the theory of concept acquisition adopted in this book that infants innately possess *some or other* set of low-level or core or categorial concepts by which they get the concept acquisition process off and running, by which they build up a conceptual scheme in the face of their experience of

16 Via the sub-concepts of the causally operative and background intentional states that figure in the concept of an intentional state.

17 See the discussion of this point in Chapter 1.

the world and their developing reasoning abilities.[18] All human infants innately possess some or other set of the kinds of concepts which serve as part of the 'deep' sub-conceptual content of all theoretically possible human concepts. Such innate categorial concepts give human infants the capacity to develop into fully blown agents over time in response to the world. On the account of concept acquisition given here there is no other way for human infants to acquire concepts of the environmental phenomena they encounter in the world following birth than by possessing at birth some or other (by definition, innate) categorial conceptual base.[19] As one would expect, given the soundness of the physicalist-functionalist account of things, empirical research in developmental psychology on how infants build up a conceptual scheme and worldview supports the existence of such innate categorial concepts.[20]

Further, given the nature of these innate concepts as fundamental to all subsequently acquired concepts, there is theoretically sound reason to think that their possession by human agents continues after infancy and that they are relied upon on an ongoing basis over the course of an agent's life to acquire further concepts in the development of her conceptual scheme. To possess a concept is to be in a physical state which is (as a component of an associated background intentional state) able to figure in the acquiring or causing of other concepts (intentional states containing those other concepts) in response to appropriate environmental or intentional inputs. Hence, it follows from the proposition that the judge possesses innate concept-acquiring concepts that it is possible that a judge is still able to rely upon those concepts to acquire new concepts, that those concepts are still functional as concept-acquiring into adulthood. That is, there is theoretically sound reason to believe that necessarily *some or other* innate set of categorial, scheme-acquiring concepts is possessed by and is practically utilizable

18 That is, in response to their environmental-intentional trajectory through the world. I have argued above that the necessarily shared set of agency concepts includes a set of categorial concepts – namely, those at the core of the various agency concepts. Here I am including in my reference those categorial concepts which are not implicated in the necessarily shared set of agency concepts.

19 Or the innate potential (a genetic, neurophysiological predisposition, perhaps) to develop such a concept-acquisitive conceptual base automatically over a period following birth.

20 Spelke (1985), Baillargeon (1999), Gelman and Wellman (1999), Botterill and Carruthers (1999) ch. 3, Nichols and Stich (2003) ch. 3. Intriguingly, there even appears to be evidence of late-term human foetuses possessing simple (perhaps prototypically so) concepts of their environmental surroundings whilst in the womb. See Hepper (1995), DiPietro et al. (1996a and 1996b), Pallas (2005).

by all agents – including judges and culturally different agents.[21] Again, findings in the psychological literature seem to support this.[22]

The key question for our purposes, though, is whether there is reason to hold that necessarily all adult agents possess the *same* set of innate categorial concepts.[23] Unlike the argument in support of necessarily shared agency concepts, an argument in support of necessarily shared categorial concepts is not as readily formulable. It does not follow from anything I have said in general about concepts and their possession that any innate concepts are necessarily shared by all agents. What is clear from what I have said is that it is theoretically *possible* within the physicalist-functionalist schema that all adult agents are neuro-physically structured such that they possess the same set of innate concepts, including categorial concepts.[24] One of the most compelling pieces of empirical evidence in support of the proposition that, as a theoretically contingent matter, all normal human infants – from both dominant and minority cultures – possess the same set of innate categorial concepts, is the fact that a dominant societal infant raised in a culturally different minority community (as well as an infant from a minority culture raised in a dominant cultural community) encounters no innate difficulties in acquiring the full set of that community's concepts, all things being equal as far as her upbringing (or lifelong environmental-intentional trajectory) goes. This fact supports the proposition that there is, as a matter of contingent empirical fact, no

---

21 Notwithstanding empirical evidence that as an agent gets older and more embedded in her own conceptual scheme it becomes more difficult to gain access to substantially different alternative schemes (witness the relative ease with which children learn alien languages as compared to adults), there appears no good reason to believe that *necessarily* once one's innate categorial concepts are utilized in the initial construction of a conceptual scheme those concepts can not be subsequently relied upon in adulthood to gain access to other conceptually different schemes – even at the limits of conceptual difference. We can, therefore, at least, establish the *possibility* of such categorial concepts being accessible in adulthood and this is enough for the purpose of rebutting the radical conceptual difference thesis, though not for establishing a limit on the possible amount of such difference. See Davidson (1974c).

22 See, for example, Wellman (1988) pp. 67–8 and Astington et al. (1988) p. 12 in relation to innate agency concepts. Wellman (1998) pp. 33–4 acknowledges the possibility of complex adult agency concepts differing significantly from the simple innate concepts of young children, though not at their sub-conceptual core. On the other hand, Gopnik's (1996) Neurathian approach to the possession and development of a theory of agency in an interpretive agent appears to be consistent with the loss of innate agency concepts over time in response to environmental experience and socialization.

23 Of course, some set of categorial concepts will be necessarily shared, at least, by interpretive agents – namely, those implicated in the necessarily shared set of agency concepts. That is, the set of necessarily shared agency concepts may be a sub-set of a larger necessarily shared set of concept-acquiring categorial concepts.

24 Of course, it is theoretically possible that they do *not* possess the same set of innate categorial concepts.

innate conceptual difference between minority and non-minority infants at birth in this regard.[25]

Given that these innate categorial concepts are necessarily maintained by an agent into adulthood, it follows that all judges and all culturally different agents, possess as a matter of contingent empirical fact, the set of such concepts.[26] The evidence indicates that there is at least one theoretically possible world where some set of concepts is shared by all judges and all culturally different agents – namely, the actual world. The possession of a shared body of such concepts is actual and, hence, possible. Indeed, even if it is merely *possible* (rather than theoretically necessary) that all agents maintain their innate categorial concepts into adulthood, it remains theoretically possible that all judges and all culturally different agents possess the same set of such concepts. Independently of our previous agency-based argument, this is enough within the physicalist-functionalist schema to rebut the assertion by incommensurabilists of a necessary global conceptual difference obtaining between judges and culturally different agents. It doesn't, though, contribute to the setting of any *limits* on the degree of conceptual difference which might obtain between judges and such agents, as our agency-based argument does. An argument for the *necessity* of shared categorial concepts would be required in order to do that.

Getting from the possibility of all judges and all culturally different agents possessing the same set of concept-acquiring concepts to the theoretical necessity of this being the case requires a more sustained engagement with the nature of concepts and their possession than I can or need offer here.[27] Any such argument would need to establish that necessarily one and only one set of innate categorial concepts was capable of enabling a human agent to construct a conceptual scheme which was in turn capable of enabling that agent to behaviourally interact with the external world in a manner which largely realizes his desires given his largely true beliefs. That is, any such argument would need to establish a theoretical link between being an agent in the world and the possession of a single set of categorial concepts. Were such an argument mountable within the terms of physicalist-functionalism, then we might plausibly add those necessarily shared categorial concepts which are not already implicated in the necessarily shared set of agency concepts to that set, and fix the limits of theoretically possible conceptual difference at a point comprising

25 Subject to any conceptual differences which might have arisen in response to environmental input differences *in utero*.

26 Additional to this argument, linguistics theorists such as Rosch (1974), Rosch and Mervis (1975), Hawkins (1988), Wierzbicka (1992 and 1994), Vosniadou (1994) and Kirby (1999), claim to have empirically established the existence of universal (if not innate) concepts, some of which might be conceived of as categorial in the terms set out here. Were such findings to be sufficiently empirically established and justified as logically central and possibility-defining within the physicalist-functionalist schema, these concepts might find a place in the necessarily shared set of concepts provided for by that schema and might further circumscribe the limits of possible conceptual difference within that schema.

27 Interpretationists have mounted such arguments over the years. See Child (1994).

global conceptual difference less this combined set of necessarily shared concepts. It is not clear to me that any such argument is available. In any event, I need not pursue the question here because I have already established the implausibility of the radical conceptual difference thesis on interpretive-agency based and innate categorial grounds and have already established a limit to the degree of conceptual difference possible between judge and culturally different agent, a limit which though less than global, is nonetheless substantial and, in any event, quite capable of meeting all reasonable descriptive demands and all reasonable ethical concerns about conceptual difference in the legal sphere, including many of the concerns held by those cultural incommensurabilists mentioned in Chapter 1.

Even if we were to establish the existence of a necessarily shared set of categorial concepts, given their inherent role as fundamental building blocks for the construction and acquisition of all possible higher level concepts, these are unlikely to be numerically substantial relative to the total number of concepts an adult agent possesses at large – even when combined with any necessarily shared agency concepts. The number of necessarily shared categorial concepts is theoretically significant in that it rebuts the radical conceptual difference thesis and further circumscribes the limits of conceptual difference. As the body of necessarily shared concepts possessed by agents increases in number, the limit of possible conceptual difference between agents decreases accordingly. But that number is not so substantial as to seriously challenge the possibility of a substantial though not global degree of conceptual difference obtaining between judges and culturally different agents. It remains a theoretical possibility that a substantial proportion of any indigenous conceptual scheme – a vast set of culturally different concepts – remains outside any judge's conceptual ken at any given point in time.[28]

A further point worth mentioning here in regard to whether we can establish the theoretical necessity of a universally shared set of categorial concepts is that for physicalist-functionalists the theoretical necessity of any state of affairs depends upon the degree to which a proposition describing that state of affairs is empirically grounded and logically central to one's possibility-defining physicalist-functionalist theory of things.[29] To the extent that physicalist-functionalism is a metaphysically contingent doctrine grounded itself to a significant degree upon empirical evidence,

28 This raises the issue of whether there might plausibly be any categorial concepts not already implicated in the set of necessarily shared agency concepts discussed earlier – which is to say, whether the categorial content of the set of necessarily shared agency concepts contains all an agent needs in order to develop a conceptual scheme capable of enabling her to rationally engage with the world over the course of her lifetime. In order to establish whether it does or not, a full analysis of the categorial content of that necessarily shared set of agency concepts, as well as an inquiry into the set of categorial concepts necessarily common to all concepts and conceptual schemes would be required. I do not have the resources to engage in any such analysis or inquiry here. Nor, again, for the reasons mentioned in the previous paragraph, do I need to.

29 Quine (1953b) and Henderson (1993) pp. 95–6.

a physicalist-functionalist might well argue that certain empirically well-grounded propositions – for example, the aforementioned proposition that, by virtue of their equal innate capacity to acquire the conceptual scheme of any conceptual community, all human agents share the same set of scheme-acquiring categorial concepts – are rightfully accorded the status of being possibility-defining. That is, a physicalist-functionalist might argue that the proposition that all human agents share the same set of categorial concepts is so empirically well-grounded and so logically fundamental to some significant sector of the propositions comprising the physicalist-functionalist and scientific system of knowledge, as to be theoretically necessary within that system and that it follows as a matter of theoretical necessity, then, that all judges and all culturally different agents possess the same set of categorial concepts, the actual identity and number of which remain to be established by sound physicalist-functionalist inquiry. Were such an argument successful then again we would have grounds, again, for establishing the upper limit or maximal degree of possible conceptual difference at a point constituting global difference less the set of necessarily shared categorial and agency concepts.

Of course, there would be no need to stop at the set of categorial concepts if there were other concepts – non-categorial and non-agency concepts – the universal possession of which was both solidly empirically evidenced and fundamentally embedded within the physicalist-functionalist system of knowledge. For example, there is an interesting body of evidence and argument in linguistics and anthropology pointing to the possession by all human agents of certain non-categorial and non-agency concepts as a nomological matter.[30] Again, were such findings to be sufficiently empirically established and justified as logically central and possibility-defining within the physicalist-functionalist schema these concepts too might find a place in the necessarily shared set of concepts provided for by that schema and might further circumscribe the limits of possible conceptual difference within that schema. As I have argued, the limits of theoretical possibility are determined by the content of our possibility-defining theory of things. The content of that theory is a matter of argument. The more empirically supported and systemically compatible our propositions about human concept possession are, the more theoretical necessity they are capable of generating in our understanding of the issues, the more capable they are of delimiting the bounds of possibility in this field. The more propositions asserting or entailing the existence of necessarily shared concepts are admitted to the possibility-defining theory, the less the degree of possible conceptual difference. This is merely to say that the conceptual schemes of a judge and a culturally different agent can be as different as one's possibility-defining theory of things says they can be.

This is all to say that a physicalist-functionalist can admit of degrees of theoretical necessity and can hold that the more a theoretical proposition is backed

30 See Rosch's (1974) discussion of the literature on colour, form and emotion concepts. See also Lukes (1982) pp. 267–8, Hawkins (1988), Wierzbicka (1992 and 1994), Vosniadou (1994) and Kirby (1999).

by empirical evidence and the more securely it fits within the overall physicalistic system of knowledge, the more that proposition is justifiably accorded possibility-defining status within the physicalist-functionalist system of knowledge.[31] The more empirically grounded and central a proposition is within the physicalist-functionalist scheme of things, the more it is capable of determining how the world is or even might be for such a theorist.[32] Certain of the propositions mentioned so far in this discussion – the proposition that all interpretive agents possess a shared set of agency concepts, the proposition that all human agents possess *some or other* set of innate categorial concepts – are more possibility-defining than others – for example, the proposition that all human agents possess the *same* set of innate categorial concepts or the proposition that all humans agents possess a shared set of higher-level concepts additional to the set of categorial and agency concepts. The limits of possible conceptual difference may be more justifiably set at one point rather than another depending upon which of these propositions we are willing to accept as possibility-defining within our metaphysical framework. If cogent evidence contradicting any of these propositions comes to light – for example, if empirical evidence emerges that agents lose possession of their innate concept-acquiring concepts as they mature and develop a conceptual scheme of any complexity[33] – or if relevant changes are made in other parts of the physicalist-functionalist system of knowledge, then the strength of any argument to necessity offered on the basis of such proposition will be compromised and the limits of possible conceptual difference may need to be reconsidered and revised.

There is, then, a *limit* on the degree of conceptual difference which may obtain between any judge and any indigenous or testimonial agent. This limit arises out of the terms of the physicalist-functionalist account of agency, intentionality and interpretation adopted here, including the findings of our best empirical inquiry into these things. For the physicalist-functionalist, a culturally different agent can be as conceptually different from a judge as is consistent with that agent being an agent (or more specifically, an interpretive agent) according to the possibility-defining terms of that account. This is to say that any such agent can be as different from a judge as is consistent with cogent relevant empirical evidence and as is consistent with the terms of the physicalist-functionalist system of knowledge at large, including the metaphysical doctrine of physicalism itself. Within the

31 This is consistent with the Quinean dimensions of the physicalism articulated throughout this book.

32 See Henderson (1993) pp. 95–6 on this point.

33 I am not aware of any such evidence. As mentioned earlier, there is some evidence to suggest that it does become more difficult for an agent to acquire a conceptually different scheme or significant parts of one as she gets older and more embedded in her own scheme (again, witness the relative ease with which children learn alien languages as compared to adults). Such evidence does not sufficiently rule out, though, the possession of innate categorial concepts by adults and their use by adults (to some degree) in the acquisition of substantially different concepts and schemes.

physicalist-functionalist framework, the parameters of possible conceptual difference between any judge and any culturally different agent range from there being no conceptual difference at all[34] to there being a degree of conceptual difference consistent with the existence of whatever necessarily shared concepts physicalist-functionalists can soundly argue for. This latter degree constitutes the upper limit of possible conceptual difference for any such agents. No more difference than this is theoretically possible for any such agents.

On the physicalist-functionalist approach to things adopted in this book, certain types of concept are necessarily shared between judges and culturally different agents and certain types of concept are possibly shared between them. It is not the case that no concept is possibly shared. It is not the case that global difference necessarily obtains between them. At this point, pending the provision of a sustained and sound argument for the necessity of a shared set of categorial concepts or other concepts, the only necessarily shared concepts I am committing to are the set of agency concepts mentioned earlier. Whatever the content of the necessarily shared set of concepts, the maximal degree of conceptual difference possible on the physicalist-functionalist schema remains quite substantial though, in any event, less than global. Despite being less than global, the maximal theoretically possible degree of conceptual difference between a judge and culturally different agent may, *whilst it lasts*, be enough to undermine many, if not all, of the cognitive and interpretive endeavours of any judge under any circumstances in relation to such agent. It may be enough to undermine the vast majority of a judge's cognitive and interpretive endeavours over the course of the legal hearing.

Finally, it is worth keeping in mind that whilst the existence of necessarily shared agency, categorial or other innate concepts admits of the possibility of substantial conceptual difference it does not necessitate substantial conceptual difference. Within the parameters established above, the extent of the conceptual difference which obtains between a judge and culturally different agent depends upon the environmental-intentional trajectories those agents take over the course of their lives. And the nature of those trajectories depends upon the nature of the environmental and intentional inputs – the evidence and reasoning – those agents are causally subject to over the course of their lives. It depends upon the amount and quality (relevance to concept acquisition) of the environmental or evidential events those agents have causal contact with over the course of their lives, upon the functionality of their sensory and cognitive apparatus and upon their capacity to behave in an effective concept-acquisitive manner over that time. It depends upon the amount and quality of the reasoning (intentional inputs) those agents are capable of and engage in over that time, and so on. We can conceive of all of this in terms of the nature of the epistemic conditions those agents are subject

34 Though it is implausible to think that two agents could be conceptually identical, even within the same conceptual community, nonetheless it is not impossible on a physicalist-functionalist approach.

to over the course of their lives.[35] Within the parameters set above, the extent of the conceptual difference actually obtaining between judges and indigenous and testimonial agents and the nature of the environmental-intentional trajectories taken or epistemic conditions obtaining as far as those agents are concerned, are all contingent matters to be determined by physicalistically sound inquiry.[36]

The Limits of Judicial Concept Acquisition

The existence of the set of necessarily shared concepts mentioned in the previous section presents problems not only for the global difference dimension of the radical cultural incommensurability thesis but also for the global concept-acquisitive incapacity dimension of that thesis – the proposition that necessarily no judge can acquire *any* culturally different concept, including over the course of a legal hearing. We saw in the previous section that the necessity of a global concept-acquisitive incapacity on the part of all judge and all culturally different concepts is entailed by the necessity of global conceptual difference between all judges and all culturally different agents. With the failure of general global conceptual difference as either a necessary or possible state of affairs on the physicalist-functionalist schema, the argument that a general global concept-acquisitive incapacity necessarily or possibly obtains *as an entailment of such difference* also fails. This does not mean, though, that the necessity of some degree of general concept-acquisitive incapacity cannot be established on other grounds. The failure of the antecedent in a conditional does not entail the failure of the consequent.[37] Those who wish to advocate the necessary incapacity of all judges to acquire any

35 I will have more to say about these conditions below. Note though that the term 'epistemic conditions' should not be taken to include the degree of conceptual difference which obtains between any two agents or sets of agents.

36 This is all entirely consistent with the account of concept possession offered in Chapter 4, according to which not only is conceptual difference between the conceptual scheme of any judge and any culturally different agent theoretically possible, but a *range* of degrees of conceptual difference (including no difference – that is, global conceptual identity) between such schemes is theoretically possible. Because it is possible on the account offered here for any judge and any culturally different agent to take one of a range of such trajectories – each trajectory differing to varying degrees from the others in relation to its environmental and intentional content and, therefore, each differing in relation to the set of concepts it causes an agent taking that trajectory to possess – it is possible for judges and culturally different agents to differ to *varying degrees* in the concepts they possess. It is possible for conceptual difference between such agents to take one of a number of theoretically possible degrees.

37 The conditional 'If radical conceptual difference, then radical concept-acquisitive incapacity' and the proposition 'not radical conceptual difference', does not entail the conclusion 'not radical concept-acquisitive incapacity'.

culturally different concept must seek to do so on grounds independent of any radical conceptual difference.

Of course, given the existence of a set of necessarily shared concepts, the most extreme position a cultural incommensurabilist can logically take on the question of the limits of possible judicial concept-acquisitive incapacity within the physicalist-functionalist framework is that, as a matter of theoretical necessity, no judge can acquire any culturally different concept which is not necessarily shared by judges and culturally different agents. That is, there is no theoretically possible world in which any judge acquires any (what I will term) non-necessarily-shared culturally different concept. I will, from this point on, then, construe the radical concept-acquisitive incapacity thesis as maintaining this revised proposition. Further, when discussing the judicial acquisition of culturally different concepts from this point on, I will be referring to the acquisition of *non-necessarily-shared* culturally different concepts, it not being possible for the judge to acquire, over the course of a legal hearing, concepts she necessarily possesses from birth. Of course, from time to time, I may have cause to expressly refer to non-necessarily-shared culturally different concepts as such.

In this section, then, I explore the plausibility of this revised thesis from the physicalist-functionalist point of view. My ultimate conclusion is that it too is implausible. In the course of reaching this conclusion, I identify the limits of theoretically possible judicial incapacity in relation to the acquisition of culturally different concepts. I conclude that it is not *necessarily* the case that no judge can acquire any culturally different concept, though it is contingently *possible* that no judge can acquire any culturally different concept, including over the course of a legal hearing.[38] The corollary of this conclusion, though, is that it is also theoretically possible that some or all judges *can* acquire some or all culturally different concepts, including a practically adequate set of such concepts over the course of a legal hearing. As was the case in the previous section, what is theoretically possible or necessary in relation to the judicial capacity to acquire culturally different concepts depends upon the propositional content one ascribes to one's possibility-defining theory of things. I will have more to say on this below.

We saw in earlier chapters that where a culturally different concept is not possessed by a judge it may be acquired where the judge engages in an appropriate cognitive response to appropriate environmental inputs or intentional inputs – where the judge appropriately engages with or in appropriate evidence and reasoning – *provided that* sufficient sub-concepts of that concept are already possessed by the judge.[39] And such sub-concepts may be acquired, if needed, in the same manner,

38 This is by virtue of the theoretical possibility that the necessarily shared concepts provide no basis for the acquisition of any other culturally different concepts under any possible epistemic conditions.

39 As we saw in Chapter 2, an intentional state containing a concept is typically caused by one of a set of environmental or intentional inputs but only provided that an associated set of background intentional states is in place.

provided that the judge possesses sufficient sub-concepts of those sub-concepts. A judge may acquire whatever sub-conceptual content of a culturally different concept is necessary for possession of that concept by coming into appropriate cognitive contact with evidence or engaging in reasoning appropriate to acquiring that sub-conceptual content but always on the basis of possessing relevant, lower-order, sub-conceptual content. In this way a judge may build up to possession of a culturally different concept, sub-concept by sub-concept over a period of time. She may acquire a culturally different concept by a multi-staged process of sub-concept acquisition in response to appropriate evidence and reasoning.

Thus, there are two individually necessary and jointly sufficient conditions for acquiring a culturally different concept – the possession of appropriate and adequate sub-conceptual content, on the one hand and appropriate cognitive engagement with appropriate evidence or appropriate reasoning in relation to one's present beliefs, on the other. We can redescribe these conditions in terms of the obtaining of an acquisition-enabling degree of conceptual difference and an acquisition-conducive set of epistemic conditions.[40] If either or both of the conditions necessary for the acquisition by a given judge of a given culturally different concept fail, then that concept cannot be acquired by that judge. If either or both of these conditions fail as a general matter for all culturally different concepts and all judges then no culturally different concept can be acquired by any judge. The obtaining of merely one or the other of these does not enable the acquisition of a culturally different concept. If some or all judges are not properly engaged with appropriate evidence or in appropriate reasoning – that is, if conducive epistemic conditions do not obtain – then those judges will not be able to acquire an associated concept no matter how much of that concept's sub-conceptual content they possess. Likewise, if some or all judges do not possess sufficient of a concept's sub-conceptual content, they will not (whilst that lack continues) be able to acquire that concept no matter what evidence or reasoning they engage with or in. Judicial concept-acquisitive success depends upon the degree of conceptual difference which obtains between the judge and the culturally different concept in question – how much of the sub-conceptual content of that concept she possesses at the commencement of the hearing and how much of that content she has to acquire over the course of the hearing – as well as upon the nature of the epistemic conditions which obtain in relation to the judge and the concept over the course of the hearing.

Those who advocate the revised radical concept-acquisitive incapacity thesis are committed to arguing that either or both of these conditions necessarily do not obtain for any judge in regard to any and all culturally different concepts.

---

40 Recall my earlier stipulation that the epistemic conditions informing a situation of concept acquisition do not include the degree of conceptual difference which obtains in that situation. Note also that global conceptual difference is necessarily an acquisition-*disabling* degree of conceptual difference for any and all culturally different concepts as far as any judge is concerned.

They must, for example, argue that necessarily no judge possesses a set of sub-conceptual content which would enable the acquisition of any culturally different concept under any possible epistemic circumstances – that as a matter of theoretical necessity neither the necessarily nor the possibly shared set of concepts and sub-concepts mentioned in the previous section contains an acquisitively adequate set of the sub-conceptual content of any non-shared culturally different concept. They must hold that a degree and kind of conceptual difference necessarily obtains which, though not global given the critique mounted in the previous section, nonetheless disables judges from acquiring any culturally different concept. Alternatively, or additionally, they must argue that necessarily no judge comes into appropriate cognitive engagement with evidence or engage in appropriate reasoning causal of the acquisition of any culturally different concept. This is to say that necessarily, epistemic conditions conducive to the acquiring of any culturally different concept by any judge do not obtain. I want to argue in this section that it is not the case that either or both of these conditions necessarily do not obtain for any judge and any culturally different concept. On the contrary, the obtaining of both of these conditions, for all judges and all culturally different concepts, is theoretically possible. Let me consider the first of these conditions now – namely, the judicial possession of an appropriate and adequate set of sub-conceptual content for non-necessarily-shared culturally different concepts.

The Possibility of an Adequate Conceptual Base

In thinking through the possibility or impossibility of this condition obtaining we should focus upon the most extreme of possible circumstances, that in which maximal possible conceptual difference obtains between the judge and culturally different agent in question. In order for a judge to acquire a non-shared culturally different concept under conditions of maximal possible conceptual difference between that judge and a culturally different agent it must be the case that the necessarily or possibly shared set of concepts possessed by a judge includes an acquisition-adequate set of sub-conceptual content for that non-shared concept. That is, it must be the case that the necessarily or possibly shared set of concepts includes concepts which, in conjunction with appropriate evidence or reasoning, cause the acquisition of that non-shared indigenous concept. This is to say, of course, that it must be the case that an acquisition-disabling degree of conceptual difference between the judge and the culturally different concept under acquisition does not obtain.[41]

41 In order to acquire *any* given culturally different concept, a judge needs an acquisition-adequate sub-conceptual base for that concept. In order to acquire *some set* of culturally different concepts, a judge needs an acquisition-adequate sub-conceptual base for that set of concepts In order to acquire *all* culturally different concepts, a judge needs an acquisition-adequate sub-conceptual base for all culturally different concepts. Of course, possession of such base is not necessarily sufficient for concept acquisition. Conducive epistemic conditions for each of the concepts in question also need to obtain.

If it turns out that the necessarily or possibly shared set of concepts mentioned in the previous section either necessarily or possibly includes sub-concepts sufficient for the acquisition of *some or other* non-shared culturally different concept, then the incommensurabilist proposition that necessarily any such shared set does not include such sub-concepts will be rendered implausible. Likewise, if it turns out that the necessarily or possibly shared set of concepts mentioned in the previous section either necessarily or possibly includes sub-concepts sufficient for the acquisition of *all* non-shared culturally different concepts, then again the incommensurabilist proposition that necessarily any such set does not include such sub-concepts will fail.[42] Whether a necessarily or possibly shared set of concepts can enable the acquisition of any or all non-shared culturally different concepts in conjunction with appropriate evidence or reasoning is an empirical and interpretive matter to do with the semantic relations which exist between that shared set and the non-shared indigenous concept or concepts in question. Let me, at this point, examine each of the categories of necessarily or possibly shared concepts discussed in the previous section and make some comments on their capacity to enable the judicial acquisition of any or all non-shared culturally different concepts (should conducive epistemic conditions obtain).

Consider, firstly, the innate concept-acquiring or categorial concepts which I argued all agents necessarily possess on the physicalist-functionalist schema. Some set of those categorial concepts provided culturally different agents with a sub-conceptual means to post-natally acquire some set of simple non-innate culturally different concepts in response to those agents' post-natal epistemic conditions.[43] If we accept the theoretical possibility argued for in the previous section that those same categorial concepts are possessed by all judges and remain functional in those judges in the acquisition of new concepts[44], then we have grounds for arguing that judges possess as a theoretical possibility a sub-conceptual base for the acquisition of some simple set of non-shared culturally different concepts. Further, if we accept (as I shall soon argue we should) the possibility that epistemic conditions relevantly analogous – though not necessarily identical – to the post-natal epistemic conditions which obtained for those culturally different agents might obtain for any and all judges over the course of a legal hearing, then we are logically committed to the possibility that all judges may acquire any and all of

42 And if we can establish the theoretical possibility of the 'conducive epistemic conditions' condition of judicial concept-acquisition obtaining in relation to any culturally different concept, the theoretical possibility that any judge might acquire any culturally different concept will be confirmed.

43 In response to some set of evidence and reasoning or environmental and intentional inputs.

44 As I argued above, there is no sound reason to think that the concept-acquisitive functionality of innate categorial concepts in adults is theoretically impossible. Indeed, there is reason to believe that their functionality in adults follows from their possession as a theoretical necessity.

those simple post-natally acquired culturally different concepts, even at the limits of possible conceptual difference, rebutting the revised radical concept-acquisitive incapacity thesis in relation to its denial of the judicial acquisition of, at least, *some or other* set of culturally different concepts.

We need not stop here, though. Given that these simple non-innate culturally different concepts together with the innate categorial concepts provided culturally different agents with a sub-conceptual base for the acquisition of all the non-shared concepts possessed by them, their possible possession by all judges together with the possible judicial possession of the set of innate categorial concepts possessed by culturally different agents opens up the possibility of all judges possessing a sub-conceptual base for the acquisition of any and all culturally different concepts – provided, of course, that it is possible that those judges be subject to acquisitively conducive epistemic conditions analogous to those that enabled the culturally different agents to acquire those concepts in the first place. Having acquired a set of simple non-shared culturally different concepts on the basis of a shared set of categorial concepts, it is possible that any judge might then go on to build up and acquire more complex non-shared culturally different concepts in response to appropriate evidence and reasoning, in a manner analogous to the way the culturally different agents did.[45] Indeed, if her environmental and intentional situation were conducive enough the judge might proceed to acquire any and all elements of the culturally different conceptual scheme by pursuing an environmental-intentional trajectory into that scheme similar to or equivalent to that taken by a culturally different agent.[46]

If, again, we accept the possibility (soon to be argued for) that acquisitively conducive epistemic conditions might obtain for any and all judges over the course of a legal hearing in relation to any or all culturally different concepts, then we are logically committed to the possibility that given their possible possession of the innate categorial concepts possessed by culturally different agents, all judges might acquire any or all culturally different concepts – including a set of practically adequate culturally different concepts as far as her judicial purposes were concerned. This possibility rebuts the revised radical concept-acquisitive incapacity thesis in relation to its denial of the judicial acquisition of any or all culturally different concepts. The judicial acquisition of any part or the whole of the culturally different conceptual scheme remains a possibility here, grounded ultimately in the possible possession of a shared set of innate concept-acquiring concepts, as well as the possibility of conducive epistemic conditions obtaining over the course of the hearing. Of course, the possibility argued for here is a contingent one. As a corollary of this possibility it is also possible that all judges

45 There is no reason to think that a particular concept-acquisitive trajectory is off limits to a judge, as I shall argue below.

46 It is worth noting here that this capacity to acquire non-shared culturally different concepts would exist even if it turns out that concepts are not initially acquired by infants by means of innate concepts but by some other innate and cross-culturally shared mechanism.

and all culturally different agents do *not* possess the same set of innate categorial concepts and that conducive epistemic conditions for acquiring non-necessarily-shared culturally different concepts do not obtain for any judge in relation to any indigenous concept. That is, it is contingently possible for the physicalist functionalist that no judge can acquire any culturally different concept under any possible epistemic conditions.

Were we to take the various propositions elaborated here in relation to the possession and functionality of a shared set of innate categorial concepts as not merely contingent possibilities but as central and possibility-defining tenets of the physicalist-functionalist theoretical framework (and we might mount an argument that we should take them as such)[47], then not only would it be possible for a judge to acquire any and all culturally different concepts under conducive epistemic conditions but it would be necessary that she does, under such conditions. Such a theoretical manoeuvre on our part would, in conjunction with other theoretical propositions, not merely enable us to rebut the radical concept-acquisitive incapacity thesis (as the previous possibility-based argument did), but it would also circumscribe the limits of possible judicial concept-acquisitive incapacity. Under the possibility based argument just outlined, it is theoretically possible that either or both of the necessary conditions for judicial concept acquisition fail to obtain. And so it is possible on that less circumscribing approach that, even where conducive epistemic conditions obtain a judge may not acquire a culturally different concept by virtue of the possibility of her not possessing an acquisitively adequate sub-conceptual base. However, where it is necessarily the case that the judge possesses an acquisitively adequate sub-conceptual base – as follows from rendering the judicial possession of a functional, universally shared categorial set a theoretical necessity – then necessarily *where conducive epistemic conditions obtain* a judge acquires any and all culturally different concepts.

Of course, it remains theoretically possible even on this more circumscribing approach that conducive epistemic conditions not obtain and so it remains a possibility on this approach that no judge acquires any culturally different concept. Nonetheless, the limits of possibility established in this necessity-based approach differ from those at work in the weaker possibility-based approach mentioned earlier. The range of epistemic conditions under which a judicial concept-acquisitive incapacity is possible is restricted if this necessity-based approach to innate categorial concepts is taken. Under the weaker approach, an acquisitive incapacity is possible under any possible epistemic conditions. Under the stronger, more circumscribing approach, an acquisitive incapacity is possible only under non-conducive epistemic conditions. And as far as comparisons with the radical concept-acquisitive incapacity thesis goes, this necessity-based approach renders a

47 Again, relevant arguments here would have to do with the degree to which the proposition in question is supported by sound empirical evidence as well as with the degree to which is implicated in the body of other propositions constituting the physicalist-functionalist scheme of knowledge.

judge necessarily unable to acquire a culturally different concept only where non-conducive epistemic conditions necessarily obtain, rather than necessarily unable to acquire a culturally different concept under any possible epistemic conditions whatsoever. Pending a more compelling set of evidence or line of argument in relation to the theoretical necessity at stake here, I do not intend to adopt or pursue this line of thought any further.

Notwithstanding some similarities in relation to the comments just made about innate categorial concepts, importantly different issues about the limits of judicial concept-acquisitive incapacity emerge when we consider the role played in concept acquisition by the necessarily shared set of *agency* concepts mentioned above. I made the point earlier that this set of concepts implicates a significant number of concepts and sub-concepts – including categorial concepts. Whilst it is true that without a detailed analysis of the necessarily shared set of agency concepts it cannot be clearly established that it contains the full set of innate human categorial concepts, it nonetheless is clear that it contains *some* set of those categorial concepts, as well as a number of higher level concepts. Given the absence of any persuasive physicalist-functionalist argument that this set of agency concepts necessarily does not contain the full set of human categorial concepts, we are justified in holding (at least, for the time being) that it is possible within the physicalist-functionalist schema that it does so.[48] Given both the amount and the diversity of the conceptual content implicated in the necessarily shared set of agency concepts, as well as the possibility that that content implicates all of the categorial concepts available to human agents, it is implausible to suppose that *necessarily* that set does not provide a sub-conceptual basis for the acquisition by any judge of *any* non-necessarily-shared culturally different concept, even were appropriate epistemic conditions to obtain. What reason would we have for thinking so – even independently of the possibility that in addition to these shared agency concepts, judges and culturally different agents possess the same full set of categorial concepts?

It is implausible within the physicalist-functionalist framework to think that it is theoretically impossible for the set of agency concepts and sub-concepts to provide a basis for the acquisition of other concepts, given the right environmental and intentional inputs. Rather, it is consistent with all we know about concepts and their acquisition within that framework to suppose that it is, at least, theoretically *possible* that the necessarily shared set of agency concepts provides a sub-conceptual basis for the acquisition of some or other set of (and, indeed, possibly any and all) non-necessarily-shared indigenous concepts by a judge – specifically, those non-shared indigenous concepts which maintain an appropriate semantic relationship with those agency concepts and sub-concepts.[49]

48 And that, therefore, that full set of categorial concepts is necessarily shared by all *interpretive* agents.

49 One would have to perform a detailed analysis of those shared agency concepts and the culturally different conceptual scheme to determine which non-shared culturally

And, of course, it is possible that it does not. This is because it is not theoretically necessary that the set of necessarily shared agency concepts provides a sub-conceptual base for the judicial acquisition of any set of non-shared culturally different concepts. Why? Because it is not necessarily the case that the agency set contains the full set of culturally different categorial concepts. Consequently, it is not necessarily the case that the judge possesses the *same* set of other non-agency implicated categorial concepts which the culturally different agent relied upon in building his theory of mind and subject agent. It may be the case that all of the non-necessarily-shared culturally different concepts are acquirable only on the condition that the judge possesses a set of categorial concepts which are not implicated in the set of agency concepts. And, as I have just argued above, it is possible that the judge does not possess those categorial concepts. In which case, the necessary possession of the set of agency concepts does not entail the necessary possession of all categorial concepts (and hence all non-agency-based categorial concepts) nor any higher-level concepts implicating those non-agency-based categorial concepts. It is possible that the set of agency concepts does not contain categorial concepts sufficient to acquire any – let alone each and every – culturally different concept, even were conducive epistemic conditions for those concepts to obtain.

Independently of the argument mounted above in relation to the innate set of categorial concepts, the necessary possession by all judges of the set of agency concepts possessed by culturally different agents when coupled with both the contingently possible capacity of some part of that set to comprise a sub-conceptual basis for the acquisition by any or all judges of some or other set of (and, indeed, all) non-agency culturally different concepts and the (soon to be argued) contingent possibility of conducive epistemic conditions obtaining over the course of a legal hearing, provides a rebuttal of the revised radical concept-acquisitive incapacity thesis. It is not necessarily the case that no judge can acquire any non-necessarily-shared culturally different concept under any possible epistemic conditions. Rather, it is merely contingently possible that no judge can acquire any non-necessarily-shared culturally different concept under any possible epistemic conditions. It is worth noting that this conclusion follows not merely from the discussion of agency concepts mounted just here but also from the discussion of innate categorial concepts mounted earlier. It expresses the limits of possible judicial concept-acquisitive incapacity for physicalist-functionalists.

Let me repeat, though, were we to take it as a theoretical necessity rather than a mere possibility that the necessarily shared set of agency concepts provides a sub-conceptual basis for the acquisition of some or all culturally different

different concepts those shared agency concepts might provide acquisitive access to, which further non-shared culturally different concepts those initially acquired concepts might provide access to, and so on. Were it theoretically necessary that the agency set does so, then it would follow that under conducive epistemic conditions it is necessary that a judge acquire those non-necessarily-shared culturally different concepts.

concepts (say, because necessarily that set of agency concepts contains the full set of human categorial concepts) then not only would it be merely possible for a judge to acquire those culturally different concepts semantically grounded in those agency concepts under conducive epistemic conditions, but it would be necessary that she does so under such conditions. Again, such a theoretical tactic would, in conjunction with other theoretical propositions, not only enable us to rebut the radical concept-acquisitive incapacity thesis (as the previous possibility-based argument did), but it would also circumscribe the limits of possible judicial concept-acquisitive incapacity. Rather than it being be possible that no judge acquires any culturally different concept under any epistemic conditions, it would merely be possible that no judge acquires any culturally different concept not semantically grounded in the set of agency concepts under any set of epistemic conditions nor acquires any culturally different concept which *is* semantically grounded in the set of agency concepts under non-conducive conditions. This is a more circumscribed limit upon possible concept-acquisitive incapacity than that discussed just now. It is also a more circumscribed limit than that advocated by the revised radical concept-acquisitive incapacity thesis. As was my position earlier, pending a more compelling set of evidence or line of argument in relation to the theoretical necessity at stake here, I do not intend to proceed any further with this line of argument.

Within the physicalist-functionalist schema, the possibility of a general judicial concept-acquisitive incapacity obtaining in relation to non-necessarily-shared culturally different concepts, turns on the possibility of the necessarily or possibly shared set of concepts mentioned above constituting a acquisition-adequate sub-conceptual component of those culturally different concepts. There is no good reason within the terms of that schema to think that as a matter of theoretical necessity those shared concepts do not do so. Nor is there sufficiently strong reason to think that necessarily they do. Thus, I am content to maintain the proposition that within the physicalist-functionalist schema, by virtue of the possibility of the judge not possessing an acquisitively adequate sub-conceptual base, it is contingently possible that no judge can acquire any non-necessarily-shared culturally different concept – including any practically adequate culturally different concept – under any possible epistemic conditions. According to the physicalist-functionalist model of things advocated throughout this book, a general and virtually global degree of judicial concept-acquisitive incapacity is possible within the legal hearing process. All the physicalist-functionalist may plausibly deny is that any degree of judicial concept-acquisitive incapacity between judges and culturally different concepts is theoretically necessary.

We should not forget, of course, that the corollary of the possibility advocated here is that given the possibility of conducive epistemic conditions obtaining, it is contingently possible that any or all judges *can* acquire any or all non-necessarily-shared culturally different concepts. To the extent that it is possible that such conditions obtain over the course of a legal hearing, then it is possible that all judges can acquire all non-necessarily-shared culturally different concepts –

including that practically adequate set of culturally different concepts the judge needs to acquire in order to properly interpret testimonial evidence, understand culturally different actions and perform her determinative role – over the course of a hearing. To the extent that it is possible that conducive epistemic conditions obtain over the course of a hearing, there are no grounds for pessimism about the potential of the legal process to provide culturally different parties with the recognition and protection they seek. Let me turn now to the issue of whether it is possible for conducive epistemic conditions to obtain over the course of a legal hearing.

The Possibility of Conducive Epistemic Conditions

In order to acquire a concept an agent must either come into appropriate sensory and cognitive contact with a set of environmental phenomena causal of that concept or must engage in a process of reasoning which is causal of the acquisition of that concept, all against the background of a set of conceptually relevant intentional states or, as I have also been terming it, a set of acquisition-adequate sub-conceptual content. Since raising this issue in Chapter 4, I have been conceiving of the various environmental, sensory, cognitive, behavioural and other phenomena implicated in the process of judicial concept acquisition, other than the judge's possession of the background set of intentional states or sub-conceptual base in terms of the epistemic conditions surrounding the judge in relation to the acquisition of the culturally different concept in question. A situation of judicial concept acquisition is dualistically analysable in terms of the set of epistemic conditions and the degree of conceptual difference which obtain in that situation.

We saw in Chapter 4 that these epistemic conditions may, in turn, be categorized in terms of the internal capacities of the judge and the external circumstances she is subject to. The former category includes, for example, those conditions to do with the quality of the judge's sensory, cognitive and reasoning apparatus (including her capacity to see and hear properly, as well as her capacity to properly conceptualize sensory data); the quality of the judge's bodily motor skills (including her capacity to seek out and manipulate conceptually relevant evidence, as well as move her body into a state or position conducive to cognitively appropriating that evidence); the quality of the judge's reasoning skills (including, most importantly, her capacity to interpretively reason within the parameters of the various theories of agency and mind mentioned in the previous chapter); and the quality of the judge's motivation to sensorily and cognitively engage with evidence and to reason appropriately (including the nature and strength of her desires to do so). The latter category includes those conditions to do with the nature of the environmental phenomena which causally interact with the judge (including the identity and amount of the evidence presented to her, as well as the lighting and auditory conditions surrounding her engagement with that evidence); the nature and quality of any sensory, cognitive or reasoning aids available to the judge and other relevant agents (including the availability of microphones, video conferencing facilities, and computers); and the time available to her for concept acquisition.

It is clear that in acquiring the various culturally different concepts they possess, culturally different agents were subject to one or other of the range of sets of epistemic conditions which are conducive to the acquisition of those concepts. At some point in time, those agents possessed some concept-acquiring set of internal capacities and were subject to some concept-acquiring set of external circumstances. They possessed adequate sensory apparatus and came into appropriate sensory contact with concept-causing evidence under suitable conditions of light and sound, they possessed suitable cognitive and reasoning faculties and properly conceptualized that evidence and reasoned about it, they possessed motor skills which enabled them to behaviourally manipulate that evidence for their concept-acquisitive ends, and they had at their disposal sufficient time to do all of these things and acquire the concepts in question. Further, given that culturally different concepts continue to be acquired by culturally different agents, epistemic conditions conducive to the acquisition of each and every culturally different concept continue to obtain. By virtue of the fact that culturally different agents have acquired and continue to acquire culturally different concepts, it follows that the obtaining of epistemic conditions conducive to the acquisition of every culturally different concept is theoretically possible.[50]

Additionally, given that within the physicalist-functionalist schema there is no 'in principle' difference between the internal capacities and external circumstances a member of a dominant culture (including a judge) may possess or be subject to and those a member of a culturally different minority may possess or be subject to, the possibility of conducive epistemic conditions obtaining for culturally different agents entails the possibility of their obtaining for dominant societal agents, including judges. Because no impossibility attaches within physicalist-functionalism to the obtaining of conducive internal capacities and external circumstances for judges, it follows *as a general matter* that it is theoretically possible within that schema that epistemic conditions conducive to the acquisition of any and all culturally different concepts obtain for any and all judges. Nothing within the physicalist-functionalist schema necessitates the isolation of any dominant societal agent, including any judge, from the influence of any of the epistemic conditions causal of a culturally different concept, given possession of an appropriate sub-conceptual base.

Whether or not it is theoretically possible for conducive epistemic conditions to obtain over the course of a legal hearing (as distinct from obtaining generally), depends upon whether there are any features specific to a legal hearing which theoretically necessitate the non-obtaining of such conditions as far as the presiding judge is concerned. Quite simply, there are not. At a very basic level, we can conceive of a legal hearing as comprising a complex and interrelated series of actions performed by relevant agents, including the judge, within the context

50 No cultural incommensurabilist would deny this.

of some or other external environment. Part of that overall series of actions may be distinguished as a judicial concept-acquiring series of actions. Such series might include the actions of parties to the matter tendering evidence to the judge about the content of a culturally different concept, the testimonial actions of witnesses testifying about that concept and, most importantly for our purposes, the interpretive actions of the judge in making sense of the evidence of any such witness.[51] All of this takes place within an environmental context comprising the behaviour of relevant agents, objects of real evidence, lighting and auditory conditions, and the rest. In this respect, the judicial concept-acquiring process which takes place over the course of a legal hearing is no different from that which might occur generally. Both primarily involve a concept-acquiring judicial agent possessing and exercising some or other set of internal capacities whilst being subject to some or other set of external circumstances.

Where, though, the process of judicial concept-acquisition at hearing may be said to differ from that carried on generally, is that at hearing the actions of all the participating agents, including the judge, as well as the internal capacities of and external circumstances surrounding the judge are, to some degree, regulated by a set of legal norms. That some set of these things is legally norm-governed is a necessary feature of a legal hearing. Such norms might include, for example, ones prescribing that judges must, as a pre-requisite of holding judicial office, possess some practically adequate set of sensory, cognitive, behavioural and reasoning capacities; rules of evidence regulating the kinds of testimony and real evidence which might be tendered to or relied upon by a judge over the course of a hearing; ones prescribing (roughly) the time which might be spent by a judge in engaging with any given piece of evidence or in acquiring any given concept at hearing; and ones prescribing certain lighting and auditory standards for a hearing or permitting the use by participants of sensory, reasoning or behavioural aids such as microphones, computers and (when holding the hearing 'on country') vehicles. We can conceive of the actions of all the various agents involved in the judicial concept-acquisition process over the course of a legal hearing, including those of the judge, as being informed both by beliefs about those states of affairs prescribed by applicable legal norms and by desires to make one's own and others' internal capacities,[52] actions and external circumstances conform to some degree with those (believed) states of affairs.[53]

---

51 The tendering of a range of non-testimonial actions or real evidence, together with their interpretation or cognitive appropriation by the judge may additionally or alternatively be involved in this process, as we saw in Chapters 4 and 5.

52 The parties and the judge, for example, will desire and will act to ensure that testimonial agents have vocal motor skills and cognitive capacities adequate to their testimonial role.

53 This account of legal norms builds upon and is consistent with the account of norms given in Chapters 2 and 3.

Such legal norms may be taken not only to regulate but also to constitute a component of the epistemic conditions obtaining in relation to the judicial acquisition of culturally different concepts over the course of a legal hearing.[54] As we saw in Chapters 2 and 3, though, norms are no more than complexes of human thought and action. As such, the contents of legal norms – the standards, including the epistemic conditions, they prescribe – are contingent upon the nature of the thoughts and actions of those agents who actively constitute them. And within the parameters of the physicalist-functionalist theory of action adopted here, the thoughts and actions of the agents who actively constitute the legal norms regulating the epistemic conditions which obtain at a legal hearing – like those of any complex of thought and action – are contingent phenomena which may take a wide variety of forms, including epistemically conducive forms as far as the judicial acquisition of culturally different concepts is concerned – though always within the bounds of general theoretical possibility. By virtue of there being no basis within physicalist-functionalism upon which to maintain the proposition that non-conducive epistemic conditions are necessitated by the legal norms operative within legal hearings, we may confidently assert the proposition that it is theoretically and contingently possible for epistemic conditions conducive to the judicial acquisition of any culturally different concept to obtain within any legal hearing. It is theoretically possible for the epistemic conditions which obtain at a legal hearing as far as any judge is concerned to mirror any of those which might obtain in general as far as any agent is concerned. Within the physicalist-functionalist schema, there is no reason why *necessarily* the legal norms regulating judicial practice over the course of a legal hearing do not enable the judge to engage in precisely the same series of actions a dominant societal agent might engage in generally in order to acquire a culturally different concept.

As such, it is possible for the epistemic conditions which obtain at a legal hearing (including the legal norms regulating those conditions) to be entirely non-conducive to the judicial acquisition of any or all culturally different concepts or entirely conducive to such acquisition, or merely to some degree conducive or non-conducive to such acquisition. The possibilities in this sphere are as vast as they are in general. Given their contingency, a notable feature of the epistemic conditions and associated norms operative within the legal process is that they are reformable. Where they are not conducive to judicial concept acquisition and where those agents whose practice constitutes those conditions and norms so desire, those conditions and norms may be changed so as to be more conducive to judicial concept acquisition. Law reform – even radical law reform – in the service of an enhanced judicial interpretive capacity, concept-acquisitive capacity and capacity to understand culturally different actions is a theoretically live option within the physicalist-functionalist scheme of things. If it is theoretically possible for conducive epistemic conditions to obtain as a general extra-legal matter, there

54 There is no problematic circularity in this statement given the dialectic nature of norms, as outlined in Chapters 2 and 3.

is no good reason to hold that necessarily the legal hearing process is not or cannot be rendered epistemically conducive to the acquisition of any and all culturally different concepts by any and all judges. This is a very important feature of the physicalist-functionalist approach elaborated in this book which I will take up in the concluding chapter.

There is good reason, then, for physicalist-functionalists to maintain that the obtaining of the second of the aforementioned conditions of culturally different concept acquisition – that the judge be subject to conducive epistemic conditions – is possible for any or all judges in relation to any or all culturally different concepts. A radical incommensurabilist argument that such condition is not possible – that a failure of conducive conditions is necessary – is implausible. There is no good reason to believe that *necessarily* over the course of a legal hearing no judge can engage in appropriate sensory and cognitive relations with appropriate evidence nor engage in appropriate reasoning (given the possession of appropriate concepts and intentional states), as far as a given culturally different concept is concerned. Again, though, the possibility in question here is a contingent one. It is not theoretically necessary that an appropriate sensory or cognitive engagement with relevant evidence or an appropriate engagement in relevant reasoning obtains for any or all judges and any or all culturally different concepts. It is not theoretically necessary that conducive epistemic conditions obtain for any or all judges in relation to any or all culturally different concepts. It is theoretically possible on the physicalist-functionalist theory of agency, intentionality and interpretation adopted in this book that the condition in question here does *not* obtain at any time for any or all judges and any or all culturally different concepts. It is theoretically *possible* (but not necessary), by virtue of the possibility of the failure of the necessary condition of there being conducive epistemic conditions, that any and all judges be incapacitated from acquiring any and all culturally different concepts, independently of whether or not an acquisitively adequate degree of conceptual difference obtains.

Conclusion

The acquisition of a culturally different concept by a judge is possible only if both of the two individually necessary and jointly sufficient conditions for that acquisition are possible – namely, that the judge possesses an acquisition-adequate set of sub-conceptual content for that concept and that the epistemic conditions under which the judge thinks and acts are conducive to the acquisition of that concept. Judicial concept acquisition is possible if the degree of conceptual difference which exists between the judge and culturally different concept or culturally different agent in question is not so great as to render acquisition under any epistemic conditions impossible and if epistemic conditions enabling acquisition at that degree of conceptual difference are possible. I have endeavoured to show that given the truth of the physicalist-functionalist account of things offered in this book it *is* theoretically possible for both of these conditions to concurrently obtain for all judges and all culturally different concepts – even under conditions of maximal possible conceptual difference – over the course of a legal hearing. Thus, it is theoretically possible for any judge to acquire any culturally different concept at any possible degree of conceptual difference, provided that over the course of the hearing she is subject to conditions which enable her to cognitively appropriate evidence and reason in a manner causal of the acquisition of that concept. It is not the case that all judges are necessarily incapacitated from acquiring any culturally different concept under any epistemic conditions, including those obtaining at hearing. The radical concept-acquisitive incapacity thesis is not plausible from the physicalist-functionalist point of view.

Indeed, if we step back from the detail of the preceding argument about the limits of judicial concept-acquisitive incapacity and think about what culturally different concepts *are* within the physicalist-functionalist scheme of things, both the consistency of that argument with the basic tenets of physicalist-functionalism and the implausibility of the radical cultural incommensurability thesis becomes clear. For a start, the very idea that there could exist in the world a higher-order phenomenon (namely, a culturally different concept or intentional state), the identity – which is to say, the functional role or content – of which is necessarily unknowable to every actual and possible inquirer who is not a member of a specific cultural group, including those operating within our best sciences, is fundamentally inconsistent with the monistic ontological and epistemological ethos of the physicalist project.

Because both the radical conceptual difference thesis and the radical concept-acquisitive incapacity theses are not plausible, neither is the radical cultural incommensurability thesis which, as we saw, is comprised of these. As far as the limits of incommensurability are concerned in relation to judges and culturally different agents and their concepts, it remains theoretically possible that the non-necessarily-shared part of the conceptual schemes of any judge and any culturally different agent be incommensurable under any theoretically possible epistemic conditions. As a contingent possibility though, this proposition entails that it is also theoretically possible that the conceptual schemes of any judge and any culturally different agent be *commensurable* under certain possible (acquisition conducive) epistemic conditions. The interpretation of culturally different agents by judges and the judicial acquisition of concepts testified about by those agents – even to a practically adequate degree as far as the judge's determinative purposes are concerned – is a theoretical possibility for a physicalist-functionalist such as myself, even if the maximal possible degree of conceptual difference obtains between the judge and any such agents at the commencement of the interpretive encounter between them. Consequently, the judicial understanding of any and all culturally different actions and the proper determination of legal matters implicating cultural difference is possible on the physicalist functionalist approach. There is no need to be pessimistic about the recognitional and protective potential of the legal system – at least on metaphysical grounds.

Chapter 7
Judicial Understanding and Law Reform

The Possibility of Interpretive Law Reform

The ultimate finding of this book in relation to the limits of judicial understanding is that judges have a contingent capacity to acquire any culturally different concept and understand any culturally different action over the course of a hearing and that the claims of the radical cultural incommensurability thesis that they do not are not plausible. That is, it is contingently possible that any judge acquires any culturally different concept and understands any culturally different action over the course of a legal hearing. Equally, though, it is contingently possible that any judge does not and that an epistemically and adjudicatively disabling degree of conceptual incommensurability obtains in some or all hearings. Everything here depends upon the content of the conceptual scheme possessed by the judge at the commencement of a hearing – which is to say, the degree of conceptual difference which obtains at the hearing's commencement between the judge's scheme and that of the culturally different participants – and upon the epistemic conditions which obtain for the judge over the course of the hearing.

I argued in Chapter 6 that certain of the content of a judge's conceptual scheme is theoretically necessitated but that it is a theoretically contingent matter as to the remaining content of her scheme. At the commencement of a determination hearing, the non-necessarily possessed part of a judge's conceptual scheme may exhibit a degree of difference from that of any culturally different agent ranging from complete identity to complete difference. It is a theoretically contingent matter where on the spectrum of conceptual difference between these extremes a judge's scheme actually lies vis-à-vis that of such an agent. Likewise, I argued that the nature of the epistemic conditions which obtain for a judge in any given situation (including that obtaining over the course of a legal hearing) is a theoretically contingent matter, capable of taking a variety of forms within the bounds of theoretical possibility ranging from unconducive to conducive of the acquisition of culturally different concepts. On the argument mounted in Chapter 6, it is theoretically possible for the epistemic conditions which obtain over the course of a legal hearing to mirror the most ideal conditions generally possible in the world.

Both the content of a judge's conceptual scheme at the commencement of a hearing and the epistemic conditions which obtain for a judge over the course of a hearing are (and, therefore, can be) subject to some degree of regulation by legal norms. On the account of things offered in this book, legal norms are theoretically contingent, socially constructed phenomena capable of being formulated, reformulated and repealed so as to provide for the obtaining of a range of situations, all within the bounds of theoretical possibility. There is no reason to believe that any theoretical necessity operates upon the content of legal norms preventing them from providing for a degree of judicial conceptual difference or for a set of epistemic conditions conducive to the acquisition of any culturally different concept. Thus, the system of legal norms presently operative within a legal process both prior to and during a hearing is capable of being *interpretively reformed* so as to enable any of the range of theoretically possible judicial conceptual schemes and epistemic conditions to obtain, including those schemes and conditions most conducive as a general matter to the acquisition of any culturally different concept.[1] Within the limits of theoretical possibility, the norms regulating the content of a judge's conceptual scheme at the commencement of a hearing are amenable to reform so as to ensure a greater or lesser degree of conceptual difference between judge and culturally different agent at that point in time. Likewise, the legal norms regulating the epistemic conditions which obtain for a judge over the course of a determination hearing are, within the limits of theoretical possibility, amenable to reform so as to ensure that the epistemic conditions which obtain at hearing are conducive – even ideally so – to the judicial acquisition of culturally different concepts and understanding of culturally different actions.[2]

Thus, it is possible on our analysis for the system of norms constituting and regulating the legal system to sustain a degree of relevant conceptual difference and a set of epistemic conditions which will enable the judicial acquisition of any of those culturally different concepts, the possession of which is necessary for her to understand culturally different actions.[3] If such difference or such conditions do not actually obtain as a general matter under the present normative regime governing legal hearings (and it is possible on our analysis that they do not), then it is possible that that regime be reformed so as to ensure that they do obtain. It is possible that the norms regulating the legal process be reformed in a manner oriented towards both the reduction of the degree of relevant conceptual difference

1 By interpretive reform I mean reform oriented towards facilitating the judicial interpretation of testimonial evidence about culturally different concepts, the judicial and acquisition of such concepts and the judicial understanding of culturally different actions implicating such concepts.

2 Further, by virtue of the fact that, like all concepts, the concept of indigenous land title adopted by relevant judiciary is itself a product of the contingent practices of some authoritative set of agents, the indigenous land title system is also open to the effective reform of its capacity to formally recognize and protect indigenous actions, including conceptually different actions. As I have previously mentioned, the rebuttal of the radical cultural incommensurability thesis pursued in Chapter 6 also enables me to rebut a consequence of that thesis, namely that necessarily no legally valid concept of indigenous land title describes any claimant set of actions.

3 Likewise, of course, it is possible on our analysis for the norms regulating the legal system to sustain a degree of relevant conceptual difference and a set of epistemic conditions which *disable* such judicial acquisition.

between judge and culturally different actions which obtains at the commencement of legal hearings and the cultivation of interpretively and concept-acquisitively conducive epistemic conditions over the course of such hearings.

What I want to do in this chapter is provide a brief critical overview of certain key norms which presently regulate the judicial acquisition of culturally different concepts within the indigenous land title hearing process of a number of common law jurisdictions with the intention of clarifying some (at least) of the applied, legal reformist potential of the preceding philosophical analysis, as well as providing some indication of the direction which any sustained legal analysis of reform options might wish to take in the future. In order to keep the discussion manageable, I will use the concrete norms presently operative within the Australian native title system as my predominant – though not exclusive – focus. These norms are largely representative of those operating in the indigenous land title jurisdictions of most other contemporary common law jurisdictions. Additionally, they give the reader a useful sense of the kind of norms generally operative and the kinds of reform options more generally available in regard to the judicial understanding of cultural difference in legal systems throughout the world. Despite this focus, I will, where appropriate, make reference from time to time to relevant aspects of the law and procedure of other common law jurisdictions. The discussion in this chapter is intended to be suggestive rather than comprehensive in relation to the relevant norms and avenues of reform operative and available in this sphere. It is intended to give a preliminary and partial indication of the kind of substantive legal analysis and institutional reform, which might be engaged in in pursuing a critical and remedial agenda in relation the cross-cultural capacity of a legal system.

Legal Norms and the Content of the Judge's Conceptual Scheme

Consider, to start, the relationship between legal norms and the first element of the overall conditions determinative of the judicial capacity to acquire culturally different concepts – namely, the content of the judge's conceptual scheme vis-à-vis the culturally different agent's scheme. The degree of conceptual difference which obtains between a judge and a set of culturally different concepts and actions at the commencement of a legal hearing might be 'lessened' – that is, a judge might come to a legal hearings in possession of a greater store of relevant culturally different concepts and sub-concepts – were judges to be subject over the course of their career to an ongoing process of education about those culturally different concepts, actions, ways of life and other aspects of culture which are likely to come before them over the course of their tenure. That is, rather than rely upon ad hoc judicial enculturations into culturally different conceptual schemes on a hearing by hearing basis, the process of enculturation might be pre-empted to some extent by a sustained process of cross-cultural education both immediately prior to a person taking on the role of judge, as well as on an ongoing basis.

By such means, the amount of interpretive and concept-acquisitive work demanded of a judge over the course of a hearing – whatever the epistemic conditions which actually obtain at hearing – might be reduced and the acquisition of culturally different concepts facilitated. It follows from the analysis provided earlier in this book that the more pre-existing knowledge a judge has of a culturally different group's worldview and way of life, the less additional knowledge she need acquire over the course of a hearing in order to interpret relevant testimony and acquire a culturally different concept. Though some moves towards judicial education of this kind are, in fact, currently underway within the legal systems of a number of jurisdictions, they are limited.[4] In light of the analysis of judicial understanding offered in earlier chapters, further reform of the norms regulating such education so as to improve its quality and amount and regularity would only improve things.

Alternatively, or additionally, the norms presently regulating the selection of persons for duty as judges likely to be involved in intercultural proceedings might be reformed so as to ensure that judges are chosen exclusively from a field of persons already enculturated to some degree into some or all of the culturally different ways of life likely to come before such judges.[5] For example, relevant anthropological expertise might be made a prerequisite for appointment to the indigenous land title bench. Indeed, in such an area of law the field of candidates might be restricted to indigenous persons – assuming that the impartiality and fairness concerns which lie at the heart of the present legal prohibition on members of indigenous groups serving as land title judges in their own cases were addressed.[6] This is to say that the legal norms at work here might be reformed so as to reduce, prior to hearing, any conceptual gap which might obtain between judge and culturally different claimants. In the indigenous rights sphere, the norms regulating judicial selection and the ongoing education might be reformed with a view to *indigenizing* judges to some degree. There is no denying the extent of the challenge involved here – the number of distinct and distinctive cultural groups in a jurisdiction and the extent to which the various minority groups share concepts in common are important factors in the success of any such scheme. Nonetheless, some amelioration of the epistemic task facing judges may, as a general matter, be gained by some degree of law reform along these lines.

---

4 These jurisdictions include Canada, Australia and the US. See Armytage (1993), Gregorczuk (1996), Williams-Mozley (1999), Kirby (2000), Fryer-Smith (2002), Cooke (2002), Wallace (2003), Smith (2005).

5 See Kirby (2000) on this.

6 So, indigenous persons who are not members of a given indigenous claimant group in an indigenous land title matter might hear the claim of such group. Indeed, if the impartiality and fairness concerns which lie at the heart of the present legal prohibition on members of claimant groups serving as judges in their own cases could be otherwise addressed, legal practice in this regard might be reformed so as to enable even members of claimant groups to serve as adjudicators of their group's claim. Though, perhaps, unlikely given the present state of legal norms, it is within the realm of theoretical possibility.

Legal Norms and the Epistemic Conditions of the Legal Hearing

As far as the epistemic conditions which generally obtain over the course of legal hearings are concerned, all of which are regulated by some or other set of legal norms, a range of law reform opportunities present themselves by which the interpretive, concept-acquisitive and epistemic capacities of judges might be improved. Recall that in Chapters 4 and 6, I analysed these conditions in terms of the internal capacities of the judge and the external circumstances surrounding her over the course of a hearing. Relevant internal capacities include the functionality of the judge's sensory, cognitive, reasoning and behavioural apparatus; the strength of her desires or motivation to sensorily engage with relevant evidence, cognitively appropriate that evidence and reason about it; and the quality of the theoretical and practical skills she possesses in relation to culturally different concept acquisition (particularly, those relied upon in the interpretation of relevant testimonial evidence).[7] Relevant external circumstances fall broadly under categories to do with the amount and quality of relevant evidence which is available to and appropriated by the judge; the visual and auditory quality of her surroundings; the availability of sensory, bodily and reasoning aids and assistance; and the time available to her for interpretation, concept acquisition and understanding.

The Judge's Internal Capacities

As far as the internal capacities of judges go, the legal system might be rendered more interpretively and concept-acquisitively effective if the norms regulating the selection, dismissal and ongoing functionality and motivation of judges were such as to ensure the employment of persons who possess and maintain a high standard in relation to these capacities. On this approach, only persons with suitable faculties, motivation and theoretical and practical skills would be appointed to and retained on the bench. Those without these would be liable to dismissal and all judges would be subject to ongoing support in maintaining their faculties, motivation and skills by way of ongoing skills training and education, the provision of employment conditions conducive to ensuring good mental and physical health, and so on.[8] Most legal systems are, at present, already largely oriented towards the appointment of persons with suitable faculties and motivation. They may not, though, be sufficiently oriented towards the ongoing maintenance of those faculties or to the ready dismissal of those whose faculties

7 Including, most importantly, here the judge's capacity to interpretively reason within the parameters of the various theories of agency, mind, and the testimonial agent mentioned in Chapter 5.

8 This statement should not be taken as implying that some generic set of sensory faculties is required of judges. Persons with non-standard sensory endowments (the visually or aurally challenged, for example) may be entirely suitable to the role with or without extrinsic aids, making up in one area of sensory capacity what they might lack in another.

have fallen below an acceptable standard.[9] So too, it might be argued, the present norms regulating many legal spheres adequately ensure neither the appointment of persons adequately skilled enough in cross-cultural concept acquisition nor the ongoing education of existing judges in developing and perfecting such skills.[10] From a purely concept-acquisitive perspective, further reform may be necessary in this area of law across a range of jurisdictions.

The Judge's External Circumstances

The other category of epistemic conditions surrounding a judge over the course of a hearing is that to do with those circumstances external to her. Perhaps the most important of these concern the availability and cognitive accessibility of evidence relevant to the judge's acquisition of culturally different concepts. As a preliminary point, the capacity of a judge to acquire a culturally different concept depends crucially upon the very *existence* of evidence about that concept adequate to her acquisitive task. If there is no (or no practically adequate) real or documentary evidence in the world informative of the content of culturally different concepts or no (or no practically adequate set of) agents capable of testifying about the content of such concepts, then the judge will not be able to acquire such concepts by evidential means over the course of a hearing. Hence, general extra-legal circumstances surrounding the production and preservation and acquisition of relevant evidence importantly condition the ability of a judge to acquire culturally different concepts. To the extent that legal norms are capable of regulating such matters, law reform might be engaged in oriented towards ensuring the preservation and acquisition of any such evidence.[11]

---

9 Judicial tenure norms, though justifiable with reference to desirable political ends, may not serve purely inter-cultural communicative ends as effectively.

10 Nor the dismissal of those judges whose concept-acquisition skills have become inadequate and who cannot or will not be educated back up to standard. This point intersects with the point made earlier about the enculturation of judges into culturally different conceptual schemes. See on this, the Royal Commission into Aboriginal Deaths in Custody (1991) Vol. 3 pp. 71–80, New South Wales Law Reform Commission (2000) ch. 7, Kirby (2000), Williams-Mozley (2002).

11 As far as the preservation of relevant real evidence goes, for example, cultural heritage protection legislation throughout many jurisdictions, concerned as it is with the protection and preservation of significant minority cultural places and artefacts, offers an instance of the kind of legal norms which might presently apply here and which might be reformed. In Canada and the US, indigenous cultural protection is governed by a number of federal and provincial/state statutes, as well as by treaties and other agreements between government and indigenous groups. See Bell and Paterson (1999) and Kiers and Bell (2003) on relevant Canadian legislation and Phelan (1993) and Gerstenblith (1995) for a comprehensive overview of relevant US legislation. See Paterson (1999) on the New Zealand situation and McRae et al. (2003) ch. 8 on the situation in Australia. As far as the availability of suitable witnesses is concerned (particularly witnesses who are members of

Closer to home, the resources available to the parties involved in a legal matter in making relevant evidence available to the judge (including the knowledge and skills of their legal counsel in effectively identifying and tendering such evidence) are also germane external circumstances here. Laws ensuring that minority groups are more adequately resourced so as to effectively make out the evidential elements of their case might be enacted or improved.[12] Any such reforms might include mechanisms for the more regular engagement by culturally different groups of highly competent counsel, expert witnesses and other advisers.[13] Alternatively, replacing the present adversarial mode of inquiry presently provided for at law with a more inquisitorial mode might render the judicial interpretive and epistemic role more effective, provided the judiciary and its investigative staff were adequately resourced. In any event, the judiciary and its adjudicative support staff should be adequately resourced to enable them to perform their role more effectively.[14]

Additionally, the quality of witnesses as far as their capacity and willingness to effectively impart information about culturally different concepts to a judge is an important factor here. The selection of those witnesses best able to convey pertinent information to the judge may be affected by legal norms regulating the quality of legal counsel and their advice on suitable witnesses.[15] The quality of witnesses may also be affected by norms providing for the education of culturally

---

the relevant culturally different group), this is especially significant in the area of indigenous land title where the transmission of claim-related cultural knowledge from elders to the young may be vulnerable to interference or extinction. Addressing this threat invokes a series of complex and structural issues in relation to law reform – including, for example, issues to do with those laws affecting minority health, life-expectancy and education.

12 Asch and Bell (1994) pp. 532–3, Neate (2001) pp. 33–4. Kirby P in the Australian case of *Mason v Tritton* (1994) 34 NSWLR 572 at 600 referred to the 'exacting nature of the evidential burden established by [the law of indigenous land title]' and of the 'difficult evidentiary task' facing indigenous land title claimants in Australia. See also comments of Chief Justice Lamer for the majority in the Canadian Supreme Court case of Van der Peet (at para. 62).

13 In Australia, such mechanisms presently exist by virtue of those sections of the Native Title Act 1993 (Cth) (especially, Part 11) and related rules providing for legal representation to claimants by representative bodies. The rules on this might be reformed so as to improve both the availability and quality of counsel, experts and other advisors. See Perry and Lloyd (2003) pp. 661–726 and Bartlett (2004) ch. 29.

14 Relevant resources in the indigenous land title sphere include those necessary for the judge and the parties to travel to relevant geographic locations 'on country' where appropriate, as well as the provision of sensory, motor and reasoning aids for the use of the judge and others over the course of a hearing (such as binoculars, motor vehicles, aircraft, laptop computers, and so on). The present Chief Justice of the Federal Court of Australia, Michael Black, has commented that the logistical requirements of holding indigenous land title hearings on country is enormous and may limit the court's capacity to carry such hearings out to an interpretively necessary standard. Black (2002) p. 19. See also Neate (2001) p. 32.

15 Neate (1996) pp. 281–2.

different parties and witnesses about the operative legal process, both specific and general.[16] Further, educating culturally different witnesses in relation to the effects which their culturally-specific mode of interaction might have on dominant societal agent such as the judge or examining counsel may also be of use in improving the quality of information provided to the judge.[17] Overall, the better relevant witnesses understand the legal system and the dominant culture at large, the better able they will be to navigate that system's evidentiary demands and provide the judge with what she needs to properly perform her role. Where legal regulation affects the quality of that cross-cultural understanding, legal reform may be able to make a positive difference here.

One factor which can assist here and which is presently subject to legal regulation in many jurisdictions[18] is the provision of interpreters at hearing, tasked with the job of assisting both culturally different witnesses in effectively conveying their evidence, as well as the judge, counsel and others in understanding that evidence.[19]

---

16 The degree to which culturally different witnesses are enculturated into a dominant culture and are familiar with the operation of the dominant legal system more generally may also play a role in the quality of their evidence. The President of the National Native Title Tribunal in Australia himself has noted this very fact in commentary. 'The greater the differences between that person's culture and the culture on which the language is based, the greater the danger of that person misunderstanding the language and the culture to which is belongs.' Neate (2003) p. 34. This is, of course, only to make a point argued for throughout this book.

17 Eades (1994) and others (for example, Cooke (1995) pp. 87–8 and Neate (2003) p. 16) have noted the way in which certain of the interaction styles of certain indigenous persons may be misinterpreted by non-indigenous agents, compromising communication between them. These have been identified by theorists as including a failure to make eye contact during conversation (Eades (1994) p. 243), an indirect style of providing information, an aversion to 'either-or'-type questions (ibid. p. 247), and gratuitous concurrence to certain non-indigenous questions and assertions (ibid. p. 244). '[A] common Aboriginal response to inappropriate non-Aboriginal questioning is 'I don't know' or 'I don't remember'. Often this is not a statement concerning the speaker's knowledge or memory, but it is a comment on the communicative strategy, and would translate into Standard English as something like: 'This is not an appropriate way for me to provide information of this nature.' Eades (1994) p. 242.

18 Again, in the Australian context, see the Evidence Act 1995 (Cth) Section 30. This section has been interpreted generously by the Australian native title judiciary. Justice O'Loughlin in *De Rose v South Australia* [2002] FCA 1342 at para. 370, (hereafter referred to as the De Rose case) at para. 252 held that the legal value of fairness require that 'all parties to a dispute and their witnesses be given every reasonable opportunity to give their evidence in a manner that makes clear the information that the witness wishes to impart … In those cases where there may be doubts about the ability of a witness to express himself or herself in the English language, it is better to err on the side of caution and to permit witnesses to give their evidence in their first language' by means of an interpreter. See also Neate (2003) p. 15 on this.

19 Eades (1994) p. 236, and Neate (2003) p. 34.

Within the normative regime regulating their actions at hearing, interpreters may serve not only as translators of alien languages (including minority dialects of English) into standard English (indeed, legal English) and vice versa, but also in a more general explanatory role as mediators and facilitators of communication between culturally different witnesses and the judge and other agents involved in the hearing. For example, they might advise culturally different witnesses on the cultural and specifically legal practices and interactional styles of those dominant societal agents involved in the hearing, as well as advise those agents involved about the cultural practices and interactional styles of culturally different witnesses.[20] To the extent that the present set of legal norms in a given jurisdiction inhibits the capacity of interpreters to facilitate cross-cultural understanding between the agents in question (and a number of commentators have argued that it does[21]), that set may and should be reformed so as to better facilitate such understanding. This might occur by making interpreters more available, by loosening up the conditions under which they may be relied upon and by improving the quality of their bi-lingual, bi-cultural and legal understanding.[22]

Another issue relevant to the quality of the evidence about culturally different concepts provided by minority claimants and other culturally different witnesses, concerns the operation of minority secrecy norms upon the provision of such evidence.[23] Such norms operate within some minority groups to regulate the conveying of information about aspects of the group's worldview and way of life, whether by group members or by others.[24] So, for example, indigenous secrecy norms might prohibit or otherwise regulate the conveying to judge in an indigenous land title hearing by a knowledgeable witness of information about a claimant religious ritual. Where acquiring a concept of some aspect of that ritual

---

20 Neate (1996) p. 21. Neate (2003) pp. 37–8 points out that '[w]hen translating a question or an answer the interpreter may, quite properly, wish to give a detailed explanation of the concepts used. This will, on the one hand, go beyond a strict translation (if such a translation be possible) and may tend to be an explanation incorporating the interpreter's view about the information sought or the answers being given'. Eades (1994) p. 254 argues that interpreting involves more than translating. '... where the two speakers have rather different cultures, then the process of interpretation necessitates much paraphrasing and explaining of the concepts and ideas being translated.' Cooke (1995) pp. 67–76 shows how interpreters can shield culturally different witnesses from the anti-communicative and strategic practices of opposing counsel in cross-examination.

21 See, for example, Eades (1994) and Cooke (1995).

22 Neate (1981) p. 190, Byrne 2003 p. 4.

23 Fisher (1985), Walsh (1994), Eades (1994), Keen (1994), Neate (1996 and 2003).

24 Such as anthropologists who may have gained knowledge of secret aspects of the group's worldview and way of life. Norms regulating which persons may speak on which issue or concept also operate within many minority groups, including indigenous groups. These should and may be accommodated by counsel in selecting witnesses and by the judge and other agents in interpreting and otherwise interacting with culturally different witnesses. Neate (1981) p. 205.

is a necessary condition of the judge adequately understanding a claimant action implicating that concept (say, a ritual action), the reluctance of claimants and others in possession of knowledge about the ritual to impart their knowledge to the judge may prevent the judge acquiring the concept and understanding the action in question, with all the consequences which that entails for the action's legal recognition and protection. Now, it is clear that the legal norms of the dominant society do not *directly* regulate the operation of minority secrecy norms upon relevant agents. Minority secrecy norms subsist within an alternative normative regime to the dominant legal system. This is not to say, though, that dominant legal norms can have no effect on the compliance of relevant minority and non-minority agents with minority secrecy norms. A range of options are, in principle, available here which might broadly be categorized as either coercive or cooperative. Given the recognitional ethos of the legal system, coercive options – though not theoretically impossible – would generally be considered as unacceptable on moral or political grounds and will be ignored in the discussion to follow.[25] In any event, cooperative legal mechanisms may be just as effective as – indeed, may be more effective than – coercive ones. These involve establishing (through the introduction and development of relevant legal norms) a context within the hearing process which mitigates the extent of any breach of secrecy posed by the giving of sensitive information by imposing strict limits upon the extent of the actual and potential dominant societal (or minority) audience for any such information. It is then left to the minority group to choose whether or not to authorize the presentation of such information under such conditions.

Such mechanisms may take a variety of forms. One key form provided for under existing legal norms in a number of jurisdictions involves restricting the number of non-minority agents who may be present at the giving of sensitive testimony or who may view sensitive real or documentary evidence.[26] Thus, sensitive evidence might

25 For example, imposing criminal sanctions upon claimants or witnesses for any withholding on secrecy grounds of relevant information about culturally different concepts.

26 Fisher (1985). In Australia, Federal Court Rules Order 78, rule 31(3) empowers the hearing judge to make orders relating to the manner in which evidence may be presented to the court or relating to the presentation of evidence about a cultural or customary subject. This enables the court to restrict the hearing and publication of evidence. Black (2002) p. 23. Federal Court Rules Order 78, rules 32, 33 and 36 also allow the court to ensure a degree of confidentiality for culturally different evidence. Additionally, Section 50 of the Federal Court of Australia Act 1976 (Cth) states that 'The Court may, at any time during or after the hearing of a proceeding in the Court, make such order forbidding or restricting the publication of particular evidence, or the name of a party or witness, as appears to the Court to be necessary *in order to prevent prejudice to the administration of justice* or the security of the Commonwealth'. Section 17(4) of that Act also provides that 'The Court may order the exclusion of the public or of persons specified by the Court from a sitting of the Court where the Court is satisfied that the presence of the public or of those persons, as the case may be, would be contrary to the interests of justice'. Section 82(2) of the Australian Native Title Act 1993 (Cth) has also been interpreted so as to allow the court to exclude persons of

be (and indeed, has been) given by culturally different witnesses to a relatively small group of dominant societal agents involved in the hearing comprising, for example, only the judge, her associate, counsel for the minority parties and, perhaps, counsel for select other parties. In cases where minority secrecy norms have been gender-based,[27] legal norms have been enacted and applied so as to ensure that the select non-minority group accessing sensitive evidence has itself been gender restricted.[28] Another form of cooperative legal regulation on this topic has involved the restricting of subsequent general public access to records of any such evidence (including parts of the judge's written decision).[29]

Two concerns informing legislative and judicial practice internationally in this regard have been that non-minority parties to relevant legal proceedings are not unfairly prejudiced by any denial of access by them to culturally different evidence and that the public interest in knowing the basis for a judge's decision (say, to grant or not grant indigenous land title to indigenous groups) is provided for.[30] These concerns – formally provided for in a number of rules regulating the hearing process in a number of jurisdictions[31] – have resulted in less-than-ideal secrecy arrangements being imposed on or offered to culturally different parties (as far as they are concerned) in relation to certain evidence, and in some cases in such evidence not being tendered as a result.[32] To the extent that the present legal arrangements in many jurisdictions in relation to minority secrecy norms are not conducive to the provision of evidence necessary for the judicial acquisition of relevant culturally different concepts, those arrangements might be reformed so as to provide the most conducive arrangements possible – even in the face of operative fairness and public accountability concerns. At the end of the day, though, no matter what conditions are provided at law, a choice may still remain with the minority group as to whether they tender sensitive evidence under those conditions. The present system may be improved, though, so as to maximize the chances of culturally different parties making the choice to tender and enable the judge to acquire whatever concepts she needs to perform her role.[33]

---

a given gender from the adducing of certain gender-sensitive evidence, even if this means that no single legal advisor is aware of the whole of the evidence tendered in the case. Perry and Lloyd (2003) p. 495. Similar provisions exist in the equivalent legislation of other jurisdictions.

27 That is, knowledge of the aspect of the minority way of life in question is restricted to members of one or other gender within and outside the group.

28 Neate (1996) pp. 287–8.

29 Australian Law Reform Commission (1986) p. 487.

30 Neate (2003) p. 50.

31 For example, the (Australian) Evidence Act 1995 (Cth) Sections 11, 130, and 135–8.

32 Neate (1996) p. 297.

33 Indeed, the legal norms may be reformed so as to better allow for the negotiation by the culturally different parties and judge of a suitable set of procedural mechanisms in this respect.

One aspect of the present legal regime regulating indigenous land title claims in a number of jurisdictions which has facilitated conducive epistemic conditions for the acquisition of culturally different concepts through improving the quality of the hearing environment – and one linked to the preceding discussion – is the set of legal rules which authorizes the holding of all or part of the determination hearing on the claim area ('on country', as it is often put).[34] A range of interpretive and concept-acquisitive issues are addressed by the provision of this option to a judge. First, being on country may improve a judge's sensory and cognitive access to relevant real evidence of culturally different concepts – geographical locations, natural objects, performances of culturally different actions, and so on. It may also provide an environment in which culturally different witnesses may more comfortably – and, hence, more effectively – present their testimony. A number of commentators have noted the obstructive effect which the standard court environment in most modern jurisdictions has on the effective provision of evidence by witnesses unfamiliar with such environment.[35] In an indigenous land title matter, for example, there is evidence that indigenous witnesses are often more relaxed and informative when giving their evidence 'on country' than they would be in a courtroom dealing, for example, merely with photos and maps of the land under claim.[36]

On a related point, the present Chief Justice of the Federal Court of Australia has pointed out that in indigenous land title matters there the rule enabling the holding of hearings on country may go some way to addressing concerns arising out of indigenous norms regulating the tendering of evidence about the claimant culture. He notes that the 'on country' rule is 'an acknowledgment that, under traditional law, some evidence can *only* be given on country, and that there will

---

34 Most important in this respect in the Australian native title context is Federal Court Rules, Order 78, rule 35. The present Chief Justice of the Federal Court of Australia has pointed out (Black (2002) p. 18) that the capacity of a judge to hear evidence 'on country' there arises out of the flexibility afforded by this rule which provides that the court may at its discretion direct that evidence be 'taken at a time and in a manner other than in the normal course. This encompasses the holding of hearings on country'. The Chief Justice has stated (ibid.) that this provision 'is a recognition that, for many [indigenous land title] claimants, their relationship to country is *not* able to be explained in the abstract, and that it is necessary to be on country to gain a true appreciation and understanding of that relationship and the claimants' evidence about it'.

35 Neate (1996) p. 294. Justice O'Loughlin in the Australian case of De Rose referred to 'the apparent discomfort of witnesses in the context of formal court proceedings, suggesting that aspects of the evidence (some of which were unclear or confusing to the Court) may have been affected by the environment of the hearing'. Neate (2003) p. 75 quoting the De Rose case at paras 249, 428, 804, and 743. As part of the ethos underlying this approach, Australian judges have taken to adopting a less formal and hierarchical stance in that jurisdiction; sitting 'in the dust' with indigenous claimants in open necked shirts and speaking to them in a style which might be less intimidating and more intelligible.

36 Neate (1996) p. 294.

be many cases in which it would be quite wrong to expect claimants to talk about their relationship to country by reference to maps prepared by non-indigenous people; maps which may have no meaning to the claimants and which cannot begin to reflect their relationship to country'.[37] Again, to the extent that aspects of the present rules prevent the effective holding of hearings on country – out of judicial habit or concerns about the availability of resources for the Court or other parties to get onto country[38] – the rules might be reformed so as to make such holding of hearing easier.

Of course, whether 'on country' or in an urban courtroom, witnesses testifying to the content of a culturally different concept are presently subject to the norms establishing and maintaining an adversarial mode of fact finding within the legal process of many jurisdictions.[39] Under this mode, the testimonial evidence of culturally different witnesses in relation to culturally different concepts is provided to the court by way of responses to questions asked by counsel leading the evidence and is then subject to testing by way of questions asked by opposing counsel in cross-examination. It is commonly thought that this mode best serves the joint interest all legal hearings maintains in truth-finding and fairness to the parties, through enabling the parties to gather and present the evidence they think best serves their case, as well as test the reliability of the evidence gathered by other parties.[40]

However, empirical research has noted the detrimental effect that various aspects of the adversarial process have had and can have on the capacity of culturally different witnesses to effectively testify about relevant matters – the most notable of these being that set of norms which presently provide for the aggressive and manipulative cross-examination of minority and other witnesses by counsel for other parties.[41] In the indigenous land title sphere, for example, Cooke argues that,

> cross examination, as a type of discourse, is much more complex cross-culturally and contextually. It places an overwhelming demand on the witness to constantly

---

37 Black (2002) p. 18. Again, in applying this rule and in deciding whether or not to hold the hearing on country the judge may be subject to norms to do with fairness to other parties to the claim in. See the Australian Evidence Act 1995 (Cth) Section 82(2) and Federal Court Rules Order 32. Black (2002) pp. 18, 22.

38 See Justice O'Loughlin in the De Rose case at paras 8–9 and Black (2002) pp. 18–19. Black (2002) pp. 19–20 also discusses the ways in which visual, auditory and other cognitive problems arising out of 'on country' hearings can be addressed by technological means, thus, addressing another element of the judge's external circumstances identified in Chapter 6.

39 Ligertwood (1988) pp. 21–2.

40 Ligertwood (1988) pp. 21, 146, 231. The adversarial system is said to also serve fairness by ensuring that the judge stays out of the evidence gathering and testing process and maintains an impartial stance towards all parties. Ligertwood (1988) p. 21.

41 Eades (1994) pp. 241–6, Walsh (1994) p. 231.

> reorient himself as counsel jumps from one temporal, physical, interpersonal or cultural context to another; or to rapidly change from reporting, to conjecturing, to hypothesising (in succession). This often places an unreal expectation on the Aboriginal witness's level of sophistication in his knowledge of the English language and or Anglo-Australian patterns of discourse and communicative behaviour. Further to this, once it has been decided that the witness can take the stand without an interpreter, the witness is most frequently cross-examined in a manner which fails to provide an ongoing monitoring of his comprehension of what is being put to him … It is common to merely seek from the witness an affirmation of the proposition (put negatively or positively) that the lawyer wishes to establish. In some cases such propositions are contained within grammatically complex, lengthy and convoluted interrogatives. In being prompted into giving a yes/no response, and especially when cued as to which of these two alternatives is being sought, the witness is not required to demonstrate any significant degree of oral or aural competence in English and thus the court may find itself unable to evaluate the accuracy, veracity or applicability of the response.[42]

Evidence points to the members of certain culturally different groups not being skilled in the question-answer mode of interaction as a communicative strategy, even when that mode is engaged in in examination-in-chief (let alone under the strategic pressure of cross-examination). Rather, many such people maintain an alternative mode of communication – an alternative *pragmatics* of action, if you like, akin to the alternative semantics of action we have been concerned with throughout this book – which is often interfered with by the question and answer demands of the adversarial mode.[43] As a result, the capacity of culturally different witnesses to provide information about culturally different concepts and actions within the adversarial mode may be compromised. To the extent that the legal rules and the application of those rules by judges permits such a mode of interaction, interpretive and epistemic effectiveness on the part of the judge would demand the reform of those rules and their application so as to provide for a less adversarial approach to the giving of testimony. It must be noted, though, that

42 Cooke (1995) p. 77. Neate (2003) pp. 28–9 makes a similar point, as do a number of Australian judges, including Justice O'Loughlin in the De Rose case at para. 804.

43 Eades (1988 and 1992). In the Australian indigenous land title context, Neate (2003) p. 25 states that 'the elicitation of information by direct questioning is generally foreign to Aboriginal people and indirect discourses are often preferred'. Cooke (1996) p. 279 argues that 'narrative testimony is what conforms to Aboriginal speech registers and is conducive to a more thorough elicitation of evidence'. Cooke provides a graphic account of the differences in the story of an indigenous woman charged with murder about the circumstances of the killing when given in narrative form and when given in response to police questions. Walsh (1994) p. 231 similarly states that 'Aboriginal witnesses are wont to launch into a monologue when the barrister wants to chop the discourse up into a linked series of questions and answers in which the questions have been carefully pre-arranged. From the Aboriginal perspective this approach jars …'.

fairness concerns vis-à-vis non-minority parties to the proceedings, who may be concerned about the reliability of the testimony in question and who may want the reliability of that evidence tested in the crucible of strong cross-examination, currently serve as a significant constraint on reformist tendencies in this regard.[44] These concerns are, arguably, legitimate ones, not unproblematically ignored or otherwise marginalized in the pursuit of interpretive reform in the interests of culturally different agents.[45]

In any event, in a number of jurisdictions, there has been significant reform of orthodox legal norms in relation to the questioning of culturally different witnesses. In Australia, for example, since the passage of the Native Title Act in the early 1990s, a range of statutory rules has been enacted and subsequently interpreted by the judiciary which have enabled judges to manage the questioning of indigenous witnesses so as to assist them in communicating their knowledge to the court, whilst at the same time providing for the legitimate interests of other parties to the claim.[46] Additional to these, it might be mentioned, have been a set of rules authorizing the giving of testimonial evidence by indigenous people in groups, rather than individually, as is normally the case.[47] This has the potential to reduce the communicatively distorting effects arising out of the aggressive cross-

---

44 Ligertwood (1988) pp. 321–2.

45 And, of course, fairness to the *minority parties* to a legal proceeding would demand that they and their witnesses not be questioned in a manner which is distortive of their attempts to honestly communicate their knowledge of things.

46 In Australia, Section 11 of the Evidence Act 1995 (Cth) recognizes the Federal Court's general power to control the conduct of a proceeding, subject to the other provisions of the Act. Section 26 of the Evidence Act gives the Court the power to make orders in relation to the way in which witnesses are questioned and the presence and behaviour of any person in connection with the questioning of a witness. It provides that the judge may make such orders as she considers just in relation to the way in which witnesses are to be questioned and the presence and behaviour or any person in connection with the questioning of a witness. This section has been interpreted as being subject to the other provisions of the Evidence Act and as not authorizing any control contrary to the principles of natural justice. Odgers (2000) p. 55. Finally, Section 29 of the Evidence Act allows the judge to permit a witness to give her evidence wholly or partially in narrative form upon an application from the party. In this way, culturally different witnesses may avoid the question and answer format and communicate better with the judge. 'Such an approach, it seems, should make the witness more comfortable in giving evidence and should enable more comprehensive evidence to be given, unconstrained by highly particular (and sometimes ill-informed or misdirected) questions'. Neate (2003) p. 30. Canadian common law too enables judges to attend to the special needs of indigenous parties and witnesses. See the comments of Chief Justice Lamer for the majority in the Canadian cases of Van der Peet (at para. 68) and Delgamuukw (at paras 80 and 87).

47 The Australian Federal Court Rules Order 34 allows that Court 'if it considers that in all the circumstances it is in the interests of justice to do so, [to] receive into evidence statements from a group of witnesses, or a statement from a witness after that witness has consulted with other persons'. See Neate (1996) p. 285, Black (2002) p. 22.

examination of individual witnesses, as well as addressing any indigenous norms which might apply regulating the context in which information about cultural matters may properly be articulated, especially if it is used in conjunction with the giving of evidence on country. The Australian Law Reform Commission has pointed out that,

> [a]n Aborigine may have, according to customary laws, no authority to speak on a given matter, but may be able to give evidence in conjunction with others who collectively have such authority. The land claim experience has been that the Aboriginal evidence is likely to be both fuller and more persuasive when it is given in the presence of peers who both by their own evidence and by their demeanour confirm the truth of what is said. Such group evidence may be an important way of increasing both the accuracy and the amount of evidence from a witness. It helps to overcome a situation where one person has no right to speak alone but can do so in the presence of others.[48]

Notwithstanding the various provisions presently provided by legal systems to facilitate a more communicatively effective questioning of culturally different witnesses about culturally different concepts and actions, a range of reforms to those provisions, as well as to their interpretation and application by the judiciary, are possible and worthy of further exploration. As Neate argues in the indigenous context,

> ... because Indigenous peoples choose (or are effectively compelled) to use the general legal system to prove the existence and content of their traditional legal systems we need to provide legal processes that are administered or adapted to ensure that their case is able to be put clearly and assessed on its merits. The Indigenous peoples of Australia are locked into a system of law that is still foreign to many of them. Given the difficulties often facing witnesses and counsel attempting to communicate clearly to each other, the form of questions to be asked may need to be considered carefully to ensure that they elicit comprehensive and accurate answers.[49]

---

48 Australian Law Reform Commission (1986) p. 481. See also Black (2002) p. 22, Perry and Lloyd (2003) p. 494, and Neate (2003) pp. 32–3 on this. Of course, the obstacles which such group evidence can pose to effective judicial interpretation, concept acquisition and understanding should not be ignored. Walsh (1994) p. 229. Nonetheless, norms mitigating these obstacles may be developed. See Australian Law Reform Commission (1986) p. 483 for a discussion of the ways in which the Northern Territory Land Rights Commission dealt with this issue.

49 Neate (2003) p. 17. Neate, who is currently the President of the National Native Title Tribunal in Australia, goes on at p. 30 to state that '[w]hile present practices prevail, however, we need to ensure that they are attuned to meet the particular challenges of cross-cultural communication'. See also Eades (1994) on this point, who argues we should seek to

An Interpretive Ethos?

Statements such as this one by the current President of the National Native Title Tribunal in Australia are consistent with a range of more general statements by past and serving members of the judiciaries of a number of jurisdictions about the interpretive potential and current interpretive progress of the legal system. For example, the present Chief Justice of the Australian Federal Court has stated, in noting how the indigenous land title system there is rapidly developing new practices and procedures in dealing with indigenous needs and the requirements of cross-cultural interpretation and recognition, that 'much time and thought has been devoted to ensuring that the court's procedures in native title cases are appropriate and sufficiently flexible to accommodate cultural requirements and the needs of all the parties who come before it'. He goes on to say that '[t]he emphasis on developing appropriate procedures reflects the understanding that this area of law is unique and that unique procedures are required. The process of developing such procedures is an ongoing one, and is an important part of the journey that we, as judges of the Federal Court, are making as we learn from our experiences in native title cases'.[50] In the Canadian Supreme Court, similar sentiments have been expressed by its Chief Justice who said in the Van der Peet case that,

> [i]n determining whether an aboriginal claimant has produced evidence sufficient to demonstrate that her activity is an aspect of a practice, custom or tradition integral to a distinctive aboriginal culture, a court should approach the rules of evidence, and interpret the evidence that exists, with a consciousness of the special nature of aboriginal claims, and of the evidentiary difficulties in proving a right which originates in times where there were no written records of the practices, customs and traditions engaged in. The courts must not undervalue the evidence presented by aboriginal claimants simply because that evidence does not conform precisely with the evidentiary standards that would be applied in, for example, a private law torts case.[51]

One might conclude from these various statements that the set of legal norms regulating the legal system in a number of common law jurisdictions displays what might be termed a cross-culturally interpretive ethos. It might be argued that such an ethos is evident in the semantic content of a number of its statutory rules and in the ongoing interpretation and application of those rules by the judiciary

---

make the information gathering mechanisms of the legal hearing more like the information gathering mechanisms of the culturally different group in question.

50 Black (2002) p. 17. See also the comment of Justice O'Loughlin in the De Rose case at para. 252 that, '[t]he interests of justice require that all parties to a dispute and their witnesses be given every reasonable opportunity to give their evidence in a manner that makes clear the information that the witness wishes to impart'.

51 Van der Peet at para. 68.

in the courts of those jurisdictions.[52] Further evidence of this ethos may also be found in certain doctrines of the common law of indigenous land title which, as we saw in Chapter 3, underlies many of the statutory regimes in common law jurisdictions. For example, the common law doctrine of *sui generis*, which operates as a fundamental theoretical and methodological norm informing all aspects of indigenous land title practice, commands both a recognition by judges throughout the common law world of the possibility of the obtaining of significant conceptual difference between indigenous and non-indigenous schemes and a methodological accommodation of any such difference by its overt proscription of any radical ethnocentrism (along interpretationist lines, say) and its recommendation of the adoption of a conceptually dynamic interpretive and epistemic strategy akin to that outlined in Chapter 5 of this book.[53]

The doctrine of sui generis reflects an underlying commitment of many common law legal systems to facilitating the judicial understanding of culturally different action along the lines elaborated in this book. This, in turn, reflects the commitment of those legal systems to uncovering relevant facts (including conceptual facts) in pursuing its adjudicative role – subject, of course, to sometimes countervailing commitments to fairness to the parties and to the wider public interest.[54] The aim of any effective law reform agenda should be to exploit the reformist potential inherent in the interpretive ethos of a legal system and direct it to cross-culturally

52 In Australia, see for example, Section 82 (2) of the Native Title Act 1993 (Cth) which states that '[i]n conducting its proceedings, the Court may take account of the cultural and customary concerns of Aboriginal peoples and Torres Strait Islanders', though, 'not so as to prejudice unduly any other party to the proceedings'. See Perry and Lloyd (2003) pp. 494–5 for a discussion of how this provision has been interpreted and applied by the Australian Federal Court. Further, Australian Federal Court Rules Order 78 rule.4(1) similarly states that '[a]t any time in a proceeding, the Court may give the directions and make the orders it considers appropriate to take account of the cultural or customary concerns of a party to the proceeding or another person'. See Black (2002), Neate (2003), Perry and Lloyd (2003) pp. 493–8 and the decisions of Justice O'Loughlin in the De Rose case and the High Court in the Yorta Yorta case for discussion of how the indigenous land title judiciary in Australia has interpreted and applied relevant statutory and related provisions.

53 The explicit historical roots of the doctrine lie in Canadian indigenous land title cases such as *Guerin v R* (1984) 13 DLR (4th) at 339, though it is implicit in early twentieth-century Privy Council cases such as *Amodu Tijani v Secretary, Southern Nigeria* [1921] 2 AC 399 at 403. On the dynamic interpretive methodology inherent in the doctrine, see Borrows and Rotman (1997), Bell and Asch (1997) pp. 48–9, and the decisions of Chief Justice Lamer and Justice L'Heureux-Dube in the Delgamuukw case. For example, Chief Justice Lamer states in that case at para. 82 that 'aboriginal rights are truly sui generis, and demand a unique approach to the treatment of evidence which accords due weight to the perspective of aboriginal peoples'. This interpretively dynamic approach has been cited with approval in a number of Australian cases including *Ward v Western Australia* (1998) 159 ALR 483 at 504. Chief Justice Lamer's statement has also been explicitly approved by the Chief Justice of the Federal Court of Australia in Black (2002) p. 17.

54 Odgers (2000) pp. 354–77, Bayne (2003) pp. 1–2.

effective interpretive, concept-acquisitive and epistemic ends. What this book has endeavoured to show is that such a reformist course of action is possible. Indeed, it is presently underway in many jurisdictions. On the physicalist and functionalist approach adopted in this book, we can make good sense of that possibility and its present realization within a legal system.

Final Remarks

The reform issues raised in this chapter are all important and interesting ones, deserving of a thorough and physicalistically sound exploration. Regrettably, a fully detailed exploration of those issues is a task to be pursued in another context. The primary purpose of this book has been to provide a philosophically, scientifically and legally informed *basis* for the pursuit of a sustained reformist project as far as cross-cultural understanding at law is concerned. Its grounding upon a cogent metaphysics and philosophical method, its consequent intersection with the findings and methodology of the natural and social sciences, and its orientation around solid legal doctrinal and procedural analysis increase, I would argue, the likely effectiveness of any proposals for reform such a project might engender. An important meta-theoretical aim of this book is that it provide a token of the contribution which a sound philosophical analysis might make to the cause of legal reform. Hence, this chapter.

As I stated in Chapter 1, I share the concern of the incommensurabilist critics of the legal system about the capacity of the agents of that system to adequately understand culturally different action and properly recognize and protect culturally different ways of life. It is clear from an analysis of the epistemic conditions which presently obtain within the legal systems of common law jurisdictions and many others that obstructions to the proper judicial understanding of culturally different actions – and, therefore, to their proper recognition and protection – exist. These conditions are capable of and demand reform. Any such reformist efforts, though, must be based on a sound comprehension of the nature of the phenomena involved. The radical incommensurabilist reading of those phenomena cannot, by its very nature, provide such a basis for reform. It not only fails to provide us with any cogent insight into the nature of the phenomena involved but it denies the very possibility of reform and consigns the theorists, officials and concerned citizens of societies in which culturally different minorities reside to a personal and institutional impotence in the face of those minorities urgent ethical and political demands. I have sought to argue that the physicalist-functionalist analysis of things offered here not only gives a detailed and coherent insight into the nature of all of the phenomena involved in the judicial understanding of culturally different thought and practice, but also provides us with a solid and effective basis for identifying, making sense of and actively addressing the weaknesses and strengths of the legal system in giving culturally different people some degree of what they want – the legal recognition and protection of their ways of life.

Bibliography

Adorno, T. and Horkheimer, M. (1979). *Dialectic of Enlightenment* (J. Cumming, trans.). London: Verso.

Alexander, S. (1920). *Space, Time, and Deity* (Vol. 2). London: Macmillan.

Allen, C.K. (1964). *Law in the Making*. Oxford: Oxford University Press.

Anscombe, G.E.M. (1963). *Intention* (2nd edn). Oxford: Blackwell.

Armytage, L. (1993). Policy Development in Continuing Judicial Education: An Assessment of Some Approaches Taken in NSW, USA, UK, and Canada. *Journal of Professional Legal Education*, 11(1), 51–77.

Asch, M. (ed.). (1997). *Aboriginal and Treaty Rights in Canada: Essays on Law, Equity and Respect for Difference*. Vancouver: University of British Columbia Press.

Asch, M. and Bell, C. (1994). Definition and Interpretation of Fact in Canadian Aboriginal Title Litigation: An Analysis of Delgamuukw. *Queen's Law Journal*, 19 (No. 2 Spring), 503–50.

Ashcroft, B., Griffiths, G. and Tiffin, H. (eds). (1995). *The Post-colonial Studies Reader*. London: Routledge.

Astington, J. (1996). What is Theoretical about the Child's Theory of Mind?: A Vygotskian View of its Fevelopment. In P. Carruthers and P.K. Smith (eds), *Theories of Theories of Mind* (pp. 184–99). Cambridge: Cambridge University Press.

Astington, J.W., Harris, P.L. and Olson, D.R. (eds). (1988). *Developing Theories of Mind*. Cambridge: Cambridge University Press.

Australian Law Reform Commission. (1986). *The Recognition of Aboriginal Customary Laws* (No. 31). Canberra: Australian Law Reform Commission.

Avis, J. and Harris, P.L. (1991). Belief-desire Reasoning among Baka Children: Evidence for a Universal Conception of Mind. *Child Development*, 62, 460–67.

Baillargeon, R. (1999). The Object Concept Revisited: New Directions in the Investigation of Infants' Physical Knowledge. In E. Margolis and S. Laurence (eds), *Concepts: Core Readings* (pp. 571–612). Cambridge, MA: MIT Press.

Barnes, B. (1995). *The Elements of Social Theory*. Princeton, NJ: Princeton University Press.

Barnes, B. and Bloor, D. (1982). Relativism, Rationalism and the Sociology of Knowledge. In M. Hollis and S. Lukes (eds), *Rationality and Relativism* (pp. 21–47). Cambridge, MA: MIT Press.

Barnes, J. (1987). *Early Greek Philosophy*. London: Penguin Books.

Bar-on, D. (1994). Conceptual Relativism and Translation. In F.S.G. Preyer and A. Ulfig (eds), *Language, Mind and Epistemology: On Donald Davidson's Philosophy* (pp. 145–70). Dordrecht: Kluwer Academic Publishers.

Baron-Cohen, S. (1995). *Mindblindness*. Cambridge, MA: MIT Press.

Bartlett, R.H. (ed.). (1993a). *The Mabo Decision*. Sydney: Butterworths.
Bartlett, R.H. (1993b). The Source, Content and Proof of Native Title at Common Law. In R.H. Bartlett (ed.), *Resource Development and Aboriginal Land Rights in Australia* (pp. 35–60). Perth: The Centre for Commercial and Resources Law [of] the University of Western Australia and Murdoch University.
Bartlett, R.H. (2000). *Native Title in Australia* (1st edn). Sydney: Butterworths.
Bartlett, R.H. (2004). *Native Title in Australia* (2nd edn). Chatswood, NSW: LexisNexis Butterworths.
Bauman, Z. (1993). *Postmodern Ethics*. Oxford: Blackwell.
Bayne, P. (2003). *Uniform Evidence Law: Text and Essential Cases*. Sydney: Federation Press.
Becker, L.C. (1977). *Property Rights: Philosophical Foundations*. London: Routledge and Kegan Paul.
Beckermann, A., Flohr, H. and Kim, J. (eds). (1992). *Emergence or Reduction?* Berlin: De Gruyter.
Beckett, J.R. (ed.). (1988). *Past and Present – The Construction of Aboriginality*. Canberra: Aboriginal Studies Press.
Bell, C. and Asch, M. (1997). Challenging Assumptions: The Impact of Precedent in Aboriginal Rights Litigation. In M. Asch (ed.), *Aboriginal and Treaty Rights in Canada: Essays on Law, Equity and Respect for Difference* (pp. 38–74). Vancouver: University of British Columbia Press.
Bell, C. and Paterson, R. (1999). Aboriginal Rights to Cultural Property in Canada. *International Journal of Cultural Property*, 8, 167–211.
Berger, P. and Luckman, T. (1967). *The Social Construction of Reality*. Harmondsworth: Penguin Books.
Bernstein, R. (1971). *Praxis and Action*. London: Duckworth.
Bernstein, R.J. (1983). *Beyond Objectivism and Relativity*. Oxford: Basil Blackwell Ltd.
Bhabha, H.K. (1993). *The Location of Culture*. London: Routledge.
Black, M. (2002). Developments in Practice and Procedure in Native Title Cases. *Public Law Review*, 13(March), 16–25.
Block, N. (ed.). (1980a). *Readings in Philosophy of Psychology: Volume 1*. Cambridge, MA: Harvard University Press.
Block, N. (1980b). Troubles with Functionalism. In N. Block (ed.), *Readings in Philosophy of Psychology: Volume 1* (pp. 268–305). Cambridge, MA: Harvard University Press.
Block, N. (1981). Psychologism and Behaviourism. *Philosophical Review, 90*, 5–43.
Block, N. (1994). Consciousness. In S. Guttenplan (ed.), *A Companion to the Philosophy of Mind* (pp. 210–19). Oxford: Blackwell.
Block, N. and Fodor, J.A. (1972). What Psychological States are Not. *Philosophical Review*, 81(2), 159–81.
Block, N. and Stalnaker, R. (1999). Conceptual Analysis, Dualism and the Explanatory Gap. *Philosophical Review*, 108(1), 1–46.

Boas, F. (1966). *Introduction to the Handbook of American Indian Languages*. Lincoln: University of Nebraska Press.

Bohman, J. (1991). *New Philosophy of Social Science*. Cambridge, MA: MIT Press.

Bonevac, D. (1995). Reduction in the Mind of God. In E.E. Savellos and U.D. Yalcin (eds), *Supervenience: New Essays* (pp. 124–39). Cambridge: Cambridge University Press.

Borrows, J. and Rotman, L. (1997). The Sui Generis Nature of Aboriginal Rights: Does It Make a Difference? *Alberta Law Review*, 36(1), 9–45.

Botterill, G. (1996). Folk Psychology and Theoretical Status. In P. Carruthers and P.K. Smith (eds), *Theories of Theories of Mind* (pp. 105–18). Cambridge: Cambridge University Press.

Botterill, G. and Carruthers, P. (1999). *The Philosophy of Psychology*. Cambridge: Cambridge University Press.

Braddon-Mitchell, D. and Jackson, F. (1996). *Philosophy of Mind and Cognition*. Oxford: Blackwell.

Bratman, M. (1992). Shared Co-operative Activity. *Philosophical Review*, 101(2), 327–41.

Bruner, J., Goodnow, J. and Austin, G. (1999). The Process of Concept Attainment. In E. Margolis and S. Laurence (eds), *Concepts: Core Readings* (pp. 101–23). Cambridge, MA: MIT Press.

Byrne, J.-A. (2003). Indigenous Witnesses and the Native Title Act 1993 (Cth). *National Native Title Tribunal Occasional Papers Series*(2).

Cairns, B.C. (1996). *Australian Civil Procedure* (4th edn). Sydney: Law Book Company.

Campbell, K. (1970). *Body and Mind*. London: Macmillan.

Cane, P. (2002). *Responsibility in Law and Morality*. Oxford: Hart Publishing.

Carnap, R. (1959). The Elimination of Metaphysics through Logical Analysis of Language. In A.J. Ayer (ed.), *Logical Positivism* (pp. 60–81). New York: The Free Press.

Carruthers, P. (1996). Simulation and Self-knowledge: A Defence of Theory-theory. In P. Carruthers and P.K. Smith (eds), *Theories of Theories of Mind* (pp. 22–38). Cambridge: Cambridge University Press.

Carruthers, P. and Smith, P.K. (eds). (1996). *Theories of Theories of Mind*. Cambridge: Cambridge University Press.

Castle, G. (ed.). (2001). *Postcolonial Discourses: An Anthology*. Oxford: Blackwell.

Chalmers, D.J. (1996). *The Conscious Mind: In Search of a Fundamental Theory*. New York: Oxford University Press.

Charles, D. and Lennon, K. (eds). (1992). *Reduction, Explanation, and Realism*. New York: Oxford University Press.

Cherniak, C. (1986). *Minimum Rationality*. Cambridge, MA: MIT Press.

Child, W. (1994). *Causality, Interpretation and the Mind*. Oxford: Clarendon Press.

Chomsky, N. (1994). Noam Chomsky. In S. Guttenplan (ed.), *A Companion to the Philosophy of Mind* (pp. 153–67). Oxford: Blackwell.

Churchland, P.M. (1979). *Scientific Realism and the Plasticity of Mind.* Cambridge: Cambridge University Press.

Churchland, P.M. (1981). Eliminative Materialism and the Propositional Attitudes. *Journal of Philosophy*, 78, 67–90.

Churchland, P.M. (1994). Folk Psychology. In S. Guttenplan (ed.), *A Companion to the Philosophy of Mind* (pp. 308–16). Oxford: Blackwell.

Churchland, P.S. (1986). *Neurophilosophy: Towards a Unified Science of the Mind/Brain.* Cambridge, MA: MIT Press.

Clark, E. (1973). What's in a Word? On the Child's Acquisition of Semantics in His First Language. In T.E. Moore (ed.), *Cognitive Development and the Acquisition of Language* (pp. 65–110). New York: Academic Press.

Clark, M. (1990). *Nietzsche on Truth and Philosophy*. Cambridge: Cambridge University Press.

Clifford, J. (1988). *The Predicament of Culture: Twentieth-century Ethnography, Literature, and Art*. Cambridge, MA: Harvard University Press.

Connolly, A. (2005). Conceiving of Tradition: Dynamics of Judicial Interpretation and Explanation in Native Title Law. In S. Corcoran and S. Bottomley (eds), *Interpreting Statutes* (pp. 118–46). Sydney: Federation Press.

Connolly, A. (2006). Conceptual Incommensurability and the Judicial Understanding of Indigenous Action. Unpublished PhD Thesis. Canberra: Australian National University.

Connolly, W.E. (1991). *Identity/Difference: Democratic Negotiations of Political Paradox*. Ithaca, NY: Cornell University Press.

Connor, S. (ed.). (2004). *The Cambridge Companion to Postmodernism.* Cambridge: Cambridge University Press.

Cooke, M. (1995). Aboriginal Evidence in the Cross-cultural Courtroom. In D. Eades (ed.), *Language in Evidence: Issues Confronting Aboriginal and Multicultural Australia* (pp. 55–96). Sydney: UNSW Press.

Cooke, M. (2002). *Indigenous Interpreting Issues for Courts*. Melbourne: The Australian Institute of Judicial Administration.

Cornell, D. (1992). *The Philosophy of the Limit*. London: Routledge.

Cornell, D., Rosenfeld, M. and Carlson, D.G. (eds). (1992). *Deconstruction and the Possibility of Justice*. New York: Routledge.

Cowie, F. (1999). *What's Within: Nativism Reconsidered.* Oxford: Oxford University Press.

Crane, T. (1994). Physicalism (2): Against Physicalism. In S. Guttenplan (ed.), *A Companion to the Philosophy of Mind* (pp. 479–84). Oxford: Blackwell.

Crane, T. and Mellor, D.H. (1990). There is No Question of Physicalism. *Mind*, 99(394), 185–206.

Culler, J. (1989). *On Deconstruction: Theory and Criticism after Structuralism.* London: Routledge.

Cusset, F. (2008). *French Theory: How Foucault, Derrida, Deleuze and Co Transformed the Intellectual Life of the United States*. Minneapolis: University of Minnesota Press.

Davidson, D. (1963). Actions, Reasons, and Causes. In *Essays on Actions and Events* (pp. 3–19). Oxford: Clarendon Press.

Davidson, D. (1967). Causal Relations. In *Essays on Actions and Events* (pp. 149–62). Oxford: Clarendon Press.

Davidson, D. (1969). The Individuation of Events. In *Essays on Actions and Events* (pp. 163–180). Oxford: Clarendon Press.

Davidson, D. (1970a). Mental Events. In *Essays on Actions and Events* (pp. 207–27). Oxford: Clarendon Press.

Davidson, D. (1970b). Events as Particulars. In *Essays on Actions and Events* (pp. 181–7). Oxford: Clarendon Press.

Davidson, D. (1971). Agency. In *Essays on Actions and Events* (pp. 43–61). Oxford: Clarendon Press.

Davidson, D. (1973). Radical Interpretation. In *Inquiries into Truth and Interpretation* (pp. 125–39). Oxford: Clarendon Press.

Davidson, D. (1974a). Psychology as Philosophy. In *Essays on Actions and Events* (pp. 229–39). Oxford: Clarendon Press.

Davidson, D. (1974b). Belief and the Basis of Meaning. In *Inquiries into Truth and Interpretation* (pp. 141–54). Oxford: Clarendon Press.

Davidson, D. (1974c). On the Very Idea of a Conceptual Scheme. In *Inquiries into Truth and Interpretation* (pp. 183–98). Oxford: Clarendon Press.

Davidson, D. (1975). Thought and Talk. In *Inquiries into Truth and Interpretation* (pp. 155–70). Oxford: Clarendon Press.

Davidson, D. (1978). Intending. In *Essays on Actions and Events* (pp. 83–102). Oxford: Clarendon Press.

Davidson, D. (1980). *Essays on Actions and Events*. Oxford: Clarendon Press.

Davidson, D. (1984). *Inquiries into Truth and Interpretation*. Oxford: Clarendon Press.

Davidson, D. (1986a). Empirical Content. In E. LePore (ed.), *Truth and Interpretation: Perspectives on the Philosophy of Donald Davidson* (pp. 320–31). Oxford: Basil Blackwell.

Davidson, D. (1986b). A Nice Derangement of Epitaphs. In *Truth, Language and History* (pp. 89–107). Oxford: Clarendon Press.

Davidson, D. (1986c). A Coherence Theory of Truth and Knowledge. In E. Lepore (ed.), *Truth and Interpretation: Perspectives on the Philosophy of Donald Davidson* (pp. 307–19). Oxford: Basil Blackwell.

Davidson, D. (1989). The Myth of the Subjective. In *Subjective, Intersubjective, Objective* (pp. 39–52). Oxford: Clarendon Press.

Davidson, D. (1997). Seeing through Language. In J. Preston (ed.), *Thought and Language* (pp. 15–27). Cambridge: Cambridge University Press.

Davies, M. and Stone, T. (1995). *Mental Simulation: Evaluations and Applications*. Oxford: Blackwell.

Davies, M. and Stone, T. (eds). (1995). *Folk Psychology: The Theory of Mind Debate*. Oxford: Blackwell.
Davis, L.H. (1994). Action. In S. Guttenplan (ed.), *A Companion to the Philosophy of Mind* (pp. 111–17). Oxford: Blackwell.
Dennett, D. (1978a). *Brainstorms: Philosophical Essays on Mind and Psychology*. Cambridge, MA: MIT Press.
Dennett, D. (1978b). Beliefs about beliefs. *Behavioral and Brain Sciences*, 1, 568–70.
Dennett, D. (1980a). Headaches. *Philosophical Books*, 21(2), 65–73.
Dennett, D. (1980b). Reply to Professor Stich. *Philosophical Books*, 21(2), 73–6.
Dennett, D. (1981). Making Sense of Ourselves. *Philosophical Topics*, 12(1), 63–82.
Dennett, D. (1987). *The Intentional Stance*. Cambridge, MA: MIT Press.
Derrida, J. (1976). *Of Grammatology* (G.C. Spivak, trans.). Baltimore, MD: Johns Hopkins University Press.
Derrida, J. (1978). *Writing and Difference* (A. Bass, trans.). London: Routledge and Keegan Paul.
Derrida, J. (1992). Force of Law: The 'Mystical Foundation of Authority' (M. Quaintance, trans.). In D. Cornell, M. Rosenfeld and D.G. Carlson (eds), *Deconstruction and the Possibility of Justice* (pp. 3–67). New York: Routledge.
Derrida, J. (1998). *Monolingualism of the Other: or, The Prosthesis of Origin* (P. Mensah, trans.). Stanford, CA: Stanford University Press.
Devitt, M. (1991). *Realism and Truth* (2nd edn). Princeton, NJ: Princeton University Press.
Devitt, M. and Sterelny, K. (1987). *Language and Reality: An Introduction to the Philosophy of Language*. Cambridge, MA: MIT Press.
Dews, P., (1987). *Logics of Disintegration: Post-Structuralist Thought and the Claims of Critical Theory*. London: Verso. .
DiPietro, J.A., Hodgson, D.M., Costigan, K.A., Hilton, S.C. and Johnson, T.R.B. (1996a). Fetal Neurobehavioral Development. *Child Development*, 67(5), 2553–67.
DiPietro, J.A., Hodgson, D.M., Costigan, K.A. and Johnson, T.R.B. (1996b). Fetal Antecedents of Infant Temperament. *Child Development*, 67(5), 2568–83.
Divers, J. (2002). *Possible Worlds*. London: Routledge.
Doherty, J., Graham, E. and Malek, M. (eds). (1992). *Postmodernism and the Social Sciences*. New York: St Martin's Press.
Donnellan, K. (1966). Reference and Definite Descriptions. *Philosophical Review*, 75(3), 281–304.
Douzinas, C. and Warrington, R. (1994). *Justice Miscarried: Ethics, Aesthetics and the Law*. London: Harvester Wheatsheaf.
Douzinas, C., Warrington, R. and McVeigh, S. (eds). (1991). *Postmodern Jurisprudence: The Law of Text in the Texts of Law*. London: Routledge.
Dray, W. (1957). *Laws and Explanation in History*. Oxford: Clarendon Press.

Dretske, F. (1988). *Explaining Behaviour: Reasons in a World of Causes*. Cambridge, MA: MIT Press.

Dretske, F. (1995). *Naturalizing the Mind*. Cambridge, MA: MIT Press.

Eades, D. (1984). Misunderstanding Aboriginal English: The Role of Socio-cultural Context. In G.R. McKay and B.A. Sommer (eds), *Further Applications of Linguistics to Australian Aboriginal Contexts* (Vol.'Occasional Papers No. 8, pp. 24–33). Melbourne: Applied Linguistics Association of Australia.

Eades, D. (1991). Communicative Strategies in Aboriginal English. In S. Romaine (ed.), *Language in Australia* (pp. 84–93). Cambridge: Cambridge University Press.

Eades, D. (1992). *Aboriginal English and the Law: Communicating with Aboriginal English Speaking Clients: A Handbook for Legal Practitioners*. Brisbane: Queensland Law Society.

Eades, D. (1994). A Case of Communicative Clash: Aboriginal English and the Legal System. In J. Gibbons (ed.), *Language and the Law* (pp. 234–64). London: Longman.

Eades, D. (1995). *Language in Evidence: Issues Confronting Aboriginal and Multicultural Australia*. Sydney: UNSW Press.

Enc, B. (1995). Nonreducible Supervenient Causation. In E.E. Savellos and U.D. Yalcin (eds), *Supervenience: New Essays* (pp. 169–86). Cambridge: Cambridge University Press.

Evnine, S. (1991). *Donald Davidson*. Stanford, CA: Stanford University Press.

Feigl, H. (1958). *The 'Mental' and the 'Physical': The Essay and a Postscript* (Vol. 2). Minneapolis: University of Minnesota Press.

Feleppa, R. (1988). *Convention, Translation and Understanding: Philosophical Problems in the Comparative Study of Culture*. Albany, NY: State University of New York Press.

Fish, S. (1989). *Doing What Comes Naturally: Change, Rhetoric and the Practice of Theory in Literary and Legal Studies*. Oxford: Clarendon Press.

Fisher, M. (1985). Secrecy, Proof and Confidentiality of Aboriginal Customary Laws in the Legal System. *Aboriginal Law Bulletin*, 1(17), 14–16.

Fodor, J.A. (1974). Special Sciences, or the Disunity of Science as a Working Hypothesis. *Synthese*, 28.

Fodor, J.A. (1975). *The Language of Thought*. New York: Crowell.

Fodor, J.A. (1987). *Psychosemantics: The Problem of Meaning in the Philosophy of Mind*. Cambridge, MA: MIT Press.

Fodor, J.A. (1990). *A Theory of Content and Other Essays*. Cambridge, MA: MIT Press.

Fodor, J.A. (1991). You Can Fool Some of the People All of the Time, Everything Else Being Equal: Hedged Laws and Psychological Explanations. *Mind*, 100, 19–34.

Fodor, J.A., Garrett, M.F., Walker, C.T. and Parkes, C.H. (1980). Against Definitions. *Cognition*, 8, 263–367.

Fodor, J.A and Lepore, E. (1992). *Holism: A Shopper's Guide*. Oxford: Blackwell.

Foley, W.A. (1997). *Anthropological Linguistics: An Introduction.* Oxford: Blackwell.

Follesdal, D. (1982). The Status of Rationality Assumptions in Interpretation and in the Explanation of Action. *Dialectica*, 36(4), 301–16.

Forster, M.N. (1997). On the Very Idea of Denying the Existence of Radically Different Conceptual Schemes. *Inquiry*, 41, 133–85.

Foucault, M. (1971). *The Order of Things: An Archaeology of the Human Sciences.* New York: Vintage Books.

Foucault, M. (1977). *Discipline and Punish: The Birth of the Prison* (A. Sheridan, trans.). London: Penguin Books.

Foucault, M. (1980). *Power/Knowledge: Selected Interviews and Other Writings 1972–1977.* New York: Pantheon Books.

Fryer-Smith, S. (2002). *Aboriginal Benchbook for Western Australian Courts.* Melbourne: The Australian Institute of Judicial Administration.

Gadamer, H.-G. (1989). *Truth and Method* (J. Weinsheimer and D.G. Marshall, trans. 2nd revised edn). New York: The Continuum Publishing Company.

Gamst, F.C. and Norbeck, E. (eds). (1976). *Ideas of Culture: Sources and Uses.* New York: Holt, Rinehart and Winston.

Gasche, R. (1986). *The Tain of the Mirror: Derrida and the Philosophy of Reflection.* Cambridge, MA: Harvard University Press.

Geertz, C. (1973). *The Interpretation of Cultures.* New York: Basic Books.

Geertz, C. (1979). From the Native's Point of View: On the Nature of Anthropological Understanding. In P. Rabinow and W.M. Sullivan (eds), *Interpretive Social Science* (pp. 225–41). Berkeley: University of California Press.

Geertz, C. (1988). The Uses of Diversity. *Michigan Quarterly Review*, 23, 105–23.

Geertz, C. (1989). Anti Anti-Relativism. In M. Krausz (ed.), *Relativism: Interpretation and Confrontation* (pp. 12–34). Notre Dame: University of Notre Dame Press.

Gelman, S.A. and Wellman, H.M. (1999). Insides and Essences: Early Understandings of the Non-obvious. In E. Margolis and S. Laurence (eds), *Concepts: Core Readings* (pp. 613–37). Cambridge, MA: MIT Press.

Gerstenblith, P. (1995). Identity and Cultural Property: The Protection of Cultural Property in the United States. *Boston University Law Review*, 75, 559–688.

Gibson, R.F. (ed.). (2004). *The Cambridge Companion to Quine.* Cambridge: Cambridge University Press.

Gilbert, M. (1989). *On Social Facts.* Princeton, NJ: Princeton Univerisity Press.

Goldflam, R. (1995). Silence in Court! Problems and Prospects in Aboriginal English Interpreting. In D. Eades (ed.), *Language in Evidence: Issues Confronting Aboriginal and Multicultural Australia* (pp. 28–54). Sydney: UNSW Press.

Goldman, A. (1970). *A Theory of Human Action.* Englewood Cliffs, NJ: Prentice-Hall.

Goldman, A.I. (1986). *Epistemology and Cognition*. Cambridge, MA: Harvard University Press.

Goldman, A.I. (1989). Interpretation Psychologized. *Mind and Language*, 4(3), 161–85.

Gopnik, A. (1993). How We Know Our Minds: The Illusion of First-person Knowledge of Intentionality. *Behavioural and Brain Sciences*, 16, 1–14.

Gopnik, A. (1996). Theories and Modules: Creation Myths, Developmental Realities, and Neurath's Boat. In P. Carruthers and P.K. Smith (eds), *Theories of Theories of Mind* (pp. 169–83). Cambridge: Cambridge University Press.

Gopnik, A. and Melzoff, A.N. (1993). The Role of Imitation in Understanding Persons and Developing a Theory of Mind. In S. Baron-Cohen, H. Tager-Flusberg and D.J. Cohen (eds), *Understanding Other Minds: Perspectives from Autism* (pp. 335–66). Oxford: Oxford University Press.

Gopnik, A. and Wellman, H.M. (1992). Why the Child's Theory of Mind Really is a Theory. *Mind and Language*, 7, 145–71.

Gopnik, A. and Wellman, H.M. (1994). The 'Theory Theory'. In L.A. Hirshfield and S.A. Gelman (eds), *Mapping the Mind: Domain-Specificity in Cultural Cognition* (pp. 257–93). New York: Cambridge University Press.

Gordon, R.M. (1986). Folk Psychology as Simulation. *Mind and Language*, 1(2), 158–71.

Grace, G. (1987). *The Linguistic Construction of Reality*. London: Croom Helm.

Grandy, R. (1973). Reference, Meaning and Belief. *Journal of Philosophy*, 70, 439–40.

Gregorczuk, H. (1996). The Desirability of Judicial Education in Australia. *Journal of Professional Legal Education*, 14, 77–95.

Grimes, T.R. (1991). Supervenience, Determination, and Dependency. *Philosophical Studies*, 62, 81–92.

Guttenplan, S. (ed.). (1994a). *A Companion to the Philosophy of Mind*. Oxford: Blackwell.

Guttenplan, S. (1994b). An Essay on Mind. In S. Guttenplan (ed.), *A Companion to the Philosophy of Mind* (pp. 3–107). Oxford: Blackwell.

Habermas, J. (1987a). *The Theory of Communicative Action, Vol.1: Reason and the Rationalisation of Society* (T. McCarthy, trans.). Cambridge: Polity Press.

Habermas, J. (1987b). *The Theory of Communicative Action, Vol. 2: Lifeworld and System: A Critique of Functionalist Reason* (T. McCarthy, trans.). Cambridge: Polity Press.

Habermas, J. (1987c). *The Philosophical Discourse of Modernity: Twelve Lectures* (F. G. Lawrence, trans.). Cambridge: Polity Press.

Habermas, J. (1988). *On the Logic of the Social Sciences* (S.W. Nicholsen and J.A. Stark, trans.). Cambridge, MA: MIT Press.

Habermas, J. (1992). *Between Facts and Norms* (W. Rehg, trans.). Cambridge: Polity Press.

Habermas, J. (1994). Struggles for Recognition in the Democratic Constitutional State. In A. Gutman (ed.), *Multiculturalism: Examining the Politics of Recognition* (pp. 107–48). Princeton, NJ: Princeton University Press.
Habermas, J. (1998). *On the Pragmatics of Communication.* Cambridge, MA: MIT Press.
Hacker, P.M.S. (1996). On Davidson's Idea of a Conceptual Scheme. *The Philosophical Quarterly*, 46(184), 289–307.
Haebich, A. (1992). *For Their Own Good: Aborigines and Government in the South West of Western Australia 1900–1940.* Nedlands: University of Western Australia Press.
Harman, G. (1978). Studying the Chimpanzee's Theory of Mind. *Behavioral and Brain Sciences*, 1, 576–7.
Hart, H.L.A. (1954). Definition and Theory in Jurisprudence. *Law Quarterly Review*, 70, 37–60.
Hart, H.L.A. (1961). *The Concept of Law* (1st edn). Oxford: Clarendon Press.
Harvey, D. (1989). *The Condition of Postmodernity*. Oxford: Blackwell.
Haugeland, J. (1982). Weak Supervenience. *American Philosophical Quarterly*, 19, 93–103.
Hawkins, J.A. (ed.). (1988). *Explaining Language Universals*. Oxford: Basil Blackwell.
Heal, J. (1986). Replication and Functionalism. In J. Butterfield (ed.), *Language, MInd and Logic* (pp. 135–50). Cambridge: Cambridge University Press.
Heal, J. (1989). *Fact and Meaning: Quine and Wittgenstein on Philosophy of Language*. Oxford: Basil Blackwell.
Heal, J. (1995). How to Think About Thinking. In M. Davies and T. Stone (eds), *Mental Simulation: Evaluations and Concepts* (pp. 33–52). Oxford: Blackwell.
Heal, J. (1996). Simulation, Theory, and Content. In P. Carruthers and P.K. Smith (eds), *Theories of Theories of Mind* (pp. 75–89). Cambridge: Cambridge University Press.
Heal, J. (1997). Radical Interpretation. In B. Hale and C. Wright (eds), *A Companion to the Philosophy of Language* (pp. 175–96). Oxford: Blackwell.
Heidegger, M. (1993a). On the Essence of Truth. In D.F. Krell (ed.), *Basic Writings: Martin Heidegger* (pp. 115–38). London: Routledge.
Heidegger, M. (1993b). The Question Concerning Technology. In D.F. Krell (ed.), *Basic Writings: Martin Heidegger* (pp. 311–41). London: Routledge.
Heil, J. (1998). *Philosophy of Mind: A Contemporary Introduction*. London: Routledge.
Hellman, G. (1985). Determination and Logical Truth. *Journal of Philosophy*, 82, 607–16.
Hellman, G. and Thompson, F.W. (1975). Physicalism: Ontology, Determination, Reduction. *Journal of Philosophy*, 72, 551–64.
Hempel, C.G. (1962). Rational Action. *Proceedings and Addresses of the American Philosophical Association*, 35, 5–23.

Hempel, C.G. (1965). *Aspects of Scientific Explanation and other Essays in the Philosophy of Science*. New York: The Free Press.
Hempel, C.G. (1966). *Philosophy of Natural Science*. Englewood Cliffs, NJ: Prentice-Hall Inc.
Hempel, C.G. (1969). Reduction: Ontological and Linguistic Facets. In S. Morganbesser, P. Suppes and M. White (eds), *Philosophy, Science and Method: Essays in Honor of Ernest Nagel* (pp. 179–99). New York: St Martin's.
Henderson, D.K. (1993). *Interpretation and Explanation in the Human Sciences*. Albany, NY: SUNY Press.
Henderson, D.K. (1994). Conceptual Schemes After Davidson. In G. Preyer, F. Siebelt and A. Ulfig (eds), *Language, Mind and Epistemology: On Donald Davidson's Philosophy* (pp. 171–97). Dordrecht: Kluwer Academic Publishers.
Hepper, P.G. (1995). The Behaviour of the Fetus as an Indicator of Neural Functioning. In W.P.F. Jean-Pierre Lecanuet, N.A. Krasnegor and W.P. Smotherman (eds), *Fetal Development. A Psychobiological Perspective* (pp. 405–17). Hillsdale, NJ: Lawrence Erlbaum.
Heydon, J. (2000). *Cross on Evidence* (6th edn). Sydney: Butterworths.
Hirst, R.J. (1967). Realism. In P. Edwards (ed.), *The Encyclopedia of Philosophy* (Vol. 7, pp. 77–83). New York: Macmillan.
Hohfeld, W.N. (1919). *Fundamental Legal Conceptions*. New Haven, CT: Yale University Press.
Hollis, M. (1970). The Limits of Irrationality. In B. Wilson (ed.), *Rationality* (pp. 214–20). Oxford: Basil Blackwell.
Hollis, M. and Lukes, S. (1982). *Rationality and Relativism*. Oxford: Basil Blackwell.
Hookway, C. (1988). *Quine: Language, Experience and Reality*. Cambridge: Polity Press.
Horgan, T. (1984). Jackson on Physical Information and Qualia. *Philosophical Quarterly*, 34, 147–53.
Horgan, T.E. (1994). Physicalism. In S. Guttenplan (ed.), *A Companion to the Philosophy of Mind* (pp. 471–79). Oxford: Blackwell.
Hornsby, J. (1980). *Actions*. London: Routledge and Keegan Paul.
Humboldt, W. v. (1988). *On Language: The Diversity of Human Language-structure and its Influence on the Mental Development of Mankind* (P. Heath, trans.). Cambridge: Cambridge University Press.
Humphries, P. (1996). Aspects of Emergence. *Philosophical Topics*, 24, 53–70.
Hutcheon, L. (1989). *The Politics of Postmodernism*. London: Routledge.
Hylton, P. (1994). Quine's Naturalism. *Midwest Studies in Philosophy*, 19, 261–82.
Hylton, P. (2004). Quine on Reference and Ontology. In R.F. Gibson (ed.), *The Cambridge Companion to Quine* (pp. 115–50). Cambridge: Cambridge University Press.
Jackendoff, R. (1983). *Semantics and Cognition*. Cambridge, MA: MIT Press.
Jackson, F. (1982). Epiphenomenal Qualia. *Philosophical Quarterly*, 32, 127–36.
Jackson, F. (1986). What Mary Did Not Know. *Journal of Philosophy*, 83, 291–5.

Jackson, F. (1998). *From Metaphysics to Ethics: A Defence of Conceptual Analysis*. Oxford: Clarendon Press.

Jackson, F., Pargetter, R. and Prior, E. (1982). Functionalism and Type-Type Identity Theories. *Philosophical Studies*, 42, 209–25.

Jackson, F. and Pettit, P. (1990). Causation in the Philosophy of Mind. *Philosophy and Phenomenological Research*, 50, 195–214.

Jay, M. (1973). *The Dialectical Imagination: A History of the Frankfurt School and the Institute of Social Research 1923–1950*. Boston, MD: Little, Brown and Company.

Jubien, M. (1997). *Contemporary Metaphysics: An Introduction*. Oxford: Blackwell.

Katz, J. (1972). *Semantic Theory*. New York: Harper and Row.

Keen, I. (1994). *Knowledge and Secrecy in an Aboriginal Religion*. Oxford: Clarendon Press.

Keesing, R.M. (1974). Theories of Culture. *Annual Review of Anthropology*, 3, 73–97.

Keon-Cohen, B. (2000). Native Title in the New Millenium. Paper presented at the Native Title Representative Bodies Legal Conference, Melbourne.

Kerruish, V. and Purdy, J. (1998). "He Look Honest – Big White Thief". *Law Text Culture*, 4(1), 146–71.

Kiers, B. and Bell, C. (2003). Canadian Legislation Relating to First Nations Cultural Heritage. http://www.law.ualberta.ca/research/aboriginalculturalheritage/CanadianLegislation.pdf.

Kim, J. (1984). Concepts of Supervenience. *Philosophy and Phenomenological Research*, 45(2), 153–76.

Kim, J. (1993). *Supervenience and Mind: Selected Philosophical Essays*. Cambridge: Cambridge University Press.

Kim, J. (1998). *Mind in a Physical World*. Cambridge, MA: MIT Press.

Kim, J. (1999). Multiple Realisation and the Metaphysics of Reduction. In J. Kim and E. Sosa (eds), *Metaphysics: An Anthology* (pp. 515–30). Oxford: Blackwell.

Kim, J. (2003). Supervenience, Emergence, Realization, Reduction. In M.J. Loux and D.W. Zimmerman (eds), *The Oxford Handbook of Metaphysics* (pp. 556–84). Oxford: Oxford University Press.

Kirby, M. (2000). Modes of Appointment and Training of Judges – A Common Law Perspective. *Commonwealth Law Bulletin*, 26, 540–49.

Kirby, S. (1999). *Function, Selection, and Innateness: The Emergence of Language Universals*. Oxford: Clarendon Press.

Kirk, G.S. and Raven, J.E. (1966). *The Presocratic Philosophers*. Cambridge: Cambridge University Press.

Kirk, R. (2004). Indeterminacy of Translation. In R.F. Gibson (ed.), *The Cambridge Companion to Quine* (pp. 151–80). Cambridge: Cambridge University Press.

Kitcher, P. (1981). Explanatory Unification. *Philosophy of Science*, 48, 507–31.

Koch, H. (1991). Language and Communication in Aboriginal Land Claim Hearings. In S. Romaine (ed.), *Language in Australia* (pp. 94–103). Cambridge: Cambridge University Press.

Krausz, M. (ed.). (1989). *Relativism: Interpretation and Confrontation.* Notre Dame, IN: University of Notre Dame Press.

Kripke, S. (1980). *Naming and Necessity*. Cambridge, MA: Harvard University Press.

Kuper, A. (1999). *Culture: The Anthropologists' Account*. Cambridge, MA: Harvard University Press.

Lampert, J. (1997). Gadamer and Cross-Cultural Hermeneutics. *The Philosophical Forum*, 28(4), 351–68.

Lane, C. (1985). Mis-communication in Cross-examinations. In J.B. Pride (ed.), *Cross-Cultural Encounters: Communication and Mis-communication* (pp. 196–211). Melbourne: River Seine Publications.

Laurence, S. and Margolis, E. (1999). Concepts and Cognitive Science. In E. Margolis and S. Laurence (eds), *Concepts: Core Readings* (pp. 3–81). Cambridge, MA: MIT Press.

Leiter, B. (1997a). Rethinking Legal Realism: Towards a Naturalised Jurisprudence. *Texas Law Review*, 76, 267–315.

Leiter, B. (1997b). Why Quine is Not a Postmodernist. *Southern Methodist University Law Review*, 50, 1739–54.

Leiter, B. (1998). Naturalism and Naturalized Jurisprudence. In B. Bix (ed.), *Analyzing Law: New Essays in Legal Theory* (pp. 79–104). Oxford: Clarendon Press.

Leiter, B. (2002, Fall, 2002). *Naturalism in Legal Philosophy*, from http://plato.stanford.edu/archives/fall2002/entries/lawphil-naturalism/>.

Lennon, K. (1990). *Explaining Human Action.* London: Duckworth.

Lepore, E. (ed.). (1986). *Truth and Interpretation: Perspectives on the Philosophy of Donald Davidson.* Oxford: Basil Blackwell.

Lepore, E. and McLaughlin, B. (eds). (1985). *Action and Events: Perspectives on the Philosophy of Donald Davidson.* Oxford: Basil Blackwell.

Leslie, A.M. (1991). The Theory of Mind Impairment in Autism: Evidence for a Modular Mechanism of Development? In A. Whiten (ed.), *Natural Theories of Mind: Evolution, Development and Simulation of Everyday Mindreading* (pp. 63–78). Oxford: Basil Blackwell.

Levi, E.H. (1949). *An Introduction to Legal Reasoning*. Chicago: University of Chicago Press.

Levinas, E. (1969). *Totality and Infinity: An Essay on Exteriority* (A. Lingis, trans.). Pittsburgh, PA: Duquesne University Press.

Levinas, E. (1985). *Ethics and Infinity* (R.A. Cohen, trans.). Pittsburgh, PA: Duquesne University Press.

Levy-Bruhl, L. (1979). *How Natives Think* (L.A. Clare, trans.). New York: Arno Press.

Lewis, D. (1966). An Argument for the Identity Theory. *Journal of Philosophy*, 63, 17–25.
Lewis, D. (1972). Psychophysical and Theoretical Identifications. *Australasian Journal of Philosophy*, 50, 249–58.
Lewis, D. (1974). Radical Interpretation. *Synthese*, 27, 331–44.
Lewis, D. (1980). Mad Pain and Martian Pain. In N. Block (ed.), *Readings in Philosophy of Psychology: Volume 1* (pp. 216–22). Cambridge, MA: Harvard University Press.
Lewis, D. (1983). New Work for a Theory of Universals. *Australasian Journal of Philosophy*, 61(4), 343–77.
Lewis, D. (1986a). Events. In *Philosophical Papers: Volume 2* (pp. 241–69). New York: Oxford University Press.
Lewis, D. (1986b). *On the Plurality of Worlds*. Oxford: Basil Blackwell.
Lewis, D. (1990). What Experience Teaches. In W.G. Lycan (ed.), *Mind and Cognition: A Reader* (pp. 447–60). Oxford: Basil Blackwell.
Lewis, D. (1994). Reduction of Mind. In S. Guttenplan (ed.), *A Companion to the Philosophy of Mind* (pp. 412–31). Oxford: Blackwell.
Ligertwood, A. (1988). *Australian Evidence*. Sydney: Butterworths.
Lillard, A.S. (1997). Other Folks' Theories of Mind and Behaviour. *Psychological Science*, 8(4), 268–74.
Lillard, A.S. (1998). Ethnopsychologies: Cultural Variations in Theory of Mind. *Psychological Bulletin*, 123, 3–32.
Locke, J. (1975). *An Essay Concerning Human Understanding*. New York: Oxford University Press.
Lombard, L.B. (1986). *Events: A Metaphysical Study*. London: Routledge and Kegan Paul.
Loux, M. J. and Zimmerman, D.W. (eds). (2003). *The Oxford Handbook of Metaphysics*. Oxford: Oxford University Press.
Lucretius. (1951). *On the Nature of the Universe* (R.E. Latham, trans.). Harmondsworth: Penguin Books.
Lucy, J.A. (1992). *Language Diversity and Thought: A Reformulation of the Linguistic Relativity Hypothesis*. Cambridge: Cambridge University Press.
Lukes, S. (1970). Some Problems About Rationality. In B. Wilson (ed.), *Rationality* (pp. 194–213). Oxford: Basil Blackwell.
Lukes, S. (1982). Relativism in its Place. In M. Hollis and S. Lukes (eds), *Rationality and Relativism* (pp. 261–305). Oxford: Basil Blackwell.
Lycan, W.G. (1987). *Consciousness*. Cambridge, MA: MIT Press.
Lynch, M.P. (1997). Three Models of Conceptual Schemes. *Inquiry*, 40, 407–26.
Lyons, W. (1995). *Approaches to Intentionality*. Oxford: Clarendon Press.
Lyotard, J.-F. (1988). *The Differend: Phrases in Dispute* (G.V.D. Abbeele, trans.). Minneapolis: University of Minnesota Press.
MacCormick, N. (1981). *H.L.A. Hart*. London: Edward Arnold Publishers.
MacCormick, N. (1990). Reconstruction after Deconstruction: A Response to CLS. *Oxford Journal of Legal Studies*, 10, 539–58.

Macdonald, C. (1995). Psychophysical Supervenience, Dependency, and Reduction. In E.E. Savellos and U.D. Yalcin (eds), *Supervenience: New Essays* (pp. 140–57). Cambridge: Cambridge University Press.

MacDonald, G. and Pettit, P. (1981). *Semantics and Social Science*. London: Routledge and Kegan Paul.

Malpas, J.E. (1992). *Donald Davidson and the Mirror of Meaning: Holism, Truth and Interpretation*. Cambridge: Cambridge University Press.

Mantziaris, C. and Martin, D. (2000). *Native Title Corporations: A Legal and Anthropological Analysis*. Leichhardt: Federation Press.

Margolis, E. (1999). How to Acquire a Concept. In S. Laurence and E. Margolis (eds), *Concepts: Core Readings* (pp. 549–67). Cambridge, MA: MIT Press.

Margolis, E. and Laurence, S. (eds). (1999). *Concepts: Core Readings*. Cambridge, MA: MIT Press.

Marx, K. (1978). Theses on Feuerbach. In R.C. Tucker (ed.), *The Marx-Engels Reader* (pp. 143–5). New York: W.W. Norton and Company.

McCorquodale, J. (1986). The Legal Classification of Race in Australia. *Aboriginal History*, 10(1), 7–24.

McDowell, J. (1985). Functionalism and Anomalous Monism. In E. Lepore and B. McLaughlin (eds), *Actions and Events: Perspectives on the Philosophy of Donald Davidson* (pp. 389–98). Oxford: Blackwell.

McDowell, J. (1994). *Mind and World*. Cambridge, MA: Harvard University Press.

McGinn, C. (1977). Charity, Interpretation and Belief. *Journal of Philosophy*, 74, 521–35.

McGinn, C. (1982). *The Character of Mind*. New York: Oxford University Press.

McGinn, C. (1991). *The Problem of Consciousness*. Oxford: Basil Blackwell.

McGregor, R. (1997). *Imagined Destinies: Aboriginal Australians and the Doomed Race Theory, 1880–1939*. Carlton South: Melbourne University Press.

McNicol, S.B. and Mortimer, D. (2001). *Evidence* (2nd edn). Chatswood: Butterworths.

McRae, H., Nettheim, G., Beacroft, L. and McNamara, L. (2003). *Indigenous Legal Issues: Commentary and Materials*. Sydney: Lawbook Co.

Mele, A. (1992). *The Springs of Action*. New York: Oxford University Press.

Melnyk, A. (1994). Being a Physicalist: How and (More Importantly) Why. *Philosophical Studies*, 74(2), 221–41.

Melnyk, A. (1997). How to Keep the 'Physical' in Physicalism. *Journal of Philosophy*, 94(12), 622–37.

Melnyk, A. (2001). Physicalism Unfalsified: Chalmers' Inconclusive Conceivability Argument. In C. Gillett and B. Loewer (eds), *Physicalism and its Discontents* (pp. 329–47). Cambridge: Cambridge University Press.

Melnyk, A. (2003). *A Physicalist Manifesto: Thoroughly Modern Materialism*. Cambridge: Cambridge University Press.

Miller, J.G. (1984). Culture and the Development of Everyday Social Explanation. *Journal of Personality and Social Psychology*, 46, 961–78.

Miller, S. (2001). *Social Action: A Teleological Account*. Cambridge: Cambridge University Press.
Mills, S. (2001). The Idea of Different Folk Psychologies. *International Journal of Philosophical Studies*, 9(4), 501–19.
Mongia, P. (ed.). (1996). *Contemporary Postcolonial Theory: A Reader*. London: Arnold.
Moore, G.E. (1922). *Philosophical Studies*. London: Routledge and Keegan Paul.
Moore, M. (2000). *Educating Oneself in Public*. Oxford: Oxford University Press.
Moore, M. (2002). Legal Reality: A Naturalist Approach to Legal Ontology. *Law and Philosophy*, 21, 619–705.
Moreland, J.P. (1998). Should a Naturalist Be a Supervenient Physicalist? *Metaphilosophy*, 29(1/2), 35–57.
Moser, P.K. and Trout, J.D. (eds). (1995). *Contemporary Materialism: A Reader*. London: Routledge.
Motha, S. (1998). Mabo: Encountering the Epistemic Limit of the Recognition of Difference. *Griffith Law Review*, 7(1), 79–96.
Muir, K. (1999). Reconciling Through Understanding. *Australian Institute for Aboriginal and Torres Strait Islander Studies – Native Title Research Unit Newsletter* 4, 3–4.
Nagel, E. (1961). *The Structure of Science: Problems in the Logic of Scientific Explanation*. New York: Harcourt, Brace and World Inc.
Nagel, T. (1974). What Is It Like to Be a Bat? *Philosophical Review*, 83, 435–50.
Nagel, T. (1986). *The View From Nowhere*. New York: Oxford University Press.
Neate, G. (1996). Proof of Native Title. In R.H. Bartlett (ed.), *Commercial Implications of Native Title* (pp. 240–319). Perth: Centre for Commercial and Resources Law, UWA.
Neate, G. (2001). Management of Native Title Case by the Federal Court – Does This Affect the Anthropologist's Role? Paper presented at the Native Title Conference: Expert Evidence in Native Title Court Cases: Issues of Truth, Objectivity and Expertise, Adelaide University, South Australia.
Neate, G. (2003). Land, Law and Language: Some Issues in the Resolution of Indigenous Land Claims in Australia. Paper presented at the Conference of the International Association of Forensic Linguists, Sydney.
Neate, G.J. (1981). Legal Language Across Cultures: Finding the Traditional Aboriginal Owners of Land. *Federal Law Review*, 12(3), 187–211.
New South Wales Law Reform Commission. (2000). *Sentencing: Aboriginal Offenders* (No. 96). Sydney: New South Wales Law Reform Commission.
Ney, A. (2008). Physicalism as an Attitude. *Philosophical Studies*, 138, 1–15.
Nichols, S. and Stich, S.P. (2003). *Mindreading: An Integrated Account of Pretence, Self-Awareness and Understanding Other Minds*. Oxford: Clarendon Press.
Nichols, S., Stich, S., Leslie, A. and Klein, D. (1996). Varieties of Off-line Simulation. In P. Carruthers and P.K. Smith (eds), *Theories of Theories of Mind* (pp. 39–74). Cambridge: Cambridge University Press.

Nisbett, R.E., Peng, K., Choi, I. and Norenzayan, A. (2001). Culture and Systems of Thought: Holistic Versus Analytic Cognition. *Psychological Review*, 108(2), 291–310.

Norris, C. (1993). *The Truth About Postmodernism*. Oxford: Blackwell.

Nunn, K.B. (1997). Law as a Eurocentric Enterprise. *Law and Inequality*, 15, 323–71.

Odgers, S. (2000). *Uniform Evidence Law*. Sydney: LBC Information Services.

Pallas, S.L. (2005). Pre- and Postnatal Sensory Experience Shapes Functional Architecture in the Brain. In B. Hopkins and S.P. Johnson (eds), *Prenatal Development of Postnatal Functions* (pp. 1–30). Westport, CT: Praeger Publishers.

Papineau, D. (1978). *For Science in the Social Sciences*. New York: St Martins Press.

Papineau, D. (1993). *Philosophical Naturalism*. Oxford: Blackwell Publishers.

Parret, H. and Bouveresse, J. (eds). (1981). *Meaning and Understanding*. Berlin: Walter de Gruyter.

Paterson, R.K. (1999). Protecting Taonga: The Cultural Heritage of the New Zealand Maori. *International Journal of Cultural Property*, 8, 108–32.

Patterson, D. (2003). From Postmodernism to Law and Truth. *Harvard Journal of Law and Public Policy*, 26, 49–65.

Patton, P. (1995a). Mabo, Freedom and the Politics of Difference. *Australian Journal of Political Science*, 30, 108–19.

Patton, P. (1995b). Post-structuralism and the Mabo Debate: Difference, Society and Justice. In M. Wilson and A. Yeatman (eds), *Justice and Identity: Antipodean Practices* (pp. 153–71). Wellington: Bridget Williams Books Ltd. – Allen and Unwin.

Patton, P. (1996). Sovereignty, Law and Difference in Australia: After the Mabo Case. *Alternatives*, 21(2), 149–70.

Patton, P. (1997). Justice and Difference: The Mabo Case. In P. Patton and D. Austin-Broos (eds), *Transformations in Australian Society* (pp. 83–98). Sydney: Research Institute for Humanities and Social Sciences.

Peacocke, C. (1992). *A Study of Concepts*. Cambridge, MA: MIT Press.

Perner, J. (1996). Simulation as Explicitation of Prediction-implicit Knowledge about the Mind: Arguments for a Simulation-theory Mix. In P. Carruthers and P.K. Smith (eds), *Theories of theories of mind* (pp. 90–104). Cambridge: Cambridge University Press.

Perry, M. and Lloyd, S. (2003). *Australian Native Title Law*. Sydney: Lawbook Co.

Pether, P. (1998). Principles or Skeletons? Mabo and the Discursive Constitution of the Australian Nation. *Law Text Culture*, 4(1), 115–45.

Pettit, P. (1978). Rational Man Theory. In C. Hookway and P. Pettit (eds), *Action and Interpretation* (pp. 43–63). Cambridge: Cambridge University Press.

Pettit, P. (1982). Habermas on Truth and Justice. In G.H.R. Parkinson (ed.), *Marx and Marxisms* (pp. 207–28). Cambridge: Cambridge University Press.

Pettit, P. (1992). The Nature of Naturalism. *Supplementary Volume of the Aristotelian Society*, 66.
Pettit, P. (1993a). *The Common Mind: An Essay on Psychology, Society and Politics*. Oxford: Oxford University Press.
Pettit, P. (1993b). A Definition of Physicalism. *Analysis*, 53(4), 231–23.
Phelan, M. (1993). A Synopsis of the Laws Protecting Our Cultural Heritage. *New England Law Review*, 28, 63–108.
Pinker, S. (1989). *Learnability and Cognition: The Acquisition of Language Structure*. Cambridge, MA: MIT Press.
Place, U.T. (1956). Is Consciousness a Brain Process? *British Journal of Psychology*, 47, 44–50.
Poland, J. (1994). *Physicalism: The Philosophical Foundations*. New York: Oxford University Press.
Poole, R. (1996). On Being a Person. *Australasian Journal of Philosophy*, 74(1), 38–56.
Popper, K. (1968). *The Logic of Scientific Discovery*. London: Hutchinson.
Post, J.F. (1987). *The Faces of Existence: An Essay in Nonreductive Metaphysics*. Ithaca, NY: Cornell University Press.
Post, J.F. (1991). *Metaphysics: A Contemporary Introduction*. New York: Paragon House.
Povinelli, E.A. (2002). *The Cunning of Recognition: Indigenous Alterities and the Making of Australian Multiculturalism*. Durham, NC: Duke University Press.
Premack, D. and Woodruff, G. (1978). Does the Chimpanzee have a Theory of Mind? *The Behavioural and Brain Sciences*, 1, 515–26.
Prinz, J.J. (2002). *Furnishing the Mind: Concepts and Their Perceptual Basis*. Cambridge, MA: MIT press.
Putnam, H. (1960). Minds and Machines. In S. Hook (ed.), *Dimensions of Mind* (pp. 136–64). New York: New York University Press.
Putnam, H. (1962). The Analytic and the Synthetic. In *Mind, Language and Reality: Philosophical Papers, Volume 2* (pp. 33–69). Cambridge: Cambridge University Press.
Putnam, H. (1967). Psychological Predicates. In W.H. Capitan and D.D. Merrill (eds), *Art, Mind and Religion*. Pittsburgh, PA: University of Pittsburgh Press.
Putnam, H. (1975). The Meaning of Meaning. In *Mind, Language and Reality: Philosophical Papers Volume 2* (pp. 215–71). Cambridge: Cambridge University Press.
Putnam, H. (1981). *Reason, Truth and History*. Cambridge: Cambridge University Press.
Putnam, H. (1983). *Realism and Reason: Philosophical Papers Volume 3*. Cambridge: Cambridge University Press.
Quine, W.V.O. (1953a). *From a Logical Point of View*. Cambridge, MA: Harvard University Press.
Quine, W.V.O. (1953b). The Two Dogmas of Empiricism. In *From a Logical Point of View* (pp. 20–46). Cambridge, MA: Harvard University Press.

Quine, W.V.O. (1960). *Word and Object*. Cambridge, MA: MIT Press.
Quine, W.V.O. (1969). *Ontological Relativity and Other Essays*. New York: Columbia University Press.
Quine, W.V.O. (1970). Philosophical Progress in Language Theory. *Metaphilosophy*, 1, 2–19.
Raz, J. (1984). Legal Rights. *Oxford Journal of Legal Studies*, 4, 1–21.
Raz, J. (1990). *Practical Reason and Norms*. Princeton, NJ: Princeton University Press.
Rescher, N. (1980). Conceptual Schemes. In P. French, T. Uehling and H. Wettstein (eds), *Midwest Studies in Philosophy: Studies in Epistemology* (Vol. 5, pp. 323–45). Minneapolis: University of Minnesota Press.
Rey, G. (1983). Concepts and Stereotypes. *Cognition*, 15, 237–62.
Rey, G. (1985). Concepts and Conceptions: A Reply to Smith, Medin and Rips. *Cognition*, 19, 297–303.
Rey, G. (1994). Concepts. In S. Guttenplan (ed.), *A Companion to the Philosophy of Mind* (pp. 185–93). Oxford: Blackwell.
Reyna, S.P. (2002). *Connections: Brain, Mind and Culture in a Social Anthropology*. London: Routledge.
Reynolds, H. (1992). *The Law of the Land*. Ringwood: Penguin Books Australia.
Reynolds, H. (1996). *Aboriginal Sovereignty: Three Nations or One Australia?* St Leonards, NSW: Allen and Unwin.
Ripperger, B. (1998). Law, Authority and Critique in the Wake of Terra Nullius: A History of 'Profane Illumination' or an Economy of Violence? *Law Text Culture*, 4(1), 172–95.
Root, M. (1986). Davidson and Social Science. In E. Lepore (ed.), *Truth and Interpretation: Perspectives on the Philosophy of Donald Davidson* (pp. 272–304). Oxford: Basil Blackwell.
Rorty, R. (1970). In Defence of Eliminative Materialism. *The Review of Metaphysics*, 24, 112–21.
Rorty, R. (1972). The World Well Lost. *Journal of Philosophy*, 69, 649–65.
Rorty, R. (1986). Pragmatism, Davidson and Truth. In E. LePore (ed.), *Truth and Interpretation: Perspectives on the Philosophy of Donald Davidson* (pp. 333–55). Oxford: Basil Blackwell.
Rorty, R. (1989). *Contingency, Irony and Solidarity*. Cambridge: Cambridge University Press.
Rorty, R. (1991). Solidarity or Objectivity? In *Objectivity, Relativism and Truth: Philosophical Papers Volume 1* (pp. 21–34). Cambridge: Cambridge University Press.
Rosaldo, M.Z. (1982). The Things We Do With Words: Ilongot Speech Acts and Speech Act Theory in Philosophy. *Language and Society*, 11, 203–37.
Rosch, E. (1974). Linguistic Relativity. In A. Silverstein (ed.), *Human Communication: Theoretical Explorations*. New York: Halsted Press.
Rosch, E. and Mervis, C.B. (1975). Family Resemblances: Studies in the Internal Structure of Categories. *Cognitive Psychology*, 7, 573–605.

Rosemont, H. (1988). Against Relativism. In G.J. Larson and E. Deutsch (eds), *Interpreting Across Boundaries: New Essays in Comparative Philosophy*. Princeton, NJ: Princeton University Press.

Rosenfeld, M. (1992). Deconstruction and Legal Interpretation: Conflict, Indeterminacy and the Temptations of the New Legal Formalism. In D. Cornell, M. Rosenfeld and D.G. Carlson (eds), *Deconstruction and the Possibility of Justice* (pp. 152–210). New York: Routledge.

Royal Commission into Aboriginal Deaths in Custody. (1991). *National Report*. Canberra: Australian Government Publishing Service.

Ruben, D.-H. (1998). The Philosophy of the Social Sciences. In A.C. Grayling (ed.), *Philosophy 2: Further Through the Subject* (pp. 420–69). Oxford: Oxford University Press.

Ryle, G. (1949). *The Concept of Mind*. London: Hutchinson and Co.

Sabates, M. (2002). MInd in a Physical World? *Philosophy and Phenomenological Research*, 65(3), 663–70.

Said, E. (1984). *The World, the Text and the Critic*. London: Faber and Faber.

Said, E. (1993). *Culture and Imperialism*. London: Chatto and Windus.

Sapir, E. (1949). *Selected Writings*. Berkeley: University of California Press.

Savellos, E.E. and Yalcin, U.D. (eds). (1995). *Supervenience: New Essays*. Cambridge: Cambridge University Press.

Schiffer, S. (1991). Ceteris Paribus Laws. *Mind*, 100, 1–17.

Schwarz, H. and Ray, S. (eds). (2000). *A Companion to Postcolonial Studies*. Oxford: Blackwell.

Searle, J.R. (1983). *Intentionality: An Essay in the Philosophy of Mind*. Cambridge: Cambridge University Press.

Searle, J.R. (1990). Collective Intentions and Actions. In P.R. Cohen, J. Morgan and M.E. Pollack (eds), *Intentions in Communication* (pp. 401–15). Cambridge, MA: MIT Press.

Searle, J.R. (1992). *The Rediscovery of the Mind*. Cambridge, MA: MIT Press.

Searle, J.R. (1995). *The Construction of Social Reality*. New York: The Free Press.

Searle, J.R. (1999). *Mind, Language and Society: Philosophy in the Real World*. London: Phoenix.

Segal, G. (1996). The Modularity Theory of Mind. In P. Carruthers and P.K. Smith (eds), *Theories of Theories of Mind* (pp. 141–57). Cambridge: Cambridge University Press.

Sharp, N. (1996). *No Ordinary Judgment: Mabo, The Murray Islanders' Land Case*. Canberra: Aboriginal Studies Press.

Shoemaker, S. (1975). Functionalism and Qualia. *Philosophical Studies*, 27, 291–315.

Simons, P. (2003). Events. In M.J. Loux and D.W. Zimmerman (eds), *The Oxford Handbook of Metaphysics* (pp. 357–85). Oxford: Oxford University Press.

Smart, J.J.C. (1959). Sensations and Brain Processes. *Philosophical Review*, 68, 141–56.

Smart, J.J.C. (1978). The Content of Physicalism. *Philosophical Quarterly*, 28, 339–41.

Smith, J.C. (1968). The Unique Nature of the Concepts of Western Law. *The Canadian Bar Review*, 46(N2), 191–225.

Smith, J.C. (1974). The Concept of Native Title. *University of Toronto Law Journal*, 24, 1–16.

Smith, L. (2005). Judicial Education On Context. *University of British Columbia Law Review*, 38, 569–82.

Smith, N. (1997). Incommensurability and Alterity in Contemporary Jurisprudence. *Buffalo Law Review*, 45, 503–53.

Spelke, E.S. (1985). Perception of Unity, Persistence and Identity: Thoughts on Infants' Conceptions of Objects. In *Neonate Cognition: Beyond the Blooming Buzzing Confusion* (pp. 89–113). Hillsdale, NJ: Lawrence Erlbaum Associates.

Stich, S.P. (1981). Dennett on Intentional Systems. *Philosophical Topics*, 12(1), 39–62.

Stich, S.P. (1983). *From Folk Psychology to Cognitive Science: The Case Against Belief.* Cambridge, MA: MIT Press.

Stich, S. (1990). *The Fragmentation of Reason: Preface to a Pragmatic Theory of Cognitive Evaluation.* Cambridge: MIT Press.

Stich, S.P. (1996). *Deconstructing the Mind.* Oxford: Oxford University Press.

Stich, S.P. and Nichols, S. (1992). Folk Psychology: Simulation or Tacit Theory? *Mind and Language*, 7, 35–71.

Stoljar, D. (2005). *Physicalism*, from http://plato.stanford.edu/archives/win2005/entries/physicalism/.

Stone, T. and Davies, M. (1996). The Mental Simulation Debate: A Progress Report. In P. Carruthers and P.K. Smith (eds), *Theories of Theories of Mind* (pp. 119–37). Cambridge: Cambridge University Press.

Taylor, B. (1985). *Modes of Occurrence: Verbs, Adverbs and Events.* Oxford: Basil Blackwell.

Taylor, C. (1964). *The Explanation of Behaviour.* London: Routledge and Keegan Paul.

Taylor, C. (1985a). *Human Agency and Language: Philosophical Papers 1.* Cambridge: Cambridge University Press.

Taylor, C. (1985b). *Philosophy and the Human Sciences: Philosophical Papers 2.* Cambridge: Cambridge University Press.

Taylor, C. (1985c). Interpretation and the Sciences of Man. In *Philosophy and the Human Sciences: Philosophical Papers 2* (pp. 15–57). Cambridge: Cambridge University Press.

Taylor, C. (1985d). Rationality. In *Philosophy and the Human Sciences: Philosophical Papers 2* (pp. 134–51). Cambridge: Cambridge University Press.

Taylor, C. (1992). The Politics of Recognition. In A. Gutmann (ed.), *Multiculturalism and 'The Politics of Recognition'* (pp. 25–73). Princeton, NJ: Princeton University Press.

Taylor, C. (1995). *Philosophical Arguments*. Cambridge, MA: Harvard University Press.

Thalberg, I. (1977). *Perception, Emotion and Action: A Component Approach*. Oxford: Blackwell.

Thompson, J.B. (1981). *Critical Hermeneutics*. Cambridge: Cambridge University Press.

Tuomela, R. (1984). *A Theory of Social Action*. Dordrecht: Reidel.

Tuomela, R. (1995). *The Importance of Us*. Stanford, CA: Stanford University Press.

Turner, S.P. (1980). *Sociological Explanation as Translation*. Cambridge: Cambridge University Press.

Turpel, M.E. (1990). Aboriginal Peoples and the Canadian Charter: Interpretive Monopolies, Cultural Differences. *Canadian Human Rights Yearbook*, 6, 3–45.

Tye, M. (1995). *Ten Problems of Consciousness: A Representational Theory of the Phenomenal Mind*. Cambridge, MA: MIT Press.

Ullmann-Margalit, E. (1977). *The Emergence of Norms*. Oxford: Clarendon Press.

Vosniadou, S. (1994). Universal and Culture-specific Properties of Children's Mental Models of the Earth. In L.A. Hirschfeld and S.A. Gelman (eds), *Mapping the Mind: Domain Specificity in cCgnition and Culture* (pp. 412–30). Cambridge: Cambridge University Press.

Wallace, J.C. (2003). Globalisation of Judicial Education. *Yale Journal of International Law*, 28, 355–64.

Walsh, M. (1994). Interactional Styles in the Courtroom: An Example from Northern Australia. In J. Gibbons (ed.), *Langauge and the Law* (pp. 217–33). London: Longman.

Walters, M.D. (1999). The 'Golden Thread' of Continuity: Aboriginal Customs at Common Law and Under the Constitution Act, 1982. *McGill Law Journal*, 44, 711–52.

Wellman, H.M. (1990). *The Child's Theory of Mind*. Cambridge, MA: MIT Press.

Wellman, H.M. (1998). Culture, Variation, and Levels of Analysis in Folk Psychologies: Comment on Lillard (1998). *Psychological Bulletin*, 123(1), 33–6.

White, S.K. (1991). *Political Theory and Postmodernism*. Cambridge: Cambridge University Press.

Whorf, B. (1956). *Language, Thought and Reality: Selected Writings of Benjamin Lee Whorf*. Cambridge, MA: MIT Press.

Wierzbicka, A. (1992). *Semantics, Culture, and Cognition: Universal Human Concepts in Culture-Specific Configurations*. New York: Oxford University Press.

Wierzbicka, A. (1994). Cognitive Domains and the Structure of the Lexicon: The Case of the Wmotions. In L.A. Hirschfeld and S.A. Gelman (eds), *Mapping the Mind: Domain Specificity in Cognition and Culture* (pp. 431–52). Cambridge: Cambridge University Press.

Williams-Mozley, J. (2002). *Overview Report on the National Aboriginal Cultural Awareness Program 1993–2000*. Melbourne: The Australian Institute of Judicial Administration.

Wilson, B. (1970). *Rationality*. Oxford: Basil Blackwell.

Wimmer, H. and Perner, J. (1983). Beliefs about Beliefs: Representation and Constraining Function of Wrong Beliefs in Young Children's Understanding of Deception. *Cognition*, 13(1), 1–134.

Winch, P. (1958). *The Idea of a Social Science and its Relation to Philosophy*. London: Routledge and Kegan Paul.

Winch, P. (1964). Understanding a Primitive Society. *American Philosophical Quarterly*, 1(4), 307–24.

Wittgenstein, L. (1953). *Philosophical Investigations* (G.E.M. Anscombe, trans.). Oxford: Blackwell.

Wollheim, R. and Hopkins, J. (eds). (1982). *Philosophical Essays on Freud*. Cambridge: Cambridge University Press.

Wright, G.H. v. (1971). *Explanation and Understanding*. Ithaca, NY: Cornell University Press.

Young, I.M. (1990). *Justice and the Politics of Difference*. Princeton, NJ: Princeton University Press.

Index

For Product Safety Concerns and Information please contact our EU representative GPSR@taylorandfrancis.com
Taylor & Francis Verlag GmbH, Kaufingerstraße 24, 80331 München, Germany

www.ingramcontent.com/pod-product-compliance
Ingram Content Group UK Ltd.
Pitfield, Milton Keynes, MK11 3LW, UK
UKHW021514250926
475702UK00043B/500
9780754679523